This book challenges standard accounts of early Christian exegesis of the Bible. Professor Young sets the interpretation of the Bible in the context of the Graeco-Roman world – the dissemination of books and learning, the way texts were received and read, the function of literature in shaping not only a culture but a moral universe. For the earliest Christians, the adoption of the Jewish scriptures constituted a supersessionary claim in relation to Hellenism as well as Judaism. Yet the debt owed to the practice of exegesis in the grammatical and rhetorical schools, especially as Christian scholarship developed in the third century, was of overriding significance. Methods were philological and deductive, and the usual analysis according to 'literal', 'typological' and 'allegorical' is inadequate to describe questions of reference and issues of religious language. The biblical texts shaped a 'totalising discourse' which by the fifth century was giving identity, morality and meaning to a new Christian culture.

BIBLICAL EXEGESIS AND
THE FORMATION OF
CHRISTIAN CULTURE

BIBLICAL EXEGESIS AND THE FORMATION OF CHRISTIAN CULTURE

FRANCES M. YOUNG

Edward Cadbury Professor of Theology
University of Birmingham

PUBLISHED BY THE PRESS SYNDICATE OF THE UNIVERSITY OF CAMBRIDGE
The Pitt Building, Trumpington Street, Cambridge CB2 1RP, United Kingdom

CAMBRIDGE UNIVERSITY PRESS
The Edinburgh Building, Cambridge CB2 2RU, United Kingdom
40 West 20th Street, New York, NY 10011–4211, USA
10 Stamford Road, Oakleigh, Melbourne 3166, Australia

First published 1997

Printed in the United Kingdom at the University Press, Cambridge

Typeset in Baskerville 11/12½ pt

*A catalogue record for this book is available from
the British Library*

Library of Congress cataloguing in publication data

Young, Frances M. (Frances Margaret)
Biblical exegesis and the Formation of Christian culture: the
speaker's lectures delivered in the University of Oxford in 1992 and
1993 / Frances M. Young.
p.   cm.
Includes bibliographical references.
ISBN 0 521 58153 2 (hardcover)
1. Bible – Hermeneutics. 2. Civilization, Christian.
3. Christianity and culture. I. Title.
BS476.Y68 1996
220.6'09'015 – dc20   96–26085 CIP

ISBN 0 521 58153 2

To Maurice Wiles, a great encourager,
with affection and thanks

Generalisation is the death of art.
It's in the details where God resides.

(These words, attributed to Arthur Miller, playwright,
appeared as a 'Saying of the Week' in *The Observer*, 9 April 1995.)

Contents

Preface

The Speaker's Lectures in Biblical Studies in the University of Oxford for 1992 and 1993 provided the opportunity to draft most of this book. I was assured that I could use the lectures to try something out, and that is what I did. I trust that this version reflects a more mature, and indeed coherent, stage in my thinking: in Oxford, I contested the whole idea of 'typology' in 1992, only to restore it in 1993!

Although the original drafts provided the basis for what appears here, none has remained unchanged, not least because the integration of the two sets of lectures has effected an almost total transformation of the original order. In several cases, there has been substantial rewriting, with the inclusion of additional material; in some, the omission of repetitive recapping, which was necessary for a lecture audience; and, in most, a recasting of link paragraphs. Furthermore, one previously published paper has been incorporated in slightly revised form, others plundered at various stages.

I am grateful to Professor Ernest Nicholson and those who elected me to the Speaker's Lectureship for giving me the stimulus to develop this work. Others, for whom I have a great respect, did me the honour of faithfully coming to the lectures and offering encouragement; to these too I would express my thanks, especially Professor John Barton, Professor Christopher Rowland and Dr Sebastian Brock. I hope this version will not disappoint them, or Professor Maurice Wiles, my Cambridge *Doktorvater* and career-long mentor. To him I dedicate this volume.

Abbreviations

ACW	*Ancient Christian Writers.* New York: Newman Press
addit. vol.	additional volume
Adv. haer.	*Adversus haereses*
Adv. marc.	*Adversus Marcionem*
ANCL	*Ante-Nicene Christian Library*, Edinburgh: T. & T. Clark
Apol.	*Apology*
Apost. const.	*Apostolic constitutions*
BJRL	*Bulletin of the John Rylands Library.* Manchester: John Rylands Library
C. Arianos	*Contra Arianos*
Cat. orat.	*Catechetical oration(s)*
CC	*Corpus Christianorum.* Turnhout: Brepols
CCL	*Corpus Christianorum. Series Latina.* Turnhout: Brepols
C. Cels.	*Contra Celsum*
C. Eunom.	*Contra Eunomium*
I/II Clem.	*I/II Clement*
Comm.	*Commentary*
Comm. in Ps.	*Commentary on the Psalms*
Comm. Jn.	*Commentary on John*
Comm. Matt.	*Commentary on Matthew*
CSCO	*Corpus Scriptorum Christianorum Orientalium.* Louvain: Secretariat to *CSCO*
CSEL	*Corpus Scriptorum Ecclesiasticorum Latinorum.* Vienna: Tempsky
CWS	*The Classics of Western Spirituality.* New York: Paulist Press
De doct. Christ.	*De doctrina Christiana*

Dem. Evang.	*Demonstratio evangelica*
De princ.	*De principiis*
De Trin.	*De Trinitate*
Dial.	*Dialogue with Trypho*
Ep. Barn.	*Epistle of Barnabas*
ET	English translation
FC	*Fathers of the Church.* Washington, DC: Catholic University of America Press
GCS	*Die griechischen christlichen Schriftsteller.* Berlin: The Berlin Academy
HE	*Historia ecclesiastica*
Hom. Cor.	*Homilies on the Corinthian Letters*
Hom. in Matt.	*Homilies on Matthew's Gospel*
Hom. Jer.	*Homilies on Jeremiah*
Inst. orat.	*Institutio oratoria*
Jaeger	*Gregorii Nysseni Opera.* Ed. W. Jaeger *et al.*, Leiden: Brill
JSNT	*Journal for the Study of the New Testament.* Sheffield: Sheffield Academic Press
JTS	*Journal of Theological Studies.* Oxford: Oxford University Press
LCC	*Library of Christian Classics.* London: SCM Press
LCL	*Loeb Classical Library.* London: William Heinemann, Cambridge, Mass.: Harvard University Press
Mart. Pol.	*Martyrdom of Polycarp*
Nov. T.	*Novum Testamentum.* Leiden: Brill
NPNF	*A Select Library of Nicene and Post-Nicene Fathers.* 1st and 2nd Series. Oxford and London: Parker & Co. Reprinted Grand Rapids: Eerdmans
NS	New Series
NTS	*New Testament Studies.* SNTS. Cambridge: Cambridge University Press
Orat.	*Oration*
PG	*Patrologia Graeca*
Praep. evang.	*Praeparatio evangelica*
prol.	prologue
SC	*Sources Chrétiennes.* Paris: Editions du Cerf
serm.	sermo(nes)
SNTS	Society for New Testament Studies
SP	*Studia Patristica.* Papers presented at the Oxford

	Patristic Conferences. Publishers various: formerly TU, latterly Leuven: Peeters
Strom.	*Stromateis*
TPI	Trinity Press International
TS	*Texts and Studies*. Cambridge: Cambridge University Press
TU	Texte und Untersuchungen. Berlin: Akademie-Verlag
VC	*Vigiliae Christianae*. Amsterdam: North Holland Publishing Co.

Introduction

This book is an attempt to reconfigure standard outlines of patristic exegesis of the Bible. This it seeks to effect by presenting not a linear argument or chronological account, but something more like a spider's web. Such a web is made up of strands carefully placed in relation to one another. The radiating segments of the web are analogous to the sections of the book: they represent the major themes, each of which is traced in second-century material and then broadened out by consideration of material from subsequent centuries. These segments, however, are interlinked by connecting threads, issues which keep recurring, and which defy simple organisation. Scattered over the web are dew-drops that highlight issues by providing depth of focus through detailed inspection of particular texts. The hope is that by a combination of panoramas and close-ups, new perspectives may emerge as the complete web is contemplated.

It has been suggested that 'anyone engaged in studies related to the Fathers of the Church has not had readily available any historical outline of patristic exegesis'.[1] The writer of those words, Manlio Simonetti, set out to fill the gap. Certainly, a great deal of the requisite material lies in studies of particular outstanding exegetes or scholarly monographs on the treatment of specific texts. So the translation of Simonetti's work is a useful addition to the introductory literature available in English.[2] It is not my intention

---

[1] Manlio Simonetti, Preface to *Biblical Interpretation in the Early Church: An Historical Introduction to Patristic Exegesis*, ET John A. Hughes, with Anders Bergquist and Markus Bockmuehl as editors, and William Horbury as Consultant Editor (Edinburgh: T. & T. Clark, 1994), p. vii.

[2] Other standard literature that students may use as introductions includes: Robert M. Grant with David Tracy, *A Short History of the Interpretation of the Bible* (2nd edn, revised and enlarged, London: SCM Press, 1984) (chapters 1–15 originally published in 1963); P. R.

to duplicate such an account. Rather my discussion presupposes acquaintance with earlier work. As indicated, the material is selective, for truly comprehensive coverage of the patristic material would be impossible in a single study. But there is sufficient, I hope, to reconfigure our diagrams of the exegetical process.

Fundamentally, exegesis explicates the meaning of a 'text', usually written but potentially anything in words, potentially even a symbolic artefact without words. This process is always complex, involving usually language and its usage, context, reference, background, genre, authorial intention, reader reception, literary structure and so on. The Fathers were more aware of these complexities than standard accounts suggest. The traditional categories of 'literal', 'typological' and 'allegorical' are quite simply inadequate as descriptive tools, let alone analytical tools. Nor is the Antiochene reaction against Alexandrian allegory correctly described as an appeal to the 'literal' or 'historical' meaning. A more adequate approach needs to be created.

This might be regarded as a specialised patristic matter, but I hope it is also a contribution to biblical studies. Recent developments have challenged the once predominant historico-critical approach to exegesis. Canon criticism, structuralism and literary-critical studies have produced new perspectives and methods. Hermeneutical discussion and liberation theologies have questioned the basis and value of what are increasingly, but erroneously, regarded as the 'traditional' methods. It is in this context that a reassessment of patristic exegesis seems timely, and relevant to the central questions of modern biblical interpretation. In an earlier book,[3] I endeavoured to use patristic material in discussion of these issues. As indicated, I now wish to refine our understanding of what the Church Fathers were doing as they used and interpreted the scriptures.[4]

Ackroyd and C. F. Evans (eds.), *The Cambridge History of the Bible*, vol. 1 (Cambridge: Cambridge University Press, 1970), pp. 412–563; J. Daniélou, *From Shadows to Reality: Studies in the Biblical Typology of the Fathers* (London: Burns & Oates, 1960); R. M. Grant, *The Letter and the Spirit* (London: SPCK, 1957); G. W. H. Lampe and K. J. Woollcombe, *Essays in Typology* (London: SCM Press, 1957); K. Froehlich, *Biblical Interpretation in the Early Church*, Sources of Early Christian Thought (Philadelphia: Fortress Press, 1984).

[3] *The Art of Performance: Towards a Theology of Holy Scripture* (London: Darton, Longman & Todd, 1990).

[4] The work which appears in this book has generated further papers which bear more directly on these wider issues. My purpose is not to repeat such discussions, but to

The articulation of the range of things that were actually going on in patristic exegesis cannot but illuminate many current exegetical assumptions: for, as Edwin Hatch pointed out a century ago,[5] scriptural commentary is still derived from the practice of commenting on literature which was the basis of ancient education, ancient education being the ancestor of the educational traditions of mediaeval universities and of the classical tradition which predominated throughout Europe until comparatively recently. The art of exegesis was partly taught, partly caught, as pupils read texts with their masters. Scriptural exegetes sought meaning and truth in their texts just as literary exegetes did in classical texts. The loss of that tradition has impoverished awareness of all the things involved, and reinforced preoccupation with but one element – namely the historical reference.

The results of the Fathers' exegetical methods have often been dismissed because of their so-called disregard of history. Indeed, the standard English account of Origen's exegesis[6] virtually organises the material around the view that Origen never really understood the Bible because he sat too loosely to history. Since that book was written, the shift in biblical studies has helped us to recognise that concern about 'history' has a very modern ring. The Fathers would condemn much modern exegesis for its exclusive focus on the 'earthly', and its lack of concern with the 'heavenly' dimension of the text. A reassessment of their assumption that the Bible has a 'spiritual meaning' is necessary, as is a review of the procedures whereby they unravelled the symbols discerned in the text. Debate is needed about potential criteria for distinguishing justifiable and unjustifiable 'allegory'. This is important not only for patristic interpretation but also for modern hermeneutics. Without a form of allegory that at least allows for analogy, the biblical text can only be an object of archaeological interest. Recent trends suggest that there is considerable dissatisfaction with the limitations

contribute to current debates indirectly by providing further insight into the exegetical processes we can trace in the early Church. See: 'Allegory and the Ethics of Reading', in Francis Watson (ed.), *The Open Text* (London: SCM 1993), pp. 103–20; 'Typology', in Stanley E. Porter, Paul Joyce and David E.Orton (eds.), *Crossing the Boundaries. Essays in Biblical Interpretation in Honour of Michael D. Goulder* (Leiden: Brill 1994), pp. 29–48; 'Interpretative Genres and the Inevitability of Pluralism', *JSNT* 59 (1995), pp. 93–110.

[5] *The Influence of Greek Ideas on Christianity* (New York: Harper, 1957, reprinted by arrangement with Williams & Norgate, London).

[6] By R. P. C. Hanson, *Allegory and Event* (London: SCM, 1959).

of historico-critical research precisely because it yields no hermeneutic.

We may not always find the conclusions of patristic exegesis satisfactory or plausible, but this is more often than not because of a different estimate of what seems problematic, or of what constitutes a valid cross-reference. From the Fathers' methods and their endeavour we might learn much. The fundamental exegetical question is: what does it mean? The answer may be obvious, or it may be arrived at by rational enquiry about word usage, about signification and metaphor, about syntax, about reference and about truth. There is no escape from that complexity.

Nowadays, the principal vehicle of exegesis remains the commentary, while the primary locus of interpretation is still in fact the pulpit. The origin of both homily and commentary lies in the patristic period, and a reassessment of the influences that produced these forms could illuminate the relationship between them. To what extent does the interpretative genre shape the interpretation offered and the interests of the interpreter, creating conventions which predetermine the approach to and perception of the text and its meaning? The Bible functioned in many genres in the patristic period. Much work is also required on the interrelationship between biblical material and theological thinking, the understanding of one undoubtedly affecting the other. The modern divorce between biblical exegesis and systematic theology, or indeed between biblical exegesis and *praxis*, would have been unthinkable in the days of the Fathers. The question of meaning was deeply affected by the issue of truth, by what was conceptually possible given the limitations of religious language, and by what was the perceived reference outside the text. To deplore the influence of Greek philosophy or contrast the Hellenic and Hebraic approaches, as scholars have done in this century, is to do less than justice to the fascinating cultural interpenetration which took place as the Bible became the literary foundation of a new 'totalising discourse'.[7]

This book is not intended, then, as a review of the very considerable amount of recent specialist study of patristic exegesis, but rather has a twofold aim: (1) to challenge accepted generalisations, so, hopefully, alerting a wider theological readership to the pitfalls

---

[7] Averil Cameron, *Christianity and the Rhetoric of Empire. The Development of Christian Discourse* (Berkeley/Los Angeles/Oxford: University of California Press, 1991).

of uncritical acceptance of summary accounts, and (2) to work with certain key texts and authors to provide living examples of the exegetical process, its principles, underlying assumptions and practice. In the process, light will be shed on the crucial function of the Bible in the formation of Christian culture.

PART I

Exegesis and the unity
of the scriptures

The unity of the scriptures is recognised to have been a 'dogma' among the Fathers. The effect of this on exegesis, however, has not previously been discussed. Yet exegesis cannot but reflect funda-mental hermeneutical principles which derive from the larger process of reception and appropriation. This is evident as soon as one articulates the interaction between understanding particular sentences or passages and discerning the perceived overarching plan, plot or argument of a literary work. The one affects the other: if the one modifies or confirms the other, then we may speak not of a hermeneutical circle, but rather a hermeneutical spiral as the whole and parts are brought into meaningful coherence.

Part I shows how the dogma was formed by considering how second-century readers received and read the scriptures; and then how exegesis was slanted by the assumption that the scriptures formed a unity.

CHAPTER I

Reception and appropriation

I

By 'reception and appropriation' I mean the exegetical process whereby readers make the text their own.

According to scholarly tradition, 'reception' of the biblical material in the early Church has been studied through the search for allusion and quotation. Debate has centred on the question whether such material evidences oral tradition or knowledge of particular documents, especially in relation to the reception of Christian-authored texts.[1] If knowledge of particular documents is claimed, then the issue of the status accorded to them becomes important, and so, in the case of Christian-authored documents, the process of reception is associated with the formation of the canon in most modern scholarship. The assumption has been that the canonical process was one in which Christian-authored documents were gradually lifted to the same inspired status as the inherited Jewish ones. The reception and appropriation of the Jewish scriptures has usually been taken for granted. True, questions have been raised about which scriptures, and to what extent they were mediated through memory or testimony-books. But the assumption

---

[1] E.g. Helmut Koester is especially associated with the view that in the Apostolic Fathers knowledge of specific New Testament documents is not proven, rather form-critical analysis discovers the deposit of oral tradition: *Synoptische Überlieferung bei den Apostolischen Vätern* (TU 65, Berlin: Akademie-Verlag, 1957). Other scholars, however, have persisted in arguing for knowledge of this or that canonical text on the basis of apparent allusion: the continuing vitality of this opposing view is indicated by the theme of the Leuven Colloquium of 1986, papers edited by J.-M. Sévrin and published in 1989 under the title *The New Testament in Early Christianity* (Leuven: Leuven University Press, 1989), and also the recent English translation of Massaux's classic thesis of 1950, *The Influence of the Gospel of Saint Matthew on Christian Literature before Saint Irenaeus* (Macon, Ga.: Mercer University Press, and Leuven: Peeters, 1990).

that Christians inherited a canon to which they then added their own literature meant that there was nothing surprising in Origen's adoption of the Jewish traditions that every jot and tittle mattered, or that inspired texts could be interpreted by means of other inspired texts. Thus, the unity and inerrancy of the Bible, however problematic for modern scholars, have been taken to be, for the early Church, unsurprising dogmas.

Meanwhile, however, reader-response theory has posed other questions about reception and appropriation.[2] We are now alerted to the fact that the way in which texts are read determines their meaning, for a text 'says' nothing until the reader 'realises' the black-and-white patterns on the page. Reader expectation invests a text with coherence, so prior assumptions about the nature of a text and how it is to be read will deeply affect what is found in the process of reading and interpreting. Our mental and physical attitudes are different depending on whether we are curled up in a corner of the settee with a novel, or standing for the Gospel lection in church.

Of course, in the early Church there were not many post-Kantian autonomous selves with freedom to select and criticise, to adopt a hermeneutic of retrieval or a hermeneutic of suspicion as suited them. But attention to reader-reception issues does suggest that, while literary allusion and canon formation may tell us much, they too often presume a literary environment and a reading culture which may be entirely anachronistic. Paper, printing and copyright belonged to the future. Insufficient attention has been paid to the cultural and social – indeed practical – realities of 'reading' in the ancient world. Reception of texts must have been affected by the character and format of books, the kind of people who used them, and the mechanics of book production, as well as their composition, publication and distribution, not to mention the extent of literacy, especially in the social circles amongst which Christianity spread.

---

2 Some of the classic discussions of reader-reception theory can be found in David Lodge (ed.), *Modern Criticism and Theory: a Reader* (London: Longman, 1988). Reader-response theories are associated particularly with the literary-critical work of Wolfgang Iser and Stanley Fish. Their effect on biblical and theological studies may be followed up through, e.g., Edgar V. McKnight, *Postmodern Use of the Bible. The Emergence of Reader-Oriented Criticism* (Nashville: Abingdon, 1988); Mark G. Brett, 'The Future of Reader Criticisms?', in Francis Watson (ed.), *The Open Text*; and Werner Jeanrond, *Text and Interpretation as Categories of Theological Thinking* (ET Thomas J. Wilson, Dublin: Gill & Macmillan, 1988).

Yet we leave the physical reality of ancient books to specialists in textual criticism. They may at least supply us with some information.[3]

It is evident that upper-class literati had private libraries, enjoyed what we might describe as country-house literary weekends, patronised the equivalent of literary societies and reading circles, composed literary works which they read to one another, and communicated with one another in highly wrought literary letters, often intended for collection and circulation as literary works themselves. For such people what we now call 'intertextuality' was an important feature of literature, one text achieving its status by its allusive and mimetic relationship with others that had the status of classics.

There was a book-trade to serve the needs of such readers, and possessing classics written in gold letter was one way of conspicuous consumption. In the absence of printing, however, book production could not be effectively controlled, and just as people now pirate tapes or computer software, private individuals had their own private copies made and distributed, whether of their own work or that of others. Interpolation, incision and plagiarism were commonplace hazards. The author's control over his text was perceived as a problem, and some philosophers, like Aristotle, vested their deposit in an authorised community or school in order to protect it.

Reader reception was universally through the oral medium, and reading even in private was aloud. Consequently, as George Kennedy has stressed,[4] texts were received in a linear way, the overall thrust becoming evident as the structure unfolded in succession.

---

[3] C. H. Roberts, 'The Codex', in *Proceedings of the British Academy* 40 (1954), pp. 169–204; (with T. C. Skeat), *The Birth of the Codex* (London: Oxford University Press for the British Academy, 1983); 'Books in the Greco-Roman World and in the New Testament', in Ackroyd and Evans (eds.), *The Cambridge History of the Bible*, vol. 1 (Cambridge: Cambridge University Press, 1970), pp. 48–66; and 'The Writing and Dissemination of Literature in the Classical World', in David Daiches (ed.), *Literature and Western Civilisation*, vol. 1 (London: Aldus, 1972); to Roberts I am indebted for the specific items of information underlying the outline that follows here. But now see Harry Y. Gamble, *Books and Readers in the Early Church* (New Haven and London: Yale University Press, 1995).

[4] E.g. in *New Testament Interpretation through Rhetorical Criticism* (Chapel Hill and London: University of North Carolina Press, 1984), pp. 5–6. Cf. George Kennedy's other works on rhetoric, such as *The Art of Rhetoric in the Roman World* (Princeton: Princeton University Press, 1972); *Classical Rhetoric and its Christian and Secular Tradition from Ancient to Modern Times* (Chapel Hill and London: University of California Press, 1980); and *Greek Rhetoric under Christian Emperors* (Princeton: Princeton University Press, 1983).

Exordium, narrative, proof and peroration provided a recapitulative framework which carried the listener to conviction by reminder and variation. Reference back depended upon memory, reference forward upon expectation, or known classic outcome. As the roll gradually unwound, so a narrative or argument moved towards its climax or ending.

In such circles, all real books were written on papyrus rolls. Notes and drafts would be made on wax tablets, and in the West these cumbersome aids, often linked with thongs into the kind of thing we call a book, were already being replaced by parchment notebooks in New Testament times. From this would emerge the codex, but it was never used at this early date for a real book. To have 'pocket-editions' in codex form is recommended as a novelty by Martial at the end of the first century, and he stresses their convenience for travel and for saving space in the library. But his endorsement did not produce a consumer switch. As Roberts put it, 'the fashionable author or discriminating bibliophile would not favour a format that suggested the lecture room or the counting house'.[5]

For that is where the codex format belonged. In the grammatical and rhetorical schools, pupils made their notes and drafts on tablets, in the world of business, accounts and other notes were similarly inscribed, as were the *aides-mémoire* of lawyers and doctors. When Paul is represented in 2 Timothy 4.13 as asking Timothy to bring the books, especially the notebooks, a distinction is made between rolls and parchment folders, using the Latin loan-word *membranas*, one of a number of indications that it was the practical Romans who introduced this more convenient substitute for linked tablets. The codex belonged to the day-to-day world, where a basic level of literacy was probably more widespread than in any period prior to the twentieth century.[6] The roll belonged to the world of the ancient revered classics which shaped a sophisticated high-class literary culture, which in turn filtered down to the urban masses through theatre and public oratory.

In the schools, pupils would make jottings in notebooks, but they would learn to read the classics from papyrus rolls. Rhetorical education encouraged reading aloud as practice for declamation,

---

5 Roberts, 'The Codex', p. 178.
6 Though see William V. Harris, *Ancient Literacy* (Cambridge, Mass.: Harvard University Press, 1989).

and the use of literature as great speech to emulate in composition. Reading a manuscript without word division or punctuation required the kind of oral realisation that most of us need to read a musical score:[7] it is not easy to do it in one's head. The end-product would be like the performance of a concerto by a virtuoso – from memory without the score.

That, it seems, is where Jewish practice differed. As to this day, the *bar mitzvah* boy learned how to perform the text correctly with his eyes on the script. Though most often referred to as a *proseuchē* (prayer-house), the synagogue could be described as an ethnic meeting-place for reading; with its library and school, it preserved a culture based on a body of ancient literature, different from that which shaped the Hellenised world, yet just as much, if not more, grounded in books and their reading aloud. Its 'real books' have remained inscribed on parchment rolls to this day.

The Jewish community exercised tight internal control over the wording of the text and its book production, which was never done by mass dictation, always by painstaking copying from a master-roll. The scrolls, paraded ceremonially in liturgy, almost came to take the ritual place of a pagan image. This was a very considerable heightening of the 'aura' attributed to books in the ancient world in general. Jewish children, like other children of the time, used wax tablets and notebooks in school. The oral traditions and rulings of Jewish teachers seem sometimes to have been recorded on tablets or in notebooks. But it would be unthinkable that the 'scriptures' be inscribed on anything but rolls.

It is therefore something of a shock to discover that Christians were producing copies of the Torah and Psalms in papyrus codices as early as the middle of the second century – sacred books in notebook format! As Roberts states, 'the transference of the Law from its sacrosanct form to a format of no antiquity and little regard . . . must have seemed to the Jew an act of sacrilege'.[8] So the question for us

---

[7] Cf. *The Art of Performance*, p. 96.

[8] 'Books in the Greco-Roman World', p. 61. It is also clear that Christians did not maintain careful authorisation of the text, or indeed its preservation in the original Hebrew. Translations into various vernaculars, not only of the inherited scriptures, but also of the Christian materials which became the New Testament, were made early, and the texts of those Christian documents seem to have been fluid in the second and third centuries. The use of texts by 'heretics' both provoked accusations of text-tampering, and, it would seem, judicious modification: see Bart D. Ehrman, *The Orthodox Corruption of Scripture. The Effect of Early Christological Controversies on the Text of the New Testament* (Oxford: Oxford University Press, 1993).

is this: what does that say about Christian reception and appropriation of the Jewish scriptures?

The answer to that may depend on the answer to Roberts'
question, namely: why did Christians adopt the codex form for their
books far in advance of it becoming the norm? Indeed, long after
the codex was established as the form for Christian scriptures,
Christian scholars like Origen and Jerome reverted to the roll for
their literary works, thus confirming the peculiarity of Christian
custom. It makes sense that the earliest Christians used notebooks
for odds and ends, perhaps collections of testimonies or sayings of
Jesus. It is unlikely that the majority were poor and marginalised,
but on the other hand few came from among the privileged or
leisured literati. They largely came from the urban commercial
classes, craftsmen, traders, travelling salesmen, as far as we can
make out. Few were literary, but many, in all probability, were
literate, and accustomed to making notes on tablets or parchment
folders.[9]

The use of such a medium for the dissemination of 'real books',
however, demands explanation. Is it any wonder that cultivated
pagans regarded the Christian scriptures as crude and unworthy of
attention, that Origen had to defend Christians from the charge
of unlettered barbarity? Their books simply were not books in the
proper sense at all. It is hardly surprising that neither the argument
from economy, nor the suggestion of easier reference for apologetic
argument with Jews, satisfies Roberts, who canvassed alternative
views in his various writings, both of which assumed that Christian
writings in codex form influenced the adoption of this format for the
books of scripture.

Now if one or other of these hypotheses were proved correct, it
would imply that Christian-authored books had a certain priority
– the very opposite of the usual view of canon-formation. And, in
any case, the use of the codex has dramatic implications for the
reception and appropriation of the Jewish books. They were
physically 'taken over' – not just re-read but re-formed. In the act
of appropriation, they were subordinated, demoted, long before

---

[9] In *Manuscript, Society and Belief in Early Christian Egypt* (Oxford: Oxford University Press for
British Academy, 1979), C. H. Roberts indicates that the 'hands' of our earliest papyrus
texts are 'documentary' rather than 'literary', thus confirming this point.

they were accorded the title 'Old Testament'.[10] They had been, as it were, wrested away from their original community, and another community was taking charge of this literary heritage. These books were informing a new culture for a new community which received them differently, and accorded them a different kind of status.

In these new Christian assemblies, it was not scrolls and reading which had primacy. The word written and read was testimony to something else, and the living and abiding voice of witness had the greater authority.[11] There was no reason why, like the oral testimony, this written testimony should not be recorded in note-books so that reminders could be turned up more readily and carried about with less difficulty, perhaps be more easily concealed if necessary. We are witnessing, it seems, not the gradual elevation of recent Christian books to the sacred status of the Jewish scriptures, but rather the relativising of those ancient scriptures. Certainly they retain an undeniable aura, both because of the respect accorded literature in the general culture of the Graeco-Roman world, and because of the specific legacy of their sacred place in Jewish tradition. But they have become secondary to the Gospel of Christ.[12]

The ambiguities implicit in all this become explicit in the struggle with Marcion and the Gnostics. But already Ignatius, like Paul, wrestles with the appropriate response to those who overestimate the importance of these books:

[10] My argument was partially anticipated by Peter Katz in his article, 'The Early Christians' Use of Codices Instead of Rolls', *JTS* 46 (1945), pp. 63–5. He argues that Christ and the eucharist replaced the 'veiled sacred rolls', kept in niches or 'later in a richly ornamented temple-like ark', at the centre of Christian worship, and that self-conscious differentiation from Judaism is the key to explaining Christian adoption of the codex.

[11] As is well known, Eusebius (*HE* III, 39, 4; *GCS*, vol. II.1, p. 286) quotes the early second-century Christian Papias of Hierapolis as saying: 'I thought that it was not so much what was taken from books that would help me as that which came from a living and abiding voice.'

[12] The discussion of the *nomina sacra* in C. H. Roberts, *Manuscript, Society and Belief*, suggests the same conclusion. Christian scribal practice here is unlikely to derive from Jewish usage; rather the Jewish texts taken over by Christians are written in such a way as to draw attention to the 'Name' of Jesus, and to suggest number symbolisms pointing to fulfilment in Christ. Jewish veneration of the Tetragrammaton provides a general cultural background. This confirms the sense of 'aura' ascribed to texts which point to Christ, but which have nevertheless ceased to become more directly the object of veneration. The revelatory importance of the (secret) 'name' in a Gnostic text such as *The Gospel of Truth* merely reinforces this observation.

Certain people declared in my hearing, 'Unless I can find a thing in our ancient records (*archeia*), I refuse to believe it in the Gospel'; and when I assured them that it is indeed in the ancient scriptures (*gegraptai*), they retorted, 'That has got to be proved'. But for my part, my records are Jesus Christ; for me the sacrosanct records are His cross and death and resurrection, and the faith that comes through Him. And it is by these, and by the help of your prayers, that I am hoping to be justified.[13]

The 'sacrosanct records' are in Greek *ta athikta archeia* – they are 'untouchable'. This is a remarkable reminiscence of the Rabbinic definition of sacred books as those which 'defile the hands', and the phrase confirms that the *archeia* meant are the written scriptures of the Jews.

Thus the passage demonstrates that the Gospel of Jesus Christ, not apparently a written Gospel but what people have called the 'kerygma', has become equivalent to sacred books, within which, in any case, whatever is to be believed is found written. As already for Paul and the Epistle to the Hebrews, Christ has become the hermeneutical key which relativises the texts, even as they confirm the Christian testimony. (Corresponding to this, maybe, is the retention of their reading and interpretation in the liturgy, but subordinated to the eucharist.)

The sacred glow on the scrolls consequently begins to fade while they remain important as proof of faith. Before we know where we are, they are transcribed into notebooks, a more convenient format for their new, more utilitarian role. So is it surprising that Marcion raises the question whether these books are after all indispensable, indeed whether they really are about the same God as revealed by Apostle and Gospel? Once disseminated in notebooks, is it surprising that little study circles got to work debating the esoteric applications which this new attitude fostered? And would not such study inevitably focus piecemeal on intriguing puzzles or congenial texts? Are Valentinus and Justin Martyr all that different in this regard, though one seems to have been intrigued by prophecy and the other by cosmology? The physical reception of these texts, first transformed by the hermeneutical attitude adopted towards them, then in turn affects their interpretation. And it all happens even faster than we might have imagined.

---

[13] *Philadelphians* 8. ET Maxwell Staniforth, rev. Andrew Louth, *Early Christian Writings* (London: Penguin Classics, 1987), p. 95.

II

Meanwhile, however, Christian assemblies had adopted not only the Jewish scriptures, but also much of the character of Jewish synagogue gatherings.[14] Even if the eucharist became the climax, Christians still had public readings of books and teachers who provided commentary. Presumably, to begin with, books would be owned by the community and not widely disseminated, even if key texts, or testimonies, were more widely available in notebooks. How was such a complex body of literature, even in translation, to be made accessible to aural recipients for whom this was foreign and unknown, who had no prior acquaintance with the plots, characters, heroes, contexts? How would they 'follow' a text, presumably read piecemeal according to some kind of lectionary system? How would they retain a sense of direction and overview as each extract was heard?

Some centuries later, the need to summarise scripture is made quite explicit by Cyril of Jerusalem, faced with his class of catechumens and the pressure to 're-educate' the masses of the Roman Empire. In that day, church buildings would begin to be covered with the visual representation of biblical narrative in mural and mosaic, rivalling the traditional art of the Roman world which had communicated the heroes and tales of the ancient pagan culture. Many had neither the leisure nor the capacity to read the biblical codices. This, for Cyril, justifies the existence of the creed as a brief summary committed to the memory.

In learning the Faith and in professing it, acquire and keep that only, which is now delivered to you by the Church, and which has been powerfully composed out of all the Scriptures. For since all cannot read the Scriptures, some being hindered as to the knowledge of them by want of learning, and others by want of leisure, in order that the soul may not perish from ignorance, we comprise the whole doctrine of the Faith in a few lines. This summary I wish you both to commit to memory when I recite it, and to rehearse with all diligence among yourselves, not writing it out on paper, but engraving it by the memory upon your heart . . . For the articles of the Faith were not composed on the basis of human preferences; rather the most important points were collected out of all the Scripture to make up one complete teaching of the Faith. And just as the mustard seed in one

---

[14] Cf. James Tunstead Burtchaell, *From Synagogue to Church. Public Services and Offices in the Earliest Christian Communities* (Cambridge: Cambridge University Press, 1992).

small grain contains many branches, so also this Faith has embraced in few words all the knowledge of godliness in the Old and New Testaments.[15]

It would, of course, be anachronistic simplistically to read this back to the initial process of reception and appropriation. But something analogous must have been the situation. The 'hypothesis' of scripture had to be articulated to enable its 'hearing'.

In *The Art of Performance*,[16] I stressed the importance of the Rule of Faith or the Canon of Truth as providing the extra-canonical framework or 'overarching story' by which the scriptures were to be read and interpreted. Irenaeus appealed to this public tradition, authorised by the apostles, as the guaranteed deposit which ensured that the private esoteric interpretations of the heretics and their censored or contaminated texts could not be reliable. The issues of proper reception and appropriation had become a matter for contention, and the concept of an authorised tradition preserving the literary deposit is reasserted against the private 'piracy' that was beginning to develop as a result of re-forming the scriptures in notebooks.

What has not been explicitly noted before is that all along creed-like statements and confessions must in practice have provided the hermeneutical key to public reading of scripture before Irenaeus articulated this. An addition to the many factors in the formation of creeds explored by J. N. D. Kelly[17] must be the need to provide the 'hypothesis' which gave sense and meaning to the collection of scrolls or notebooks from which the community read aloud in its gatherings. Kelly's insistence that a linear evolution from one-clause to two-clause or three-clause forms of confession cannot be traced is an important observation: for each of the three forms provided important ways of access to the texts. The one-clause form gave Jesus Christ and the story of his life, death and resurrection primacy over the books which nevertheless testified to him; the two-

---

[15] *Cat. orat.* v.12. Migne, *PG* 33.520–1. ET a modified version of *NPNF*, 2nd series, vol. VII, p. 32.
[16] Ch. 3. NB Wayne Meeks in his Speaker's Lectures (published as *The Origins of Christian Morality. The First Two Centuries* (New Haven and London: Yale University Press, 1993)) also explored in an interesting way the importance of this overall plot, and attributed to Irenaeus the credit for making it explicit 'as the guiding theme for reading scripture and understanding the moral contest in which every person is engaged'. Irenaeus was consciously conservative, but perhaps in this, as in other ways, innovatory in the face of his opponents. What he made explicit, however, I would see as already implicit.
[17] *Early Christian Creeds* (London: Longmans, 2nd edn, 1960).

clause form drew attention to the continuity between promise and fulfilment, and the revelation through Christ of the God already known in the Jewish scriptures; the three-clause form reinforced the inspired nature of the words which testified to the Word of God. All were ways of affirming the unity of the scriptures as testimony to the revelation of God in Christ.

Thus, long before the formation of the canon of two Testaments, Old and New, or the listing of the authorised books that belonged to it, the unity of the Bible and its witness to Christ was the assumption underlying its 'reception' by readers and hearers in the 'public' assembly of the community. Irenaeus drew on this tradition and developed it in response to Marcion and the Gnostics.

With received tradition behind him as the ultimate court of appeal, Irenaeus could accuse his opponents of not understanding the *hypothesis* of scripture.[18] They have their own *hypothesis*, which neither the prophets heralded, nor the Lord taught, nor the apostles passed down. They read from what Irenaeus refers to as *agrapha* (taken to mean non-scriptural sources). Using a common proverb, Irenaeus suggests that they strive to weave ropes of sand, attempting to harmonise to their claims the Lord's parables, the prophetic sayings and the apostolic words, so that their *plasma* (a word implying their own creation, invention or fiction) should not seem to lack testimony. He suggests an analogy: gemstones or mosaic pieces, intended to construct the beautiful image of a king, being rearranged into the form of a dog or a fox. In the same way, he suggests, the heretics patch together old wives' tales; then lifting sayings, terms and parables from their context, they want to harmonise with their tales the oracles of God.

In a subsequent passage,[19] Irenaeus accuses the heretics of behaving like the literary sophisticates who made 'centos' out of Homer, stringing together verses abstracted from context to make a new narrative. The word 'cento' is thought to have meant a 'patchwork cloak', and the idea was to take a series of discrete poetic lines from the classic epic and put them together so that they made sense as a new narrative.[20] Of the Valentinians, then, Irenaeus says:

---

[18] *Adv. haer.* i.viii.1; Harvey, vol. i, p. 66; *SC* i.2, pp. 112 ff.; ET *ANCL*, vol. i, p. 32.

[19] *Adv. haer.* i.ix.4; Harvey, vol. i, pp. 84 ff.; *SC* i.2, pp. 146 ff.; ET *ANCL*, vol. i, pp. 40–1.

[20] One of the few literary works to come down to us from the pen of an early Christian woman author is a work of this kind: Proba's *cento*, using Virgil's works to provide 694 lines for a Christian poem, possibly composed in response to Julian's decree against Christians

Taking terms and names scattered here and there in scripture, they transfer them . . . from their natural sense to a non-natural sense. Thus they behave just like those who propose *hypotheseis* which happen to occur to them, and then try to do an exercise out of Homer's poems. The result is that the ignorant imagine Homer composed the verses for what is in fact a newly constructed *hypothesis*, and many others are carried away by the neat sequence of the verses into wondering whether Homer actually did compose it in this way.

Irenaeus gives an example, and then asks,

What simpleminded hearer would not be carried away by these verses, and would consider Homer had composed in this way according to this *hypothesis?* The hearer who is experienced in Homer's *hypothesis* would recognise the verses but not the *hypothesis*, knowing that one referred to Odysseus, another to Heracles, [and so on; Irenaeus multiplies his examples]. If such a person takes each verse and restores it to its proper context, he gets the [strange] *hypothesis* out of the way. So the person who holds to himself unswervingly the Canon of Truth he received in baptism, will recognise the names and terms and parables as being from the scriptures, but will not recognise this blasphemous *hypothesis* of theirs. Though he will detect the mosaic pieces, he will not accept the fox instead of the king's image. Restoring each of the expressions to its own rank, and accommodating it to the body of truth, he will expose as naked and unsubstantiated their fiction.

Thus it was that the notion of the Bible having a particular *hypothesis*, which Irenaeus here identified with the Canon of Truth or Rule of Faith, and characterised implicitly as 'the king's face' or the Christological reference, emerged along with the doctrine of the unity of the Bible, both being quite specifically articulated in response to those who would reject or misread some of the books in the community's communal library, claiming that they did not all emanate from the same one God. Books on the Bible in the early Church invariably comment upon these doctrines, pointing out the unfortunate 'flattening' effect they had on exegesis. But their overriding significance for the reception and appropriation of the biblical material, both prior to this crisis and subsequent to it, has hardly been recognised.

teaching classical literature in 362, tells the 'overarching story' of the Bible as perceived by the early Christian tradition – the creation and fall, the birth of Christ and some episodes in his life, and his death and resurrection. See Elizabeth A. Clark, *Ascetic Piety and Women's Faith* (New York: Edwin Mellen, 1986), pp. 124–71.

Neither the Rule of Faith nor the creed was in fact a summary of the whole biblical narrative, as demonstrated earlier in *The Art of Performance*.[21] They provided, rather, the proper reading of the beginning and the ending, the focus of the plot and the relations of the principal characters, so enabling the 'middle' to be heard in bits as meaningful. They provided the 'closure' which contemporary theory prefers to leave open.[22] They articulated the essential hermeneutical key without which texts and community would disintegrate in incoherence.

III

The treatment of many books as one was bound to affect the reading of each and every constituent part. The scholars of the Church, notably the Antiochenes, would ask about the *hypothesis* of a particular prophetic book or Pauline Epistle, or the *skopos* (intent) of a particular Psalm, but, as we shall see in the next chapter, Athanasius in confuting the Arians would look for the mind (*dianoia*) or aim (*skopos*) of scripture as a whole. This he probably inherited from Origen, in whose work the dogma of the Bible's unity had a profound effect upon its exegesis. Origen required that each detailed verse or problem be understood in the light of the Bible's overarching thrust or meaning, which he took to be Christological. The rest of this chapter will explore how Origen understood this unity.

In the *Commentary on John*, Origen is concerned with the Oneness of the Logos. In fragments of Book v,[23] in particular, he turns to the multiplicity of words and 'many books' against which certain texts deliver warnings: the saints are not guilty of speaking too many words, he suggests, because they always have the *skopos* (the aim or intent) which accords with the one Word. Holy scripture is one book, he affirms. It is one book written about Christ, for Christ is written of in the Pentateuch, the prophets, the Psalms, indeed in all the scriptures.

In Book x,[24] Origen is faced with the narrative of the Cleansing

---

[21] *The Art of Performance*, pp. 49ff.
[22] See e.g. Gabriel Josipovici, *The Book of God* (New Haven and London: Yale University Press, 1988).
[23] *GCS*, vol. IV, pp. 102–3; ET *ANCL*, addit. vol., pp. 346ff.
[24] *Comm. Jn.* x.19; *GCS*, vol. IV, p. 175; ET *ANCL*, addit. vol., pp. 399ff.

of the Temple, and the inconsistencies between the Gospel of John and what we call the Synoptic Gospels. Origen suggests that the evangelists dealt with the details freely, shaping them to the underlying truth. He speaks of their 'mystical' (*mystikos*) intent. The heretics have mistaken the underlying object of scripture, often because they could not hold the contradictions together: Christ is son of David and yet not son of David. Origen indicates that he wants to be free to explain material difficulties in the scriptures by the deeper truth which the words of scripture clothe.

The multiplicity, indeed the significance of every jot and tittle, has to be related to the unity. In a fragment of the *39th Homily on Jeremiah*,[25] Origen speaks of the stumbling-blocks in scripture. You should never give up hope that each rock of offence has meaning, he says. Every single word, every letter, has its effect. He compares this with gathering herbs: each has its particular powerful effect on the health of the body, but you have to be an expert to know which herb is required and how to apply it. The interpreter is a sort of spiritual herbalist. Similarly physicians understand the function of all the various parts of the body. So you should think of the scriptures as one complete body of the Word, and those who desire to devote themselves to study should not let a single letter pass without examination and enquiry. If you cannot see how it fits, you should not imagine that it has no purpose. Origen's view of the unity of scripture does not exclude its variety.

In another fragment, this time from the *Commentary on Matthew*, Book II,[26] Origen includes among the peacemakers those who show that what seems the discord of the scriptures is no discord, those who make the harmony and peace of scripture evident, whether the harmony of Old Testament with New, or of Law with Prophets, or of one passage in the Gospels with another, or of one Apostolic writing with another. Referring to a text in Ecclesiastes, he speaks of all the scriptures being the words of the wise that act like goads, and these goads are all applied by the one Shepherd, the Word or Logos. He then turns to another image, that of the lyre with its different strings. Untrained people may think that because the notes are different they are discordant; but one trained in the music of God knows how to strike the strings in time, now the strings of the Law,

[25] From the *Philocalia*; *GCS*, vol. III, p. 196, *SC*, vol. 302, pp. 366–70, ET Tollinton, pp. 49ff.
[26] From the *Philocalia*; *SC*, vol. 302, pp. 308ff. ET Tollinton, p. 46ff.

now harmoniously with them the strings of the Gospel, now the strings of Prophecy, and when occasion demands the Apostolic strings in harmony with one or the other. For he knows all scripture is the one perfect and attuned instrument of God producing from its various notes a single sound of salvation for those willing to learn.

Origen introduced his *Commentary on John*, Book I,[27] by suggesting that the Gospel is the 'first-fruits' of the scriptures, the harvest as it were, whereas Moses is the 'first-growth'. He then defines *Euangelion* as containing the promise of things which rejoice the hearer because of their benefits.[28] But that means Gospel embraces the Law and the Prophets, for they too contain such promises. However, they did not contain them in the same way prior to the coming of Christ: the Saviour caused the Gospel to appear in bodily form, and so caused all the scriptures to appear as Gospel. Every divine scripture, he will eventually conclude, is Gospel. However, as the Law was a *paidagōgos*, a 'shadow' of the good things to come, so the Gospel itself teaches a shadow of the mysteries of Christ. The mysteries are presented in the discourses, the deeds are enigmas of spiritual things. The sensible or 'bodily' Gospel is really about an intellectual and spiritual one. Origen speaks of our whole energy being directed to the effort to penetrate to the depths of the meaning of the Gospel and to search out the truth divested of 'types'. That truth is the one Logos of God.[29]

Examination of Origen's hermeneutical principles as he articulates them in the *De principiis* confirms these points. The words and teachings of Christ are not simply those recorded from his days on earth. For Moses and the prophets were filled with his spirit.[30] Amongst the apostolic doctrines which provide the Rule of Faith is the doctrine that the scriptures were composed through the Spirit of God and that they have not only that meaning which is obvious but also another which is hidden from the majority of readers. For the contents of scripture are the outward forms of certain mysteries and images of divine things. On this point, Origen affirms, the whole Church is unanimous.[31]

De principiis IV articulates Origen's fuller understanding of the

---

[27] *Comm. Jn.* 1.12(4); *GCS*, vol. IV, p. 6; ET *ANCL*, addit. vol., p. 298.
[28] *Comm. Jn.* 1.27(5)ff; *GCS*, vol. IV, p. 9ff.; ET *ANCL*, addit. vol., pp. 299ff.
[29] *Comm. Jn.* 1.46(10); *GCS*, vol. IV, p. 13; ET *ANCL*, addit. vol., p. 302.
[30] *De princ.* 1.1; *GCS*, vol. V, pp. 7–8; ET Butterworth, p. 1.
[31] *De princ.* 1.8; *GCS*, vol. V, p. 14; ET Butterworth, p. 5.

inspiration of scripture and the proper mode of its interpretation. It was after the advent of Jesus that the inspiration of the prophetic words and the spiritual nature of Moses' Law came to light.[32] Before his advent it was not possible to bring forth clear proofs of the divine inspiration of the old scriptures. The light contained in the Law of Moses was hidden under a veil. The books themselves give the clue to their interpretation: Proverbs and Paul are called in to support a threefold reading corresponding to body, soul and spirit.[33] (Origen's discussion of this point is well known.) One must think of the Holy Spirit's words not as a composition depending upon feeble human eloquence, but in accordance with the sayings of scripture: 'All the king's glory is within', and a 'treasure' of divine meanings lies hidden within the 'frail vessel' of the poor letter.[34] The enquirer has as goal the unsearchable ways of God, but no created mind possesses the capacity to understand all. Everyone who cares for truth will care more for what words signify than for the words themselves.

A number of times in the discussion we find the word *skopos* (or the Latin equivalent, *conspectus*, where we rely on Rufinus' translation). In IV.2.7–9,[35] we discover it was the Spirit's *skopos* to enlighten the prophets and apostles so that they became partakers in all the doctrines of the Spirit's counsel. These doctrines prove to be those concerning God, his only-begotten Son, and the cause of his descent to the level of human flesh. But the second *skopos* of the Spirit was to conceal the doctrine concerning these truths in a narrative dealing with the visible creation in such a way that proper examination of these records of human actions, even wars, would point to spiritual truths. The need to alert people to the deeper meaning of the texts led to the placing of stumbling-blocks in the form of impossibilities in the midst of law and narrative. So, we are told, the principal *skopos* was to announce the connection that exists among spiritual events, and where the earthly narrative did not fit, bits were woven in to represent the more mystical meaning. The coherence of scripture, we might say in summary, lies at its heart, in its soul or spirit, not its physical reality, the multiplicity of letters on the pages of many codices.

---

[32] *De princ.* IV.1.6; *GCS*, vol. v, pp. 301–2; ET Butterworth, p. 264.
[33] *De princ.* IV.2.4; *GCS*, vol. v, p. 312; ET Butterworth, pp. 275ff.
[34] *De princ.* IV.3.14–15; *GCS*, vol. v, pp. 345ff; ET Butterworth, pp. 310ff.
[35] *GCS*, vol. v, pp. 318–22; ET Butterworth, pp. 282ff.

On the basis of these passages, it has been suggested[36] that Origen owed his views on the coherence of scripture to the literary organicism of Neoplatonic exegesis, coupled with his interest in the Platonic speculations concerning the One and the Many. The contribution of the latter seems borne out by the passages already drawn from the *Commentary on John*, which clearly indicate his concern to show the interrelationship of diversity and unity. The former needs further discussion.

The necessary 'organic unity' of a composition had been noted by Plato:

It is necessary for every speech to cohere like a living thing having its own body so that nothing is lacking in head nor foot, but to have a middle and extremities suitable to each other, sketched as part of a whole.[37]

In the later Neoplatonists, the notion of literary organicism would become fundamental to their reading of texts.[38] The question that arises, however, is the precise nature of the unity sought.

If a Platonic dialogue is analogous to a living organism, and a living organism has a single *telos*, then a dialogue too should have a single *telos*, that is, one *skopos*.[39]

It has been argued[40] that this way of understanding unity is exceptional in the Greek tradition of literary criticism. Most had regarded movement from one topic to another as appropriate, and encouraged alternating tension and relaxation, the concept of unity being 'centrifugal'. Only the Neoplatonists insisted on finding a single overall *skopos*, and they advanced this view polemically, well aware that it ran counter to general rhetorical theory, which encouraged variety of intent.[41] Origen, it would seem, acknowl-

---

[36] B. Ritchie, 'The Emergence of *skopos* as an Important Technical Term in Patristic Exegesis', unpublished paper given at the Eleventh International Conference on Patristic Studies, Oxford 1991.

[37] *Phaedrus* 264c, 6–9, as quoted by Kennedy in *Classical Rhetoric*, p. 56.

[38] See J. A. Coulter, *The Literary Microcosm. Theories of Interpretation of the Later Neoplatonists* (Leiden: Brill, 1976), on which Ritchie drew.

[39] From a sixth-century Neoplatonic text quoted by Malcolm Heath, *Unity in Greek Poetics* (Oxford: Clarendon, 1989), p. 124.

[40] Heath, *Unity*.

[41] The insistence of Theodore of Mopsuestia on a single *skopos* for individual whole texts such as a Psalm would appear exceptional also, if this view were to be sustained. But clearly the discussion is standard in the fourth and fifth centuries: cf. Alexander Kerrigan, *St Cyril of Alexandria. Interpreter of the Old Testament* (*Analecta Biblica* 2, Rome: Pontifical Biblical

edged a unity of intent but saw it as underlying the variety of scripture, the One Word of God under the many words. The point is perhaps not exactly that of the Neoplatonists.

Proclus apparently criticised the notion that Plato's Dialogues were strictly historical: rather Plato selects from and supplements the record of what actually took place so that each text contains exclusively what will bear on the particular *skopos* he has in view in that text.[42] Here we are perhaps reminded of Origen's treatment of the narratives of the Gospels. Later Neoplatonists attributed to Porphyry the idea that the expression of a text is analogous to its body while its content is analogous to the soul. Such views were, of course, anticipated in the approach of the Jewish Platonist Philo, and the Christian Platonist Origen. If it is right that the conception of literary organicism, though based on Plato, was changed in Neoplatonic tradition, then we may have to conclude that Platonists interested in biblical interpretation laid some of the groundwork. Conversely, Philo and Origen might provide evidence that, though not found in extant texts, the discussion of a text's unitive thrust or *skopos* was already under way very much earlier, and, as suggested,[43] influenced Origen as he developed his views on the *skopos* of scripture.

The organic unity of a text, treated as analogous to the unity of body and soul, encouraged the search for deeper meanings, another feature that Origen and the Neoplatonists shared. In rhetorical theory, it was generally accepted that the style and diction of a speech were distinguishable from the subject-matter, that the 'idea' and order had first to be 'invented', then clothed in appropriate wording and ornament, a style fitted to that underlying idea. The idea that human language provides a metaphor for the material world is suggested by a passage with an intriguing double meaning found in Numenius, the second-century Neo-Pythagorean influenced by both Platonism and Judaism. Both language and universe are structured out of *stoicheiai* (a word which may mean the 'elements' or 'first principles' of the universe, or the letters of the alphabet, the first principles of *logoi*), and both are an unstable

---

Institute, 1952), who reviews *skopos* in Neoplatonic and Christian texts, noting that Cyril appeals to *skopos* in his prologues and in elucidating the 'literal' meaning of particular texts, pp. 87–110; but he also recognises the spiritual *skopos*, p. 224ff.

[42] According to Heath, *Unity*, p. 129.

[43] By Ritchie; cf. note 36.

inadequate expression of a permanent underlying reality.[44] Plotinus affirms that the material world expresses higher realities, and 'implied in this attitude,' suggests Lamberton,[45]

is the belief that the material universe itself constitutes a system of meaning, a language of symbols that, properly read, will yield a truth that transcends its physical substrate.

It is easy to see how these notions would contribute to the notion that a reality which pre-exists the text is placed under the veil of the narration or poem by divine intent.

Origen has clearly been subjected to the same influences as the Neoplatonists, but it is an intriguing thought that their exegesis of Homer as the inspired theologian could have owed not a little to the Judaeo-Christian treatment of the Bible, even if their desire to find the unitive *skopos* of a Platonic Dialogue may have been the outcome of rather different concerns than the Christian search for the unitive *skopos* of scripture.[46] One thing this discussion has shown is that the dynamic requiring the discernment of that unitive *hypothesis* or *skopos* was, in any case, and prior to Origen, inherent in the Christian appropriation of the Jewish scriptures.

IV

This chapter began by stating what was meant here by reception and appropriation, namely, the exegetical process whereby readers make the text their own. The appropriation of the texts that we have traced produced an exegesis of particular texts as prophetic testimony or apostolic testimony to Christ. At a later stage, we will discuss the exegetical effects of the resultant build-up of inter-textual reference. Meanwhile, let us note how we have traced a curiously paradoxical process in the appropriation of the scriptural material.

To begin with, it seems, the odour of sanctity which had been attached to the books inherited from the Jews was challenged. The texts full of words were relativised by the embodied Word, and the oral testimony had as good a claim to honour as the written

---

[44] See Robert Lamberton, *Homer the Theologian* (Berkeley and Los Angeles: University of California Press, 1986), p. 77.

[46] *Homer the Theologian*, p. 95.

[46] I remain somewhat cautious here. I am grateful for correspondence with Malcolm Heath.

testimony, as the well-known remark of Papias[47] has always suggested for the specifically Christian material. Subsequently the Bible regained its divine aura, as the dogmas of its unity and inspiration gave it the inerrancy, when understood correctly, that fundamentalists would still like to claim. But the ancient Church remained all too aware of the problems of rival readings, whether Jewish or heretical, and the need to have both an authorised text and an authorised 'reception' underlay much of the debate, discussion and controversy which produced the creeds and classic definitions of doctrine. It was crucial to these debates that the 'letter' of the text, all its contrary details, the questions and problems raised, were subjected to a perspective which did not simply amass proof-texts but discerned the unitive intent of the whole. To that extent the public community traditions embodied in liturgy provided the key mode of reception: public reading and teaching, in a context which appropriated the texts as testimony to the core claims of the community, ensured they were consistently heard in a meaningful way.

[47] 'For I did not imagine that things out of books would help me as much as the utterances of a living and abiding voice' (Eusebius, *HE* III.39: ET Williamson, p. 150).

CHAPTER 2

The mind of scripture

Given that a Christian reading of the scriptures required the discernment of their overall unity through the provision of a creed-like key,[1] and that the interpretation of particular texts was inevitably affected by this emphasis on the unity of scripture, what was the legacy of this in the doctrinal debates of the later period? This will gradually emerge as we embark on a particular case-study, analysing the exegetical aspects of Athanasius' polemic against the Arians. This involves both a chronological jump and anticipation of discussions to be undertaken in other sections of the book, especially those concerned with language, reference, deduction and genre – to that extent the proposals made in this volume are interrelated and cumulative. This chapter is placed here because the overriding conclusion of this case-study follows on from the last: discerning the unitive 'mind' (dianoia) of scripture[2] was seen as essential to reaching a proper interpretation.[3]

---

[1] As argued in *The Art of Performance*, chs. 2 and 3. See also Peter Gorday, *Principles of Patristic Exegesis. Romans 9–11 in Origen, John Chrysostom and Augustine* (New York and Toronto: The Edwin Mellen Press, 1983), pp. 34–9: he sees the character of patristic exegesis as arising from 'a real and vital wholeness', which proceeds from credal formulations 'as a frame by which to order the scriptural message'. 'This pattern is termed by the patristic writers an "economy" since the wholeness of scripture is represented in a creedal pattern reciting the progress of salvation from creation to eschaton.'

[2] Athanasius' supposed emphasis on the *skopos* of scripture has entered the literature. T. F. Torrance (*The Trinitarian Faith. The Evangelical Theology of the Ancient Catholic Church* (Edinburgh: T. & T. Clark, 1988)), for example, sees Christ as the *skopos* of scripture in *Continued on p. 30*

[3] The following exploration works through certain key Athanasian texts, and on the whole ignores scholarly discussion of Athanasius' exegesis. In fact there have been responses to Pollard's article; e.g. H. J. Sieben, 'Herméneutique de l'exégèse dogmatique d'Athanase', *Continued on p. 30*

I

The writings of Athanasius make it absolutely clear that the Arian controversy was about exegesis. This is especially the case with the *De decretis*, a letter written about AD 350, and the *Orations against the Arians*, the date of which is disputed but most probably belonging also to the 350s. The first three orations have generally been treated as genuine, though the authenticity of the third has now been

---

[2] *Continued from p. 29* Athanasius' understanding (p. 25). T. E. Pollard had argued ('The Exegesis of Scripture in the Arian Controversy', *BJRL* 41 (1958–9), pp. 414–29) that Athanasius had a number of exegetical principles which established the soundness of his argument against the Arians, one of which was the appeal to the *skopos* of scripture: he 'refutes Arian arguments based on literal interpretation of isolated verses of scripture. No doctrine, he [Athanasius] argues, can be based on an isolated verse of scripture unless it is in harmony with the general teaching of the whole of scripture' (pp. 422–3).

This principle is established by Pollard on the basis of one passage in *C. Arianos* III.28–9 (Migne, *PG* 26.384–5) where the author speaks of the *skopos* of faith which is to be used as a *kanōn* when we apply ourselves to reading the inspired scriptures. The passage goes on: 'This is the *skopos* and *charactēr* of Holy Scripture – it contains a double account of the Saviour, that he was ever God, and is the Son, being the Father's Logos and Radiance and Wisdom, and that afterwards for us he took flesh from a virgin, Mary Theotokos, and was made man.' Although Pollard comments that it is clear that the *regula fidei* is to be used as a *kanōn*, he proceeds to suggest that *skopos* is not 'scope' or 'intention', 'end' or 'purpose', but 'the general bearing or drift'. The one other passage (apart from some references to *C. Arianos* IV, which is usually regarded as Ps.-Athanasius) is *C. Arianos* III.58 (Migne, *PG* 26.445); this speaks of the ecclesiastical *skopos*, and refers to the *oikonomia* or incarnation.

Two comments may be made: (1) in the texts which we examine here, *skopos* is not the term found, but rather *dianoia*; (2) in the passages Pollard cites, *skopos* is nearer to being the 'canon of truth' than the 'general drift' of scripture. Later Pollard briefly mentions and illustrates *dianoia*, but fails to see both that it is more central in Athanasius' terminology (especially if *C. Arianos* III is not authentic; see note 4) and that it functions in the way he attributes to *skopos*.

[3] *Continued from p. 29* in Charles Kannengiesser (ed.), *Politique et théologie chez Athanase d'Alexandrie* (Paris: Beauchesne, 1974), pp. 195–214; and Christopher Stead, 'Athanasius als Exeget', in J. van Oort and U. Wickert (eds.), *Christliche Exegese zwischen Nicaea und Chalcedon* (Kampen: Kok Pharos, 1992), pp. 174–84.

Pollard had tried to claim that exegesis in the Arian controversy was literal, and that Athanasius' exegesis was more successful than that of his opponents because he adopted three principles whereby attention was to be payed (1) to the whole of scripture (see previous note); (2) to scriptural usage, and (3) to context, principles which Pollard claims are just as valid today. The 'context' principle he based on Athanasius' repeated references to the need to look at the 'person', the 'time' and the 'point' or 'subject' (*pragma*) – standard philological principles in other authors (Sieben) and clearly from the textbooks (Stead).

But Sieben argues that Athanasius consistently means by this, not the 'literary' or even

challenged by Kannengiesser.[4] We shall focus on *Orations* I and II, after first working through the argument of the *De decretis*.

This document takes up the point that Arians were objecting to the non-scriptural language of the Nicene Creed, a view shared by some who supported church doctrine. Athanasius treats this as a new issue, a new excuse for continuing the dispute when they had already been defeated by reasonable argument. However, it seems unlikely that it was in fact new – the scriptures seem to have had a key role in the debate from the beginning.[5] Of course, Athanasius cannot admit to a genuine controversy about exegesis – for in his eyes any opponent is 'double-minded' and has betrayed the unity of the truth, whose heralds are unanimous by definition! However, we are not concerned with the rhetoric of the debate, nor indeed the reconstruction of its history, but rather with the hermeneutical principles which were consciously or unconsciously in play.

The first issue Athanasius takes up is the meaning of the word 'Son'.[6] He distinguishes two scriptural senses of the word. Firstly, anyone obedient to God's commandments is God's son, as Deuteronomy 13.18–14.1 shows, and this sonship by adoption and grace is confirmed from the New Testament. On the other hand, scripture speaks of Isaac as son of Abraham, and many other examples of natural sons are cited. The question is, he suggests, which of these senses applies to the Son of God. If the Arians think the first is correct, then the Son is no different from the rest of us.

'historical' context, but rather discernment of the applicability of the text in question to the eternal or incarnate Logos – *prosōpon* is not the person 'speaking' in the text, but the person envisaged by the prophet; *kairos* concerns the issue whether it is before or after the incarnation: the 'double account of the Saviour' is indeed Athanasius' fundamental canon. In other words these 'keys' relate to the Christological meaning. Proverbs 8.22, to be discussed later in this chapter, is a case in point, and gives little confidence that Athanasius' exegetical principles can survive the test of time! Stead challenges the notion that Athanasius has consistent principles, suggesting that his position shifts in different contexts, and certainly embraces allegory.

[4] Charles Kannengiesser, 'Athanasius' *Three Orations against the Arians*: a reappraisal' in *Arius and Athanasius. Two Alexandrian Theologians* (Aldershot: Variorum Reprints, 1991); originally published in *SP* 18.3 (Oxford: Pergamon Press, 1982).

[5] See my book, *From Nicaea to Chalcedon* (London: SCM Press, 1983), p. 62; and E. Boularand, *L'hérésie d'Arius et la 'foi' de Nicée* (2 vols., Paris: Letouzey & Ane, 1972).

[6] *De decretis* 6; *Athanasius Werke II.1, De decretis Nicaenae synodi*, ed. H.-G. Opitz (Berlin and Leipzig: Walter de Gruyter, 1935), pp. 5–6; *NPNF*, 2nd series, vol. IV, pp. 153–4.

Yet they claim that though he is a creature, he is not as one of the creatures. So Athanasius embarks on a long discussion of Arian attempts to avoid the conclusion that the Son is no different from other sons, using a combination of logic and proof-texts to demolish their standpoint. He then argues that the only alternative is to take the meaning of the word in the other sense, and understand that he is the true Son of God.[7]

Now, however, Athanasius has to distance himself from the idea that there is an exact analogy between the physical generation of Isaac by Abraham and God's generation of his Son.[8] God is not as man. So even if the same terms are used in scripture, the 'clear-sighted, as Paul enjoins, will study it, and thereby discriminate': distinctions will be made with respect to what is written according to the nature of the subject, so that confusion of sense will be avoided. One must avoid conceiving of the things of God in a human way, and ascribing aspects of human nature to God; for this is to mix wine with water.

This topic is pursued at some length, and we need not dwell on the details (such matters as the nature of bodies as compounded and in a state of flux, or the loss of substance in begetting, and so on). We simply note Athanasius' conclusion that God's begetting cannot be of that kind – there is no 'effluence' of the immaterial, nor can the uncompounded be partitioned.[9] The point is that, despite looking to scripture to provide the possible range of meaning, in other words using the long-established principle of interpreting Homer by Homer or Bible by Bible, Athanasius adduces what appears an external hermeneutical principle, namely the fundamental other-ness of the divine, in order to argue for a reading which is not strictly literal. It is true that he assumes that this principle is also scriptural, but, from this point on, scriptural texts can be the starting-point of theological deductions far from the verbal sense of the biblical words.

So the argument becomes an interesting amalgam of deductions of an a priori character and texts taken in what we may describe as a quasi-literal sense. Examples will elucidate what I mean: (1) The statement, 'This is my beloved Son, in whom I am well pleased', and other texts indicating that the Father's only-begotten Word is in his

---

[7] *De decretis* 10; Opitz, p. 9; *NPNF*, 2nd series, vol. iv, p. 156.
[8] *De decretis* 10.4–6; Opitz, p. 9; *NPNF*, 2nd series, vol. iv, p. 156.
[9] *De decretis* 11.4; Opitz, p. 10; *NPNF*, 2nd series, vol. iv, p. 157.

bosom (John 1.18) and sits at his right hand (Acts 7.55; Rom. 8.34; Col. 3.1), are taken to mean genuine derivation from the Father, though not in a physical sense, and real co-adoration without literal sitting.[10] (2) The 'otherness' of God, though described in language reflecting concerns not explicit in scripture, is backed up by texts asserting that no one knows the Father except the Son.[11] Yet further scriptural material indicates that he who has seen the Son has seen the Father. Athanasius concludes that the inseparability of Father and Son is indicated in a parabolic way: how can the radiance be separated from the source of light? Even this is grounded in texts about the 'brightness of his glory'.

The assumption, then, is that the whole argument is scriptural, whereas the opposition is charged with forming ideas which are not in scripture. But then Athanasius has to meet the appeal to Proverbs 8.22.[12] He asserts that they seem to have a wrong understanding of this passage. To explain it he begins with a commonsense distinction between 'making' something external to the maker, like a house, and begetting a son. He then shows that this distinction is observed in scripture, quoting Genesis 1.1 to illustrate 'creating' and Psalms 109.3 and 2.7 (LXX) for begetting. 'I have begotten you from the womb before the morning star' and 'You are my Son, today I have begotten you' are simply taken to refer to the Son of God, and then significantly the same expression is found in the contentious Proverbs passage at 8.25: 'Before all the hills he begat me.' New Testament testimony is drawn in and Athanasius concludes: 'If son, then not creature; if creature, not son.'

But the problem is not yet solved, because the use of 'create' in Proverbs 8.22 demands an explanation.[13] Athanasius resorts to an expedient which destroys the flow in the context of the Proverbs passage, asserting that it refers to the incarnation, for then indeed one can say the Son was created. Scripture is called in to show that he became son of man as well as being eternally Son of God. We will return to this novel exegetical expedient a little later on. Meanwhile we note that the use of scripture in doctrinal debate did not lead to what we would recognise as a more literal exegesis. Texts from what

---

[10] *De decretis* 11.5–6; Opitz, p. 10; *NPNF*, 2nd series, vol. IV, p. 157.
[11] *De decretis* 12; Opitz, pp. 10–11; *NPNF*, 2nd series, vol. IV, p. 157–8.
[12] *De decretis* 13; Opitz, pp. 11–12; *NPNF*, 2nd series, vol. IV, p. 158.
[13] *De decretis* 14; Opitz, p. 12; *NPNF*, 2nd series, vol. IV, p. 159.

had become the Old Testament continued to be anachronistically read as referring to Christ, and the discussion of the meaning of words shows that a straightforward literal sense was seen to be problematic. What debate did was to provoke a theological assessment of religious language.

The next point Athanasius turns to also illustrates this.[14] Are the terms 'word' and 'wisdom' attributed to the Son as 'names' only? Again a combination of deductive reasoning and scriptural texts seeks the unity of the various terms used for the Son in the fact that they refer to the one begotten. Not to confess this betrays ignorance of the truth and inexperience in divine scripture. The attribution of these terms implies they are more than mere 'names', but their sense has to be understood in a manner appropriate to the divine reality to which they refer.

So debate made questions of meaning explicit. It also made Athanasius aware that one needed to probe behind the words to the 'mind' of scripture. He argues to this effect in the next section of the letter,[15] where he attempts to defend the use of non-scriptural terms such as *ex ousias* and *homoousios*. Of course, he first charges his opponents with themselves using non-scriptural phrases and developing plausible sophisms, because this enables him to show that the Council had to meet like with like in defence of scriptural terms and their proper sense – Eusebius (of Nicomedia) and his cronies accepted anything from scripture, interpreting it in their own blasphemous way. So the bishops were forced to collect the mind (*dianoia*) of the scriptures, and to restate it in these non-scriptural formulae.[16]

So Athanasius distinguishes between the 'wording' and the 'sense' (*dianoia*), urging those who hesitate about the Council's formula to do likewise. If they agree the sense, they should subscribe to the wording. Athanasius insists that, even if the expressions used are not, in so many words, in the scriptures, yet they contain the mind of the scriptures and so convey it to those willing to respond. If they continue to claim that it is not scriptural, that very complaint shows the disorder of their minds.[17]

---

[14] *De decretis* 15; Opitz, p. 13; *NPNF,* 2nd series, vol. IV, pp. 159–60.
[15] *De decretis* 18ff.; Opitz, pp. 15ff.; *NPNF,* 2nd series, vol. IV, pp. 161ff.
[16] *De decretis* 19.4; Opitz, p. 16; *NPNF,* 2nd series, vol. IV, pp. 162–3.
[17] *De decretis* 21; Opitz, pp. 17–18; *NPNF,* 2nd series, vol. IV, p. 164.

In all of this, he is exploiting a distinction we will meet again: rhetorical procedure differentiated between *ho pragmatikos topos* and *ho lektikos topos*.[18] The first was the subject-matter, the area determined by the author's *heuresis* or *inventio*, and the second was the verbal dress in which it was decked – the *onomata* or *verba*, or what we would call the vocabulary and style. Clearly this distinction could be employed as a hermeneutical device. Origen had already applied it to explore the fundamental unity of the biblical revelation: we noted his insistence on looking for the *skopos* of scripture behind the verbal diversity, indeed contradictions, which may appear on the surface.

In other words, Athanasius was drawing on a well-tried hermeneutical principle which made his argument quite different from a simple text-slinging match, and also meant that the 'words' of a text were relativised. Discernment of the mind of scripture meant discernment of its underlying coherence, its unitive testimony to the one true Son of God, and that discernment involved what we might call a critical stance towards a literalising view of religious language. Nevertheless, to discern the mind of scripture did involve two things: (1) the assembly of texts pointing to the same conclusion, and (2) respect for the normal or 'earthly' meaning of words, appropriately modified, or perhaps I should say 'elevated', for their theological context. The interpretation may not be literal, but, in the majority of cases, it is also far from allegorical. The categories usually used to discuss patristic exegesis are inadequate to the task.

We are also observing a fairly complex deductive process. It is complex because one element is the assembly of data from the scriptural material, and the other is a set of theological assumptions which are themselves sometimes justified by scriptural passages even though their import cannot have originally conveyed what they were taken to indicate. That God is incomposite and incorporeal, that the divine Being is incomprehensible – such ideas are grounded in God's mysterious name revealed to Moses at the burning bush. But such talk in fact introduces a whole set of anachronistic concepts and assumptions, far more than merely non-scriptural language as

---

[18] Quintilian, *Institutio oratoria* x.i and ii (in *The Institutio Oratoria of Quintilian*. 4 vols., ed. and trans. H. E. Butler, *LCL*, 1920, 1921, 1922). See Dionysius of Halicarnassus, *De Thucydide*, ed. and trans by W. Pritchett (Berkeley/Los Angeles/Oxford: University of California Press, 1975), p. xxxvi, for summary table of the rhetorical system of Dionysius; also S. F. Bonner, *The Literary Treatises of Dionysius of Halicarnassus* (Cambridge: Cambridge University Press, 1939), pp. 84ff.

Athanasius would have us believe. That the Son is immutable and unchangeable, as a genuine Son of God, is deduced from the image of light and its radiance,[19] a scriptural image by all means, but exploited to deduce the answer to problems barely conceived at the time of its writing.

But such an issue could not have occurred to Athanasius or his contemporaries. Ancient literary criticism did not grasp the notion of an anachronistic reading,[20] for it was essentially about reader reception and response. In the case of a text believed to enshrine the truth, indeed the divine accommodation to the limitations of human discourse, the notion of anachronistic reading was the more inconceivable, for the archaic features of the text were merely part of the verbal dress. The discernment of the reality behind the inadequate verbal clothing was the only proper response, and the misconception of it was nothing less than blasphemy. So this was not for Athanasius an internal exegetical debate, but a war with the clever deceit of the devil.

The human mind, then, has to apprehend the divine through the mind of scripture. But how is Athanasius' deductive exegesis to be differentiated from that of his opponents? They too assembled texts to show the truth to which scripture pointed. They too argued with a similar complexity of textual data and theological assumption. Both sides were unable to question anachronistic readings. Neither side resorted to a simple literalism or an elaborate allegorism, for these were not opposed methods but coexisting responses to different aspects of a text, and in any case the issues were not resolvable in terms of either. In the end Athanasius' discernment of the mind of scripture was found more convincing than that of the Arians, but it was a close-run thing. From now on the 'mind' of the church, as expressed in tradition, as documented from the writings of distinguished Fathers, will increasingly come into play as the struggle to discern the 'mind' of scripture continues. Athanasius ends his letter by appealing to pre-Nicene authorities in support of the Council's determination – Theognostus, Dionysius of Alexandria, Dionysius of Rome, and indeed Origen.[21] Innovation could not be admitted.

---

[19] *De decretis* 23–4; Opitz, pp. 19–20; *NPNF,* 2nd series, vol. IV, pp. 165–6.
[20] Cf. D. A. Russell, *Criticism in Antiquity* (London: Duckworth, 1981), especially chs. 8 and 11.
[21] *De decretis* 25–7; Opitz, pp. 20–24; *NPNF,* 2nd series, vol. IV, pp. 166–9.

II

Yet Athanasius was himself an innovator as he sought to reinterpret texts exploited by the opposition in the light of his hermeneutical principles. The innovatory character of Athanasius' exegesis has been highlighted by Simonetti in his article on Proverbs 8.22,[22] and, in reviewing Athanasius' treatment of this text in the *De decretis*, I hinted that here was a novelty to which we would return.[23]

Proverbs 8.22 was clearly a key text in the Arian controversy: indeed, the bulk of Athanasius' second oration is devoted to its exegesis. Tradition took this text as Christological, Wisdom, the speaker, being identified with the Logos. Everyone, up to and including Arius, took it that the whole passage referred to the creative activity of the pre-existent Logos. The fact that the text of v. 22 spoke of God 'creating' this Logos had been overlooked or minimised in the light of the fact that v. 25 used the word 'begat'. Once Arius pressed the distinction between begetting and creating, there was little in principle or context to establish the superiority of one mode of interpretation over the other. Both words were present in the text. The answer to Arius could not therefore be simply a conservative reversion to a previous exegesis. The option of denying the reference to the Logos was never entertained. It seems it was Marcellus of Ancyra who first resorted to the novel expedient of asserting that Proverbs 8.22 referred to the incarnation, rather than to the origin of the pre-existent Logos.

Simonetti's article demonstrates, then, that the notion of identifying a reference to the incarnation in this verse was undoubtedly a novel move, probably copied by Athanasius from Marcellus, but still novel, not traditional, entirely stimulated by Arius' challenge. The exigences of debate could lead further away from attention to the natural reading of the text, rather than encouraging a more literal reading. It is time we turned to Athanasius' handling of this controversial text in the *Orations against the Arians*.

As indicated earlier, the bulk of the second oration is devoted to this text, yet there is a sense in which Athanasius takes a long time

---

[22] M. Simonetti, *Studi sull'Arianesimo* (Rome: Editrice Studium, 1965), ch. 1.
[23] See further my paper, 'Exegetical Method and Scriptural Proof: The Bible in Doctrinal Debate', *SP* 24 (1989) pp. 291–304.

to get round to it. First[24] he establishes that the Son must not be called a creature, so ensuring that the perspective from which the detail of this text is examined prevents its being misread. Proper exegesis is achieved not simply by paying attention to words and syntax, but by attending to more overarching considerations about what is appropriate to the divine reality of which the text speaks, and Athanasius does not hesitate to rehearse the necessary arguments, engaging in a similar complex process of deduction to that we have already observed in *De decretis*. Only thus will 'they' learn to read properly (*kalōs*) with the 'sense' (*dianoia*) right.[25]

In the course of this prior argument, the status of words themselves is discussed.[26] Words are just collections of syllables, ephemeral expressions of a person's will. On this basis, the Arians had apparently raised the question how the Son could be 'Word'. Athanasius accepts the proffered description of mere human words, but differentiates God's Word. We see a parallel to his discussion of 'son' in the *De decretis*, a combination of a priori theological assumptions and scriptural texts being used to establish that appropriate divine meaning is not identical with literal human meaning. For Athanasius the very problem raised by the Arians is evidence of impiety, alien to what is found in scripture and to the teaching of the Fathers – the general problem of heresies which use the language of scripture but fail to grasp its sense occupies him for a while. But he offers no methodological answer to the question on what criteria there might be assessment of competing views of what the sense of scripture might be, apart from tradition and an a priori sense of what is appropriate to the divine.

Eventually Athanasius turns to the details of Proverbs 8.22, and we find a series of exegetical tactics rolling into one another. First he attends to genre.[27] These are proverbs, expressed in the way of proverbs – John 16.25 shows that there is a difference between proverbs and plain speech. Enquiry must be made about reference and the religious sense of each proverb. The sense of what is said must be unfolded and sought as something hidden. From here he moves to a discussion of scriptural usage, with proof-texts, to show

---

[24] The argument begins at the beginning of *C. Arianos* II, but is particularly at stake in II.18ff.; Bright, pp. 86ff.; *NPNF*, 2nd series, vol. IV, pp.357ff.

[25] *C. Arianos* II.1; Bright, p. 68; *NPNF*, 2nd series, vol.IV, p. 348.

[26] *C. Arianos* II.35ff.; Bright, pp.104ff.; *NPNF*, 2nd series, vol. IV, pp.367ff.

[27] *C. Arianos* II.44; Bright, pp.113ff.; *NPNF*, 2nd series, vol. IV, p. 372.

two conclusions: (1) that 'created' is elsewhere used of creatures, and not where scripture is speaking of the generation of the Son;[28] (2) that there are two scriptural senses of the word, one concerning origin, the other renewal, as in the text, 'Create in me a new heart.'[29] So he suggests that the 'proverb' in question is to be understood not as referring to the generation of the Word, but rather as relating to renewal, and so as referring not to the essence but to the manhood of the Word.

The next tactic is to consider the syntax. He argues that 'The Lord created me a beginning of his ways' is equivalent to 'My Father prepared for me a body.'[30] The LXX text could allow taking the two accusatives 'me' and 'a beginning of his ways' as a double object similar to that necessary with a verb like 'appoint'; presumably Athanasius intends something of that kind, for he speaks of the proverb calling the Son a 'beginning of his ways', and compares this text with 'The Word became flesh.' Neither speaks of an absolute becoming or creation, but of one relative to 'us' or to 'his works'. Here Athanasius notes that whereas *ektisen* in v. 22 is modified by an expression of purpose, 'for his works', the use of *gennā(i)* in v. 25 does not have a similar modifier.[31] So here, as elsewhere in scripture (a point illustrated lavishly), the 'begetting' is stated absolutely, whereas the word 'created' is relative; it is relative to the 'Economy' – that is, the incarnation as an expression of God's providential and saving plan.

This distinction between speaking absolutely of the Son's Being and speaking of him relative to the Economy is fundamental to Athanasius' discernment of the mind of scripture, and is explored at length. This enables the interpretation in terms of renewal or re-creation to be elaborated: 'we are his workmanship, created in Christ Jesus', he suggests, using Ephesians 2.10 among many other passages. Thus he arrives at a classic distinction, which he regards as fundamental to scripture: God's offspring (*gennēma*) was begotten but then made, made flesh for our salvation in the Economy, whereas creatures (*poiēmata*) were made and then begotten through Christ, becoming sons by grace.[32] This distinction, he suggests,

---

[28] *C. Arianos* II.45; Bright, p. 114; *NPNF*, 2nd series, vol. IV, pp. 372–3.
[29] *C. Arianos* II.46; Bright, p. 115; *NPNF*, 2nd series, vol. IV, p. 373.
[30] *C. Arianos* II.47; Bright, pp. 116–17; *NPNF*, 2nd series, vol. IV, p. 374.
[31] *C. Arianos* II.56–61; Bright, pp. 125–32; *NPNF*, 2nd series, vol. IV, pp. 379–81.
[32] *C. Arianos* II.62–3; Bright, pp. 132–3; *NPNF*, 2nd series, vol. IV, pp. 382ff.

applies to this text. He is 'first-born of all creation' as being the origin of the new creation; he could not be first-born of God, since he is only-begotten of God.

But now the problem of context demands attention.[33] How can his reading of v. 22 be satisfactory in the light of v. 23, where it states: 'before the world, he founded me in the beginning'? Athanasius appeals again to the proverbial character of the material; then he appeals to the text 'No other foundation can anyone lay . . . ', and indicates that Proverbs is speaking of the providential preparation of this grace for us before the foundation of the world. So the essence of Wisdom was not created; what was created was the impress of Wisdom in the works of God as a copy of the divine image. His triumphant conclusion is that thus the whole world will be filled with the knowledge of God. And it must be admitted that he takes a lot longer to get there than my brief survey of his material would suggest!

So what are the exegetical strategies and hermeneutical principles that Athanasius evidences? Clearly his exegesis is neither literal, nor typological, nor allegorical. Rather it is deductive. The deductive process involves attention to the meaning of words, their particular biblical sense, the syntax and the context of the text in question – the basic techniques of the *grammaticus* attending to the verbal configuration of a passage. But the overriding principle concerns the discovery of a proper way of reading what is proverbial according to a sense which accords with both the unitive mind of scripture and the appropriate conception of the one God. The irony is that that concern demands innovative exegesis. Time and again we find Athanasius struggling with those texts which the Arians could more naturally exploit, and producing explanations that were neither obvious nor traditional. How then could he be so sure his mind reflected the mind of scripture?

III

There is, I believe, an answer to the question how Athanasius knew that he was the one who knew the 'mind' of scripture, but to find it we must search the repetitive rhetoric of the anti-Arian orations,

---

[33] *C. Arianos* II.72–8; Bright, pp. 142–9; *NPNF*, 2nd series, vol. IV, pp. 388ff.

repetitive in itself and repetitive of the *De decretis*. We shall not attempt to work through the orations as we did the shorter work, but rather to identify the main lines of argument, most of which will be found already familiar.

Athanasius is convinced that the difference between the Arian view and his orthodox interpretation is the difference between blasphemy and piety, between deceit and truth.[34] He recognises that both sides claim to be offering a scriptural understanding, and that both sides use non-scriptural terms. But one produces an appropriate exegesis, the other does not. The difficulty in distinguishing between truth and deceit lies in the fact, attested by scripture itself, that the devil himself can quote scripture; and the warnings found in I Timothy and Titus, for example, predict departure from sound teaching when people are seduced by deceiving spirits.[35]

Athanasius would probably accept that ultimately he is claiming that no criteria of human reason can provide the necessary differentiation between the deductive exegetical argument of their side and that of his own side. Irrespective of exegetical method, and despite rational arguments (indeed, resort to syllogism and 'Greek' reasoning was a point against the Arians), their doctrine is impious and fundamentally alien to the scriptures – as he keeps asserting, and as his own deductive arguments repeatedly endeavour to show. The standard is simply his own perspective on true piety: 'Which of the two theologies sets forth our Lord Jesus Christ as God and Son of the Father', he asks, 'this which you vomited forth or that which we have spoken and maintain from the scriptures?'[36] The question presupposes that the theology Athanasius is defending is the necessary outcome. What we seek then is the grounds of Athanasius' confidence that he knows what constitutes proper piety, and what devilish blasphemy.

Clearly Athanasius regards his argument as scriptural, yet on its own that hardly provides the answer. For his argumentation is rarely conducted by appeal to proof-texts:

You see, it is from the divine scriptures that we speak with confidence of the 'pious' faith, and set it like a light on a lampstand, saying, 'He is true Son of the Father, natural and genuine, proper to his Being, only-begotten

---

[34] *C. Arianos* 1.8–10; Bright, pp. 8–11; *NPNF*, 2nd series, vol. iv, pp. 310–12ff.
[35] *C. Arianos* 1.8; Bright, p. 8; *NPNF*, 2nd series, vol. iv, p. 310.
[36] *C. Arianos* 1.10; Bright, pp. 10–11; *NPNF*, 2nd series, vol. iv, p. 311.

Wisdom, true and only Word of the Father; he is not a creature or a work
(*poiēma*), but the offspring (*gennēma*) proper to the Being of the Father.'[37]

This statement, claimed as scriptural, is certainly not quotation of
texts or even simply scriptural terms and expressions. Appeal to
John 14.9, 'He that has seen me has seen the Father', is slipped in,
but essentially here Athanasius meets the slogans of the *Thalia* with
his own watchwords.

In much of the material, the sort of thing already documented
from the *De decretis* is developed at greater length – such things as
summary statements, or deductive arguments concerning the
meaning of such terms as 'Son' and 'Word' when applied to the
divine. In large part this is done without 'proof-texts', or directly
exegetical discussion. Quotation of scriptural passages is, in
general, concentrated in blocks rather than integral to the argument. Fundamental to the deductive process, however, are the three
elements already illustrated from the *De decretis*: (1) a concern with
what properly pertains to the divine Being; (2) catenae of key texts,
taken to refer to the divine Being in the 'quasi-literal' way we have
already noted, and distinguished from others referring to creatures;
and (3) a sense that differing scriptural terms, like Wisdom, Word
and Radiance, united in their ascription to the 'Son', create a
conception of God's *gennēma* beyond human language or creaturely
correspondence. Clearly Athanasius is again valuing the mind of
scripture more highly than the verbal expressions of particular
texts, and that is why he can regard his watchwords as scriptural and
prefer them to proof-texts. In a sense he knows that one proof-text
can always be met by another. Indeed, one-third of the first oration
and the whole of the second are devoted to providing orthodox
exegesis of Arian proof-texts. So the basis of Athanasius' confidence
that he knows what constitutes proper piety must correspond to
his grounds for giving priority to what we might call the 'elevated
face-value' meaning of his catena of texts, and seeing their amalga-
mation as expressive of the mind of scripture. What are these?

The answer is to be found, I suggest, in the way he handles the
texts which at first sight favour Arian exegesis. The first of these is
Philippians 2.9–10.[38] The fact that God exalted him meant to the

---

[37] *C. Arianos* 1.9; Bright, p. 9; *NPNF*, 2nd series, vol. IV, p. 311.
[38] *C. Arianos* 1.37ff.; Bright, pp. 38ff.; *NPNF*, 2nd series, vol. IV, pp. 327ff.

Arians that he received a promotion, and so his nature is alterable; also that being called 'Son' and 'God' was the result of that promotion, without him being 'true Son'. Athanasius appeals not so much to the immediate context, involving humiliation before promotion, though he does do that, but to the whole plot that that passage summarises – in other words to the *hypothesis* of scripture Irenaeus had identified, the overarching story outlined in the 'Canon of Truth'. His promotion is part of the story of salvation: he was God and he became man for us. How is he exalted who was Most High before his exaltation? This is not an *ainigma*, but a *mysterion theion*. His exaltation is our exaltation.[39] At considerable length, and with many quotations, particularly from the Gospel of John, but also from Paul and Hebrews, what we might call 'salvation-history' is rehearsed. 'This then I consider the sense (*dianoia*) of the saying (*rhēton*), and a very ecclesiastical sense it is too', concludes Athanasius.[40]

Next Athanasius turns to Psalm 45.7, 8, a text quoted in Hebrews and normally treated as Christological, but embarrassingly speaking of the 'anointing' of the Son.[41] For the Arians this implied he received grace, and so it was linked with the text just discussed as evidence of the Son's promotion. Context helps again, since the text addresses the one anointed as 'God', but Athanasius' fundamental argument is repetition of the last. In the context of the incarnation, he receives grace, is sanctified, anointed, receives the Spirit and so on, so that we might be sanctified and receive the Spirit and other such benefits. Arian exploitation of the 'wherefore' reveals their inexperience of scripture: in the case of the Word, it implies not reward of virtue, but the reason he came down to us.[42] Athanasius is not neglectful of the details of the text. But fundamentally it is his sense of the overarching plot, a sense inherited from the past and ingrained in the tradition of the Church, which allows him to be innovative in exegetical detail and confident of providing the correct and 'pious' reading. The 'Canon of Truth' or 'Rule of Faith' expresses the mind of scripture, and an exegesis that damages the coherence of that plot, that *hypothesis*, that coherence, that *skopos*, cannot be right.

---

[39] *C. Arianos* 1.41; Bright, pp. 42–3; *NPNF*, 2nd series, vol. IV, p. 330.
[40] *C. Arianos* 1.44; Bright, p. 45; *NPNF*, 2nd series, vol. IV, p. 331.
[41] *C. Arianos* 1.46ff.; Bright, pp. 47ff.; *NPNF*, 2nd series, vol. IV, pp. 333ff.
[42] *C. Arianos* 1.49; Bright, p. 51; *NPNF*, 2nd series, vol. IV, p. 335.

Athanasius is not absolutely explicit about this. But deeds speak louder than words, we might say. It is built into his exegetical practice. It has become a commonplace to say that Athanasius' exegesis distinguishes those things pertaining to the divinity and those things pertaining to the flesh, or divides aspects of the Gospel story between what Jesus did *qua* God and what he did *qua* Man. But I would suggest that, while it is true that the Antiochenes would use Athanasian passages of this kind to good effect to defend their own dualistic exegesis,[43] and that much in *Contra Arianos* III supports that estimate, that procedure is not so evident in I and II. Cyril's appeal to Athanasius reflects his mind better: the Alexandrian way was to distinguish the Being or Essence of the Word from what the Word accepted in the 'Economy', that is, the providential saving plan of God worked out in the incarnation.[44] So undergirding Athanasius' exegesis is the unitive story or plot which is the mind of scripture expressed in its many words and images, and of which the one 'Son' is the subject.

At one point Athanasius characterises the Arian approach to scripture, and ironically he provides us, I suggest, with a mirror-image of his own hermeneutical principle:

> Dislodged from the conceptions, or rather mis-conceptions, of their own hearts, they resort to the words of the divine scriptures, and here too from their usual want of discernment, they do not see the mind (*nous*) in those words. But laying down their own impiety as a kind of canon, they twist all the divine oracles into accordance with it. Those who talk in this way, deserve to hear nothing other than 'You are in error, not knowing the scriptures, nor God's power' (Matt. 22.29). And if they persist, they deserve to be shamed and to hear, 'Render to man the things that are man's and to God the things that are God's' (Matt. 22.21).[45]

Athanasius claims to replace their canon of impiety with the Canon of Truth, and it is on these grounds alone that his hermeneutic can claim to be different.

In the last analysis, then, Athanasius is confident that his interpretation is correct because he has received insight into the 'mind' of scripture through the Canon of Truth received from his

---

[43] Theodoret makes plentiful use of Athanasius in the Florilegia of the *Eranistes*; see further my 'Exegetical Method and Scriptural Proof'.

[44] The Christological debate was about the exposition of the Nicene Creed; cf. my *From Nicaea to Chalcedon*, pp. 216ff. and 26off.

[45] *C. Arianos* 1.52; Bright, p. 55; *NPNF*, 2nd series, vol. IV, p. 337.

predecessors. Paradoxically, interpretations of particular texts may be novel and recent if they cohere better with the teaching that elucidates the unity of the Bible through discerning the overarching narrative from creation through incarnation to the eschaton.

PART II

The Bible as classic

The fact that patristic exegesis took for granted principles of interpretation and composition drawn from classical rhetoric has already been hinted at in Part I. Here we examine the way in which the scriptures came to be treated as an alternative body of literature, to be subjected to the same scholarly examination as the Greek classics, and to replace those classics in providing authoritative examples, quotations and allusions for exploitation by Christian orators. Christian culture mirrored classical culture, but its discourse was formed by reference to another set of texts and stories – a novel intertextuality.

CHAPTER 3

Cultures and literatures

I

The perception that the Jewish scriptures became a substitute set of classics gives us a very different perspective on Christian appropriation of this 'barbarian' literature. It meant not just their Christological interpretation, not simply a supersessionary claim in relation to Jews, but potentially a supersessionary claim in relation to all of ancient culture. With astonishing audacity, a small persecuted community of oddly assorted persons with no natural kinship, no historical identity, claims a universality which challenges the most powerful tradition in ancient society, the Hellenic *paideia* which had taken over the world and colonised other traditions, Latin and Hebrew, Eastern and Western. In the course of this process the very concept of religion was redefined and philosophy reminted. Not only did the Christians prove themselves in the intellectual power struggle, but, to a traditionalist world shaped by unquestioned obligations to a society both human and divine in its constituents (the very word *religio* reflects that element),[1] they introduced the concept of religion as a particular faith-commitment, truth-claim or '-ism' as we understand it.

Hellēnismos, *Ioudaismos* and *Romanitas* were originally terms referring to culture; only in response to Christianity did paganism or Judaism, or for that matter at a later date Hinduism, become a

---

[1] The persistence (from the second century BC to the time of Augustine, fourth century AD) of the belief that the gods had made Rome great as a reward for Roman *pietas* bears witness to this attitude. According to J. H. W. G. Liebeschutz, *Continuity and Change in Roman Religion* (Oxford: Clarendon Press, 1979), p. 6, Livy suggests that 'Roman religion was a discipline which yoked individuals and the people as a whole to an exacting round of duties, and obliged individuals to submit to the expert guidance of priests who were also leading figures in public life.'

49

belief-system as distinct from a whole culture. To characterise religion in the ancient world is increasingly recognised as a very difficult task because we approach it with Christianising presuppositions.[2] Ancient religion was indistinguishable from culture, and the process of Hellenisation involved the assimilation of a mass of local pious practices to the dominant perspective of the Greek classics, while retaining local variety.[3] Religion consisted of a vast plethora of traditional practices for which aetiological myth or rationale might or might not be offered. It meant respect for inherited custom; a sense of duty and piety towards gods, ancestors and parents; and belonging to a community, with service to that community often projected into 'liturgies' or rituals involving the local gods.[4] What an individual or group believed was irrelevant, and those who overdid it by adopting new-fangled additional insurances were regarded as superstitious.[5] Philosophers might be sceptical and play games with symbols, but even they would uphold pious practices for the sake of social stability.[6]

So ancient revered literature and civic pride conspired to create a

[2] Robin Lane Fox, *Pagans and Christians in the Mediterranean World from the Second Century AD to the Conversion of Constantine* (Harmondsworth: Penguin, 1988), pp. 31ff. Ken Dowden, *Religion and the Romans* (London: Bristol Classical Press (an imprint of Duckworth), 1992), pp. 8–9, 65. Louise Bruit Zaidman and Pauline Schmitt Pantel, *Religion in the Ancient Greek City*, ET Paul Cartledge (Cambridge: Cambridge University Press, 1992), chs. 1 and 2 particularly (though treating the earlier classical period, much would still apply centuries later).

[3] The equation of Zeus and Baal, Zeus and Jupiter, etc., is but the simplest manifestation of Hellenistic syncretism. Hellenistic philosophies, especially Stoicism and Middle Platonism, encouraged the notion of a single divine in many manifestations. See e.g. Robin Lane Fox, *Pagans and Christians*; Moses Hadas, *Hellenistic Culture, Fusion and Diffusion* (New York: Norton, 1972); Luther H. Martin, *Hellenistic Religions* (Oxford: Oxford University Press, 1987); Martin Hengel, *Judaism and Hellenism*, 2 vols. (ET London: SCM Press, 1974); Robert Grant, *Gods and the One God. Christian Theology in the Graeco-Roman World* (London: SPCK, 1986).

[4] Plutarch's many works reveal how meaningful these religious ceremonies could be, as well as the philosopher's tendency to understand them all as symbolic. For helpful secondary literature, see previous notes.

[5] There are some good satires of religion in classical literature: e.g. Theophrastus (c. 371–288 BC, Aristotle's successor) wrote a series of thirty *Characters*, including the Superstitious Man (ed. and ET J. M. Edmonds, *LCL*, 1929; ET Philip Vellacott, Harmondsworth: Penguin Classics, 1967). Among Plutarch's *Moralia* is an essay *De superstitione* (text and ET by F. C. Babbitt, *LCL*, 1965). Lucian of Samosata (second Century AD) is particularly known for *Peregrinus* (probably satirising the typical Christian prophet taking advantage of the gullible) and *Alexander of Abounoteichos* (the religious impostor) (ed. and ET A. M. Harmon, K. Kilburn, M. D. McLeod, *LCL*, 1911–67). Noteworthy also is *The Life of Apollonius of Tyana* by Philostratus (c. 175–249 AD) (ed. and ET F. C. Conybeare, *LCL*, 1912).

[6] See e.g. Cicero, *De natura deorum*, ed. A. S. Pease, 2 vols. (Cambridge, Mass.: Harvard University Press, 1955); ET H. C. P. McGregor (Harmondsworth: Penguin Classics, 1972).

living culture in which people inhabited a socially constructed world with a population of visible and invisible beings, a sacred order that had to be respected, and appropriate rituals performed to maintain natural and social harmony. Education for life in such a world was based on 'imitation' of the classics which provided models of sublime style and diction, but also with proper critical attention, appropriate moral exemplars, embodying virtue and *eusebeia* (piety). Judaism also was just such a local commonwealth with its local divine patron and its own ancestral customs. If Jews claimed their God was the one King of the Universe, then Greeks and Romans claimed the same for Zeus and Jupiter, and each had its court of divine acolytes. So was not the same High God behind them all? A theoretical unity could be philosophically discerned behind the diversity and pluralism. Jews, too, usually acknowledged that Gentiles had their own virtue and piety given by God,[7] though they remained jealous of their particular obligations to the divinely given covenant, and maintained a literary culture of their own rather than developing the kind of Hellenised classical tradition which Rome happily adopted.

The radical shift which Christianity brought in how religion is understood owed not a little to the adoption by choice of that alternative literary culture, the commitment to it as the truth revealed by God, and the challenge thus offered to the literary culture that shaped the ancient world. The title of Arthur Droge's book, *Homer or Moses?*, neatly makes the point.[8] What Droge examines in that book is an apologetic claim I had long been aware of, namely the argument that the Greeks got their insights into truth from Moses, who predated their own important lawgivers and philosophers. His work has provoked me into seeing the deeper significance of this in terms of what we might call a potential cultural take-over bid.

The debate about culture was one which had already been under way long before the rise of Christianity.[9] The question of how civilisation arose had fascinated Greeks of the classical period. In Plato's day genealogies of heroes and cities already constituted a

---

[7] Martin Goodman, *Mission and Conversion. Proselytizing in the Religious History of the Roman Empire* (Oxford: Clarendon Press, 1994).

[8] Arthur J. Droge, *Homer or Moses? Early Christian Interpretations of the History of Culture*, Hermeneutische Untersuchungen zur Theologie 26 (Tübingen: J. C. B. Mohr (Paul Siebeck), 1989).

[9] Ibid., pp. 3ff.

science, *archaiologia*, and in the Hellenistic period it flowered among
Hellenistic and Roman literati. Jews joined in: Josephus' *Antiquities*
is a case in point. Tacitus, Droge notes, concedes the legitimacy of
Jewish religion, despite his criticism, on the basis of its extreme
antiquity. Many eastern peoples shared with the Jews the advantage
of being ancient in their heritage, and the Greeks themselves had
developed a theory of the barbarian origin of their culture. This was
taken up by Hellenised easterners who in Greek challenged the
Greek claim to have civilised the world. Apologetic histories of
Egyptians, Babylonians, Phoenicians, Jews – such provide the
context into which the writings of Christian apologists fit, suggests
Droge.

Nothing could be both new and true: such was the assumption,
such the challenge Christian apologists had to meet. As is well
known, Tacitus charged the followers of Chrestus with following a
new superstition. Plotinus met the Gnostic challenge by demonstrating that their books were recent forgeries, not, as they claimed,
documents of ancient oriental wisdom. In response to charges of
novelty, Christians followed Jews in adopting the theories of an
earlier Greek scholar, Hecataeus, which demonstrated the priority
of the barbarians, and then claimed the barbarian Moses as their
ancient inheritance, superior even to Homer since he predated the
Trojan War and gave the Egyptians their culture.[10] Like Stoics and
other philosophers, Christians found their doctrines in ancient
poems, collections of oracles, and wisdom-books, for which divine
inspiration was assumed. The Bible was ranged against Homer,
Hesiod, Orpheus and the Sibyl.[11]

The process is evident in the works of Justin, Tatian and
Theophilus, with the reverse side of the argument presented around
the same period by Celsus. Further developments occur in the
Alexandrians Clement and Origen, with the culmination in
Eusebius' grandly conceived history of culture in his *Praeparatio
evangelica*. Droge works through all this material, documenting on
the one hand its adoption of Greek assumptions, methods and
theories, while on the other hand indicating the implicit claim to a
superior tradition based on a body of literature which had priority
over the accepted classics.

Justin, of course, is recognised as highlighting similarities

[10] Ibid., p. 8.   [11] Ibid., pp. 10–11.

between Christianity and philosophy, and as suggesting that the universal Logos inspired such as Socrates and Heraclitus as well as Abraham, Elijah and many others. But, Droge points out,[12] these similarities were meant to prove the superiority of Christianity. Greek philosophy, indeed Plato himself, had only an imperfect understanding of the truth, whereas Christianity was the truth in all its fullness. What the Greeks read in Moses, they imitated. Tatian[13] lists the inventions that the Greeks copied from others: divination through dreams from the Telemessians, astrology from the Carians, augury from the Phrygians, astronomy from the Babylonians, magic from the Persians, geometry from the Egyptians, writing from the Phoenicians and so on. Using Greek sources for his information, Tatian argues that the Greeks should recognise their unoriginality. Like their contemporary Numenius of Apamea, Justin and Tatian subscribe to the view that prior to the break-up of philosophy into competing schools, there was a primitive, unitive wisdom known to the barbarians – Brahmans, Jews, Magi and Egyptians – which Plato had learned from them. Tatian regarded Moses as the earliest representative of this universal wisdom.[14]

Indeed, where Justin had contented himself with assertion, and with the adducing of literary parallels to prove Plato had read Moses, Tatian advances a chronological argument to establish his point that Moses is more ancient than all the Greek writers, indeed even than Homer, the oldest of poets and historians.[15] He appeals to Phoenician and Egyptian evidence to date Solomon and Moses, eventually showing that Moses lived four hundred years before the Trojan War, the date he assumes for Homer.[16] His methods are thoroughly Greek, in their own way 'scientific' – at least, Droge suggests,[17] as an exercise in their science of 'archaeology'. What we are observing, I suggest, is the adoption of a contemporary preoccupation with the history of culture for the purposes of relativising that culture in relation to an alien body of literature offered as a substitute for the established classics.

---

[12] Ibid., ch. 3, pp. 49–72.
[13] *Oratio ad Graecos* 1.1–2. *Tatian: Oratio ad Graecos and Fragments*, ed. M. Whittaker, Oxford Early Christian texts (Oxford: Clarendon, 1982), p. 2. Droge, *Homer or Moses?*, ch. 4, especially pp. 86–96.
[14] Droge, *Homer or Moses?*, pp. 90–1.   [15] *Oratio ad Graecos* 31; Whittaker, pp. 54–8.
[16] *Oratio ad Graecos* 35–40; Whittaker, pp. 64–72. Droge, *Homer or Moses?*, pp. 92–5.
[17] *Homer or Moses?*, p. 96.

Both Justin and Tatian were answering the charge of novelty, and essential to their argument were not only the common assumptions they share with those they address, but the appropriation of an ancient barbarian collection of texts as the foundation documents, the classics, of this 'third race', the Christians.[18] This was scandalous on both counts, namely the appropriation of an alien canon of literature to which these 'upstarts' might be regarded as having no claim and the attempt to subvert the established basis of Hellenistic culture. No wonder scripture figures so large in Apologies addressed to the pagan world. There is a real issue not merely as to whether Justin's *Dialogue with Trypho* is a genuine report of inter-religious dialogue, but even as to whether it is really a debate with Jews at all: after all, the argument from prophecy already figures in the *Apology*,[19] and Christians had to justify their extraordinary expropriation of texts which were not similarly interpreted by their true owners. This is the broader context of the supersessionary claim in relation to the Jewish people.

The process whereby this 'take-over bid' took place was various. We have observed that Tatian, like others engaged in the history-of-culture debate, exploited the Greeks' own material against them. Theophilus engages in another kind of expropriation, reading Genesis as if it were Hesiod, and as if a cultural history could be found in this alternative text.[20] If we survey *Ad Autolycum* II,[21] the overall context of this becomes apparent. The book begins with a critique of idols, which is clearly influenced by (Second) Isaiah, and a series of arguments against not only the generation and location of the gods as presented in Greek mythology, but also the gods' morality. Here he utilises standard philosophical criticisms. Poets and philosophers are at variance, Theophilus suggests, and the so-called 'inspired' poets were evidently inspired by a spirit of error.

The prophets, on the other hand, were inspired by the Spirit of Truth.[22] Theophilus counts among these not only the Hebrew

---

[18] Harnack's treatment of the 'third race' has itself become 'classic', but the consequences drawn out here have not been made explicit. See *The Mission and Expansion of Christianity*, vol. I (London: Williams & Norgate, 1908), ch. 7, with its excursus.

[19] *I Apology* 31ff.; Migne, *PG* 6.376ff.

[20] Droge, *Homer or Moses?*, ch. 5, pp. 102–18. Following Droge's observations, we look again at the text in the following paragraphs.

[21] *Theophilus of Antioch. Ad Autolycum*, ed. and ET Robert M. Grant, Oxford Early Christian texts (Oxford: Clarendon, 1970), pp. 23ff.

[22] *Ad Autolycum* II.9; Grant, p. 38.

prophets but the Sibyl. They are consistent with one another, and the accuracy of their predictions has already been established in some cases, so we can rely on them for the rest. He turns to Genesis,[23] quoting the creation story at length and then commenting on it. He upholds the power of the Creator in bringing everything into being out of nothing rather than pre-existent matter. He contrasts Hesiod with Genesis,[24] for Hesiod begins from below, Genesis with God and the Logos which was the instrument of God's creating activity. He provides some fascinating exegeses of elements of the creation, seeing signs of the resurrection in the way seeds turn into plants, and baptism prefigured in the production of living creatures from the waters; he had already found the sea a kind of parable of the world, fed by the springs of God's words flowing from the prophets, and containing islands of safety and fertility in the holy churches. But to pursue these features would distract from our main purpose.

The point here is that Theophilus proceeds to quote the Genesis account of Paradise,[25] and, in both his discussion of the creation of human beings and his interpretation of the story that follows, he introduces features which suggest Hesiod's Golden Age. Adam is innocent, happy and free from hard toil, and the animals were not originally created evil or poisonous. Theophilus in subtle ways reworks Genesis: Adam was not yet perfect, but had the potential for advancement to perfection; the tree of knowledge was good and its fruit good – what was wrong was the act of disobedience; Adam was neither mortal nor immortal, but potentially created for an ascent to the divine nature, and Theophilus implies an etymological account of the term *anthrōpos* (man) as one who runs upward (*ta anō trechein*).[26]

In fact, Droge suggests, Theophilus indulges in some curious etymologising which suggests that he believed that language was not arbitrary, but that primitive man named things according to nature (the *physis* theory vs. the *thesis* theory of language), a view found in Plato's *Cratylus*, among the Stoics and in Cicero, here attributed to Adam who names things in Genesis. Babel accounts for

[23] *Ad Autolycum* II.10ff; Grant, pp. 38ff.   [24] *Ad Autolycum* II.12–13; Grant, p. 46.
[25] *Ad Autolycum* II.20ff.; Grant, pp. 58ff.
[26] *Ad Autolycum* II.24; Grant, p. 66. Cf. Droge, *Homer or Moses?*, p. 106.

the loss of this primitive natural language. Droge goes on[27] to trace how Theophilus comments on the vegetarian diet of primitive man, another topic among Greek anthropologists, and ascribes hunting to the result of the Fall; then to show how in summarising the following chapters of Genesis he gives a programmatic history of culture dealing with the beginning of shepherding, agriculture, murder, city-building, polygamy, music and metalwork, warfare and priesthood, all much discussed topics among the Greeks. So theories of cultural history lead up to the elaborate scientific calculation of chronology in Book III,[28] in which the more ancient and superior calculations of the world's history since the creation are claimed for Moses, as well as moral superiority and greater philosophical consistency.

So, as Droge shows, contemporary scientific interests are addressed by Theophilus in terms of the Genesis material. Theophilus, so far from using Genesis to produce cosmogonical myths like those of the Gnostics, challenges on the basis of Genesis the intellectual assumptions and interests of the period concerning creation, loss of the Golden Age and the evolution of culture. Set in the context of a critique of pagan gods, mythologies and literature, which itself exploits the philosophical critique of religion, Theophilus exemplifies the Christian adoption of an alternative barbarian culture, and paves the way for that new understanding of religion. No longer would it be simply inherited practices, rituals and stories, for it necessarily became a commitment to the truth of the way things are as revealed by the inspired prophecies found in this alternative literature.

As Christianity became more established and influential, the scandal of its displacement of the dominant literary heritage on which Hellenisation and its educational system were based would become the more apparent. As Droge shows,[29] the issue regarding

---

[27] Droge, *Homer or Moses?*, pp. 108–18. *Ad Autolycum* II.17, 29–32; Grant, pp. 54, 72–82.

[28] *Ad Autolycum* III.16–29; Grant, pp. 120–46. Theophilus begins with the dating of the Flood, correlating Plato's allusions to the Greek myth with Moses' account and polemicising against recurrent cataclysms (cf. Droge, *Homer or Moses?*, p. 113). Then he discusses chronological reckoning of the Israelites' sojourn in Egypt, with criticisms of the chronological vagueness of Manetho, establishing that Moses was 900–1,000 years earlier than the Trojan War. Then he correlates the building of the Temple with Phoenician chronology. The 'true chronology' he finds in the Bible.

[29] Each of the chapters referred to here ends with a discussion of Celsus' reply to the case made by these Christian apologists.

the origin and history of culture already underlies Celsus' anti-Christian treatise, *Alēthēs Logos*, which represents the reverse side of the argument. A century or so later, the rival literatures have become ever more explicitly exposed to criticism as the two sides polarise the conflict, and Porphyry set about the kind of literary-critical exercise that challenged the antiquity of the book of Daniel, and, by a process of reasoning not unlike that of modern historico-critics, came to the same conclusions as they do, demonstrating its pseudepigraphical character and its relatively recent date. The battle of the literatures was on.[30]

II

But such a battle of the literatures was not a foregone conclusion. In the second century, the status and interpretation of the ancient scriptures of the Jews was controversial among those claiming the true revelation in Christ. It is intriguing that these 'internal' battles coincide with the development of the major cultural claim just outlined, and probably highly significant with respect to the future enculturation of Christianity that the 'orthodox' future lay with those who were committed to a text-based version of revealed truth.

Second-century Christianity is really rather obscure, not least because identifying a 'mainstream' is problematic. With the twentieth century's burgeoning interest in Gnostic studies, and the more recent concern with Christian–Jewish relations, it has become more and more apparent that in the first and second centuries we have to think not of two clearly defined, quickly separated religions, but rather of a variety of 'Judaisms', and of 'Christian' groups of various sorts, some Jewish, some Gentile, some mixed, some loosely connected, some disconnected, some competing. Probably many of these networks, Jewish and Christian, overlapped, but a good deal of rivalry and hostility was also

---

[30] For Porphyry, see R. L. Wilken, *The Christians as the Romans saw Them* (New Haven and London: Yale University Press, 1984), ch. 6; he also has a chapter on Celsus. Since writing this, I have been intrigued by Dennis MacDonald's attempt to show that the *Acts of Andrew* 'transvalues' Homer, especially the Odyssey, modelling Andrew's adventures on Homeric tales, but shifting the moral horizons and values: see D. R. MacDonald, *Christianizing Homer. The Odyssey, Plato and the Acts of Andrew* (Oxford: Oxford University Press, 1994).

generated between these related communities.[31] Attitudes to and use of the scriptures reflected this complex social reality. For, as we have seen, culture was expected to reside in books, and if a person or group claimed to 'teach', the message would usually be invested with authority by the claim that it was to be found in ancient literature. As already noted, Ignatius encountered people who said they would accept nothing but what was in the *archeia*.[32]

Around the middle of the second century, three teachers came to Rome. They apparently 'joined' the Roman church, arriving presumably with recommendations through the network. One, being a rich shipowner, contributed a huge sum to the treasury for charitable work among widows and orphans – he came from the Black Sea.[33] The others came from Samaria and Alexandria in Egypt. Of the three, two were to be excommunicated for false teaching, the other was to become a revered teacher. He apparently practised as a professional 'philosopher' without any particular ecclesiastical 'office' or *imprimatur*, teaching nevertheless a 'Christian philosophy' of a rather Middle Platonic flavour. The shipowner got his money back when excommunicated and founded his own 'church', an organisation which spread across the then known world and lasted for some centuries. The other heretic had followers who seem to have continued to operate on the fringes of the Church in esoteric study groups in various locations from Gaul to Egypt. The careers of these three characters, Justin, Marcion and Valentinus, show something of both the coherence and the diffuseness of the Christian community.[34] Their 'doctrines', as we

---

[31] New Testament scholarship has itself been deeply affected by (1) the history of religions approach which posited pre-Christian Gnosticism, and (2) recent interest in 'the parting of the ways' between Judaism and Christianity. The result is that both these subjects have generated a huge bibliography. They may be followed up by reference to e.g. Kurt Rudolf, *Gnosis*, ET R. McL. Wilson (Edinburgh: T. & T. Clark, 1983); Simone Pétrement, *A Separate God? The Christian Origins of Gnosticism*, ET Carol Harrison (London: Darton, Longman & Todd, 1991); J. D. G. Dunn, *The Parting of the Ways Between Christianity and Judaism and their Significance for the Character of Christianity* (London: SCM Press, 1991); Jack T. Sanders, *Schismatics, Sectarians, Dissidents, Deviants. The First One Hundred Years of Jewish–Christian Relations* (London: SCM Press, 1993).

[32] See above, p. 16.

[33] Marcion is reputed to have donated 200,000 sesterces, which were returned when his heretical views became apparent and he was excommunicated: Tertullian, *Adversus Marcionem* iv.4, ed. and trans. E. Evans, Oxford Early Christian Texts (Oxford: Clarendon, 1972), p. 268, *ANCL* p. 184; *De praescriptione haereticorum* 30, *CSEL*, p. 36, *ANCL*, vol. ii, p. 34.

[34] C. H. Roberts, *Manuscript, Society and Belief*, is important for providing evidence of similar coherence and diffuseness in Egypt and Alexandria. We should not deduce from the

shall see, demonstrate something of the cultural ambivalence of converts to this new movement, especially with regard to the embodiment of 'teaching' in ancient authoritative literature.

Ignatius had appeared to 'demote' the ancient scriptures by comparison with Christ, and the reduction of the biblical texts to the codex form suggested an equivalent 'de-sacralising' of these texts.[35] Both Marcion and Gnostics like Valentinus indicate the logical outcome of Ignatius' position: the new revelation either supersedes and displaces the old, literature and all, or it supersedes and reconfigures ancient texts of all kinds, all of which but dimly anticipate it.

One of the most interesting readings of Valentinus appears in David Dawson's book, *Allegorical Readers and Cultural Relativism in Ancient Alexandria*. Using the fragments and the *Gospel of Truth* as clues, Dawson shows how Valentinus 'erases the line between text and commentary, as interpretation becomes new composition'.[36] He talks in terms of an 'Apocalypse of the Mind', and the implied comparison is apposite: Valentinus, we might say, imaginatively reconfigures texts such as Genesis in a manner not unlike the creative reminting of biblical language and images found in works such as the book of Revelation. Here, however, the resultant cosmic myth does not concern what we might call the world-stage, beginning with divine creation and ending with an eschatological new creation; rather, the story of fall and redemption is recast in the interests of what Dawson calls 'psychodrama'. This 'revisionary freedom' Dawson regards as 'the authentically Gnostic spirit',[37] but he draws attention to the fact that the new composition 'gains much

presence of Valentinus and Basilides that Egyptian Christianity was in origin Gnostic (Walter Bauer, *Orthodoxy and Heresy in Earliest Christianity* (ET London: SCM Press, 1972), followed by many scholars since). Rather it seems to have been largely Jewish (and non-Pauline), with the papyri providing clear evidence of regard for the scriptures. Quoting R. M. Grant (*Cambridge History of the Bible*, p. 286), who characterised 'common core Christianity' in the second century as rejecting docetism, accepting the Old Testament and being non-elitist, and saw this 'embryonic orthodoxy as related to a common core of books accepted by most Christians, Gnostics included', Roberts suggests that 'the reading list of the provincial Church in Egypt [as evidenced in the papyri] ... answers remarkably well to Professor Grant's definition' (p. 72). On the other hand, he accepts that the lines between gnosticism and orthodoxy were clearly blurred throughout the second century in both Rome and Alexandria.

35 See above, pp. 13–16.
36 David Dawson, *Allegorical Readers and Cultural Revision in Ancient Alexandria* (Berkeley/Los Angeles/Oxford: University of California Press, 1992), p. 128.
37 Ibid., p. 131.

of its effectiveness precisely because the new story contains oblique, sometimes nearly subliminal, echoes of the old story'.[38]

Much of the detailed argument that Dawson offers depends upon the assumption that Valentinus was revising an older Gnostic myth, taken to be present in the *Apocryphon of John*. That analysis may be shaky: Simone Pétrement[39] has not only challenged the widespread scholarly assumption that Gnosticism has a pre-Christian origin, but also argued that the Gnosticism of the Sethians and the *Apocryphon* developed from Valentinianism, not vice versa. But, details apart, Dawson's suggestion implies much more. For it is not just Gnostic myth, but the classics and the scriptures which Valentinus apparently reconfigured in accordance with his own visionary experience:

In a sermon entitled *On Friends*, Valentinus claims that the wisdom common to both classical Greek literature ('things written in publicly available books') and Christian literature ('the writings of god's church'), whether conceived as speech ('utterances') or writing (the 'written' law), is first available in the hearts of 'the people of the beloved' (frag. G). One does not need to go to derivative sources, for the truth originally lies in the very interior of one's being.[40]

The manifestation of the Word, Dawson concludes, so purifies the visionary's heart that the Christian can see God.

As a result, the visionary possesses those insights from which the shared wisdom of classical and Christian literature is derived; he or she is enabled not merely to comment (like Philo or Clement), but to create (like Cornutus's mythologists, Heraclitus's Homer, Philo's Moses, or Clement's *logos*).[41]

Dawson has already shown how these allegorists regarded themselves as discerning the true authorial intention; his point here is that the Gnostic sense of being in touch directly with the truth meant even greater creative freedom with respect to existing texts, even though those texts were assumed to contain that truth when read with the right 'Gnostic' spectacles. Now if this is a right reading of Valentinus it explains the many seeming allusions or parallels to Genesis and the Gospels, as well as to Plato, in material which is not strictly derivative. Nor is it surprising that Valentinus' successors

---

[38] Ibid., p. 130.   [39] *A Separate God?*
[40] Dawson, *Allegorical Readers*, p. 167.   [41] Ibid., p. 168.

would need to elucidate key texts in relation to the new vision: Ptolemy explains the Law to Flora, Heracleon produces the earliest commentary on John's Gospel.

But even more significant, perhaps, is the suggestion that this is the authentic Gnostic spirit: for that explains how other Gnostic texts can show dependence on scriptural material while not being at all tied to the text, nor exclusive with respect to other religious texts, symbols and images. The crucial thing for the Gnostic was the insight which discerned through any and all ancient texts truths which had actually been received from elsewhere. Gnostic doctrine is revelatory rather than traditional, textual or rational. The Valentinians may have been close to the Church, but other Gnostics were both more syncretistic and more counter-cultural. The Gnostic demotion of the 'Creator' is now perceived by scholars as a strong anti-Jewish streak, but the anti-cosmic thrust of Gnosticism also implies an alienation from all earthly wisdom. Gnostics expressed their cultural marginalisation in terms of a 'superiority' to contemporary culture, both Greek and Jewish, which would ultimately permit unbridled eclecticism.

So, once one had the gift of *gnōsis*, one could apparently create new texts which drew the truth out of ancient writings, whether Jewish or otherwise. The serpent of the Genesis narrative could become the embodiment of the female principle of wisdom, bringing knowledge to humanity (as in the *Hypostasis of the Archons*), a not unreasonable reading if one already thought the Creator was other than the true God, and one associated wisdom with the serpent according to the symbolism of ancient mythology.[42] Likewise, Valentinus could conflate Genesis and the crucifixion:

He [Jesus Christ] was nailed to a tree and became fruit of the father's acquaintance. Yet it did not cause ruin because it was eaten. Rather, to those who ate of it, it gave the possibility that whoever he discovered within himself might be joyful in the discovery of him.[43]

As Dawson puts it,[44] the crucifixion enables Christians to eat the fruit (Jesus) and discover they are actually in the Father and

---

[42] The only work I know which begins to explore this is Elaine Pagels, *Adam, Eve and the Serpent* (London: Penguin, 1988).
[43] *Gospel of Truth* 18.24: *The Gnostic Scriptures*, ed. Bentley Layton (London: SCM Press, 1987) p. 254.
[44] *Allegorical Readers*, p. 167.

the Father in them. In both cases the import of the Genesis narrative is strikingly reversed.

I have long been inclined to doubt the consensus that Gnosticism was a pre-Christian movement and I therefore welcome Pétrement's study,[45] though with some reservations about detail. Still for our purposes it is not absolutely necessary to decide whether the roots of Gnosticism are syncretistic or Jewish, whether they lie inside or outside Christianity, or whether de-Christianisation or re-Christianisation is a more plausible account of Gnostic history. The significant thing seems to be that, despite their exegetical activities, on the whole Gnostics stood apart from the battle of the literatures, having no firm commitment to any particular 'canon'. They may have used whatever was useful, but all texts were, for them, de-sacralised and superseded. They were above 'culture', neither Jew nor Greek. This stance the Valentinians seem to have justified on the basis of Pauline material.

Indeed, there is emerging a good deal of evidence that the second century witnessed a battle over the Pauline heritage.[46] This is not the place to go into this in detail, except in so far as it affects attitudes towards the Jewish scriptures, but it is interesting to note how modern scholarly debate about the interpretation of Pauline theology parallels the struggle in the second century. Was Paul a Gnostic or was he anti-Gnostic? Was Paul negative or affirmative about the 'world' and the 'flesh', and if negative, was this because of expectations concerning the imminent end of the world, or because of leanings towards a Gnostic spirituality? What was the implication of his rejection of the Law? It is not insignificant that the Pauline heritage is claimed by Valentinians, by Marcion, by the *Acts of Paul*, which reflects an extreme asceticism but is seemingly anti-Gnostic, and, apparently, by other groups of more socially conformist Christians whose literature eventually entered the ecclesiastical canon, namely the so-called Pastoral Epistles.[47] No wonder 2 Peter 3.15–16 could speak of 'our dear brother Paul' while warning that much of what he wrote is hard to understand, and that ignorant and

---

[45] *A Separate God?*

[46] See e.g. Elaine Pagels, *The Gnostic Paul. Gnostic Exegesis of the Pauline Letters* (Philadelphia: TPI, 1992 (originally, Fortress, 1975)); C. K. Barrett, 'Pauline Controversies in the Post-Pauline Period', *NTS* 20.3 (1974), pp. 229–45; D. R. MacDonald, *The Legend and the Apostle: The Battle for Paul in Story and Canon* (Philadephia: Westminster, 1983).

[47] See my *The Theology of the Pastoral Letters* (Cambridge: Cambridge University Press, 1994).

unstable people twist his words, along with other scriptures, to their own destruction. The letters to Timothy provide further clues that the reception of the Jewish scriptures was one of the contentious issues surrounding the Pauline heritage.[48]

That Valentinians claimed to be followers of Paul is increasingly obvious. Valentinus, they claimed, was instructed by Theudas, one of Paul's pupils. One of the Nag Hammadi codices which contains only Valentinian works (the Jung codex) is prefaced by a *Prayer of Paul*, which invokes the one from whom he emanated, who is his intellect, treasure, fullness and repose, in the name above every name, Jesus Christ, then prays for authority, redemption and inspiration, and requests access to the mystery and majesty which is 'after the image of the animate god when he was modeled in the beginning'.[49] Elaine Pagels has demonstrated how Paul was read by Valentianian Gnostics, as speaking of those who are spiritual receiving *gnosis* and access to secret wisdom.[50] Paul provided the authority for subordinating the Law to the Gospel, the Jewish scriptures to the new revelation in Christ. Yet he also demonstrated how this new revelation could be discerned if the veil over the scriptures was removed. Paul validated the new compositions produced by 'allegorical' reading of existing texts, both Jewish and philosophical.

Paul also validated a quite different response to the scriptures, namely their rejection. It is no accident that Tertullian in replying to Marcion devoted a whole book[51] to showing that Paul's Epistles are consistent with the Creator's scriptures. This was a debate between two different readings of Paul, and both are different from that of the Valentinians. Marcion, far from privileging a religious vision which can then reconfigure ancient texts, rather used certain Christian texts in a critical way to introduce a hermeneutic of suspicion with respect to texts still treated as authoritative by the emerging Christian network.

For Marcion it was crucial to clarify which texts were to provide the authoritative basis of Christian culture, and since this culture was both anti-pagan and anti-Jewish, neither traditional body of literature was appropriate to Christian use. He hazarded a replacement

---

[48] 1 Timothy 1.7–11; 4.3–5; 4.13; 5.18; 2 Timothy 2.15; 3.8; 3.15–17.
[49] Layton, *Gnostic Scriptures*, p. 305.
[50] *The Gnostic Paul*.   [51] Book v: Evans, vol. II, pp. 508ff.

'canon' of relatively recent literary compositions, incurring the inevitable charge of 'novelty'. Though nothing like so innovative as Valentinus in one sense – for he did accept the need for authoritative texts – he was also counter-cultural in that he selected texts that for society in general were marginal. Some of his resultant 'doctrines' have a family resemblance to those of the Gnostics, at least sufficient for the anti-heretical writers to rehearse many of the same arguments and attribute many of the same false teachings to both, justifiably or not.

Are Tertullian and Irenaeus[52] fair in focussing on the unity of God as the principal issue, and attributing docetism to Marcion? It is marginal to our interest to engage in the debate whether Marcion is to be regarded as a Gnostic or not; for our purposes, it is his hermeneutic which is important. Irenaeus and Tertullian may well have discerned correctly the theological consequences of Marcion's hermeneutic, but it could be that Marcion's principal interest lay elsewhere. There are reasons for thinking that Marcion's concerns were initiated by the problems of scriptural consistency, not least because it was those issues which, a generation or so later, exercised the first scholarly exegete, Origen, and there are reasons for thinking that he was responding to Marcion's arguments. This is also borne out by the concrete information Tertullian gives us about Marcion's own literary activity.

Marcion apparently wrote a work called the *Antitheses*. The aim of this work, according to Tertullian,[53] was to show a diversity of gods by setting the Gospel at variance with the Law. Yet Tertullian argues in the same breath that the opposition between Law and Gospel is what suggested the idea that the God of the Gospel is different from the God of the Law, and that, if this is the case, the opposition between the two gods must owe its origin to Marcion's own analysis and cannot have been revealed by Christ. It is, of course, in Tertullian's interests to insist on the novelty of Marcion's position, but it also contradicts his first statement of Marcion's purpose. That Marcion's theology was derived from exegetical

---

[52] Irenaeus promised in the *Adversus haereses* to write a book on Marcion, thus suggesting that he saw Marcion's challenge as different from that of the Valentinians. Such a work does not survive, if it was ever written. Tertullian's large work against Marcion is therefore the principal source for Marcionite views, apart from brief notices in the anti-heretical literature.

[53] *Adv. Marc.* 1.19; Evans, vol. I, p. 48.

concerns rather than vice versa, seems highly likely. Galatians suggested a difference of opinion between Peter and Paul with respect to the law which Marcion seems to have exploited, for Tertullian next needs to affirm that Peter and Paul made it up, and to explain that though Paul was opposed to circumcision and Jewish festivals, this was because a new dispensation had been inaugurated according to the purpose of the Creator God himself, and all this was in any case predicted by the prophecies of a new covenant.[54] The debate strongly suggests that Marcion saw himself as properly understanding the Pauline tradition. By delaying his treatment of Pauline exegesis to Book v and turning to the unity of God in Book ii, Tertullian has perhaps reversed Marcion's priorities.

Tertullian very occasionally allows us to glimpse specific examples of Marcion's *Antitheses*. Apparently he pointed out that the Law prohibited touching a leper, whereas Christ touched in order to heal, reinforcing this with the point that Elisha needed water applied seven times to heal Naaman, whereas Christ healed the leper by a word only.[55] He also contrasted the responses of David and Jesus to blind people: David was offended at the blind who blocked his entrance to Jerusalem (2 Sam. 5.6–8), whereas Christ succoured the blind, thus demonstrating that he was not David's son.[56] Such examples may seem trivial, but may also be an important clue. The contrasts between Law and Gospel were textually based. Marcion found real difficulty in reconciling the compassion and love revealed in Jesus Christ with the justice, judgement, wrath and punishment which constituted the world of the text as far as the Jewish scriptures were concerned.

Tertullian's detailed arguments show how many of the Marcionite arguments were objections to the character and behaviour of the God depicted in the Jewish scriptures. That God is immoral: he incited the Hebrews to defraud the Egyptians.[57] That God is fickle and unstable: there are contradictions in the laws concerning Sabbath,[58] the election and rejection of Saul shows inconsistency, and God 'repents', changing his mind about the Ninevites as well as Saul.[59] That God is ignorant: he had to call out

---

[54] *Adv. Marc.* i.20; Evans, vol. i, p. 50.   [55] *Adv. Marc.* iv.9; Evans, vol. ii, p. 290.
[56] *Adv. Marc.* iv.36; Evans, vol. ii, p. 470.   [57] *Adv. Marc.* ii.20; Evans, vol. i, pp. 140–2.
[58] *Adv. Marc.* ii.21; Evans, vol. i, p. 144.   [59] *Adv. Marc.* ii.23–4; Evans, vol. i, pp. 148–52.

'Where are you?' to Adam, and ask Cain where his brother was.[60] It is striking how closely Marcion's objections to the God of the Jews parallel the philosophical critique of the gods of Greek myths.[61]

Tertullian accuses Marcion of not discerning the goodness of God in the created order, but Marcion's primary concern was that the God of the Jewish scriptures was malignant. The Gospel becomes liberation from that God, a liberation not unlike that offered by Epicurus, who sought to free everyone from fear of the gods by proving they had no concern with human beings.[62] Since the scriptures designate God as Creator of the world, the denigration of creation is a consequence of this radical hermeneutic. In response to Marcion, Tertullian constantly affirms the importance of discipline, and the fact that love and judgement are two sides of the same coin, while Origen over and over again allegorises the wrath of God, suggesting that irrational passion should not be attributed to the divine but rather the goodness of a physician who causes pain in order to heal. These reactions indicate the seriousness of Marcion's exegetical challenge. The scriptures of the Jews depicted a god unworthy to be the Father of Jesus Christ.

In Book III of Tertullian's work against Marcion, the argument from prophecy takes centre stage. Marcion, it seems, wishes to present a 'new being in a new way' without prior announcement. This new revelation is confirmed not by prophecy but by miracle.[63] That Tertullian devotes a whole book to the argument from prophecy in this context shows how fundamental it was to the reception of the scriptures in the Church. It was not simply apologetic, whether with respect to Jews or non-Jews, though apologetic was doubtless required by the need to justify Christian appropriation of the Jewish scriptures while investing them with a new meaning; it was at the heart of Christian understanding of Christ, and Marcion undermined that. Tertullian may have devoted his last two books to an exegesis of those Christian texts that

[60] *Adv. Marc.* II.25; Evans, vol. I, pp. 154–6.
[61] See my article, 'The God of the Greeks and the Nature of Religious Language', in W. R. Schoedel and Robert Wilken, *Early Christian Literature and the Greek Intellectual Tradition, Festschrift for R. M. Grant* (Théologie Historique 53, Paris: Editions Beauchesne, 1980).
[62] This 'gospel' is the principal message of Lucretius, the Roman Epicurean who wrote a long poem promulgating Epicurean doctrine: *De rerum natura*, ed., trans. and comm. C. Bailey, 3 vols. (Oxford: Clarendon, 1947); ET R. E. Latham (Harmondsworth: Penguin, 1951).
[63] *Adv. Marc.* III.3–4; Evans, vol. I, pp. 172–4.

Marcion accepted, an exegesis geared to showing that the Creator is so written into these texts that Marcion's acceptance of them was inconsistent; but he also demonstrates the intertextual relationships between the scriptures Marcion rejected and these Christian documents (by now regarded as the New Testament, though not in Marcion's day). That demonstration largely depends on the argument from prophecy.

For our third second-century character, Justin, that argument was indispensable. He was anxious to demonstrate the inadequacy of the appeal to miracle; proof lay in the way prophecies were fulfilled, so that fulfilment and prophecy mutually confirmed each other.[64] The literature he had available on which to base his educational programme was the Jewish scriptures, now understood to enshrine the true philosophy more effectively than Plato or other philosophical schools. As is well known, in the *Dialogue with Trypho*,[65] Justin explains, according to a common literary convention, how he tried a number of philosophical schools, rejecting them all for various reasons, until with a Platonist he made real progress towards wisdom, at least prior to a strange meeting which led him to the works of the prophets who were witnesses to the 'truth above demonstration'.[66]

Justin and Trypho (the Jewish spokesman in his *Dialogue*, a useful 'type', whether or not he be a fictional character) share the same literary heritage, and the same intellectual scene, yet their 'culture' is different. Each politely accuses the other of having listened to teachers who do not understand the scriptures. Trypho even affirms admiration for the Gospel precepts. What he cannot understand is why these Christians make no effort to separate themselves from the Gentiles, or alter their mode of living in accordance with the scriptures they claim. Needless to say, the subsequent discussion is about contrary exegeses of those scriptures. But, for our purposes, the point is that this Christian philosophical teacher lays claim to an ancient literary heritage. These prophets are 'more ancient than all those esteemed philosophers'.[67] The key thing is that the revelation

---

[64] *1 Apology* 30: Migne, *PG* 6.373–6; ET in *FC*, p. 66. Justin needs to show that Christ was not a magician, and regards the argument from prophecy as more soundly based. He goes on to provide the evidence of prophetic fulfilment.

[65] *Dial.* 2; Migne, *PG* 6.476B–477C; ET in *FC*, p. 149.

[66] *Dial.* 3; Migne, *PG* 6.477D; ET in *FC*, pp. 151ff.

[67] *Dial.* 7; Migne, *PG* 6.492A; ET in *FC*, p. 159.

is not an outright novelty, but embedded in texts. To that extent Justin, though being neither 'Jew' nor 'Greek' in terms of culture, is far from adopting the counter-cultural stance of those relying entirely on a new revelation, whether enshrined in recent texts or in the hearts of believers.

So we observe the process whereby Greek literary culture was subordinated to Christian culture in the way outlined earlier. Justin follows lines already laid down by Hellenistic Jews such as Aristobulus who had been anxious to reinterpret their Greek host culture by claiming priority:

It seems to me that Pythagoras, Socrates, and Plato with great care follow him [Moses] in all respects. They copy him when they say that they hear the voice of God, when they contemplate the arrangement of the universe, so carefully made and so unceasingly held together by God. And further Orpheus also imitates Moses in verses from his (books) on the Hieros Logos.[68]

On Aristobulus, Dawson comments:

Allegorical reading transforms Jewish scripture from a parochial closed book into an interpretative lens capable of permitting readings that construe the wider Greek culture in specifically Jewish terms.[69]

Jewish interpretative subordination is in fact a hermeneutical usurpation in which classical writers are demoted to the status of Mosaic epigones, condemned merely to echo his original and sublime insights. Authentic Greek culture is actually Jewish.[70]

Philo received this bequest and, as Dawson shows, developed 'the reading of scripture as a revisionary interpretation of Greek culture' on an 'even grander scale'. This presumptuous claim would be presumptuously usurped from Jews by Christians. It was this that enabled Christian enculturation. Dawson's account stops short of Origen, but if Dawson's reading of Philo and Clement is accepted, then Origen, I suggest, is much closer to adopting Philo's legacy than Clement. Origen marks the advent of proper scholarly exegesis, and this presupposes a body of approved literature to be used for Christian *paideia*. For Origen as for Philo, Greek culture is subordinated to the scriptures.

---

[68] Aristobulus, quoted in Eusebius, *Praep. evang.* 13.12.4, quoted by Dawson, *Allegorical Readers*, p. 79.
[69] *Allegorical Readers*, p. 81.   [70] Ibid., p. 82.

The reaction to the Gnostics and to Marcion led to the definition of a scriptural canon, comparable to that of the Jews but also containing certain 'new' scriptures which provided the appropriate key to reading the old.[71] If the logical outcome of the initial de-sacralising process was the freedom of Gnostic readings and Marcion's rejection of the material, the reaction produced a re-sacralising of the Jewish scriptures, alongside the development of a collection of sacred apostolic writings enshrining witness to the fulfilment of those ancient prophecies. By the end of the second century it is clear that Christians are not only defending their adopted literature, but also substituting it for the pagan classics. The second-century struggle was for an appropriate literary 'canon' for people claiming to educate into the truth and train in the right way of life, yet belonging to a 'third race'.

III

Hellenism was a culture, a way of conceiving the world embodied in a society, articulated in a literature. Jewishness was similar. Christians were not without reason called the *tertium genus* (the third race), for they belonged to neither culture – they adopted the literature of the Jews, and claimed access to the primitive and true wisdom which both Judaism and Hellenism had fragmented and distorted. Eusebius would argue this in his *Praeparatio evangelica* and defend the scriptures in his *Demonstratio evangelica*.[72] Epiphanius[73] would create his great heresiology on the same principle: heresies – or we might call them 'options' – all stemmed from the fragmentation of the unity of humanity and distortion of the pristine truth, and they included Hellenism and its various sects, Judaism and its various sects, Scythian barbarism and so on, not just Christian deviations. With this kind of cultural embedding, religion was indistinguishable from culture, and it is not for nothing that, in Byzantine Greek, *Hellēnismos* became the word for paganism. Nor do we have to recall Tertullian's famous rhetorical exclamation, 'What

---

[71] See Hans von Campenhausen, *The Formation of the Christian Bible*, ET J. A. Baker (Philadelphia: Fortress, 1972).

[72] *Dem. evang.*; *GCS*, vol. vi, ed. I. A. Heikel (1913); *Praep. Evang.*; *GCS*, vol. viii.1 and 2, ed. K. Mras and E. des Places (1982, 1983).

[73] See my article, 'Did Epiphanius Know What he Meant by Heresy?', *SP* 18 (1982), pp. 199–205.

has Athens to do with Jerusalem?',[74] to illustrate the deep-seated sense that Christianity, based on the Bible, is a different culture from Hellenism, based on Homer and Plato.

Prior to Nicaea Christians exploited the moral and theological shortcomings of pagan literature, adopting the well-tried methods of the schools and the well-worn arguments of the philosophers to serve their exposure of traditional religion and philosophy, and to condemn the whole integrated literary and symbolic culture that surrounded them. The Bible was to provide a substitute literature, a rival *paideia*, an alternative education. The reaction of Western Europe to the rediscovery of the Greek classics at the Renaissance is an indicator of how far that substitution was successful in the centuries of Christendom. Meanwhile, however, Julian (Emperor December 361–June 363 and known as 'the Apostate') took Christians at their word, banning Christian teachers from the rhetorical schools where the traditional Hellenistic canon of classics still provided the basis of the curriculum. The Christian reaction is instructively ambivalent. Julian read the tradition aright.

Julian[75] had grown up at a Christian court, but his early experiences can hardly have been encouraging as he lost members of his immediate family to imperial jealousy and suspicion. He secretly renounced Christianity, and became a pagan fanatic with a mission. But he knew Christianity from inside, and recognised some of its strengths. The paganism he sought to restore was not the old natural culture – it was austere, moralistic, philosophic, owing not a little to ecclesiastical organisation. He did not want to create martyrs, he simply wanted the 'god-fearing' (*theosebeis*) to be favoured. On 17 June 362, he issued his notorious edict on teachers. As Bowersock notes,[76]

At first reading, the edict seems innocuous; for Julian's words were carefully chosen: 'School teachers, and professors ought to be distinguished, first by character and, second, by eloquence.' It was apparent that those who did not meet these qualifications were ineligible to teach the pagan texts which constituted the core of fourth-century education . . . when Julian issued his edict on teachers he was concerned as much with religion as with secular instruction. All this becomes clear in the explanatory

---

[74] *De praescriptione haereticorum* 7; *CSEL*, vol. II.2, pp. 9–11; ET in *ANCL*, vol. II, p. 9.
[75] See G. Ricciotti, *Julian the Apostate*, ET M. J. Costeloe (Milwaukee: Bruce, 1960); and G. W. Bowersock, *Julian the Apostate* (London: Duckworth, 1978).
[76] *Julian*, pp. 83ff.

letter which the emperor provided as an interpretation of his measure. No Christian, in his view, would qualify as a teacher because he was automatically deficient in character (*mores*). Accordingly by a single stroke Julian forbade Christians to teach grammar, rhetoric, and philosophy.

Thus Julian challenged teachers to teach the classics 'as truth'. What is significant for our purposes is to observe the Christian reaction. By now, the leadership of the Church was drawn from the leadership of society. The best education was vital, and taken for granted. How was the need for Christian education to be met? Was the process of catechesis and instruction through exegetical homily adequate to produce the Christian teachers of the next generation? The Bible was not stylistically up to the classics – could it, or should it, become an appropriate vehicle for rhetorical emulation? Two responses feed later developments.

Detailed study of the first response is hampered by lack of extant texts, but there is plenty of evidence that some, notably Apollinarius of Laodicea and his father, created a new set of classics, based on biblical stories but composed in Greek literary styles. The Apollinarii were first-class rhetoricians. Jerome[77] tells us that he went to the lectures of Apollinarius in Antioch, and comments, 'While he instructed me in scripture, I never accepted his disputable dogma on Christ's human mind.' But Jerome's attendance demonstrates the continuing repute of a man described by Kelly[78] as 'one of the most acute and versatile minds of the century'. Apollinarius had been associated with Athanasius in the anti-Arian struggle, and had also written thirty books against Porphyry's attack on Christianity. He had been a voluminous writer, producing a whole library of scripture commentaries. But as indicated, the significant point for us is that he and his father, in the crisis of 362 under Julian, set about rewriting the Bible in classical forms. Sozomen describes this reaction:

[Julian's] sole motive for excluding the children of Christian parents from instruction in the learning of the Greeks, was because he considered such studies conducive to the acquisition of argumentative and persuasive power. Apollinaris, therefore, employed his great learning and ingenuity in the production of a heroic epic on the antiquities of the Hebrews to the reign of Saul, as a substitute for the poem of Homer. He divided this work into twenty-four parts, to each of which he appended the name of one of the

---

[77] *De viris illustribus* 104.   [78] J. N. D. Kelly, *Jerome* (London: Duckworth, 1975), p. 59.

letters of the Greek alphabet, according to their number and order. He also wrote comedies in imitation of Menander, tragedies resembling those of Euripides, and odes on the model of Pindar. In short, taking themes of the entire circle of knowledge from the scriptures, he produced within a very brief space of time, a set of works which in manner, expression, character and arrangement are well approved as similar to the Greek literatures.[79]

Socrates adds the information that he composed Platonic Dialogues out of Gospel material. The only surviving material,[80] whose authenticity is in any case doubtful, is a *Paraphrase of the Psalms* in hexameters, richly interwoven with reminiscences of the old Hellenic poets.

The production of such a substitute literature was, according to our sources, a deliberate response to a crisis, and the Apollinarii were not alone in producing this sort of material. Another example is that of Nonnus of Panopolis. He is reputed to be the author of a metrical *Paraphrase of St John's Gospel*, composed in hexameters in the fifth century.[81] This case is particularly intriguing, since the poet Nonnus of Panopolis is the author of the longest extant Greek epic, forty-eight books long, celebrating Dionysus. As Bowersock has argued,[82] this work gives contemporary insight into the survival of pagan rites throughout Asia Minor and the Near East. So where did this verse paraphrase of St John come from? It is very much in Nonnus' style, and hence the assumption that he must have later converted, and written it as a Christian. But there are literary problems in regarding the *John Paraphrase* as later than the *Dionysiaca*. Is it inconceivable that a Christian could have written the latter? Bowersock thinks not.

Christian piety, at least in certain people, was entirely compatible with a profound appreciation of pagan traditions.[83]

The fact is that the battle-lines were much less clear than has often been supposed. One might compare the Neoplatonist Synesius who became bishop of Cyrene and, as far as belief is concerned, preached Christian mythology in church, but kept his own philosophical understanding in private.[84] The *Dionysiaca* shows no trace of

---

[79] Sozomen, *HE* 5.18; *GCS*, p. 222.
[80] As J. Quasten notes in *Patrology* (Utrecht and Antwerp: Spectrum, 1963), vol. III, p. 380.
[81] Ibid., p. 116.
[82] *Hellenism in Late Antiquity* (Cambridge: Cambridge University Press, 1990), pp. 42ff.
[83] Ibid., p. 43.   [84] *From Nicaea to Chalcedon*, pp. 170–7.

anti-Christian polemic, and Bowersock argues that in this period there are many traces of Christian influence on pagan mythology and practice. The development of the Dionysus figure, in art as well as Nonnus' epic, reflects the pagan response to Christian monotheism: Bowersock cites, among others, an instance in which Dionysus is depicted on the lap of Hermes, very much like the child in the lap of the virgin. He thinks

we should certainly be prepared to countenance the possibility that the same man wrote those two poems. As Gregory of Nazianzus clearly understood even though he never said so, the Hellenism of Christians could also be no less Hellenic in the sense of 'pagan' than it was in the sense of 'Greek'.[85]

Indeed, in his study of Julian, Bowersock repeats several times that 'the Christian style of life had an old-fashioned pagan zest to it'.[86] Julian's 'austerity and the fanatical zeal of its advocate portended the end of the way of life which had not only replaced the old paganism but actually absorbed its *joie de vivre*'.[87] In other words, Julian harked back to the period of confrontation. But the inter-penetration of cultures was already so deep that such distinctions were increasingly difficult to make. This explains both the capacity of Christians to respond with a rival literature in the classical forms, and also the second reaction, to which we now turn.

The other response was that of the Cappadocians,[88] which in a different way demonstrates this interpenetration producing a new attitude towards pagan literature. In his *Orations against Julian*, Gregory Nazianzen insists on making a distinction: *logos*, he says, is not a matter of *thrēskeia* (worship) but of *glossē* (tongue, language).[89] Why should Julian presume to cut Christians off as foreigners from the language and culture which is their own? Of course, Gregory particularly objected to Julian's underhand way of getting at Christians without openly persecuting them. It was a manoeuvre, which Julian hoped no one would notice, to deprive Christians of Attic eloquence.[90]

---

[85] *Hellenism*, p. 53.   [86] *Julian*, p. 94.
[87] Ibid., p.80.
[88] And others, though their work will not be explored here: see *The Emperor Julian. Panegyric and Polemic*, ed. Samuel N. C. Lieu (Liverpool: Liverpool University Press, 1986), which includes translations of work against Julian by John Chrysostom and Ephrem Syrus.
[89] *Orat.* 4.5; *SC*, vol. 309, p. 92.
[90] *Orat.* 4.61–3; *SC*, vol. 309, pp. 168ff.

In developing this theme,[91] Gregory affirms that he is prepared to give up anything except *logos*, demanding to know where Julian got the idea for depriving Christians of *logoi*, and what the arguments are for it.

Logoi [words and culture] are ours, he claims, along with *to hellēnizein* [to speak, think and live 'Greek'], of which worship of the gods is a part; yours are *alogia* and *agroika* [irrational and rural!], and nothing beyond 'Believe' is your wisdom.[92]

Julian reflects back exactly what we know Tertullian affirmed, and Gregory reports this without noting the irony. He goes on demanding that Julian demonstrate that *logoi* belong exclusively 'to you', insisting that particular people cannot claim exclusive right to use the Greek language, for speech and thought. Does *to hellēnizein* refer to religion, nation or language? If it is to be treated as referring to religion, where is it located? Where are its priests? If that is not what Julian means, then he is confusing two different realities. Besides, what exactly is Julian claiming? Is the alphabet Greek? No, it is Phoenician.[93] Is arithmetic Greek? No, it is Euboean; and Gregory exploits the old material noted earlier about Greeks borrowing all their culture from others. Even poetry and religion were borrowed, Gregory suggests, and launches into the well-worn arguments against the gods and myths of Greek tradition, with the old criticism of allegorical sophistications to get round the problems.

But let us not be misled by the old apologetics. There is now a new kind of apologetics, which claims the Hellenic cultural heritage as part of the Christian world. It is subsumed in a 'totalising discourse' which we will explore further later on.[94] It is evidenced not only in the capacity of Christians to turn the Bible into the genres of the Greek literary heritage, but also in the composition of Christian works in those genres. Gregory of Nyssa reflected on Christian doctrines in the form of Platonic Dialogues. Gregory of Nazianzus would eventually retire to pour out his soul and his philosophy in imitative Greek poetry. Before he did so, he addressed the world

---

[91] *Orat.* 4.100ff.; *SC*, vol. 309, pp. 248ff.   [92] *Orat.* 4.102; *SC*, vol. 309, p. 250.
[93] *Orat.* 4.107; *SC*, vol. 309, p. 258.
[94] The phrase comes from Averil Cameron, *Christianity and the Rhetoric of Empire*; the theme will be explored in ch. 11 below.

in the best Atticising orations, of which these two against Julian, judiciously composed after his death, are important examples.

The theme of *Hellénisme et Christianisme*[95] in the Cappadocians is hardly a new one, and we should return to the place of the Bible in all this. My purpose has been to show a shift in the issue of 'Bible and culture' from the pre-Nicene confrontation of cultures to an interpenetration which superficially gainsaid, yet largely effected, the supersession which the earlier claims had implied. Pagan literature was, we might say, 'secularised'. The traditions of moral criticism enabled Basil to affirm it for educational means, and Gregory to claim that same inheritance independent of its religious connotations. Yet the Bible replaced Homer as the authoritative religious or philosophical text, despite the survival of the old educational curriculum. In order to explore the consequences of that substitution for exegesis, we shall turn the clock back to the third century.

---

[95] I borrow the title of the book by E. Fleury, *Hellénisme et Christianisme. S. Grégoire de Nazianze et son temps* (Paris: Beauchesne, 1930).

CHAPTER 4

The advent of scholarship

I

Once the biblical literature became established as an alternative body of classics, it would soon be seen as the basis of a new *paideia*. That Origen is reputed to have established a Christian school with a curriculum embracing the standard subjects of an advanced education is an indication that this development did indeed take place. It would be surprising if this did not mean the adoption of the exegetical practices of Graeco-Roman schools. To demonstrate that Origen's exegesis drew on such standard procedures is the object of this chapter. An initial difficulty, however, is reconstructing what those procedures were.

In the ancient world, secondary literature was much sparser than it is in our world. Sometimes these days it seems that students, especially in Biblical Studies, spend so much time on secondary sources that they rarely read the original texts. It is true that ancient schools also fostered the production of handbooks, compendia and collections of extracts, but the equivalent of our secondary literature was largely oral. Exegesis and commentary went on in class, as indeed to a fair extent it does still. The oral practice of exegesis was so much taken for granted that it is quite difficult to reconstruct exactly how exegesis was done.

A certain amount of material roughly equivalent to our literary criticism has survived among the essays of people like Plutarch, and rhetorical textbooks discuss style and other features of literature. The work of D. A. Russell and M. Winterbottom[1] has done much to make such material accessible. There survive also scholia, or

---

[1] *Ancient Literary Criticism* (Oxford: Oxford University Press, 1972), a collection of material in translation; see also D. A. Russell, *Criticism in Antiquity*.

marginal notes on texts, and commentaries from various sources, which throw light on the equivalent Christian material. But far more important is the largely inaccessible oral practice in the schools, from which the scholars of the early Church learned their trade. Before we turn to Christian scholarship, it is necessary to do what we can to find out about what went on in the schools.[2]

Quintilian is our most informative source.[3] A Latin rhetor in the Greek tradition, he composed a textbook in his retirement. Where Greek textbooks can be compared, he proves a reliable purveyor of tradition. From our point of view, Quintilian's chief value is that he does not assume we know what went on in the elementary stages, as most sources do. He provides the only summary account we have of the use of literature in the school classes of the *grammaticus*.

Correct reading precedes interpretation, says Quintilian. But he makes it clear that correct reading involved an interpretative process. Words were not divided in the texts, there was no punctuation and not all handwritten copies contained the same wording. Teachers had to begin by establishing an agreed text and rejecting spurious material. Then how that agreed text was to be read would need to be discussed. Where did the sentences begin and end? Where should the stress come? As noted earlier, all reading in the ancient world was reading aloud, a kind of performance. A text was a form of recorded speech, and it had to be realised to make sense, rather like the playing of a musical score. *Diorthōsis* and *anagnōsis*, as the Greek tradition named the establishment and construal of the text, were the primary tasks of attending to the letter.

The next stage was to attend to the language. In Quintilian's view, this requires considerable scholarship, since much literature, being ancient, contains unfamiliar archaic words and forms: vocabulary and parsing are bound to occupy the class, as well as parts of speech, construing sentences and so on. The ancient Homeric dialect must have stretched even Greek-speaking pupils of antiquity. Much school comment on literature was concerned with

---

[2] This task I attempted in my article, 'The Rhetorical Schools and their Influence on Patristic Exegesis', in Rowan Williams (ed.), *The Making of Orthodoxy. Essays in honour of Henry Chadwick* (Cambridge: Cambridge University Press, 1989) pp. 182–99. The following account for the most part draws on that paper. On ancient education, the classic work is H.-I. Marrou, *L'éducation dans l'antiquité* (Paris: Editions du Seuil, 1948; ET London: Sheed & Ward, 1956). On rhetoric, see the works of George Kennedy referred to earlier, ch. 1, note 4.

[3] Quintilian, *Institutio oratoria* i.iv–ix, especially.

basic linguistic correctness. The origin and meaning of names
occupied the class: tracing etymologies was an important part of this
examination of texts at the linguistic level.

Quintilian regrets that many teachers do not pay enough attention to these preliminary mechanical foundations, but rush on to
more interesting matters like style. In reading literature, pupils
were to accumulate experience of styles to emulate when they came
later to do rhetorical compositions. So teachers would point out
'sublime' vocabulary and felicitous verbal combinations, while
noting barbarisms, grammatical solecisms and ugly combinations of
syllables – such were only to be imitated if a particular effect were
desired. Foreign words would be explained, metaphor and
archaisms elucidated. Thus, in the first place, reading a classic in
school meant analysing its sentences into parts of speech and its
verses into metre, noting linguistic usage and style, discussing
different meanings of words, elucidating figures of speech or
ornamental devices. This is what was meant by attending to *ta rhēta*,
the things stated, the letter of the text, and understanding *pros lexin*,
according to the word, the letter, the reading. Quintilian's word,
methodike, reflects the Greek rhetorical terminology for this preliminary linguistic analysis – *to methodikon*.

To this sketch we may add another exercise which can be traced
in the scholia and the fragments gleaned from them of works like
Porphyry's *Homeric Questions*, namely the attempt to resolve
'problems' in Homer by reference to other Homeric verses. The
fundamental assumption was that Homer explains his own
meaning. As far as one can see this exercise was conducted very
much at the textual and lexical level, and relates to the school
analysis *pros lexin*, the resolving of inconsistencies of meaning or
incompatibilities of detail. Someone like Porphyry had a reputation
as a philologist as well as being associated with philosophy by being
Plotinus' editor: he was engaged in this kind of basic exegetical
exercise, as well as more elaborate symbolical allegory.[4]

The other aspect of school exposition was explaining the stories,
unpacking allusions to classical myths, gods, heroes, legends,
histories – not in too much detail, advises Quintilian, nor in too
many versions. The mind must not be swamped. Commentaries
are full of such erudition. Nevertheless, the exploration of these

---

[4] See further Lamberton, *Homer the Theologian*.

background points is important.[5] Quintilian's word, *historike*, again represents technical vocabulary, but to jump to the conclusion that *to historikon* is some kind of historico-critical exegesis is misplaced: I submit that too many discussions of patristic exegesis have jumped to conclusions about historical interest where such terminology is used, for it does not necessarily imply what we mean by historical. *Historia* in the first place has to do with enquiry, the knowledge acquired by investigation, and in some contexts at least it is more likely to have that kind of meaning than to imply any claim to historical factuality in our sense. Indeed, it is acknowledged that ancient literary criticism had no true historical sense.[6]

Having said that, however, it is clear that *historia* could refer to an ancient literary genre not totally dissimilar to what we mean by history. Herodotus, the 'Father of History', had assembled the results of his investigations into a great narrative, with many sub-narratives often told in more than one version, without any attempt to distinguish critically between them, and including local 'myths'; in fact, a good deal of his information we would regard not as historical but rather as geographical or cultural. Some of his successors claimed to try and restrict themselves to what we might call 'the facts' in constructing narratives of the past (e.g. Thucydides and Polybius); but a common motif was the reporting of rhetorical speeches by the main characters, and even Thucydides confesses to having composed such speeches, inventing what seemed appropriate when no information was available.[7]

Indeed, Arnaldo Momigliano, the classical historian, once published an article on 'Pagan and Christian Historiography'[8] in which he proposed that Eusebius, the first Christian historian, changed the whole way in which history was written, and paved the way for the modern documentary approach. Up to Eusebius, history had been a literary form, 'a rhetorical work with a maximum of invented speeches and a minimum of authentic documents'. In his

---

[5] NB the discussion in Adam Kamesar, 'The Evaluation of the Narrative Aggada in Greek and Latin Patristic Literature', *JTS* NS 45 (1994), pp. 37–71. He suggests that patristic commentators wrongly understood Aggada as *to historikon*.

[6] See particularly D. A. Russell, *Criticism in Antiquity*, especially chs. 8 and 11.

[7] Thucydides, *History* (LCL, 4 vols., ET Charles Forster Smith, 1919–23) 1.22.

[8] 'Pagan and Christian Historiography in the Fourth Century AD', in A. Momigliano (ed.), *The Conflict between Paganism and Christianity in the Fourth Century* (Oxford: Clarendon, 1963), pp. 79–99. NB p. 89.

reliance on documentary evidence, Eusebius was inventing a new kind of historical presentation, which was intended to convince of the truth of Christian claims – its roots were in apologetic. That is why evidence was piled up to prove points, and an erudition displayed which is not found in pagan historical writing.

'History' as a literary genre,[9] then, was closely akin to rhetoric and tragedy: there was more interest in fate and fortune, in moral lessons,[10] in creative composition and effective style, than in historicity. It is no accident that our word 'story' is derived from *historia*; for the narrative was meant to be a good, improving story (*ktēma es aei* – a 'possession for ever', according to Thucydides[11]). *To historikon* involved the investigation of the 'story' presented in the text being studied.

However, some narrative or historical criticism, designed in practice to prepare the budding orator to challenge the narrative given by the opposing lawyer in the courts, was practised in the schools.[12] The critical question about narrative was whether it was probable or persuasive, and the methods of assessment were *anaskeuē* (refutation) and *kataskeuē* (confirmation). Three types of narrative were distinguished: true history, or an accurate account of real events; fiction, or what could have happened but did not; and myth, what could not have taken place, a 'false account portraying truth', as Theon described it. The methods of criticism were based in logic and comparison: Heracles could not have killed Bousiris as some say, since, according to Hesiod, Bousiris lived eleven generations earlier than Heracles. A narrative may be incredible because of the character to which the action is attributed, the nature of the action, its time, its mode of performance, or the motive or reason adduced. There may be omissions or contradictions in the narrative which suggest the author is not to be trusted. Dio Chrysostom applied such criteria to Homer, arguing that the story of the Trojan War is implausible; there we can see these critical techniques in

---

[9] See further below, ch. 8, especially note 20.

[10] Glenn F. Chesnut, *The First Christian Histories*. Théologie Historique 46 (Paris: Beauchesne, 1977) has a useful summary chapter on pagan historiography, before showing how much these issues continued to play a role in Christian historiography from Eusebius on, though modified by Christian beliefs.

[11] 1.22; *LCL*, vol. I, p. 40.

[12] The evidence is examined in detail by R. M. Grant in *The Earliest Lives of Jesus* (London: SPCK, 1961), ch. 2, to which the following account is largely indebted.

operation. Defence of many traditional, but implausible or immoral, narratives was offered through their allegorisation.

From the *grammaticus*, the pupil would proceed to the *rhētōr* for secondary education. Here exegesis would be even more pragmatic, geared towards the practice of composition. Rhetorical teachers explained how to set about this, and no doubt sought object-lessons in the classical texts. So texts must have been assessed in the light of the distinction already noted, namely that between *ho pragmatikos topos* (or *res*), in other words, the subject-matter, and *ho lektikos topos* (or *onomata, verba*), that is, the style and vocabulary.[13] Noting the author's skill in organising and manipulating the subject-matter, his *heuresis* or *inventio*, and then his choice of the appropriate style in which to present it, was all-important for the provision of object-lessons in successful communication.

Rhetorical criticism would always be 'audience-oriented', looking for the effect produced. The intention of the author was taken to be the production of that effect. Most interpretation was anachronistic to the extent that there was little awareness of the possibility of distinguishing authorial intention and what the interpreter discerned.[14] The intent was to effect a response. Literature was expected to be morally edificatory, and the exercise of moral judgement, or *krisis*, became an important aspect of the school tradition.[15] Because of Plato's attack on the poets as morally subversive, echoed indeed by Plutarch who spoke of poetry as a seductive form of deception, much effort was expended in extracting acceptable moral advice from classical texts, and Plutarch's essays *On the Education of Children* and *How the Young should Study Poetry* demonstrate how text was critically weighed against text, how admonition and instruction were found in tales and myths, and how the inextricable mixture of good and bad in poetry was taken to be true to life, and therefore useful for exercising moral discrimination.[16]

---

[13] See above, ch. 2, note 18. The distinction is common to the rhetorical handbooks: e.g. Quintilian, *Inst. orat.* x.i and ii. W. Rhys Roberts clarifies the components of *ho pragmatikos topos* and *ho lektikos topos* in his introduction to Dionysius of Halicarnassus, *The Three Literary Letters* (ed. and trans. by W. Rhys Roberts; Cambridge: Cambridge University Press, 1901), p. 9; cf. also *On Literary Composition* with introd., text, trans. and notes by W. Rhys Roberts (London: Macmillan, 1910).

[14] D. A. Russell, *Criticism in Antiquity*.

[15] See my article, 'Rhetorical Schools'.　　[16] *Moralia*; *LCL*, vol. 1.

II

It is time to turn to Christian material. No commentaries or works of a scholarly kind from the second century are extant among Christian literature. Formal exegetical material emerges in the first part of the third century in the West with Hippolytus, in the East with Origen. We know that Origen was aware of other exegetes, and that he argued with the Commentary of the Gnostic Heracleon in his own *Commentary on John*. We can also trace the influence of school methods and concerns in some earlier theological writings where texts are appealed to and given an exegesis, in polemical contexts such as Irenaeus' anti-heretical books, or expository contexts such as his *Demonstration of the Apostolic Preaching*, or the argumentative treatises of a Tertullian. In practice, however, the advent of Christian scholarship belongs to the early third century.

Hippolytus' exegetical work survives only in fragments, so inevitably Origen claims primary attention. Traditionally books on Origen have leapt to discussion of his allegorical method,[17] tracing the background in Stoic philosophy, the *Quaestiones Homericae* of Heraclitus (first century AD) and the near contemporary works of the Jew, Philo, even Rabbinic precedent being drawn in. For purposes of contrast and correction, I wish to focus, as indicated earlier, on the ways in which even the greatest allegorist was rooted in the school tradition I have described.[18]

Origen's interest in textcritical questions is well known, evidenced not least in the fact of the *Hexapla*. It is notoriously difficult to give a precise account of the *Hexapla* since over the centuries it has disappeared, perhaps not surprisingly – how many copies are likely to have to been made?[19] It seems it was an important reference work in the library at Caesarea, for Eusebius says 'he left us copies',[20] but no doubt it disappeared with that

---

[17] E.g. Hanson, *Allegory and Event*.
[18] My argument was anticipated by Bernhard Neuschäfer, *Origenes als Philologe* (Basel: Friedrich Reinhardt Verlag, 1987). He shows how Origen follows the standard form of prologue, the methods of *diorthōsis* (textcriticism), of *glōssēmatikon* (explanation of words), of *historikon* (explanation of points or facts), of technical matters such as metre and style, and also engages in *krisis poiēmatōn*, the identification of the *prosōpon* speaking in the text, and the practice of clarifying 'Homer by Homer', all features of 'pagan' exegetical practice.
[19] I owe this observation to a conversation with Ron Heine.
[20] *HE* VI.16; *GCS*, vol. II, p. 554.

library at some point in the vicissitudes of history. Eusebius calls it the *Hexapla* (sixfold), and speaks of Origen collecting the Hebrew and the well-known translations of Aquila, Symmachus and Theodotion as well as the LXX; we understand that this would make six columns with a transliteration of the Hebrew. But Eusebius also mentions Origen unearthing some other odd translations, and reports that in the *Hexapla of the Psalms*, after the four well-known editions, Origen placed not merely a fifth, but even a sixth and a seventh translation, one of which was found in a jar at Jericho.

We also understand that Origen marked divergences in the text by using the scholarly device of the obelus and asterisk: he tells us so in the *Commentary on Matthew* xv.14.[21] In this passage he is remarking on the apparent addition of 'You shall love your neighbour as yourself' to the Matthaean text in 19.19, which gives the list of commandments offered by the rich young ruler. He feels the suspicion that this is an addition is confirmed by the absence of these words in Mark and Luke. He goes on to comment that it would seem irreverent to make such a suggestion if it were not for the fact there is

much diversity in our copies, whether by the carelessness of certain scribes, or by some culpable rashness in the correction of the text, or by some people making arbitrary additions or omissions in their corrections.[22]

He then explains his method of curing diversity with regard to the Old Testament. He employed as a standard other versions. Where the LXX agreed, the text was retained. Words not occurring in the Hebrew were marked with an obelus: Origen refrained from removing them, saying he did not dare, presumably because of the tradition inherited from Aristeas that the LXX was inspired. Some words Origen inserted, marking them with asterisks, to show they were additions from other versions in conformity with the Hebrew, though not found in the LXX. This sounds like a critical text of the LXX rather than the *Hexapla* as generally understood, though many have taken Origen to be referring to that work.

In the Commentaries, Origen makes reference to textcritical difficulties. An example may be offered from the *Commentary on Matthew* xii.15:[23] he notes a manuscript difference as to whether

[21] *GCS*, vol. x, pp. 385–90.   [22] ET Tollington, *Selections*, pp. 109–10.
[23] *GCS*, vol. x, pp. 103–5; *ANCL*, addit. vol., pp. 459ff.

16.20 read *diesteilato* (commanded) or *epetimēsen* (charged). Pursuing the point he discovers that Mark says, 'he charged that they should tell no one of him', and Luke, 'he charged and commanded them that they should tell no one this', whereas the Matthew text he was concerned with was not only uncertain on the first point, but continued 'that they should tell no one he was the Christ'. Origen regards these difficulties as real. By a fairly long and circuitous route, he argues that the more perfect teaching that he is Christ, the Son of the Living God, was reserved for a more appropriate time; this is implied by Luke's 'this' and made more explicit in Matthew, the point being that their testimony could only be proper in the light of the crucifixion. Neither the textcritical point nor the synoptic problem is resolved, but these critical issues clearly lead Origen into explaining the reference of the text by appeal to context – a basic exegetical exercise – as well as encouraging him to produce an illuminating cross-reference to Paul's emphasis on Christ crucified. Many other examples of Origen's concern with text, with the Hebrew original, and with the construal of sentences can be gleaned from standard works.[24] In our terms, Origen singularly fails to resolve the problems he raises, but the fact that he raises them shows he is aware of the basic philological questions which exercised school classes.

So far then we have noted examples of Origen's concern with *diorthōsis* and *anagnōsis*, with establishment of the correct text and the construal and correct reading of it. Such issues had, of course, emerged earlier: we will note Justin's concern with discrepancies between Jewish and Christian readings in a later chapter. But Origen tackles the issues in a more systematic and scholarly way. The fragments of Hippolytus show that he too was consulting other translations, and raising questions at the lexical level in a more studied fashion. The preliminaries to exegesis were beginning to be taken seriously as they would have been in Graeco-Roman schools.

The other element of *to methodikon*, namely noting figures of speech, etymologies, meanings of words and so on, is also to be found in Origen, though the lexical step is often exploited to lead on to deeper meanings. Once more using the *Commentary on Matthew* for

---

[24] Including Hanson, *Allegory and Event*, ch. 6. For examples, see his discussion of frag. vi from the catenae: *GCS*, vol. ɪᴠ, p. 488; and *Comm. Jn.* x.280–3; *GCS*, vol. ɪᴠ, p. 218; *ANCL*, addit. vol., p. 405.

examples, we may note the etymology offered for 'Canaanite': 'prepared for humiliation'. We also find a 'concordance' process whereby cross-references were assembled to establish the biblical meaning of a term; as Porphyry assumed that Homer provided his own meaning, Origen assumed that the inspired authors used language consistently, and text could be used to elucidate text. Discussing the scribe fit for the kingdom who brings out of his treasury things both old and new (Matt. 13.52),[25] Origen exhorts his students, 'by giving heed to reading, to exhortation, to teaching' (1 Tim. 4.13) and 'by meditating in the law of the Lord by day and night' (Ps. 1.2), to endeavour to gather in their heart not only the new oracles of the Gospels and the apostles and their revelation, but also the old things, in the law 'which has the shadow of the good things to come' (Heb. 10.1), and in the prophets who prophesied in accordance with them:

And these things will be gathered together, when we also read and know, and remembering them, compare at a fitting time things spiritual with things spiritual, not comparing things that cannot be compared with one another, but things which admit of comparison, and which have a certain likeness of diction (*lexeōs*) signifying the same thing, and of thoughts and of opinions, so that by the mouth of two or three more witnesses (Matt. 18.16) from the scripture, we may establish and confirm every word of God.[26]

The process of comparison may assist in the spiritualising process, but it remains an exegetical move at the level of *to methodikon*.

The discussion of figures of speech is similar. To understand something *tropikōs*, a word used at least as frequently, if not more frequently, than the derivatives of *allēgoreō*, was to observe its twist or turn, its metaphorical usage. Such was often the route to allegory, but Origen made a standard point of *to methodikon* in drawing attention to the impossibility of taking metaphorical language according to the letter. He would sometimes raise questions about the proper definition of figures of speech, as in the *Commentary on Matthew* x.4,[27] where he discusses whether there is a difference between a parable and a similitude. Scripture attaches the word 'parable' to all the previous examples in the passage under discussion (Matt. 13), but when it comes to the treasure hid in a field,

25 *Comm. Matt.* x.15; *GCS*, vol. x, pp. 18–19; *ANCL*, addit. vol., pp. 422–3.
26 ET in *ANCL*, addit. vol., pp. 422–3 (my emphasis).
27 *GCS*, vol. x, pp. 4–5; *ANCL*, addit. vol., pp. 415–16.

and the following two cases, the word 'parable' does not appear. On the basis of Mark 4.30, 'To what shall we compare the kingdom of God, or in what parable shall we set it forth?', Origen establishes a distinction between parable and similitude, the similitude apparently being generic while the parable is specific. He further deduces that, as the similitude is the highest genus of parable, it contains the parable as one of its species. Further on in the Commentary,[28] he finds Matthew 13.53 does not easily fit with his first discussion, which linked parables with teaching the multitudes and similitudes with private teaching to the disciples, so he reviews his position.

So far, then, we have demonstrated that Origen was aware of the elements of school exegesis described as *to methodikon* and sought to apply it to the reading of scripture. He also adopts *to historikon* of the schools, and he has sometimes the tendency deplored by Quintilian to show off his erudition. Still drawing on the *Commentary on Matthew*, in x.7–10 we find an elaborate discussion of pearls and their source.[29] This is ultimately to enhance the sense of the merchant's search, but we get the feeling Origen enjoyed the excuse for his enquiry (*historia*).

We find then in those who write on the subject of stones, with regard to the nature of the pearl, that some pearls are found by land, and some in the sea. The land pearls are produced among the Indians only, being fitted for signet-rings and circlets and necklaces; and the sea pearls, which are superior, are found among the same Indians, the best being produced in the Red Sea. The next best pearls are those taken from the sea at Britain; and those of the third quality, which are inferior not only to the first but to the second, are those found at Bosporus off Scythia. Concerning the Indian pearls these things further are said. They are found in mussels, like in nature to spiral snail-shells; and these are described making the sea their pasture-ground, as if herds under the guidance of some leader who is conspicuous in colour and size and different from those under him, so that he has an analogous position to what is called the queen-bee.[30]

And so it goes on, Origen telling us how they are netted, how each pearl takes periods of time to form, how the shell opens to receive the dew from heaven, but closes if the pregnant shell is struck by

---

[28] *Comm. Matt.* x.16; *GCS*, vol. x, p.20; *ANCL*, addit. vol., pp. 423–4.

[29] *GCS*, vol. x, pp. 6–11; *ANCL*, addit. vol., pp. 416–19.

[30] ET in *ANCL*, addit. vol., p. 417 (altered).

lightning, with damaging results. He describes different pearls, comparing Indian with those from Britain and the Bosporus. That is one aspect of *to historikon*.

An example of another aspect is found in x.17:[31] here details are assembled to explain the Matthaean story on which he is commenting, the rejection at Nazareth. 'Where did this man get this wisdom and these mighty works?' asks the crowd. Origen refers to the verse in the same Gospel (Matt. 12.42) which speaks of a greater than Solomon, adding that he performed greater works than Elijah and Elisha, Moses and Joshua. 'Is this not the carpenter's son?' wonders the crowd, and, 'depreciating his family', as Origen puts it, they add, 'Is not his mother called Mary? And his brothers, James and Joseph and Simon and Judas? And his sisters, aren't they all here with us?' Origen has already alerted us to the crowd's ignorance of the fact that he was son of a virgin, and he proceeds to quote from the *Gospel of Peter* and the *Protevangelium of James* to the effect that the brothers of Jesus were sons of Joseph by a former wife. After some comment on the appropriateness of Mary's purity, he explains who James was, quoting Paul in Galatians, and the, to him remarkable, testimony from the *Antiquities* of the non-Christian Flavius Josephus. He has no information on Joseph and Simon, he says.

Historia is the enquiry that produces as much information as possible with respect to the elements, actions, characters or background of the text. Hippolytus too valued information. The introduction to his *Commentary on Daniel*[32] assembles a considerable background account of the prophet's time, assuming the book's fictional setting in the Babylonian exile to be authentic. The curious word in the LXX translation of Proverbs 7.22, *kepphōtheis*, is explained:[33] the *kepphos* is a kind of wild sea-bird, and Hippolytus describes it as having certain immoderate sexual impulses, thus explaining the comparison with the young man's pursuit of the harlot, folly. These early scholars delighted in providing explanatory comment of this sort. Such information Origen does not despise, and the usual focus on his willingness to disregard 'history' in our sense fails to do justice to his exegetical practice.

---

[31] *Comm. Matt.* x.17; *GCS*, vol. x, pp. 21–2; *ANCL*, addit. vol., pp. 424–5.
[32] *GCS*, vol. I, pp. 2ff.   [33] A fragment: *GCS*, vol. I, pp. 161–2.

Origen also practiced narrative criticism.[34] In the *Contra Celsum*, *kataskeuē* (confirmation) and *anaskeuē* (refutation) are used to turn the criticisms of the opponent, though Origen seems to have regarded refutation as the easier task, no doubt because of the methods inherited from the schools. Origen regards Celsus' version of the birth of Jesus as a 'myth': it was simply not true that the mother of Jesus was turned out by the carpenter who was betrothed to her, because she had been convicted of adultery and had had a child by a certain soldier called Panthera.[35] But the myth indicates that his opponent recognises that Joseph was not the father of Jesus. He proceeds to defend the story of the virgin birth by offering 'scientific' explanations and parallels in Greek stories, which make the Christian story persuasive or plausible.

In pointing out impossibilities or inconsistencies in the Gospel-narratives, Origen was using the techniques of *anaskeuē* (refutation). In the Gospel Commentaries, these techniques are employed to show the necessity of proceeding beyond the mere story to the spiritual intent of the evangelist. In the *Commentary on John*,[36] Origen tackles the discrepancy between John and the Synoptics over the Cleansing of the Temple. He spells out John's version, followed by Matthew's, Mark's and Luke's. He then notes the difference in timing. He 'conceives it to be impossible for those who admit nothing more than the history in their interpretation to show that these discrepant statements are in harmony with one another'.[37] He demonstrates the implausibility of the Johannine narrative, and then, having explained the deeper meaning of the Johannine story by allegorising its details, Origen proceeds to apply narrative criticism to the Matthaean story, showing that that too is unpersuasive taken as it stands. In the end the deeper intent of each evangelist must be attended to, rather than the history they purport to report.

In both Commentaries and the *Contra Celsum*, it is evident that Origen believes that in the Gospels different kinds of narrative are woven together, as indeed the rhetorical critics found in the texts they were interested in: myth, fiction and historical narrative are

---

[34] As Grant fully demonstrates in *The Earliest Lives of Jesus*, a book which has not, I suggest, been recognised for the important work it is. For the example in this paragraph, see p. 72.

[35] *C. Cels.* 1.32–7; *GCS*, vol. I, pp. 83–9; ET Chadwick, pp. 31ff.

[36] *Comm. Jn.* x.119–22; *GCS*, vol. IV, pp. 191–2; *ANCL*, addit. vol., pp. 391ff.

[37] *Comm. Jn.* x.130; *GCS*, vol. IV, p. 194; *ANCL*, addit. vol., p. 393.

combined. In the Commentaries, Origen tends not to 'use the prejudicial terms "myth" and "fiction"', comments Grant.[38]

Instead, he substitutes the words 'enigma' and 'parable', since they are to be found in scripture itself. We know that these words are the equivalents of 'myth' and 'fiction' because Origen's definitions of them, provided in the *Commentary on Proverbs*, are identical with the Greek definitions of the ordinary Greek terms.

As the orator may speak falsehood for the benefit of his hearers, according to Hermogenes, so 'God makes use of the same procedure'. Origen frequently uses the analogy of the father dealing with an infant son, or a physician with a patient: 'the whole of divine scripture', he suggests, 'is full of such medicines'.[39] *Anaskeuē* gave Origen his justification for symbolic exegesis, but it was based in the rationalistic criticism of the schools.

III

Thus far, then, we have explored Origen's debt to the practice of exegesis in the grammar and rhetorical schools. The examples we have adduced display not only erudition, but a concern to solve problems of meaning and apparent inconsistencies. This begins to shift the focus somewhat towards the deductive process. Such exegesis is problem-centred, and, while there is a sense in which most comment is a response to a perceived problem, the particular issue I have in mind is where a truth or consequence is reached beyond what the immediate text actually says. Often this involves ethical or doctrinal consequences. It is a vital process in the application of an authoritative text to new conditions, especially where a 'ruling' is required whether on a legal, disciplinary or doctrinal matter.

In an example of textual criticism which we looked at earlier,[40] Origen argued that it was likely that 'You shall love your neighbour as yourself' was an erroneous insertion, since if the rich young ruler had kept all the laws he cites, including this one, he would already have been perfect, and Jesus could not have suggested that he lacked 'one thing'. Paul's summary of the Law in Romans 13 is called in evidence to substantiate this. On the other hand, if it does belong to

---

[38] *Earliest Lives*, p. 66.   [39] *Hom. Jer.* 20.3; *GCS*, vol. III, p. 180.   [40] See above, p. 83.

the text, its implication must be that Jesus did not accept the man's claim to have kept all the commandments he had listed; to sell all his goods and give to the poor would alone prove he had. Here the problem arises out of the text – deductive discussion is stimulated by a textcritical problem. But there were many other features of texts that provoked the need for a reasoned consideration of the implications.

Another example arising from passages already considered[41] is the problem raised by Mary's virginity for the statements of the crowds in the Nazareth synagogue: the implication of those statements cannot be right. The characters in the story must be ignorant, and the necessary information is sought to refute improper deduction from the text: the brothers of Jesus were Joseph's sons by a former wife. Drawing still on the *Commentary on Matthew* we may note Origen's discussion of the problem of how Herod could have thought Jesus was John the Baptist.[42] Did Herod think he was John risen from the dead? But they were two different people and could not be identical. So did Herod accept the Greek idea of transmigration of souls? Origen suggests there was insufficient time since John's death, and settles for the view that the text implies a transfer of the Spirit's power from one to the other. The debate has doctrinal implications.

The fragments of Hippolytus' work, especially the *Commentary on Daniel*, show that deduction was an important element, along with cross-reference and explanatory comment, in reaching a conclusion about the reference of the prophetic text. Here is a particularly striking example:[43] the first appearance of our Lord in the flesh took place in Bethlehem, under Augustus, in the year 5500. He suffered in his thirty-third year. It is necessary that 6,000 years be accomplished before the Sabbath-rest, which is a type of the kingdom of the saints. This scheme is demonstrated among other things from the measurements of the ark: $2\frac{1}{2}$ cubits length + $1\frac{1}{2}$ breadth + $1\frac{1}{2}$ length produces $5\frac{1}{2}$ which signifies 5,500 years. Eventually the discussion works back to identifying the time the prophet Daniel is referring to in the verse under discussion.

Such rationalistic debate about a text's implications arises from

---

[41] See above, p. 87.
[42] *Comm. Matt.* x.20; *GCS*, vol. x, pp. 26–8; *ANCL*, addit. vol., p. 427.
[43] *Comm. in Daniel* xxiii–xxiv; *GCS*, vol. i, pp. 240–8.

enquiry of the kind undertaken in the schools, and interestingly is paralleled in the Rabbinic *middot*, the exegetical rules which guided Jewish exegetical traditions, which certainly had direct or indirect influence on Christian exegesis. According to Froehlich,[44] David Daube 'has convincingly argued that all these rules reflect the logic and methods of Hellenistic grammar and forensic rhetoric'. In fact, the bulk of Daube's article is concerned with legal judgements.[45] He parallels the taking over of Greek norms in Latin jurisprudence with the systematisation of legal deductions in Rabbinic interpretation, suggesting that the borrowing took place when the Rabbis were masters, not slaves, of the new Hellenistic influences.

Daube argues that at the time of Hillel a large body of oral law existed, but was contentious. Hillel, against the Sadducean rejection of oral law, demonstrated that the tradition of the fathers was to be deduced from scripture by the most up-to-date methods, the rational norms of exegesis making it possible to clarify and extend legal provisions. He finds parallels to the first four rules, always in the same order, in Cicero and other legal texts: these establish the principles for deduction. The rules are in a sense 'natural', but specific applications and the systematisation found to be common to Cicero, Hillel and Philo are hardly 'natural'. Similar Hellenistic influences affected Ishmael and Akiba as they developed the systems at a later date. Daube also finds parallels in attitude towards the relationship between oral laws and written codes.

Daube's article, entitled 'Rabbinic Methods of Interpretation and Hellenistic Rhetoric', appeared in 1949, and did not reach Saul Lieberman until his book *Hellenism in Jewish Palestine*[46] was ready for press. Lieberman saw no reason to change anything in the chapter on 'Rabbinic Interpretation of Scripture' in the light of Daube. In different ways, they were reaching the same nuanced position: that Jewish interpretation had ancient traditional roots, but responded to the Hellenistic environment by systematising these traditions in a rationalistic way.[47]

---

[44] *Biblical Interpretation in the Early Church*, p. 4.
[45] David Daube, 'Rabbinic Methods of Interpretation and Hellenistic Rhetoric', *Hebrew Union College Annual XXII* (Cincinatti, 1949), pp. 239–64.
[46] Published in 1950 (New York: Jewish Theological Seminary of America).
[47] Discussing how far interpretation was rightly traced back through Jewish tradition to Sinai, and how far it emerged under the influence of Alexandrian scholarship, Michael Fishbane (in *Biblical Interpretation in Ancient Israel* (Oxford: Clarendon, 1985)), suggests that 'neither

What Lieberman shows is a series of remarkable parallels between the development of the activity of the Soferim in Jewish tradition and the practices of the Hellenistic grammarians. He first explores texts and book production: for scripture there were no publishing houses, the official text was 'published' by being deposited in the Temple; there were other texts, however, and Lieberman parallels the tension between official and popular texts of the Bible with the circulation of Homeric texts. The textual corrections undertaken by the Soferim began too early, he thinks, for direct Hellenistic influence, but the parallels in method are striking; both scribes and Alexandrian scholars developed systems of critical marks.

Parallels in textcritical activity thus anticipate parallels in exegetical practice. *Midrash* is 'enquiry',[48] and like the grammarians the Rabbis ask 'Why?' of the texts under discussion: *zetēmata* were the Greek equivalent. The first step of interpretation was *hermeneia*, or 'Targum', translation or interpretative paraphrase, the explanation of rare or difficult terms in simpler Hebrew or Aramaic. The introductory phrase, 'it is nothing but . . . ', followed by an equivalent, is frequent in Rabbinic comment. Parallels in the Bible were used, explanations in terms of other languages were exploited.

Lieberman then turns to the Rules. Hillel produced seven:

qal wahōmer, argument from the lesser case to the greater;

gezērah shawah, inference by analogy;

binyan āb, building a family from one passage: i.e. a form of generalisation;

shenē ketubim, the same rule as the last but based on two passages;

kelal uperat, general and specific;

kayosē' bo bemaqom ahēr, deduction from another passage;

dabār hallāmed me 'inyānō, something learned from the context.

These were elaborated to thirteen by Rabbi Ishmael. Lieberman suggests that Hillel and Ishmael merely systematised existing practices, and investigations have not been able to prove any direct Greek influence. Nevertheless, the Greeks had twelve norms of

---

answer seems particularly wrong, nor particularly right, for that matter'. Rabbinic interpretation was certainly philogical, deductive and rationalistic: see the article by Geza Vermes, 'Bible and Midrash: Early Old Testament Exegesis', in Ackroyd and Evans (eds.), *The Cambridge History of the Bible*.

48 Cf. Jacob Neusner's helpful introduction to the collections of Midrash: *A Midrash Reader* (Minneapolis: Fortress, 1990).

interpretation which were very similar, and Lieberman notes that Eusebius saw the association. He then proceeds to examine particular parallels. His conclusion is that

we have no ground to assume that the method [of logical and verbal analogy] was borrowed by the Jews from the Greeks, but the method and the definition of it are two different things.[49]

The equivalence of *gezērah shawah* and *synkrisis pros isōn* is striking, and the term may be no earlier than the first century AD. The Greeks systematised, defined and gave form to interpretations, and the Jews 'would certainly not hesitate to borrow from them methods and systems which they could convert into a mechanism for the clarification and definition of their own teachings'.[50] Lieberman adduces a series of parallels, which take him beyond the Rules. Literary problems, he concludes, were solved in a similar way in the schools of Alexandria and Palestine.

Turning to the so-called thirty-two rules of the Haggadah, he notes particularly Rules 27–31, which include *Mashal*, parable, allegory or symbol; *Paronomasia*, amphiboly or playing with homonymous roots; *Gematria*, the computation of the numeric value of letters, and others which we find very artificial. These he parallels in the techniques of dream-interpretation, citing both Rabbinic interpretations and the Hellenistic treatise of Artemidorus, *Oneirocriticon*. These games were not invented by Jews or Greeks, he suggests, but were of great antiquity, and used also for the interpretation of oracles, solving of riddles and so on. Again Lieberman concludes that what Jews learned from Greek scholars was application and systematisation of their own ancient traditions.

It was inevitable that the earliest Christians would inherit Jewish ways of deducing interpretations, at first informally, subsequently with Origen perhaps more systematically.[51] The extent of Origen's Jewish contacts may have been overestimated, but what is in any case clear is that Origen shared a common culture with the scholarly communities of the ancient world. Groups which sharply differentiated themselves from one another, in fact shared a common rationalistic heritage. The logic of deducing Halakah was parallel to the logic of deducing Christian doctrine. Although parting company

---

[49] *Hellenism in Jewish Palestine*, p. 61.   [50] Ibid., p. 64.
[51] See Nicholas de Lange, *Origen and the Jews* (Cambridge: Cambridge University Press, 1976).

in terms of their principal exegetical interests, what Christians and
Jews now shared was a parallel commitment to a unitive exegesis,
achieved by similar methods of argument seeking the coherent
biblical response to exegetical questions.[52]

IV

This chapter has largely explored the influence of the elementary
and rhetorical schools on the development of Christian scholarly
exegesis. The moral interest of the schools meant that it was natural
for Origen to find the text exemplary and draw moral lessons from
the 'letter' of a narrative, as he does for example in the *Commentary on
Matthew* when he suggests that in the description of Jesus' withdrawal to the desert (Matt. 14.13) the letter teaches us to withdraw
as far as possible from those who persecute us, a point which he
elaborates at some length with cross-references.[53] But Origen
frequently slips from the positions established by these procedures
into discerning spiritual meanings of a symbolic kind. It is
instructive to observe how this happens, and how he envisages the
connections between proper enquiry at the lexical level, and
the enquiry that discerns what was traditionally described as the
'undersense' (*hyponoia*) in philosophical exegesis. Like Plutarch[54]
and Porphyry, he apparently sees no barrier between what are
recognisably scholarly procedures and what many, including the
Antiochenes, would reject as allegory.

To explore this question we may turn again to Origen's comments
on Matthew 13.52.[55] Origen observes that Jesus seems to represent
the disciples as having been scribes before the kingdom of heaven.
His first problem is how to reconcile this with Acts' description of
them as unlearned and ignorant (Acts 4.13). After exploring one line
of enquiry, Origen tries another: it might be said that everyone

---

[52] The question concerning the extent of continuing contacts and influence between Jewish
and Christian scholarship is well discussed by William Horbury, 'Jews and Christians on
the Bible: Demarcation and Convergence [325–45]' in van Oort and Wickert (eds.),
Christliche Exegese. Adam Kamesar, 'The Evaluation of the Narrative Aggada in Greek and
Latin Patristic Literature', tends to take the view that the 'semitic' material was misunder-
stood in terms of the *historikon* by exegetes such as Origen, Eusebius, Cyril, Jerome and the
Antiochenes, who did not use the material in the same way as the Rabbis.

[53] *Comm. Matt.* x.23; *GCS*, vol. x, pp. 31–2; *ANCL*, addit. vol., pp. 429–30.

[54] E.g. *On Isis and Osiris, Moralia, LCL*, vol. v.

[55] *Comm. Matt.* x.14ff.; *GCS*, vol. x, pp. 16–17; *ANCL*, addit. vol., pp.421ff.

instructed according to the letter of the law is called a scribe, and in this sense they were ignorant, being unskilled in figurative interpretation, and not understanding what is involved in anagogical exposition of the scriptures. So one is a 'scribe made a disciple to the kingdom of heaven' in the simpler sense, when one comes from Judaism and receives the teaching of Jesus Christ as defined by the Church, but one is that scribe in a deeper sense, when, having received elementary knowledge through the letter of the scriptures, one ascends to things spiritual.[56] This is an example of the kind of expectation Origen expresses over and over again in many different contexts. But in this case it is 'deduced' from a 'problem' in the text, the unexpected link between being a 'scribe' and being a 'disciple of the kingdom'. In the course of expounding his view, Origen draws on the typical exegetical practice of calling in other texts, quoting one of the woes on the scribes, and referring to Galatians for a commendation of allegorical interpretation. Methodologically there is no difference in his procedures between this and what we have observed before.

And we can observe how the move is made by returning to the pearl of great price:[57] for, having told us all about pearls, Origen speaks of the one who seeks pearls among all kinds of words professing to announce the truth, and of the mussels conceiving the dew of heaven becoming pregnant with the word of truth from heaven, and producing the goodly pearls sought by the merchant. The pearl of great price is of course Christ, and inevitably 'Cast not your pearls before swine' is drawn into the exposition. Once the expectation is that some kind of analogy can be drawn with spiritual or moral words of truth, the argument follows. And, in this case, is Origen's discernment of the metaphor that far wrong? The trouble is that he spells it out in so much detail it becomes as boring as the explained joke. Perhaps that is the fate of all scholarship!

What I hope I have shown is that Origen's exegesis, whether text-critical, explanatory, investigative or symbolic, is grounded in the same traditions of philological scholarship as our own, somewhat differently applied. The underlying assumption was that the scriptures replaced the classics as the literature on which *paideia* was based. As noted in the last chapter, that position was modified in the

---

[56] *Comm. Matt.* x.15; *GCS*, vol. x, pp. 9–10; *ANCL*, addit. vol., p. 423.
[57] *Comm. Matt.* x.8–9; *GCS*, vol. x, pp. 9–10; *ANCL*, addit. vol., p. 418.

post-Constantinian period, when cultured bishops found they could not relinquish the classics for proper linguistic training. But, even so, the handling of the biblical texts was increasingly assimilated to classical conventions, as we shall see in the next chapter.

CHAPTER 5

Bible and culture

The fact that education was premised on the imitation of classics meant that intertextuality was an important feature of ancient literary culture. Allusions and quotations laced the correspondence of the literary élite, as well as public discourse. By the fourth century, Christian leaders such as the Cappadocians, or evenTheodoret of Cyrus, evidence the same literary culture. But they also quote the Bible. The purpose of this chapter is to explore use of the Bible in a Christianised literary form, namely panegyric, at the point of confluence between cultures that we reached at the end of chapter 3.[1]

In English and French, 'panegyric' is associated with eulogy and may therefore be deemed to cover most of what the ancients would have called epideictic oratory. Strictly speaking, of course, it should refer simply to festival orations, but in ecclesiastical literature something of a practical convergence of these forms took place with the development of feast days for saints and martyrs. It is generally agreed that the Cappadocians and John Chrysostom exemplify the adaptation of funerary orations, eulogies and festal declamations to Christian purposes.

What I propose to examine, then, is the use of the Bible in such material.

I

The features to be observed may be exemplified by an examination of Gregory Nazianzen's first (Easter) Oration:[2]

---

[1] This chapter began life as a paper presented to the Eleventh International Conference on Patristic Studies in Oxford, 1991, and was published originally in *SP* 25 (1993), pp. 194–208. Apart from this introductory paragraph and some footnotes, it is unchanged.

[2] *Grégoire de Nazianze, Discours 1–3*, ed. J. Bernardi (*SC*, vol. 247; 1978). ET *NPNF*, 2nd series, vol. VII, pp. 203–4.

The first paragraph is an exhortation to keep the feast with splendour, and Gregory suggests that this involves embracing one another and saying 'Brethren' even to those who hate us, so working in an allusion to Isaiah 66.5. A few sentences later, alluding to his reluctance to take up the responsibilities of his ordination, he refers to the tardiness of Moses and Jeremiah, and then to the ready response of Aaron and Isaiah, implicitly claiming for himself the one then the other: the texts he has in mind have been identified as Exodus 4.10, Jeremiah 1.6, Exodus 4.27 and Isaiah 1.6.

The second paragraph is a dense sentence referring to his own weakness and the possibility of Easter renewal. Biblical phrases are worked into it: putting on the new man (Eph. 4.23–4), the new creation (2 Cor. 5.17), those born of God (John 1.13), and one eager to die with Christ and be raised with him (Rom. 6.8).

The third paragraph exploits an implicit Passover typology, the Lamb being slain and the doorposts anointed, Egypt bewailing her first-born, the Destroyer passing by and 'we' escaping from Egypt and Pharaoh to keep the feast, celebrating not with the old leaven of malice and wickedness, but with the unleavened bread of sincerity and truth (1 Cor. 5.8).

So it goes on: there are no full quotations, still less acknowledged quotations, but sections of the speech, though highly wrought rhetorically, depend for their graphic effect on their relationship with scripture texts. The fifth paragraph provides a particularly striking example: to spot 2 Corinthians 8.9, Philippians 2.7 and Romans 8.21 in the following is to appreciate the point.

Let us become like Christ, since Christ became like us. Let us become gods for him, since he became man for us. He took the worse lot that he might give the better; he became poor that we through his poverty might become rich; he took the form of a slave that we might receive freedom; he came down that we might be lifted up; he was tempted that we might conquer; he was dishonoured that he might bring honour; he died that he might save.

This phenomenon becomes the more extraordinary as Gregory makes double allusion to scripture and the situation he and his congregation face. In the sixth paragraph, the good shepherd who lays down his life for the sheep (John 10.15) offers the people a shepherd. To the lifeless temple (presumably the new church his father had built) he adds a living temple (namely Gregory, his son), a high priest, an heir and the words they desire – the sort which the

Spirit writes and engraves on stone tablets or fleshy hearts, deeply, not with ink but grace. My summary is enough to reveal the allusion to 2 Corinthians 3.2–3, which itself alludes to Ezekiel 36.26, and to hint at possible allusions earlier to Paul's designation of Christians as temples of the Holy Spirit, perhaps to the living stones built into the temple of 1 Peter, not to mention the language of heirship in Christ found fairly widely in the New Testament.

Then, in the final paragraph, Gregory's father is simply designated Abraham, patriarch and head, perfection of the priesthood, who today brings to the Lord his willing sacrifice, his only son, him of the promise (I hardly need draw your attention to the application of Genesis 22), and the congregation are urged to offer obedience to God and their shepherds, enjoying the green pastures and quiet waters of Psalm 23. John 10 then provides the language of further exhortation not to listen to the voice of the stranger who climbs up like a robber, but to know the shepherd and respond when he calls openly through the door. It appears that throughout Gregory has dared to transfer to his father, the bishop, the good shepherd material which in John 10 is clearly Christological.

What we observe in this Oration is a highly developed and subtle intertextuality. What we seek is some account of how the Bible came to be exploited in this way – indeed how such a bold use of the Bible operated methodologically. The usual categories of literal, typological and allegorical are clearly inadequate to describe most of what we have observed.

II

We should surely begin by investigating what the literary theorists of the ancient world said about quotation and allusion. For Gregory was rhetorically educated, and his debt to standard rhetorical *topoi* has long been recognised.[3] So what do the textbooks tell us about the purpose of literary allusion, and how did they think it should function?

Research soon reveals how important is this preliminary investigation. Our prior assumption could well be that such material was merely ornamental, a way of enhancing the quality of the diction, of showing off the erudition of the composer, or engaging the audience

---

[3] Marcel Guignet, *Saint Grégoire de Nazianze et la rhétorique* (Paris: Alphonse Picard & fils, 1911).

in the challenge to spot the quote. It would appear, however, that the purpose of quotation in ancient texts was much more than surface embellishment.

As we have seen,[4] ancient rhetorical theory made a clear distinction between style and content. The subject-matter was one aspect of a composition which needed care; the 'dress' another. It would have been quite foreign to their conceptions to suggest that the 'medium is the message'. On the other hand, the style was an important vehicle, since the object of every discourse was persuasion, and the choice of style could enhance or damage the persuasive powers of the composition. So style was an important element in rhetorical textbook discussions.

What is interesting is that allusion or quotation is not a subject for discussion in works specifically on style, such as Longinus, *On the Sublime*, or Demetrius, *On Style*; nor is it a feature of discussion of style in more comprehensive rhetorical textbooks such as Aristotle, *The Art of Rhetoric*, or indeed, his *Poetics*.[5] In all these works, there is found much quotation from literary works to illustrate stylistic points, but no discussion of using allusion stylistically as a way of ornamentation.

In fact, intertextuality is taken for granted rather than analysed. Among general rhetorical textbooks Quintilian[6] alone mentions actual reference, but clearly represents the universal view when he treats memorising classical texts as an all-important element in education precisely to ensure that the rhetorically trained mind is well stocked and has an accumulation of usable material:

they will form an intimate acquaintance with the best writings, will carry their models with them and unconsciously reproduce the style of the speech which has been impressed upon the memory. They will have a plentiful and choice vocabulary and a command of artistic structure and a supply of figures which will not have to be hunted for, but will offer them-

[4] See above, ch. 4, p. 81.
[5] Handy access to much helpful material is provided by D. A. Russell and M. Winterbottom, *Ancient Literary Criticism. The Principal Texts in New Translations*. This contains Aristotle's *Poetics*, Demetrius, *On Style*; Longinus, *On Sublimity*, and extracts from Aristotle, Dionysius of Halicarnassus and Quintilian. Texts are available in the *LCL*, though the following editions and translations are preferable: Longinus, *On the Sublime*, ed. D. A. Russell (Oxford: Oxford University Press, 1964); Aristotle, *Poetics*, ed. D. W. Lucas (Oxford: Oxford University Press, 1968), translation and commentary, Stephen Halliwell (London: Duckworth, 1987).
[6] Quintilian, *Institutio oratoria*.

selves spontaneously from the treasure-house, if I may so call it, in which they are stored. In addition they will be in the agreeable position of being able to quote the happy sayings of the various authors, a power they will find most useful in the courts. For phrases which have not been coined merely to suit the circumstances of the lawsuit of the moment carry greater weight and often win greater praise than if they were our own.[7]

It sounds as if ornamentation might be the principal function, for quotations are set alongside vocabulary and 'figures'. Yet such a conclusion would be premature, for quotations carry 'weight'.

Earlier, discussing what reading a boy should do in school in preparation for rhetorical training, he comments in passing:

we may derive confidence from the practice of the greatest orators of drawing upon the early poets to support their arguments or adorn their eloquence . . . inserted not merely to show the speaker's learning, but to please his hearers as well, since the charms of poetry provide a pleasant relief from the severity of forensic eloquence. Such quotations have the additional advantage of helping the speaker's case, for the orator makes use of the sentiments expressed by the poet as evidence in support of his own statements.[8]

It is noticeable again that, though display and ornament feature, authority is also accorded to quotation, additional weight and support for the argument.

However, on the whole, what was explicitly encouraged was not so much direct quotation or allusion, but a kind of emulation: it would seem that the principal use of literature was in providing models to be imitated.

Longinus sees 'imitation and emulation of the great writers and poets of the past' as one route to sublimity of style. He suggests that 'many are carried away by the inspiration of another', and draws a parallel with the Pythian priestess becoming impregnated with divine power: 'so, too, from the genius of ancient writers it's as though streams from holy mouths flow into the souls of their emulators'. Several examples find their climax in 'Plato, who has irrigated his style with ten thousand channels from that Homeric spring'.[9] Longinus suggests that such borrowing is not plagiarism, but rather the reproductive impress of images and works of art taken from fine forms. Those who want to cultivate a good style

---

[7] *Inst. orat.* II.vii.3–4; ET in *LCL*.   [8] *Inst.Orat.* I.viii.10–12; ET in *LCL*.
[9] *On the Sublime* XIII.2–3; my ET, but ET available in *LCL*.

should ask themselves how would Homer, or Plato, or Demosthenes, or Thucydides, supposing they had said the same thing, have made this sublime.[10] What Longinus describes is not so much quotation, or even direct allusion, as fresh inspiration arising from imitation. Now *mimēsis* was an important feature both of literary theory and of rhetorical instruction. It is much discussed in the textbooks, and it was certainly not understood as slavish copying.[11]

This is confirmed by the works attributed to Menander Rhetor[12] which are more nearly contemporary to Gregory of Nazianzus. These are particularly apposite since they are concerned with epideictic oratory and give specific rules for composing eulogies of gods, cities, festivals, emperors and suchlike, and for wedding-speeches, funeral or commemorative orations, official welcomes and so on. The Orations which concern us fall into this category.

Praise involves the magnification of the subject, an account of the descent and exploits of the one to be extolled, and delineation of character, attributes, status, honours and virtues, in particular using comparison to bring out the superiority of the subject celebrated. These features become referred to technically as *auxēsis* or *amplificatio* and *synkrisis* or *comparatio*. Aristotle regarded these as particularly characteristic of epideictic rhetoric, indeed amplification he treated as the method of 'proof' in this form of oratory.[13] Denunciations work the same way but are designed to produce the opposite effect. The work of Menander Rhetor spells out various forms of epideictic speech, with the characteristic *topoi* of each.

Though, like the other theorists, Menander repeatedly cites examples, sometimes producing substantial model paragraphs, sometimes offering a piece from the classics, he does not at any point explicitly discuss the use of quotation and allusion, except when particularly recommending the use of old stories and literary allusions in what he calls 'talks' (*lalia*), more informal addresses, for 'sweetness' is important here and the change of tone introduced

---

[10] *On the Sublime* xiv.i; ET in *LCL*.

[11] Quintilian, *Inst. orat.* x.ii provides an interesting discussion; quoted *Ancient Literary Criticism*, p. 400. See also a fragmentary work of Dionysius of Halicarnassus entitled *Peri mimēseōs*, in *Dionysii Halicarnassei opuscula* vol. ii, ed. H. Usener and L. Radermacher (Leipzig: Teubner, 1933), pp. 197–217. For discussion, see D. A Russell, *Criticism in Antiquity*.

[12] *Menander Rhetor*, ed. D. A. Russell and N. G. Wilson (Oxford: Oxford University Press, 1981).

[13] Aristotle, *Art of Rhetoric* i.ix.38–40 and iii.xvii.3; text and ET in *LCL*.

contributes to this pleasantness.[14] Clearly creative reminiscences of the great poets are as much in mind as specific quotation, and this usage could be regarded as principally stylistic. However, literature is also expected to provide examples to substantiate the comparisons (*synkriseis*) which play an important role in 'amplifying' the subject of the epideictic discourse, and also to provide material for consolation, enjoining what we might call a philosophical attitude to bereavement. In outlining the *paramythētikos*, Menander suggests a quotation from Euripides, but adds:

You should not, however, quote the whole passage, since it is generally familiar and well known, but adapt it.[15]

As noted before, literature provides the subject-matter and lends authority, but is not to be quoted at length verbatim.

The fact that rhetorical use of quotation and allusion was not a matter of stylistic ornamentation, but a means of suggesting and reinforcing the subject-matter or content, enabled the development by Christian rhetoricians of an intertextuality which functioned in similar ways to the literary tradition of their non-Christian peers. Since the time of Origen, the literary crudity and the barbarian style of the Bible had been a matter of embarrassment – true, it could be turned to good account, for its moral superiority to the myths of pagan literature could be treated as the more remarkable, coming as it did in such crude dress, but the stylistic inferiority of the Bible remained undeniable. The Bible's superiority was a matter of content, not presentation. So appeal to its text could never be for the sake of ornamentation, but certainly could be to lend authority to the intent of the discourse.

This, coupled with the importance of emulation or *mimēsis*, accounts for much that we observed in Gregory's Oration I. The exploitation of biblical phrases in highly wrought rhetorical sentences improved the Bible stylistically while implicitly claiming its authority. The transfer of biblical phraseology to describe current situations without regard to original context, even treating Gregory's father as the good shepherd, was an appropriate *mimēsis*.

---

[14] *Treatise* II.iv.389.9ff; Russell and Wilson, pp. 114–16.
[15] *Treatise* II.ix.413.25ff.; Russell and Wilson, p. 162.

III

This observation that Gregory's usage follows that of current
literary convention is borne out by further study of a varied sample
of Orations. Like all great orators, Gregory is flexible rather than
legalistic in his use of rhetorical form and each piece is different in
detail, but allusions and quotations tend to be clustered in the
particular areas of the discourses recommended by Menander. They
provide content for certain of the standard *topoi* of epideictic
oratory.

A sample of funeral speeches may demonstrate this. The clusters
of biblical quotation or allusion function in three principal ways:
(1) in the delineation of character, in which the Bible provides
those characteristics and virtues worth praising; (2) in implicit
exhortation through proverbial maxims or general truths expressed
in quotable sentences and scattered about giving authority to
observations moral or otherwise, most particularly in the *consolatio*,
usually a regular feature of a funeral oration, where biblical
material is used to provide comfort and moral exhortation for the
mourner; (3) in *synkrisis*, that is in providing examples with which
specific comparison may be adduced in order to extol the hero of the
speech. In other words, the actual use of biblical material in these
Orations bears out the point that it is not mere ornament, but gives
weight, authority and content to the theme of the Oration, as *auxēsis*
or amplification constituting the demonstration or 'proof'. It is
also apparent that creative allusion features far more than direct
quotation. Each of these three areas will be illustrated.

The character-sketch

In his Oration[16] on his brother Caesarius, Gregory describes their
father as grafted out of the wild olive-tree into the good one.[17]
Clearly the image is drawn from Romans 11, and is intended to
indicate that their father was a convert. That this is more than mere
ornament becomes clear as the passage develops the standard *topos*
of honouring the deceased's parents: through the grafting, the

---

[16] *Grégoire de Nazianze. Discours funèbres*, ed. F. Boulenger, (Paris: Alphonse Picard & fils, 1908);
   NPNF, 2nd series, vol. VII, pp. 231ff.
[17] *Orat.* VII.3; Boulenger, p. 6; *NPNF*, vol. VII, p. 230.

convert so partook of the olive's richness that he was entrusted with the cultivation and grafting of other souls, and, through his episcopal charge, he became a second Aaron or Moses, deemed worthy to draw near to God and to mediate the divine voice to others standing afar off (Exod. 24.1–3). Turning to the mother, Gregory describes her as consecrated to God by descent from her forebears, and words reminiscent of Romans 11.16 are used: a holy lump from holy first-fruits.[18] Gregory may be far from the sense of Romans 11, but his choice of phrase gives biblical authority to the commonplace that lineage is important, and character is the fruit of a good stock.

But inherited nobility had to be confirmed by character: so the description of the parents proceeds, reinforced with specific New Testament allusion. Caesarius' parents are described as snatching many a treasure from moths and robbers and from the prince of this world, to transfer it from their visit here to their true dwelling-place, laying up in store for their children the heavenly splendour as their greatest inheritance. So instead of celebrating rich material heirlooms, Gregory focusses on another kind of legacy, exploiting Matthew 6.19; John 10.1; 14.30; together with 1 Timothy 6.19. But this legacy is the more important because their son has gone before them to heaven where it awaits him.

In his Oration[19] on his sister, Gorgonia, we find particularly striking use of biblical allusions to characterise the subject of the Oration:[20] her native land was Jerusalem above, whose citizen is Christ, and whose fellow citizens are the assembly and Church of the first-born whose names are written in heaven, and who feast around its great Founder in contemplation of his glory. Her nobility consisted in the preservation of the Image, and the perfect likeness to the Archetype. The marriage of encomiastic *topoi* and biblically based content is striking. Later[21] Gregory takes Solomon's character-sketch of the ideal wife from Proverbs 31, and makes this the basis of commendation of his sister. But here again a typical rhetorical figure effects the point: for to praise her in these terms would be to praise a statue for its shadow. Her quality of modesty and discretion surpassed even the biblical sketch.

[18] *Orat.* VII.4; Boulenger, pp. 6–8; *NPNF*, vol. VII, pp. 230–1.
[19] *Orat.* VIII; Migne, *PG* 35.789–817; *NPNF*, vol. VII, pp. 238–45.
[20] *Orat.* VIII.6; Migne, *PG* 35.796; *NPNF*, vol. VII, pp. 239–40.
[21] *Orat.* VIII.9; Migne, *PG* 35.797C–800B; *NPNF*, vol. VII, p. 240.

Gregory goes on[22] to deny her interest in any of the signs of earthly grandeur or beauty that would normally figure large in a woman's encomium. The virtues celebrated indicate how she presented herself to God as a living temple;[23] how she practised the hospitality attributed to Job, her door being open to all comers, no stranger lodging in the street, she being eyes to the blind, feet to the lame, mother to the orphan (Job 31.32; 29.15). She lavished gifts on the poor (Ps. 112.9), and, according to the infallible truth of the Gospel, she laid up much store in the winepresses above, oftentimes entertaining Christ in those she served.[24] Here is a clear example of a creative reminting or associative remoulding of biblical language, as storing up treasure in heaven is linked with the wine of the Gospel, while Abraham entertaining angels, usually understood as the pre-existent Christ, is by implication linked with the parable of the sheep and the goats. It is this quality of creative compounding, a *mimēsis* which is not straight copying, which makes it difficult to distinguish biblical allusion and current ethical model; for the latter had long been indebted to the kind of process we are here observing.

Another kind of *mimēsis* is found in Gregory's account of her life. Gorgonia, suffering a bout of illness, is said to imitate biblical characters,[25] namely the woman with the issue of blood and the woman who was a sinner. With 'pious effrontery', she laid her head on the altar and wept, refusing to leave go until her health was restored. Yet she longed for her dissolution, Gregory later affirms:[26] for she had great boldness towards the one who called her, and preferred to be with Christ, beyond all things on earth (Phil. 1.23). But one more blessing she required, the perfection of her husband. She did not even fail in this petition, from the one who fulfils the desire of those that fear him and accomplishes their request (Ps. 145.19).[27]

So we reach the deathbed scene,[28] and on her lips are the words of a Psalm: I will lie down in peace and take my rest (4.8). So she

22 *Orat.* VIII.10; Migne, *PG* 35.800B–1A; *NPNF*, vol. VII, p. 241.
23 *Orat.* VIII.11; Migne, *PG* 35.801; *NPNF*, vol. VII, p. 241.
24 *Orat.* VIII.12; Migne, *PG* 35.801C–4B; *NPNF*, vol. VII, p. 241.
25 *Orat.* VIII.18; Migne, *PG* 35.809B–12A; *NPNF*, vol. VII, p. 243.
26 *Orat.* VIII.19; Migne, *PG* 35.812; *NPNF*, vol. VII, p. 243.
27 *Orat.* VIII.20; Migne, *PG* 35.812C–13A; *NPNF*, vol. VII, p. 244.
28 *Orat.* VIII.22; Migne, *PG* 35.813C–16B; *NPNF*, vol. VII, p. 244.

receives that sleep which is due to the beloved one (Ps. 127.2), and enters into a better lot, the song of those that keep holy-day (Ps. 42.4).[29] Such phrases are embedded in Gregory's elaborate celebratory sentence as he brings this eulogy to an end without the customary *consolatio*.

So the delineation of character was achieved by creative exploitation of allusion, sometimes deliberate reference or quotation, transferring biblical material in various mimetic ways to the subject of the discourse.

General moral reflection and the consolatio

Caesarius got into difficulties at court under Julian the Apostate, but, says Gregory, the victory is with Christ who has overcome the world (John 16.33).[30] A little later,[31] we find the platitude, 'Glorious is the fruit of good labours' (Wisd. 3.15). These insertions are typical of the exploitation of maxims and commonplaces, the Christian Bible now providing the source of such useful reflections on the particularities of the discourse.

In the Oration on Gorgonia we find an interesting example of quotation used to demonstrate a general truth from a specific case: turning to the *topos* of 'action', Gregory tells a graphic narrative of a carriage accident, describing Gorgonia's suffering and recovery. Here[32] Gregory comments that to the beautiful promise to the righteous (found in Ps. 37.24), 'Though he fall, he shall not be utterly broken', has been added a further one (from Ps. 146.8), 'Though he be utterly broken, he shall be speedily raised up and glorified.' Such generalising usage soon reappears in a form affected by Christian use of texts in a prophetic way. For, in his subsequent apostrophe,[33] Gregory calls on the prophecy 'He has smitten, and he will bind us up, and revive us, and after three days he will raise us up' as 'foretelling of course a greater and more sublime event, yet no less applicable to Gorgonia's sufferings!' Gregory holds in tension a specific prophetic fulfilment, and a more general applicability of the kind that justified much literary quotation.

---

[29] *Orat.* VIII.23; Migne, *PG* 35.816C; *NPNF*, vol. VII, pp. 244–5.
[30] *Orat.* VII.13; Boulenger, p.26; *NPNF*, vol. VII, pp. 233–4.
[31] *Orat.* VII.14; Boulenger, pp. 28–30; *NPNF*, vol. VII, p. 234.
[32] *Orat.* VIII.15; Migne, *PG* 35.805C–8B; *NPNF*, vol. VII, pp. 242–3.
[33] *Orat.* VIII.16; Migne, *PG* 35.808C–9A; *NPNF*, vol. VII, p. 243.

The Oration on Caesarius is one that provides a *consolatio* for the mourners,[34] and here there appears a concentration of Biblical quotation particularly substantiating the transitoriness of life: the doctrine of creation out of nothing is coupled with characterisations of human being from the Biblical Wisdom literature and the Psalms.

We are an insubstantial dream, an intangible night-vision, the flight of a passing bird, a ship leaving no track upon the sea, a speck of dust, a vapour, an early dew, a flower that quickly blooms and quickly fades. As for man, his days are as grass, as a flower of the field.[35]

Gregory has compiled this from Job 20.8, Wisdom 5.10ff., and phrases from the Psalms, notably Psalm 103.15. This is followed by the inspired David philosophising on our frailty, 'Let me know the measure of my days', defining the days of a man as a mere span long (Ps. 39.4, 5); and Jeremiah complaining about his birth (15.10); and the Preacher, who has seen all things and reviewed all of human life and says, 'Vanity of vanities, all is vanity and vexation of spirit', yet urges, as the conclusion of the whole matter, 'Fear God' (Eccles. 1.14; 12.8, 13).

Such reflections put into perspective the fact that Caesarius will never again do what he has done or might have done if he had lived. But after developing what might have been, Gregory suggests that this is not adequate for our consolation,[36] and adds a more potent remedy: this is to be found in the doctrine of resurrection. Once more biblical allusion abounds, giving authority to the theme. The departed soul, after a waiting period, will receive its kindred flesh and in some way known to God, who knit them together and dissolved them, enter with it upon the inheritance of glory there. Life will swallow up what is mortal and immutable. Already there have been linguistic echoes, and now Ezekiel and Paul are called in as evidence: Ezekiel speaking of the knitting together of bones and sinews (37.3ff.), Paul of the earthly tabernacle and the house not made with hands (2 Cor. 5.1, 6), the one to be dissolved, the other laid up in heaven, alleging absence from the body to be present with the Lord (Phil. 1.23). Gregory claims to await the voice of the Archangel, the last trumpet (1 Thess. 4.16; 1 Cor. 15.52), the

---

[34] *Orat.* VII.18ff.; Boulenger, pp. 36ff.; *NPNF*, vol. VII, pp. 235ff.
[35] *Orat.* VII.19; Boulenger, pp. 40–2; *NPNF*, vol. VII, pp. 235–6.
[36] *Orat.* VII.21; Boulenger, p. 46; *NPNF*, vol. VII, pp. 236–7.

transformation of the heavens, the transfiguration of the earth, the liberation of the elements, the renovation of the universe (2 Peter 3.10). Then he will see Caesarius.

In the final sections, Gregory turns to exhortation, and again scriptural allusion figures large, lending content and authority to his discourse. People should not suppose life such a great thing, but look for God's salvation. While on earth, one should mortify one's members and be buried with Christ, so as to rise and be joint heir with him. This was the purpose of God who for us was made man. The generosity of God is to be received with gratitude, tears are to cease, hope in God's wisdom and providence to fill us with eagerness. Such a précis gives little sense of the weaving together of textual reminiscences into Gregory's own prose. Suffice it to say that the following texts are alluded to: Psalms 4.3, 120.4, 44.19 (LXX), 69.2, 44.20, 72.6, 7, 119.81;[37] Colossians 3.5, Matthew 7.13, Psalm 8.5, 2 Corinthians 8.9, Romans 8.11, Luke 15.9, 1 Corinthians 15.49, Colossians 3.10, Galatians 3.28, 1 Corinthians 15.28, Colossians 3.11, Romans 11.36;[38] 1 Corinthians 2.9, 13.7, 1 Thessalonians 5.18, 1 Peter 4.19, Amos 5.8 (LXX), Psalms 33.6, 32.6, 119.60 (LXX).[39] Some combinations are clearly traditional, like the association of Galatians 3.28 and Colossians 3.10–11, describing the restoration of unity to humankind, a grouping or confusion certainly found, for example, in Epiphanius.[40]

The point is clear: the rhetorical function of biblical allusion is the 'demonstration' of some parts of the theme – it is far from mere ornamentation. But this is not a proof-texting process. It is much closer to the purpose and style of intertextuality in the rhetorical literature of the Graeco-Roman world. Often it is a new statement woven out of words, phrases or ideas culled from both Old and New Testaments.

Synkrisis

In Gregory's Oration on Gorgonia, Gregory the father and Nonna his wife are likened to Abraham and Sarah.[41] He was justified by

---

[37] *Orat.* VII.22; Boulenger, pp. 48–50; *NPNF*, vol. VII, p. 237.
[38] *Orat.* VII.23; Boulenger, pp. 50–2; *NPNF*, vol. VII, p. 237.
[39] *Orat.* VII.24; Boulenger, p. 54; *NPNF*, vol. VII, pp. 237–8.
[40] See my article, 'Did Epiphanius Know What he Meant by Heresy?' *SP* 18 (1982), pp. 199–205.
[41] *Orat.* VIII.4; Migne, *PG* 35.793; *NPNF*, vol. VII, p. 239.

faith, while she dwelt with him who is faithful; he beyond all hope became father of many nations, while she travailed spiritually in their birth; he escaped from the bondage of his father's gods, she is the daughter as well as the mother of the free; he went out from his kindred and home for the sake of the land of promise, she was the occasion of his exile. In fact on this score Gregory claims an honour higher for Nonna than for Sarah, and a typically contrived series of parallels makes the *synkrisis*, drawing on Romans 4, Galatians 4.22ff., Hebrews 11 and the Genesis narratives lying behind these passages.

To illustrate *synkrisis* effectively, however, we need to turn to other speeches where the *synkrisis* is more sharply evident and developed in an elaborate way to bring out the characteristics of the Christian hero being celebrated.

In Oration xviii[42] on the death of his father, Gregory associates his father's call to succeed his bishop, miraculously predicted at the moment of his baptism, with the remarkable calls of Moses, Isaiah, Jeremiah and Paul. His father's special characteristic of simplicity and freedom from guile is enhanced by reference to the special characteristics of biblical heroes: Job's patience, the meekness of Moses and David, Samuel's prophecy, the zeal of Phineas, the eagerness for preaching found in Peter and Paul, and so on. The elder Gregory was most like Stephen in his lack of malice.

Even more striking is the range of biblical heroes called upon in Oration xxi[43] to honour Athanasius, their successor: Enoch, Noah, Abraham, Isaac, Jacob, the twelve patriarchs, Moses, Aaron, Joshua, the judges, Samuel, David, Solomon, Elijah, Elisha, the prophets before and after the captivity, John the Baptist and the disciples.[44] Later Athanasius appears as Job facing the test of George the Cappadocian.[45]

Basil, too, did the works of Moses and Elijah. Indeed, the most extended *synkrisis* is found in the eulogy of Basil,[46] where specific features of his career or character are treated as greater than the deeds of the ancients from Adam to Noah, then Abraham, Isaac, Jacob, Joseph, Job, Moses and Aaron, and most of the other figures

---

[42] *Orat.* xviii *passim*; Migne, *PG* 35.985–1044; *NPNF*, vol. vii, pp. 254–69.

[43] *Orat.* xxi *passim*; text in *Grégoire de Nazianze. Discours 20–23*, ed. J. Mossay and G. Lafontaine (*SC*, vol. 270, 1980); *NPNF*, vol. vii, pp. 269–80.

[44] *Orat.* xxi.3; *SC*, vol. 270, p. 116; *NPNF*, vol. vii, p. 270.

[45] *Orat.* xxi.17; *SC*, vol. 270, pp. 144–6; *NPNF*, vol. vii, p. 274.

[46] *Orat.* xliii.70–6; Boulenger, pp. 208–20; NPNF, vol. vii, pp. 419–21.

simply listed in Athanasius' case. So, for example, Joseph was a provider of corn, but in Egypt only and not frequently and with bodily food. Basil did so for all and at all times and with spiritual food, and therefore, in my opinion, claims Gregory, his was the more honourable function.[47] The technique of amplification whereby the hero of the discourse is presented as greater than the literary heroes called in for comparison is clearly in operation, and perhaps theologically justified by the superiority of new covenant to old. Basil was also comparable with John the Baptist and the apostles, and indeed imitated Christ who girded with a towel did not disdain to wash the disciples' feet.[48] Here we have *synkrisis* without *amplificatio*, presumably because imitation of Christ is encouraged but superiority unthinkable.

But *synkrisis* with Christ could take surprising forms: figuratively speaking, Athanasius rode on a colt and was welcomed with branches of trees and garments on his return to Alexandria.[49] He then cleansed the temple of those who made merchandise of God's word.[50] Earlier an even more daring comparison had been hinted: when we were cast down, says Gregory, a horn of salvation was raised up for us and a chief cornerstone . . . [51] This is not far from the apparently direct transfer of Christological language to Gregory's father and bishop with which we began.

III

That takes us back to festal orations, or panegyric proper. Clearly space does not permit such detailed exemplification of the important features of these, but a brief survey should be undertaken.

Festivals are an invention and gift of the gods, granted us for a relaxation from the continual labour of life . . . A god is always the leader and name-giver of any festival . . . So let the beginning of the speech be praise of this god, whoever he is . . . In general the passage will be made up of what each god invented or provided for humankind.[52]

---

[47] *Orat.* XLIII.72; Boulenger, p. 212; NPNF, vol. VII, pp. 419–20.
[48] *Orat.* XLIII.64; Boulenger, p. 192; NPNF, vol. VII, pp. 416–17.
[49] *Orat.* XXI.29; *SC*, vol. 270, p. 172; *NPNF*, vol. VII, p. 278.
[50] *Orat.* XXI.31; *SC*, vol. 270, p. 174; *NPNF*, vol. VII, p. 278.
[51] *Orat.* XXI.7; *SC*, vol. 270, p. 124; *NPNF*, vol. VII, p. 271.
[52] Excerpted from Pseudo-Dionysius, *On Epideictic Speeches*, translated as Appendix to Menander in Russell and Wilson. Text: *Dionysii Halicarnassei opuscula*, vol. II, pp. 255ff.

Eulogy of gods developed out of hymns and the textbooks indicate
how different hymns and celebrations are to be composed, providing
rather different *topoi* from those employed for the eulogy of human
heroes.[53] Focus on the being of the god, the benefits provided by
the god, and the aetiological cult-myth, or particular reason for the
festival, were obvious *topoi*, and as the form was adapted by Christian
rhetoricians, the equivalent contexts provided the locus for the use
of biblical allusion and quotation. The point and manner of their
use is much the same as in the funerary orations already reviewed.

Thus, Gregory's second Easter Oration[54] is both larger in scope
and more typical than the first. The opening summons to festivity is
couched in scriptural language, with an explicit quotation from
Habakkuk, and allusions compounded from all over the Bible
conjuring up the vision of one riding on the clouds with the heavenly
host announcing salvation: Christ is risen from the dead.

This is elaborated with a surprising collocation of texts, including
the angels' song in Luke's nativity account, and then the Lord's
Passover is introduced. The Being of God is celebrated at length,
followed by the benefits – the overarching story of creation, incarnation and salvation. Details of the Passover sacrifice are explained,
the congregation exhorted to make appropriate response, and
heretics and others chided for not appreciating the truth of Trinity
and incarnation. Thus the particular *topoi* noted are covered, and
throughout there is the now recognisable blend of scriptural
phraseology with Gregory's own rhetorical prose, the Bible lending
authority to content and exhortations, and the whole producing
extraordinary webs of intertextual connections.

Much the same observations would result from a review of
Orations xxxviii–xli,[55] covering the Feast of the Theophany or
Nativity, the Festivals of Holy Lights and of Holy Baptism, and
Pentecost. Barely a page of the *Sources Chrétiennes* edition passes
without a note of some biblical allusion, and often a considerable
number create a novel and intriguing pastiche. Gregory's Festal
Orations simply illustrate further the creative and mimetic use of
the Bible already observed.

53 Menander, *Treatise* i; Russell and Wilson edition.
54 *Orat.* xlv; Migne, *PG* 36.624–64; *NPNF*, vol. vii, pp. 422–34.
55 *Grégoire de Nazianze, Discours 38–41*, ed. C. Moreschini (*SC*, vol. 358, 1990); NPNF, vol. vii,
   pp. 345–85.

Hints that Gregory was somewhat self-consciously adopting classical forms appear in a couple of features in the sample we have used. The *epithalamium* on Caesarius opens with a disavowal of any intention of using the occasion for display, and summons biblical authority for offering a tribute of lamentation by quoting Proverbs 10.7 (LXX):

The memory of the righteous is with *encomia*;

and Sirach 38.16:

My son, shed tears for the one who has died; raise a lament for your grievous loss,

which are the opening words of an extensive passage on mourning and burial. Gregory seems to need his eulogy authorised by scripture. Then in the Oration on Holy Lights he has a lengthy passage contrasting the manner of Christian festivity with pagan feasts: the celebration is spiritual not material. It seems he is offering some kind of justification for his panegyric.

IV

Quickly, however, the forms were adopted and adapted. My final sample comes not from Nazianzen but from Gregory Nyssen and John Chrysostom, and they are panegyrical orations on a biblical character designed for the saint's day. Here the *topoi* of the two forms already examined might be expected to come together, though what we tend to find are creatively new forms emerging: Chrysostom's seven *Panegyrics on Paul*, as Piédagnel has noted,[56] develop away from the traditional *topoi* to the enlargement of a particular theme. How then is the Bible used in this kind of material?

Gregory Nyssen's two encomia on Stephen the Protomartyr[57] are remarkably different in approach and content. The first is largely a rhetorical development of the material in Acts, sometimes in summary, sometimes developed with a collage of other biblical material in the manner already observed in Nazianzen's Orations,

---

[56] *Jean Chrysostome, Panégyriques de Saint Paul*, ed. A. Piédagnel (*SC*, vol. 300, 1982), Introduction, ch. 2, pp. 21–38.

[57] *Gregorii Nysseni Sermones*, ed. G. Heil, J. P. Cavarnos, O. Lendle (Jaeger edition, vol. x.2, Leiden, 1990), pp. 73–105.

directly quoting only occasionally. A little more than two-thirds of
the way through, a dogmatic interest emerges, namely to oppose
those pneumatomachians who used Stephen's vision of the Son of
Man at the right hand of God to show that there was no third person
in heaven. Clearly this is why Gregory's narrative began with the
coming of the Spirit at Pentecost and has stressed already Stephen's
endowment with the Spirit. Now, since no human being can or has
ever seen God, it is evident that only full of the Spirit was Stephen
capable of receiving the vision, and the Trinity is involved after all.
Throughout, but especially here, relevant texts are employed to
substantiate the point. The hearers are to emulate Stephen's
eusebeia, as well as his *athlēsis* in challenging the opponents of truth
and forgiving his enemies as Christ taught.

The second briefer encomium is less closely tied to the biblical
narrative. After Christ come the Christ-bearers, of which Stephen is
the first. Already the image of light is employed: after the sun of
righteousness, lamps for the inhabited earth. The phraseology of
Malachi 3.20 and Genesis 1.14ff. is thus put to daring new use in a
way very similar to the many examples noted before. The bulk of this
piece leaves Stephen behind and is devoted to a collage of scripture
passages about light, and the light-bearing function of those who
belong to the Church: 'Let your light shine before men' (Matt.
5.14–16). Stephen provides the initial model and his particular
imitation of Christ is brought out in the description of his martyrdom, Acts 7.59 being paralleled with Luke 23.46, for example. But
over half the material draws on other examples, prophetic and
apostolic.

So, although the subject of these encomia is a biblical hero,
biblical texts are still being used in the construction of mimetic
collages of the kind we have already observed. However, there is
probably overall a slight increase in specific quotation of texts;
some traditional *topoi*, e.g. concerning parental background, are
abandoned (presumably for lack of information in the biblical text);
the pieces lack both *synkrisis* and *consolatio* (presumably the latter
was felt to be inappropriate since the subject was victory over death
and the occasion closer to a festival than a funeral); and the development of character and action becomes more specifically edificatory
rather than laudatory. This encourages focus on a spiritual or
dogmatic theme, and brings what began as an epideictic form closer
to exegetical and homiletic style. A quick look at some of Nyssen's

other panegyrics suggests that these developments have something to do with the fact that the source of the material is the Bible itself, since his use of the Bible in praising Basil and other non-biblical heroes appears close to that of Nazianzen.

In general, an examination of Chrysostom's *Panegyrics on Paul*[58] suggests similar conclusions, though these seven pieces are remarkably different. The first is an exercise in *synkrisis*: Chrysostom begins with characteristically encomiastic hyperbole, claiming for Paul all human – indeed angelic – virtues collected in one soul, and the rest of the piece demonstrates this by *synkrisis* with Abel, Noah, Abraham, Isaac, Jacob, Joseph, Job, Moses, David, Elijah, John the Baptist, indeed even the angels. Typically there is much allusion to scripture and little direct quotation. The hearers are exhorted to imitation in the final paragraph. Here is a selective use of typical encomiastic procedures, but many of the traditional *topoi* are missing. The second piece exploits the Pauline material rather more explicitly, demonstrating that Paul cared for nothing except virtue, no effort or suffering deterring his pursuit of it, by quoting 2 Corinthians 4.17, Philippians 3.13 and 2.18, and 2 Corinthians 12.10. His trials and sacrifice for love of Christ are delineated by a combination of rhetorical description and allusion to Acts and the Epistles. The number of allusions still outweighs the quotations.

In the third, however, quotation has taken over, and the piece assumes a rather different character. It is much closer to an exploration of *agapē*, beginning with exhortation to imitate Paul as Paul imitates Christ, and then demonstrating Paul's love of his persecutors, even of the Jews, this being documented from Romans 10 and 11. Paul's love of Gentiles and zeal to spread the Gospel, his spiritual love in other words, is then followed by reference to his material concern for his companions. Romans 13.8–10 then inspires a paragraph on love as the fulfilling of the Law, and the piece ends with exhortation to pursue *agapē*. The use of scripture is largely different: few collages, few allusions, many 'proof-texts'.

This piece is not entirely characteristic, however. The remaining four are more like the second in their use of scripture, with an even balance of allusion and quotation. The seventh, for example, takes as its theme the cross-centred focus of Paul's life and ministry, and draws on Acts as well as the Epistles to recount some of Paul's life.

---

[58] Text ed. Piédagnel, *SC*.

Here there is more retelling in Chrysostom's own words than direct quotation. Occasional allusions to other parts of the biblical material are woven in, but the elaborate collages found in the Cappadocian material are largely absent from these panegyrics on Paul. The developments observed in Nyssen's encomia on Stephen have proceeded further: more thematic, more edificatory. As in Gregory's case, this may partly be accounted for by the nature of the material, namely its panegyrical elaboration of heroes from the biblical material itself, but it would appear to be characteristic of Chrysostom's epideictic as it matured and found its own style.

In conclusion, suffice it to offer a reminder that turning to the Bible for the material of *synkrisis* had some surprising effects, as did also the rhetorical conventions of free and creative allusion. Such use of the Bible reflects an understanding of the text quite different from that presupposed by the usual categories of literal, typological or allegorical. The text is authoritative yet far from binding. Here is an intertextuality of imaginative and creative play, far removed from the historicism of modern interpretation whether critical or fundamentalist, yet not lacking attention to the specificity of the biblical text, or its ability to lend weight to the forging of distinctive Christian values in a particular cultural dress. Maybe here there are principles worth noting, even if panegyrical practices are utterly foreign and currently unthinkable.

PART III

Language and reference

In addition to the importance of intertextuality, critical theory has latterly reminded us of the problematic relationship between language and its referent. For the Fathers, reference constituted meaning, and inappropriate interpretations could be challenged by consideration of that to which the language referred. Although language could have a 'biblical meaning' discernible by multiplying cross-references, text being interpreted by text, ascertaining reference was far more fundamental to patristic exegesis than determining the sense of the words. Discussion of the traditional 'senses of scripture' (literal, allegorical, tropological and so on) does not provide a key to method as such. A complex grid of 'reading strategies' plotted against a typology of multiple senses illuminates a fundamentally 'sacramental' understanding of the meaning of scripture: the linguistic sign represented the reality to which it referred, whether transparently or obliquely.

CHAPTER 6

Reference and cross-reference

I

'Interpretation' meant much the same as 'translation' to the Greek who used the same word, *hermeneia*, for both. This remark is not irrelevant to the subject of this chapter, for it alerts us to an apparently commonsense feature of language which was taken for granted by the ancients. Language was assumed to refer to something other than itself: hence different verbal expressions might refer to the same things in such a way that words could be translated or interpreted by the substitution of a different form of expression. The meaning of language is in the idea behind the words, the reality to which the language refers.

Such a correspondence between *logos* and world, ideas and reality, has nowadays become problematic. Language and reality have become dissociated, especially in literary theory, but also in other philosophical movements. George Steiner, in *Real Presences*, has challenged this development.[1] True, he admits, language is 'infinite': you can literally say what you like, and both myth and fiction demonstrate that language is far from merely representational.[2] Steiner wonders, however, whether this infinity is the

---

[1] *Real Presences* (London: Faber, 1989). Behind this paragraph is allusion to the whole world of discourse in hermeneutics and literary theory arising from Saussure and the development of semiotics, not to mention Wittgenstein and the philosophy of 'language-games'. One element in this bears comparison with ancient debates about language: is it convention (the *thesis* theory) or has language a natural relationship with reality (the *physis* theory)? There is, however, a more radical claim inherent in Saussure's distinction between *langue* and *parole*: that language is a self-contained system and has no necessary reference outside itself, rather like mathematics. Gadamer's hermeneutical position would encourage Steiner's protest: Joel Weinsheimer, *Philosophical Hermeneutics and Literary Theory* (New Haven and London: Yale University Press, 1991), provides a useful discussion.

[2] Clearly his point is not to be compared with another issue, namely the difficulty (noted in ch. 2) of expressing the divine in human language which presumes 'finitude' rather than infinity. This issue will be addressed again in ch. 7.

infinity of chaos or of transcendence, whether there is actually anything in what we say. The ancients recognised that the relationship
between language and reality is complex, but without abandoning
the connection. You might play something like 'language-games'
but in the end they symbolised something, the signs were not simply
a self-contained system since they signified, and were therefore
significant.

So the fundamental question for understanding meaning was
discerning the reference. This did not mean a simplistic literalism;
for the metaphoric nature of much language was something everyone was aware of, if only because they analysed figures of speech in
their education. But the point is reinforced by the commonplace we
have already noted that one should distinguish between the content
of a speech or narrative and the dress or style in which it was
clothed.[3] The 'idea' preceded its chosen mode of expression. Yet
finding the appropriate linguistic dress in which to clothe the intent
or aim was vital. Rhetoric was not simply the cultivation of style, yet
meaning was mediated through the language, and therefore the
appropriate style was a matter of great importance. There was a
necessary connection between the *logos* and the idea it expressed,
even if the idea in some sense transcended the words in which it was
enunciated. Very often, notoriously in Platonism, not only the words
but the world itself was an imperfect copy of the reality to which
both pointed.

In other words, language was symbolic, and its meaning lay in
that to which it referred. The difference between 'literal' and
'allegorical' references was not absolute, but lay on a spectrum.
Allegory in its rhetorical usage was a figure of speech among other
figures of speech: it was to speak so as to imply something other than
what is said, and included irony. Often to interpret something
allegorically was simply to recognise metaphor rather than taking
something very woodenly according to the letter. All language
signified, and as sign was symbolic. The crucial question was what it
symbolised or referred to. The case of prophecy highlights the point.
To what does prophecy refer? Surely to the event it predicts. Even if
the discovery of that prediction implies recognising the metaphoric
nature of the language and unpacking a riddle through recognition
of symbols, ambiguities, or hidden meanings which can be discerned

---

[3] See above, chs. 2 and 4, p. 35 and p. 81.

only after the event, it is the event to which the prophecy points that gives the prophecy meaning – in other words the future event is that to which it refers.

The recognition of this must make a difference to standard descriptions of much patristic exegesis. To make the point let me take my own description of Eusebius' exegesis in *From Nicaea to Chalcedon*,[4] a description that could be regarded as typical of standard accounts but is surely, though I now say it myself, somewhat misleading:

> several features are striking: [particularly], his understanding of the *literal* meaning of a prophecy as its fulfilment in a later historical event . . . Occasionally in the *Demonstratio* he offers two interpretations, literal and figurative; an example is provided by the prophecies of peace at the coming of Emmanuel: literally they refer to the peace of the empire at the time of the incarnation, figuratively to the peace of the individual soul who receives 'God with us'. More often Eusebius distinguished between direct and veiled predictions. The latter notion permitted a rather arbitrary application of texts to future events through use of allegorical methods . . . For a pupil of Origen, Eusebius was surprisingly literal-minded.

The whole matter would be much clearer if the discussion had been in terms of the reference of the text and the use of figures of speech.

Eusebius, a scholar like Origen, takes the 'letter' of the text seriously. But the language of the text refers, and the all-important question for understanding the meaning of the text is to grasp how it refers. Whether as 'plain sense' or through figures of speech, like metaphor or symbol, the reference of the prophecy was to the future fulfilment. Symbolism, in numbers, animals and natural phenomena, was as widely accepted as the metaphoric nature of much linguistic expression. By uncovering the signification of the symbols the hidden reference of the prophecy would become manifest. As Eusebius recognised, prophecies may sometimes be direct, but they are often veiled. For him *ta rhēta*, or 'the things said', are about that to which the prophecy refers – namely, in the example mentioned,[5] the incarnation – whereas 'figurative meaning' moves into another realm – the psychological or spiritual.[6]

---

[4] *From Nicaea to Chalcedon*, pp. 21–2.

[5] The reference is *Dem. evang.* VII.1.49; *GCS*, vol. VI, p. 307.

[6] Compare Kerrigan, *St Cyril of Alexandria*, p. 234: he suggests that the difference between literal and spiritual in Cyril was not a way of signifying, but of referring – they point to the objects envisaged.

So the important difference between Origen and Eusebius is that Eusebius puts greater emphasis on the long-standing tradition of prophetic reference, whereas Origen, while incorporating that, tended to emphasise the reference to transcendent spiritual realities rather than earthly events. Origen's exegesis finds its apex in 'spiritual' meanings, Eusebius focusses on the 'oracular'. But the distinction is a matter of reference, and the attempt to distinguish through the categories of 'literal' and 'allegorical' is little more than confusing.

II

Hermeneia 'translates' the symbols by pointing out their real reference. The scholars inherited a long tradition of proof from prophecy. Let us return to the second century and consider the roots of this kind of exegesis.

The roots lie, of course, in the New Testament. Justin Martyr certainly believed that he was handing on an apostolic exposition of the scriptures, and this apostolic exegesis ultimately derived from Christ's own instruction:

Now if the prophets foretold cryptically that Christ would suffer first and then be Lord of all, it was still well nigh impossible for anyone to grasp the full meaning of such prophecies, until Christ Himself convinced His Apostles that such things were explicitly proclaimed in the scriptures.[7]

Elsewhere[8] Justin tells us that Christ appeared to the Apostles after his resurrection and taught them to consult the prophecies, in which everything was predicted. According to Oskar Skarsaune,[9] there is no contradiction between the rationality of scripture proof and the 'grace to understand'; for the 'grace to understand' is not some supernatural gift, but the apostolic proof from the scriptures. This is something received by Justin. The reference of the text, once understood, illuminates its true meaning so that text and reference confirm one another and conviction follows.

How then did Justin receive this exegetical tradition? The painstaking work of Skarsaune illuminates this question and links

---

[7] *Dial.* 76.6; Migne, *PG* 6.653C; ET in *FC*, vol. 6, p. 269.
[8] *1 Apology* 50.12; Migne, *PG* 6.404A; ET in *FC*, vol. 6, p. 87.
[9] *The Proof from Prophecy. A Study in Justin Martyr's Proof-Text Tradition: Text-Type, Provenance, Theological Profile* (Leiden, Brill, 1987), p. 12.

up with our discussion in chapter 1. For Skarsaune finds two forms of text in Justin's work,[10] both of which must be original to his texts rather than introduced by copyists, since he makes comments on the basis of each. Generally speaking the 'proof-texts' that Justin uses in the *Apology* are also quoted in the *Dialogue with Trypho*, but at greater length and in the LXX version. The Christological meaning Justin takes for granted, and 'often neglects discrepancies between his inherited exegesis and the LXX text he quotes. But sometimes he tries to adjust his interpretation to the LXX text.'[11] So Skarsaune argues that Justin received his testimonies in a traditional text-form, along with the Christological interpretation of each. This text-form must have been written, and Justin certainly believed it to be the LXX, though in fact it was not. When Justin quotes longer versions which do correspond with the LXX, he treats these texts as 'Jewish'.[12]

The source of the full text, Skarsaune suggests, was the scroll, and at this date complete manuscripts or scrolls of the scriptures originated from Jews. Justin suspected 'hebraising' recensions. The source of the variant text, to which Justin accords greater authority, was a Christian testimony-book (or maybe more than one), to which the legend recounted in the *Letter to Aristeas*[13] had been attached. Skarsaune characterises the testimony source common to *I Apology* and the *Dialogue* as a missionary document, but the supposition is that it was a codex formulated for Christian use – a notebook of Christianising Targums, we might call it, including the exegesis which saw the reference of the text as prophecy of Christ. Further careful detective work discovers the underlying pattern of this source: it is the 'creed' or 'kerygma'.[14] Our conclusions about the manner of Christian reception of the text seem confirmed: an overarching scheme or 'hypothesis' permitted the abstraction of key 'oracles' from their original context, to be recorded in notebooks, and, despite Justin's occasional recourse to the full text, this testimony had the greater hermeneutical authority.

Compared with the prophetic proof-texts of the New Testament,

---

[10] Ibid., part one, ch. 2.   [11] Ibid., p. 90   [12] Ibid., pp. 43ff.

[13] For the Fathers, this text guaranteed the inspiration of the LXX translation. It is accessible in H. B. Swete, *Introduction to the Old Testament in Greek*. Appendix: 'The Letter of Aristeas', text ed. and introd. by H. St J. Thackeray (Cambridge: Cambridge University Press, 1902); or in the French edn and trans. in *SC*.

[14] *The Proof from Prophecy*, part two, ch. 2.

however, Justin's dossier is, according to Skarsaune,[15] remarkably 'Jewish', containing those texts which appear as Messianic most often in the Talmuds: Isaiah 11.1–4, Micah 5.1–4 and Psalm 72.5–17. Here too are others that appear less frequently than those mentioned, but are nevertheless evidenced in Jewish tradition: in *Targum Onqelos*, for example, two texts are treated as Messianic, neither of which appears in the New Testament, both of which are treated by Justin, namely Genesis 49.10ff. and Numbers 24.17. Skarsaune suggests that the initial New Testament proof-texts were collected on the basis of needing to show that the unexpected features of Jesus' life were predicted, so they focus on proofs of the death on a cross, the resurrection and the ascension, while later strata like the birth-narratives begin to incorporate traditional Messianic prophecies. Justin provides evidence that this process went on. It was increasingly important to show that the traditional Messianic prophecies reached their fulfilment in Christ.

How was this exegetical task performed? Skarsaune suggests that there is a repeated pattern in this traditional collection of interpreted texts. The text is quoted, abstracted of course from context, this is followed by some exposition of symbolic material and then by the fulfilment report.[16] In other words the fundamental point is to indicate the true and proper reference of the text. The true and proper reference is also the matter of dispute between Trypho and Justin. The issue of reference is indeed the more evident in the material found only in the *Dialogue*: for here we find Trypho referring to Hezekiah and other historical kings texts which Justin would refer to Christ.

Let me illustrate this process:

I Apology 32:[17] Here Justin discusses his first example. Moses, the first of the prophets, spoke in these words (Gen. 49.10):

The sceptre shall not depart from Judah, nor a lawgiver from between his feet, until he come for whom it is reserved; and he shall be the expectation of the nations, binding his foal to the vine, washing his robe in the blood of the grape.

Enquiry is needed to understand what this is about. The first problem is to ascertain up to whose time the Jews had a lawgiver and

---

[15] Ibid., pp. 261ff.   [16] Ibid., p. 140.
[17] Migne, *PG* 6.388; ET in *FC*, vol. 6, p. 68.

king of their own. Explaining that Judah was the forefather from
whom the Jews took their name, Justin suggests that they had their
own polity up to the time of Jesus Christ, who was the one to come
for whom the sceptre was reserved. He then takes the next phrase
about him being also the expectation of the nations: this indicates
that some of all nations would look for him to come again, and that is
evident; for of all races there are believers who expect the return of
the crucified one. The final phrases Justin describes as symbols
of the things that were to happen to Christ. The foal of an ass stood
bound to a vine at the entrance of a village, and he sent his followers
to fetch it, mounted it and entered Jerusalem. 'Washing his robe in
the blood of the grape' is taken to refer to the passion, his robe being
believers who are washed by his blood, which is the power of God.

This example surely makes the point. The pattern of text,
explanation and application is evident, but the fundamental issue is
one of reference, and to distinguish between a 'literal' understanding of the first part of the text, where Justin does take the
words more at their face value, and an 'allegorical' treatment of the
last part of the text, where the symbols are asking to be unpacked,
does not help much in the characterisation of the exegetical process.
The crucial move is to take the text as a 'riddling' oracle and
discover what its reference 'really' is.[18]

Dialogue 33–4:[19] Here Justin is discussing Psalm 110, which he
quoted at the end of the previous section. He is well aware that
Trypho, the representative Jew, would understand the reference of
this Psalm to be Hezekiah. Justin wishes to prove that this reference
is wrong. He picks out the verse in which the Lord swears, 'Thou art
a priest for ever, after the order of Melchisedek.' He is confident
that Trypho cannot claim that Hezekiah was a priest of any
kind, certainly not the eternal priest of God. Justin urges that the
reference is to Christ: Melchisedek was priest of the Most High,
according to Moses, and furthermore, he was priest of the uncircum-
cised who blessed the circumcised Abraham; so Christ is priest of
those in uncircumcision, but he will bless and receive those of the

---

[18] In Theodoret's *Eranistes*, Alexandrian and Antiochene alike take this text as Christological,
and both refer the latter part to the eucharist, a move Justin does not yet make (see
discussion in my article, 'Exegetical Method and Scriptural Proof'). As we shall see, when it
comes to these traditional Messianic prophecies, there is little to choose between the
Schools which are supposed to have differed over the issue of allegory.

[19] Migne, *PG* 6.545–9; ET in *FC*, vol. 6, pp. 196ff.

circumcision who approach him. This appears surprisingly independent of Hebrews, though claiming the same Christological reference for the Psalm. Justin clinches the discussion by taking as a reference to Christ's two comings, first in humiliation then in exaltation, words which appear at the end of the Psalm: 'He shall drink of the brook by the way; therefore shall he lift up the head.'

In the following section,[20] Justin turns to Psalm 72. Trypho, he knows, would refer it to Solomon, Justin wants to refer it to Christ. He suggests that ambiguous phrases mislead. 'The law of the Lord is perfect' cannot refer back to Moses' Law since God had declared that he would establish a new law and a new covenant. The words 'O God, give judgment to the king' make the application to Solomon apparently plausible, but, Justin urges, the words of the Psalm specifically refer to the 'everlasting King'. Justin quotes the whole Psalm, claiming that none of the things mentioned happened to Solomon: neither did all kings worship him, nor did he reign to the ends of the earth, nor did his enemies lick the dust. The debate is about reference, and in some ways Justin is the one wanting to take the language more at face value, or 'by the letter', in order to confute the reference claimed by the opposition.

The Christological reference, however, was only part of the whole process of appropriation. It was a key element, but only an element; for the scriptures constantly raised questions about Christian identity, particularly the differentiation between Jew and Christian. Christian exegesis was bound to be ambivalent about the Jewish past, on the one hand positively claiming the antique heritage, on the other negating Jewish traditions to justify their own existence. The primary issue tackled by Justin in the *Dialogue* concerns the key New Testament problems of Law and circumcision. He and Trypho have agreed about the importance and mistakes of philosophy, and Trypho even admits admiration for the precepts in the Gospel, but what he cannot understand is that people claiming to be pious and to be better than others are not separated from them, and have not adopted a distinctive way of life, observing festivals and Sabbaths, practising circumcision, obeying the commandments of the God from whom they profess to expect good things.[21] There is good reason to regard this dialogue as a literary artefact rather than a

---

[20] *Dial.* 34; Migne, *PG* 6.545–9; ET in *FC*, vol. 6, pp. 197ff.
[21] *Dial.* 10; Migne, *PG* 6.496; ET in *FC*, vol. 6, p. 163.

real debate, and, if that is the case, then this provides evidence of what concerned Christians.

Justin responds to Trypho[22] by insisting that there is no other God than the Creator, and certainly not one God for the Jews and another for Christians. Christians trust in the God who led 'your fathers out of Egypt with a strong hand and a mighty arm', the God of Abraham, Isaac and Jacob. But the Law promulgated at Horeb is 'old' and belongs to the Jews alone; a new and universal covenant is now incumbent upon all. 'The true spiritual Israel, the descendants of Judah, Jacob, Isaac and Abraham, who was in uncircumcision approved of and blessed by God for his faith, and called the father of many nations [*ethnē* = nations, but also signifies Gentiles], are WE, who have been led to God through this crucified Jesus.'[23]

This provided an important clue to the reading of the scriptures, with fatal consequences. For the prophetic denunciations of Israel lost their moorings in historical circumstances and were taken to refer to all Jews of any time. So Jews in general became characterised as the stubborn, stiff-necked, disobedient people of God, while the Christians inherited the promises. This has nothing to do with allegory – the prophetic warnings are clear enough taking the texts at face value; it has everything to do with reference. Heretics and deviants, along with the Jews, become the 'outsiders' of which scripture warns.

When Christians read the Torah, they had to distinguish those commandments which were interim, intended to deal with hard-hearted Israel, no longer in force; those commandments which were moral and universal, fulfilled by the Saviour and still to be followed; and those commandments which were shadows or types of what was to come. Such a distinction is implicit in Justin's treatment, explicit in Ptolemy's *Letter to Flora*.[24] The Gnostic *Letter to Flora* only differs from what became the orthodox position in its view of the source of each type of law: the interim laws were human, introduced by Moses and the elders; the Law of God could not come either from the devil or the perfect God (that is, the good Father revealed by Jesus), so it must have come from the Creator, an inferior being. It is against such speculations, and perhaps Marcion in particular, that Justin

---

[22] *Dial*.11; Migne, *PG* 6.497A–500A; ET in *FC*, vol. 6, pp. 163–5.
[23] Ibid.
[24] This Gnostic text was preserved by Epiphanius; text in *SC*, ET in Layton, *Gnostic Scriptures*.

insists on one God, who is the God of the Jews, and the source of both Law and promises. This God is the one who dealt with disobedience by giving the interim laws, as well as foreshadowing the new covenant. The Decalogue enshrined the universal moral law fulfilled in Christ, while the ritual laws of circumcision, Sabbath, sacrifices, fasting, Passover, Unleavened Bread and so on, provided the images and symbols of spiritual realities. It was all a matter of discerning the right reference.

For Justin, the failure of the Jews lay in understanding the Law in a fleshly sense, and Justin could provide scriptural backing for this view. The true fast is giving food to the hungry that you may please God, asserts Justin,[25] quoting Isaiah 55 at length, and the plain sense of that passage, taken simply at face value, suggests exactly that. For the exegesis of this passage, the distinction between literal and allegorical reading is irrelevant – it is yet again a question of reference: are the words limited to the people of the prophet's day? Or might they make an apt comment applicable universally to religious people who put their ritual observances first, whether they be Jews, Christian, Muslims or whatever? Or is the text to be referred to the present, as by the early Christians, through setting up a salvation-historical perspective which unhistorically consigned the Jew to a negated past which was in practice still present, and so making this text confirm the Christian reading of Torah rather than the supposed Jewish reading?

So to clarify in reverse order the two points I have argued so far: the Christian reading of the Jewish scriptures was not simply prophetic or even Messianic – that does not characterise its distinctiveness, for Jews too read their scriptures prophetically. The difference lies in the perception of the reference of the text, and this involved a complex set of moves, ultimately grounded in the claim first made by Paul and the author of Hebrews that the new covenant proclaimed by Jeremiah had come into being. Taken at face value along with other texts also taken at face value, this new covenant was assumed to imply that the covenant and Law with the Jewish people were superseded by a new universal covenant with the nations, of a spiritual and moral kind. The reference of texts from both Law and Prophets could then be deduced according to this hermeneutical key.

---

[25] *Dial.* 15; Migne, *PG* 6.505D–8D; ET in *FC*, vol. 6, pp. 170–1.

In thus denying the exclusively 'prophetic' characterisation of Christian exegesis, I have also hinted at the earlier point stressed: the distinction between allegorical, typological and literal does little to clarify how this shift in reference was effected. For the wording of the text, whether in its plain sense or taken as metaphoric, mattered for indicating its reference. Our examples have proved that true for Justin.

In this respect, it is instructive to examine the terminology used by Eusebius in the passage with which we began:[26] *Rhēta men oun tade*, he writes, describing the prophetic reference of the Isaiah text which he has just described: **the words stated** are about the coming of Christ. But *pros dianoian* the word of the prophecy may be referred to the peace received by every soul which receives Emmanuel : the **'mind'** of the text underlying the words may have this kind of spiritual reference. The fact that such a 'mind' can legitimately be discerned and the text received *tropikōs* (in a turned-around kind of way, that is, metaphorically or figuratively) is grounded in the impossibility of understanding *pros lexin* (according to the letter) the following phrases in the text, which are about flies and bees from Assyria and Egypt attacking the Jewish race: they are not at all to be understood *pros lexin*, but to be discerned (*theōroumena*) according to the 'mind' alone (*kata monēn dianoian*). Eusebius' distinction is closer to that distinction between content and style, which we have noted before[27] as commonplace in rhetorical textbooks, than to our distinction between literal and allegorical. The clearest way of characterising what is going on is to distinguish two kinds of reference.

We have been examining a process of reception and appropriation which encouraged the abstraction of texts for suasorial or apologetic purposes. Prior to Origen and beyond, exegesis largely consisted in the provision of the appropriate reference of each text utilised in this way. Paraenetic exegesis drew on scriptural material to foster a certain way of life, applying the text directly to those being addressed. Oracular exegesis 'proved' the fulfilment of prophecy. Both served to delineate and reinforce identity. When more systematic commentary on whole books began, long-

---

[26] *Dem. evang.* VII.1.51; *GCS*, vol. VI, p. 307. See above, p. 121.
[27] See above, p. 81.

established hermeneutical keys, deriving from this initial process of reception and appropriation, were employed: the keys were provided by (1) the Rule of Faith, the perception of the *hypothesis* of scripture now understood as a unity;[28] (2) the supersessionary 'reading' which referred texts to 'old' or 'new' dispensation as appropriate; and (3) the prophetic 'mind' or intent of both Law and Prophets, whether the predictions were understood as direct, veiled or mimetic. Thus the scene was set for an elaborate development of cross-referencing as biblical scholarship developed.

III

Self-conscious cross-referencing belongs to the pervasive intertextuality of ancient literature. Chapter 5 has already explored ancient conventions with respect to the use of quotation and allusion. Two points became clear: (1) It was not customary to produce extended quotations from literature. It was regarded as unnecessary since any educated person would recognise the quotation. The important thing was to adapt it, to provide reminiscences, to emulate the way in which the great classical authors wrote, to put it how they would put it if they were addressing the topic in hand – in other words, to engage in *mimēsis* of the great classics. (2) The point of such intertextual reference was not primarily ornamental – quotation and allusion are not discussed in the books on style. It was recognised that such material might enhance the diction, but principally the point was to enlist the authority of the great poet, or to utilise classic examples of the virtue being extolled, in order to reinforce the content of the speech.

Now it is true that this is to call in evidence the practice of élitist literary circles and their perception of appropriate intertextuality. However, I suspect that the 'filter-down effect' in ancient urban societies should not be underestimated, nor the assimilation of Jewish traditions to Hellenistic norms.[29] Once one becomes sensitive to the importance of imitation and emulation in literary composition, the extent of allusive reminting of scriptural material becomes striking, even within the New Testament itself. Richard

---

[28] Cf. ch. 1, above.   [29] See above, ch. 4, pp. 91–4.

Hays' work on scriptural echoes in Paul reinforces my own argument for a much greater recognition of Paul's allusively scriptural language in 2 Corinthians.[30] If allusive use of scripture is more evident in the New Testament than has usually been observed, that is even more the case in the second century. Indeed, I would argue that the Two Ways tradition is such a creative re-minting of scripture through a collage of allusion and quotation.

As is well known the *Didache* opens with a contrast between Two Ways, one of life and one of death. The way of life is, firstly, to love God and one's neighbour, and not do to anyone what you would not want to have done to yourself, and, secondly, not to murder, commit adultery and so on. In each case, these are spelt out with specific injunctions. I quote part of the first:

What you may learn from these words is to bless those that curse you, to pray for your enemies, and to fast for your persecutors. For where is the merit in loving only those who return your love? Even the heathens do as much as that. But if you love those who hate you, you will have nobody to be your enemy.

Beware of the carnal appetites of the body. If someone strikes you on the right cheek, turn the other one to him as well, and perfection will be yours. Should anyone compel you to go a mile, go another one with him. If someone takes away your coat, let him have your shirt too. If someone seizes anything belonging to you, do not ask it back again (you could not get it anyway). Give to everyone that asks, without looking for repayment, for it is the Father's pleasure that we should share His gracious bounty with all.[31]

One could go on, but that is enough to make the point. Clearly much of this quotes, or at least alludes to, Gospel material such as we find in the Sermon on the Mount and elsewhere.[32] But it is conflated with other material and has a fresh complexion.

Of course it might be that this is the result of oral tradition rather than literary allusion, but we find the same thing in the next section, this time alluding to texts which would become the 'Old Testament'. Anyone in the know could hear reference not just to the Ten Commandments and the injunctions of the Law against

[30] Richard B. Hays, *Echoes of Scripture in the Letters of Paul* (New Haven and London: Yale University Press 1989); Young and D. F. Ford, *Meaning and Truth in 2 Corinthians* (London: SPCK, 1987).

[31] *Didache* 1.3; *LCL*, pp. 308–10; ET from *Early Christian Writings* (slightly altered), p. 191.

[32] As the marginal references in *LCL* make clear.

sorcery, but also to the Wisdom literature and the Psalms – for 'single-mindedness', rather than duplicity, is a value characteristic of such scriptural texts:[33]

Commit no murder, adultery, sodomy, fornication, or theft. Practise no magic, sorcery, abortion, or infanticide. See that you do not covet anything your neighbour possesses, and never be guilty of perjury, false witness, slander or malice. Do not equivocate in thought or speech, for a double tongue is a deadly snare . . . you must resist any temptation to hypocrisy, spitefulness, or superiority. You are to have no malicious designs on a neighbour.[34]

With this we may compare the version of the Two Ways tradition found in the *Epistle of Barnabas* xviii–xx. The similarities and differences certainly suggest an oral catechetical tradition, but the scriptural undergirding is significant:

Practise singleness of heart, and a richness of the spirit . . . Abhor anything that is displeasing to God, and hold every form of hypocrisy in detestation. Be sure that you never depart from the commandments of the Lord.

Do not exaggerate your own importance, but be modest at all points, and never claim credit for yourself. Cherish no ill-natured designs upon your neighbour. Forbid yourself any appearance of presumption. Commit no fornication, adultery, or unnatural vice . . .

Never be in two minds . . . Love your neighbour more than yourself. Never do away with an unborn child.[35]

This version of the Two Ways is longer and more expansive than that in the *Didache*, and much more could be quoted which would reinforce the point. Let me rather illustrate it by reference to one sentence. *Barnabas* has 'Cherish as the apple of your eye anyone who expounds the word of the Lord to you.'[36] That little phrase 'the apple of your eye' occurs five times in the scriptures (Deut. 32.10; Ps. 17.8; Prov. 7.2; Zech. 2.8; Lam. 2.18), usually implying something precious to be preserved, most frequently of God caring for his own, but in Proverbs 7.2, 'my child' is enjoined to keep 'my teachings'.

---

[33] This time *LCL*, despite producing a translation which more nearly reflects the AV than the one quoted here, fails to note potential allusions in the margin, apart from the Ten Commandments (Exod. 20) and the Gospels.

[34] *Didache* ii.2–7; *LCL*, pp. 310–12; ET from *Early Christian Writings*, pp. 191–2.

[35] *Epistle of Barnabas* xix.2–5; *LCL*, pp. 400–2; ET from *Early Christian Writings*, pp. 179–80.

[36] *Epistle of Barnabas* xix.9; *LCL*, p. 404; ET from *Early Christian Writings*, p. 180.

This example is a classic of apparent allusion without direct quotation.[37]

This 'compounding' of texts with other texts seems characteristic of second-century Christian use of the Bible.[38] By contrast, in the kind of proof-texting we were exploring in the previous section, more or less exact quotation or allusion may appear, though 'Targumic' renderings make the lines difficult to draw very precisely. This being the case, the observation of Barbara Aland,[39] that the text-form of quotations is far less exact than that found in manuscripts, has its basis in the normal way of handling literary allusion in the ancient world. Furthermore, this situation may make one inclined to give the benefit of the doubt to those who find allusion to New Testament documents already in second-century material, rather than those resorting to the theory of a looser oral tradition. To reproduce exactly was not felt to be incumbent upon one who quoted a document. Thus long-standing literary conventions may provide clues to some of the problems much discussed about second-century reception of texts.[40]

Be that as it may, once scholarship got under way and, like Homer, the Bible came to be treated as self-referential, discovering cross-reference between the various books of the Bible was a pursuit taken up with great enthusiasm. It was natural, given the acceptance of intertextuality in the ancient world, to suppose that coincidence of word or phrase was significant. The 'mind' or 'aim' of the author was to point to a truth found elsewhere in the biblical corpus, and the meaning would become clear only if this were discerned and made explicit. Cross-reference could establish reference, which, as we saw earlier, was the fundamental requirement for discerning meaning.

To illustrate the profound importance of intertextuality and cross-reference in early Christian exegesis, let me take a series of examples from Origen, where the second-century situation has certainly been influenced subsequently by the practices and intentions of the literary élite.

---

[37] This allusion is noted in the *LCL* margin, as are the references to the Ten Commandments. But once again a good deal is not noted, presumably because the allusion is too vague.

[38] See further below, ch. 10, on the production of *paraenesis* by this kind of process.

[39] Barbara Aland, 'Die Rezeption des neutestamentlichen Textes in den ersten Jahrhunderten', in Sévrin, *The New Testament in Early Christianity*, pp. 1–38.

[40] Cf. ch. 1, opening remarks on pp. 9–10.

Commentary on John, *Introd. to Book VI*[41]

A house with stability must be built in calm and quiet weather, so nothing can prevent it acquiring the necessary rigidity to resist flood and tempest.

That is not a full translation but a summary of the gist of Origen's opening words. He is about to apologise for the interruption to the composition of his Commentary, explaining the problems of storms in Alexandria and his eventual removal from Egypt. Clearly he does not quote or reproduce the Lucan parable of the house built on rock and the house built on sand, but there can be little doubt it is there below the surface of the text. A little further on he suggests that the construction of a book requires that the soul rests calm in the peace that passes understanding (Phil. 4.7).

That leads him into a meditation on the need for those with the prophetic spirit and ministers of the Gospel to receive peace for their task: Jesus said, 'Peace I leave with you . . . ' (John 14.27, quoted in full). David was told he could not build the Temple because he was a man of blood (1 Kings 5.3; 1 Chron. 22.8). Solomon, on the other hand, saw God and received wisdom in a dream (digressing slightly, Origen emphasises 'dream', for the reality was reserved for the one of whom it is said 'Behold a greater than Solomon is here'); but the point about Solomon is that he lived in a peace so deep that each had rest under his vine and under his fig-tree (Micah 4.4), and his name means 'Man of Peace' (1 Chron. 22.9), so through peace he had freedom to build God's Temple. Origen then slips to the rebuilding of the Temple in the time of Ezra, deducing that there was peace when truth had victory over wine, a hostile king and women, an allusion to 3 Esdras 4.

Origen reverts to his own 'building' of the Gospel 'tower' in literary form. He has counted the cost, and considered whether he can, after laying the foundation, complete the work, so as to avoid mockery from the onlookers – another Lucan parable. His reckoning was not encouraging, but he had confidence in God who enriches with all wisdom and knowledge (1 Cor. 1.5). Following his tower image, he speaks of ascending to the parapet. He had got as far as Book v in spite of the storm in Alexandria, Jesus rebuking the winds and waves (Matt. 8.26). Details of the troubles follow. But now that

[41] *Comm. Jn.* VI.1–12; *GCS*, vol. IV, pp. 106–8; ET *ANCL*, addit. vol., pp. 349–50.

the fiery darts aimed at him have been quenched by God (Eph. 6.16), and he has reached a measure of calm, he will proceed with the work.

This first example is intended to illustrate the allusive compounding of scripture noted. The function of such allusive material is not simply ornament, but it supplies the 'proof' or justification required by the content of what Origen has to say.

Commentary on Matthew *XII.31ff.*[42]

Origen has reached the problem text: 'there are some standing here who will not taste death before they see the Son of Man coming in his kingdom' (16.28).

Some, he says, refer this to the 'going up' which takes place six (or, according to Luke, eight) days later, for the transfiguration. Peter and the others did not taste death before seeing the kingly glory of Christ. As indicated earlier, the question of reference is fundamental to the exegetical enterprise, and it is where the reference is problematic that there arises an exegetical difficulty which requires comment. Like the modern commentator, Origen and his contemporaries realised that the apparent prediction of the Second Coming had not been fulfilled in the lifetime of the apostles.

But this interpretation Origen regards as adapted to 'new-born babes' who need 'milk not meat', alluding to 1 Peter 2.2 and 1 Corinthians 3.2. For those who are not capable of greater truths scripture flows with milk and honey (another scriptural allusion), but he who has been weaned like Isaac (Gen. 21.8) seeks for food different from what is meat indeed but not solid food (Heb. 5.12–14); Origen goes on to characterise it as 'herbs', referring to Romans 14.2 where the weak eat herbs. The weaned one, dedicated to God like Samuel by his mother (and Hannah means grace), as one nurtured in the Temple, seeks the holy food of those who are perfect and priests.

Origen then reverts to the text in question. 'Some standing here' he refers to those who have the footsteps of their soul planted with Jesus. This he unpacks by cross-reference to Moses who stood on the mountain for forty days and forty nights (Deut. 10.10) and was worthy of God saying to him, 'Stand here with me' (Deut. 5.31).

---

[42] *Comm. Matt.* XII.31–5; *GCS*, vol. x, pp. 136–50; ET *ANCL*, addit. vol., pp. 466ff.

Those who stand by Jesus are not all equal, Origen goes on. Some, especially the newly initiated, do not see him coming in the glory of his kingdom: 'we saw him, and he had no form or beauty, but his form was dishonoured, defective compared with all the sons of men' (Isa. 53.2–3). They see the Word as understood in the synagogue. But there is a royal dignity evident to some who stand by Jesus, when they have been able to follow him up the lofty mountain of his own manifestation. Origen speaks of these being deemed worthy like Peter, and develops the notion of someone against whom the Gates of Hades do not prevail, of some who are 'sons of thunder', begotten by the mighty voice of God who thunders and cries aloud from heaven great things to those who have ears and are wise. Such do not taste death, he suggests. Again the allusions packed into a *novum* are evident.

In the following sections, Origen attempts to define what 'tasting death' means. It would be instructive to work through this in detail, too. Suffice it to say, however, that his starting-point is the one who said, 'I am the life', and from there he builds up a dossier of scriptural quotations, a kind of concordance, which enables him to ascertain the biblical meaning of life and death. The verb 'taste' naturally brings in the bread of life. In the end, the whole is interwoven with the interpretation of the text in front of us: for the one who is under the orders of the king, whose kingdom is potentially 'within us', as Luke said, and actually 'with power', as Mark said, is certainly one who is no longer under the reign of sin, and therefore of death. The range of cross-reference used is considerable: Deuteronomy; Psalms; Isaiah; various Gospel passages; various Epistles, Pauline and non-Pauline; Revelation.

Such discussion of a passage is typical of Origen's procedure, and it makes very clear the fundamental importance of reference and cross-reference to the discernment of meaning. To try and define what Origen does exegetically in terms of the usual categories employed to describe patristic exegesis is to miss the essential character of what is going on, and to fail to grasp both the similarities of procedure and the crucial differences between his exegesis and that of a modern critic. Both are addressing texts which raise problems of meaning. Those problems concern reference. They are often addressed by cross-referencing. The differences lie in the kind of reference found convincing, and the range of cross-reference permitted. With Origen reference and cross-reference are taking on the characteristics of scholarly research, and this discussion needs to be taken together with chapter 4. The point here is to note that multiple meanings in Origen are really multiple referents.

v

What I have tried to do in this chapter is to show something of the character of second-century exegesis, and its importance in setting trends which would remain fundamental even as exegetical scholarship became more sophisticated in the hands of such as Origen and Eusebius. The principle of looking for the reference and exploiting cross-reference in order to substantiate proposed exegesis in a rational way remains crucial throughout the period. This becomes more than evident in the *Rules of Tyconius*[43] which served as a kind of systematisation of tradition to be handed on to the Middle Ages in the West. It is instructive to take a leap forward here (Tyconius was the Donatist contemporary who influenced Augustine)[44] for the purposes of demonstrating the fundamental and lasting importance of the process we have been observing.

The *Rules of Tyconius* are about ascertaining the reference. Tyconius' aim was to write a brief book of rules providing something like keys and windows to the secrets of the Law. He claims that if the logic of the rules is accepted, every closed door will be opened and light shed on every obscurity. He lists his rules, and tackles each in turn in the subsequent sections. They do not immediately seem to us to be 'rules'. They are: 'Of the Lord and his Body'; 'Of the Lord's Bipartite Body'; 'Of Promises and the Law'; 'Of Species and Genus'; 'Of Times'; 'Of Recapitulation'; 'Of the Devil and his Body'.[45]

The first section[46] suggests that reason alone discerns whether scripture is speaking of the Lord or his Body, that is, the Church. The appropriate referent is suggested by convincing argument or the sheer power of the truth which forces itself on the reader. Occasionally, Tyconius suggests there is a double referent, giving examples of passages which oscillate between being Christological

---

[43] *The Book of the Rules of Tyconius*, ed. F. C. Burkitt, *TS*, vol. 3 (Cambridge: Cambridge University Press, 1894); ET in Froehlich, *Biblical Interpretation*.
[44] See below, ch. 12, pp. 268–9, 276 and 284.
[45] Prologue: Burkitt, p. 1; ET in Froehlich, *Biblical Interpretation*, p. 104.
[46] Burkitt, pp. 1–8; ET in Froehlich, *Biblical Interpretation*, pp. 104–10.

and ecclesiological in their reference. What goes undiscussed is the
fundamental assumption that the reference of the text of Law and
Prophets needs to be ascertained if the passage is to be understood.
Also taken for granted is the use of cross-reference in exercising
rational assessment of appropriate reference. Thus Daniel calls the
Lord 'the stone hewn from the mountain', but when 'the stone
became a mountain and filled the whole earth', he is speaking of
the Lord's Body. 'Becoming a mountain' cannot apply to Christ
since he 'had this glory before the world was made' (John 17.5). On
the other hand, 'we grow up in all things into him who is the head,
Christ, from whom the whole Body . . . derives its increase . . . '(Eph.
4.15–16; slightly abbreviated here, though Tyconius quotes in full).
Adding Colossions 2.19, Tyconius argues that what grows is not
the head, for the head is the same from the beginning.[47] Instead the
Body grows from the head.

The second section,[48] so far from demonising the old Israel, finds
the Church to be the referent of scripture wherever it speaks of the
people of God, and therefore has to affirm the 'bipartite' nature of
the Church. After surveying many texts, the section concludes: 'the
Lord testifies in all of scripture that the one body of Abraham's seed
is growing and flourishing, but also perishing in all its various parts'.
We may discern a major shift of concern as attention is focussed on
the life of the Church and the Jewish issue recedes, and that shift
effects a shift also in the reading of scripture. Augustine's idea of the
Two Cities is likely to have been influenced by Tyconius. But my
point is: meaning relates to perceived reference.

Would that we might follow through the rest of Tyconius'
discussion, but the point is made. Suffice it to comment that even
the section on species and genus is about reference. Using a
rhetorical analogy, Tyconius indicates that what he is interested in
is the 'transfer' of reference, whereby one man stands for all men,
one nation for all nations and so on.

To conclude this chapter, let us briefly reflect on the close
relationship between intra- and extra-textual reference. We have
been observing an interaction of perceived reference and cross-
reference which builds up a picture of the meaning of scripture, but
this is also a construct of the world to which the text is taken to refer.

---

[47] *Rules* I.2; Burkitt, pp. 2–3; Froehlich, *Biblical Interpretation*, pp. 105–6.
[48] Burkitt, pp. 8–11; Froehlich, *Biblical Interpretation*, pp. 110–14.

In other words, for those who accept scriptural authority, the world
of the text gives meaning to the world outside the text. Conversely,
the world outside the text enables the meaning inside the text to be
discerned. We are not talking about 'eisegesis' so much as the
inevitable process of hermeneutics. An authoritative text is understood to refer to the world in which people live, and so its meaning is
bound to be received or contested in the light of the plausibility
structures of the culture which receives the text. A culture which
can conceive of the material universe as interpenetrated by another
reality, which is transcendent and spiritual, will read the reference
of scripture in those terms. That is far more significant for the
differences between ancient and modern exegesis than any
supposed 'method'. Methodologically exegesis involves many of the
same procedures.

CHAPTER 7

The sacrament of language

I

How can God be expressed in human language? Athanasius, we have already observed,[1] insisted that the Arian interpretation of the language about the Son of God was blasphemous. 'Son' was not an improper term, strictly speaking misapplied, nor were 'Word' and 'Wisdom' mere 'names' attributed to a son adopted by grace: their sense had to be understood in a manner appropriate to the divine reality to which they referred. By referring these terms to the one true Son, the 'earthly' meaning of the human language that scripture uses could be corrected, modified or, as I suggested, 'elevated'. This mode of interpretation is not literal, but neither is it allegorical. One of the less widely recognised effects of the Arian controversy was to highlight the problem of defining God. So many think of the process of doctrinal formation as a progressive definition of belief, but the argumentation, particularly with the neo-Arians like Eunomius, gainsays that. Gregory of Nyssa developed Athanasius' treatment of religious language, stressing in what can only be described as his theological spirituality the incomprehensibility of the infinite God: with no 'boundaries', external or internal, the divine Being was in principle indefinable and therefore unknowable. The Arian insistence on defining God as *agennētos* and making deductions from that was invalidated from the start.

How then was God to be spoken of at all? Gregory's answer seems to be twofold, and both involve ascribing a key role to scripture and its exegesis.[2] In the first place, he grounded all religious knowledge

---

[1] See above, ch. 2.
[2] What follows draws on material published in my 'The God of the Greeks and the Nature of Religious Language', but with the exegetical issue more to the fore.

in God's will to make the divine self known. So, like Clement and Origen before him, he regarded the language of scripture, along with the incarnation, as God's self-accommodation to the limits and constraints of human existence – indeed of human expression. In the second place, he established on this basis a symbolic theology through which some degree of theological knowledge was made possible. This rested in the 'names' revealed in scripture. Gregory believed that 'reason supplied us with but a dim and imperfect comprehension of the divine nature; but nevertheless the knowledge that we can gather from the names which piety allows us to apply to it, is sufficient for our limited capacity'.[3] Careful study of his discussion in *Contra Eunomium* Book II illuminates his understanding of religious language, and so the hermeneutical principles which undergird his exegesis.

Gregory grounds his theory of religious language in a general theory of language: all language depends upon created human speech, and the existence of different languages is a clear indication that God allowed people the freedom to invent and develop linguistic expression. This means that no human language is God-given, not even Hebrew, and the 'names' are inadequate and humanly contrived expressions. He thinks people have a right to such word-building (*onomatopoiia*).[4]

We allow ourselves the use of many diverse 'names' in regard to him, adapting them to our point of view. For whereas no one suitable word has been found to express the divine nature, we address God by many names, each by some distinctive touch adding something fresh to our notions of God – thus reaching by a variety of nomenclature to gain some glimmerings for the comprehension which we seek.[5]

Nevertheless, the 'names' are not arbitrary. They are grounded in the prior existence and activity of God. 'We do not say that the nature of things was of human invention but only their names.'[6] Religious language is grounded in what human beings perceive of

[3] *C. Eunom.* II.130; *Gregorii Nysseni opera* (Leiden: Brill), vols. I and II: *Contra Eunomium*, ed. W. Jaeger (1960), 1.263; ET *NPNF*, 2nd series, vol. v, p. 263. (ET usually my own, but page nos. are given to the ET in *NPNF* vol., which has the treatises against Eunomius entitled and enumerated according to the Oehler edn, which is quite different from Jaeger.)

[4] *C. Eunom.* II.148; Jaeger 1.298; ET *NPNF*, 2nd series, vol. v, pp. 264–5. Note how Gregory adopts the *thesis* rather than the *physis* theory of language: cf. ch. 4 above.

[5] *C. Eunom.* II.145; Jaeger 1.267; ET *NPNF*, 2nd series, vol. v, p. 264.

[6] *C. Eunom.* II.283; Jaeger 1.310; ET *NPNF*, 2nd series, vol. v, p. 279.

God's operations: through contemplation of the works of God, certain particular and appropriate names are derived. Creation and scripture guarantee that the names of God are more than a figment of the human imagination; for creation and scripture are expressive of God's will and God is truth. They provide an adequate but limited means of communication, like the gestures and signs used in communicating with the deaf. Though God has to accommodate the divine self to the limitations of human perception, God cannot be a party to deception. So when scripture honours the only-begotten with the same names as the Father, it must imply that he shares the dignity and honour of the Godhead. Furthermore, if the Word of God named God the Father, he must eternally and unchangeably have been Father, and therefore must have had a Son. In other words, Gregory accepts Athanasius' stance that the names revealed in scripture have sufficient grounding in reality, or perhaps we should say refer sufficiently meaningfully, to form a basis for theological argument.

The names are not, then, totally misleading, but they do have to be interpreted by indicating the similarities and differences between their application to human beings and to the divine: 'there is similarity of names between things human and things divine, revealing nevertheless underneath this sameness a wide difference in meanings'.[7] 'We think of human generation in one way; we surmise the divine generation in another.' For in the case of divine generation, the mind has to reject notions of sex and passion, time and place, and think simply of the Son as being eternally derived from the Father. So wide is the gulf between Creator and creature, finite and Infinite, that different attributes or names have to be associated together in order to correct one another. But that does not mean that these various names are merely metaphorical, as Eunomius would have it. Even though 'the infinity of God exceeds all the significance and comprehension that names can furnish, if such names are truly predicable of God, they should be understood in their most natural and obvious sense, though with a heightened and more glorious meaning'. Gregory is making the same point as Athanasius: this is a special kind of 'literalism', certainly not allegorism, but a serious attention to words without turning them into an idolatry.

---

[7] *C. Eunom.* I. 620–33; Jaeger I.205–8; ET *NPNF*, 2nd series, vol. v, pp. 93–4.

Gregory does make distinctions among the 'names' offered by scripture, however. Some are to be referred to God absolutely, others are relative. No doubt Origen's earlier discussion of the *epinoiai* played some part in this,[8] but again we can recognise the more formal development of a point stressed by Athanasius. The terms used 'relatively' are invariably those that relate to the *oikonomia*, to God's relationship with the world, to the divine activity in creation, providence and salvation, whether one speaks of Father or Son. The terms used 'absolutely' are those that refer to the Being of God, especially the eternal being in relationship which is the absolute nature of Father and Son. There seems to be some attempt then to distinguish degrees of symbolical usage in religious language: some terms, like Shepherd, are more metaphorical than others, like Son. Critical evaluation of scriptural terms is essential, and that critical evaluation is based on the fundamental distinction between *theologia* and *oikonomia*, between the transcendent God – in principle unknowable and yet revealed in so far as the divine will and human limits allowed – and the God whose loving plan involved the divine self in relationship with a created order quite other than the divine Being. There is no possibility of 'narrative' in *theologia*, but narrative constitutes *oikonomia*; one is in time, the other beyond time.

This, I suggest, gives us the hermeneutical backcloth for the debate about the Two Natures. A theological critique of the language of scripture is required for an appropriate reading of its terms. The crossing of the 'gulf' between the Creator and the created, the intersection of time and eternity, stretches human language to breaking point, but without breaking it: for, while the meaning of religious language can only be made clear by endless qualifications, through the names and attributes revealed by God's will, some grasp of and advance in understanding is made possible. The biblical narratives, read imaginatively rather than literally, but accorded an authority greater than the merely metaphorical, can

---

[8] This aspect of Origen's thought was not discussed earlier in this book, but is a standard topic in considering his Christology. The key passage is the *Commentary on John*, Book I, but it is found also elsewhere. For discussion see, e.g. Joseph Wilson Trigg, *Origen. The Bible and Philosophy in the Third-century Church* (London: SCM, 1985), pp. 97–8 and elsewhere; Henri Crouzel, *Origen*, ET A. S. Worrall (Edinburgh: T. & T. Clark, 1989), pp. 189ff. See also my article, 'Allegory and Atonement', *Australian Biblical Review* 35 (Festschrift vol. for E. F. Osborn, 1987), pp. 107–14.

become luminous of a divine reality beyond human expression. This is not so much allegorical as sacramental.

In one sense this standpoint emphasises the finitude of human language; in another it hints at the kind of 'infinity' found in post-modern linguistic and literary discussion. For it ultimately validates an 'expanding' or open-ended sense of ever more meaning to be discerned, the polyvalence recognised in poetry, rather than a defining or delimiting reduction of meaning to propositional definitions produced by deduction – the process so often assumed to be at work in the formation of doctrine. Language remains referential: ancient theory, whether it adopted the *physis* or *thesis* view, assumed a relationship between Word and World, Logos and Reality, and this was in some sense a representational relationship. But the Reality to which theological language refers transcends all possible linguistic expression, and so is explosive of both literalism and conceptual deciphering, thus bearing comparison with the generative character of metaphorical expression as understood in recent discussion.[9]

II

To explore the issue of language further, we may reflect on Northrop Frye's analysis in his book, *The Great Code*.[10] He distinguishes three linguistic phases: (1) the metaphoric phase in which 'this is that', where language has *mana*, power, where the name is presence, the word evokes the thing, and the utterance is poetry; (2) the metonymic phase in which 'this stands for that', a phase which spawns commentary and deduction, where metaphor is recognised as a figure of speech, and metaphorical images illustrate a conceptual argument; and then (3) the phase in which the verbal structure is 'beside' what it represents, the thing evokes the word, metaphor becomes 'mere metaphor', inductive reasoning replaces deductive, and the issue of truth and falsity, the factuality of the

---

[9] For discussions which consider the important contributions of Gadamer, Ricoeur and others, see Janet Martin Soskice, *Metaphor and Religious Language* (Oxford: Clarendon, 1985); Sallie McFague, *Metaphorical Theology. Models of God in Religious Language* (London: SCM, 1983); Joel Weinsheimer, 'Metaphor as a Metaphor of Understanding', in *Philosophical Hermeneutics and Literary Theory*; etc.

[10] *The Great Code. The Bible and Literature* (New York and London: Harcourt Brace Jovanovich Publishers, 1981).

statement, has primacy. The last is now dominant, he suggests, and the primary function of literature, more particularly of poetry, is to keep re-creating the first, or metaphorical, phase of language during the domination of the later phases.

Though recognising that the phases are not exactly historically successive, he would place much of the Bible in phase 1, and Christian doctrine in phase 2. What I suggest is that the understanding of language developed by Athanasius and Gregory in the heat of the Arian controversy lies between phase 1 and phase 2. Language, in the case of God, has to be distinguished from its referent whose Being transcends linguistic capacities: we are no longer in phase 1. But language is more than merely metaphorical, more than simply analogy. It is the sacramental vehicle of truth, permitting the expression of eternal Being in temporal narrative which is luminous. The Word became flesh; the word evokes the presence. We are held in a kind of tensive balance between phase 2, which is where the Arians wished to settle, and phase 1, which the biblical text demanded.

It is perhaps the poetry of Ephrem Syrus which illuminates this anti-Arian hermeneutic best.[11] Athanasius and Ephrem apparently died within a month of each other in 373. So Ephrem also lived through the years of the Arian controversy, and Syrian Christianity was no less affected. Ephrem too wrote against heresies. Ephrem too recognised the gulf, or 'chasm', between Creator and created as a fundamental theological, and therefore hermeneutical, principle. He has a horror of investigation or 'prying into' God's nature, and the grounds of this recall Gregory of Nyssa. The problem is that the investigator becomes the 'container' of what is investigated, so a 'knowledge which is capable of containing the Omniscient is greater than Him'.[12] As for Gregory, God's incomprehensibility is grounded in the divine infinity, or uncontainability.

---

[11] During the lectures in Oxford, I was challenged by Sebastian Brock to include Ephrem in my consideration of patristic exegesis. For that challenge I am grateful, since looking at Ephrem has assisted my reflections very considerably. My rusty smattering of Syriac has scarcely been equal to the task; I am largely dependent on Sebastian's own work for access to the relevant material, and to this reference is made here. But I am happy to further his interest in getting Ephrem more widely known since I believe this has for me enabled a return to the Greek exegetical tradition with fresh eyes. His suggestion of similarities with the Cappadocians is certainly borne out.

[12] *Faith* 9.16; quoted in Sebastian Brock, *The Luminous Eye* (Rome: Centre for Indian and Inter-Religious Studies, 1985), p. 13.

Like Gregory, Ephrem understands that knowledge of God is only possible because the hidden One has chosen self-revelation.

Had God not wished to disclose himself to us

there would not have been anything in creation able to elucidate anything at all about him.[13]

The process of divine self-revelation takes place primarily, of course, through the incarnation itself, but also through types and symbols which are present in both nature and scripture, and, as Gregory insisted, through the 'names' or metaphors which God allows to be used to describe the divine self in scripture. God clothes himself in human language; he 'puts on' names, as Ephrem puts it.

> Let us give thanks to God who clothed Himself in the names of
>   the body's various parts:
> Scripture refers to His 'ears', to teach us that He listens to us;
> it speaks of His 'eyes', to show that He sees us.
> It was just the names of such things that He put on,
> and, although in His true Being there is no wrath or regret,
> yet He put on these names too because of our weakness.
>
> We should realize that, had He not put on the names
> of such things, it would not have been possible for Him
> to speak with us humans. By means of what belongs to us did he
>   draw close to us:
> He clothed Himself in our language, so that He might clothe us
> in His mode of life. He asked for our form and put this on,
> and then, as a father with his children, He spoke with our
>   childish state.[14]

The repeated refrain of this hymn is: 'Blessed is He who has appeared to our human race under so many metaphors.' In the next stanzas Ephrem shows that he does not accept that God literally put on 'our metaphors', or that he actually took them off: when wearing them, he is at the same time stripped of them. He keeps adopting them and stripping them off according to what is beneficial, so telling us that the metaphor does not apply to his true Being, because that Being is hidden. A humorous image soon appears: to teach a parrot to speak, a person hides behind a mirror, so deceiving the bird into thinking it is conversing with one of its own kind. The

---

[13] *Faith* 44.7; quoted in Brock, *Luminous Eye*, p. 26.
[14] *Faith* 31; quoted in Brock, *Luminous Eye*, pp. 43ff.

divine Being in his love bent down from on high and acquired from us our own habits, labouring by every means to turn all to himself. In fact, having put on our weakness, he then 'turned round and clothed us in the names of his Majesty'.[15]

So are we dealing here with an understanding of language which is simply metonymic, the metaphors standing for, or illustrating, something other rather than expressive of reality? As we shall see, Ephrem's poetic usage precludes such a conclusion, and his theory, we find, is similar to that of Gregory.

> God has names that are perfect and exact,
> and he has names that are borrowed and transient.[16]

This parallels Gregory's distinction between those names which are absolute, which we might call true metaphors, metaphoric in Frye's phase-1 sense, and those which are relative, metonymic or illustrative metaphors. Indeed, Ephrem, like Gregory, is reminiscent of Origen in his treatment of scriptural language. Whereas anger and repentance are not properly attributed to the divine nature, Being, Creator, Father, Son and Holy Spirit, even King, are names that properly apply only to God, even though they belong to human language. Applied to human beings, they are 'borrowed names', for there is only one true Father and one true Son. The true use remains with God, the likeness applies to us.

> Accordingly, in His mercy, He provided for the discerning
> among His creatures
> His various names – not to be investigated, but to be savoured
> and enjoyed.
> So, brethren, let prying dry up and let us multiply prayers,
> for though He is not related to us, He is as though of our race,
> and though He is utterly separate, yet He is over all and in all.[17]

There are then 'perfect names', and God can only be reached by these holy and perfect names, especially those of Father, Son and Holy Spirit. The important thing is not to pry further into their Persons, but just to meditate on their names. I suggest that, as in Gregory's case, we are here witnessing the attempt to avoid the unacceptable consequences of treating metaphor literally, while

---

[15] *Faith* 54.8; quoted in Brock, *Luminous Eye*, p. 45.
[16] *Faith* 44.2; quoted in Brock, *Luminous Eye*, p. 45.
[17] *Faith* 63.9–11; quoted in Brock, *Luminous Eye*, p. 47.

being true to the poetic and truly metaphoric nature of biblical language. We are between phases 1 and 2 on Frye's scale: language is more than analogy, less than magic, most like sacrament. Words and images are neither literal nor allegorical, metaphorical but not merely metaphorical, symbolic but not merely symbolic, for the names and metaphors are 'ikons' which both reveal and conceal.

In the light of such conclusions concerning names and metaphors, we turn to the types and symbols Ephrem saw present in nature and scripture. It is of course to scripture that we need to turn our attention primarily, but first consider one from nature:

> A bird grows up in three stages
> from womb to egg, then to the nest where it sings;
> and once it is fully grown it flies in the air,
> opening its wings in the symbol of the Cross.
> But if the bird gathers its wings,
> thus denying the extended symbol of the Cross,
> then the air too will deny the bird:
> the air will not carry the bird
> unless its wings confess the Cross.[18]

This example from nature suggests a view of typology rather different from the standard one: the *typos* is more to do with the mimetic 'impress' than to do with recapitulating a past event of history. Through Ephrem we may initiate a shift in the way we understand typology, and the significance we attribute to the long tradition of typological interpretation.[19]

It is possible to read some of Ephrem's types in the way Melito of Sardis, for example, has been read:[20]

> Listen to the simple symbols that concern the Passover,
> and to the double achievements of this our Passover.
> With the Passover lamb there took place for the Jewish people
> an Exodus from Egypt, and not an entry.

> So with the True Lamb there took place for the Gentiles
> an Exodus from Error, and not an entry.
> With the Living Lamb there was a further Exodus too,
> for the dead from Sheol, as from Egypt.[21]

---

[18] *Faith* 18.2, 6; quoted in Brock, *Luminous Eye*, pp. 60 and 43.
[19] See my article, 'Typology'. This is reflected in remarks made below in ch. 9, pp. 192–201.
[20] For fuller discussion of Melito, see ch. 9 below, pp. 193ff.
[21] *Unleavened Bread* 3.5–8; quoted in Brock, *Luminous Eye*, p. 41.

One event fulfilled the other – indeed, in Ephrem's view this type was so precise that

On the tenth of Nisan . . . when the Passover lamb was confined, our Lord was conceived, and on the fourteenth, when it was slaughtered, He whom the lamb symbolised was crucified.[22]

In other words, as Brock comments, 'Christ, the "true Passover lamb", enters Mary's womb on 10th Nisan, in conformity with the law of Exodus 12.3.'

It is also possible to read some of Ephrem's types as Irenaeus has been read:[23]

> Just as from the small womb of Eve's ear
> Death entered in and was poured out,
> So through a new ear, that was Mary's,
> Life entered and was poured out.
> In the month of Nisan our Lord repaid
> the debts of that first Adam:
> He gave his sweat in Nisan in exchange for Adam's sweat,
> the Cross, in exchange for Adam's Tree.[24]

What is assumed to be an event at the beginning of history is recapitulated and reversed in its antitype.

> He gave his hands to be pierced by the nails
> in place of the hand that had plucked the fruit;
> He was struck on the cheek in the judgement hall
> in return for that mouth that had devoured in Eden.
> Because Adam had let slip his foot
> they pierced his feet.

But the lines which surround that last passage indicate that Ephrem's typology is not simply to be understood in terms of a historical-eschatological model. The Lord's living death was to give life to Adam, and 'we' are Adam:

---

[22] *Commentary on Exodus* 12.2–3; quoted in Brock, *Luminous Eye*, p. 87.

[23] Irenaeus' theology of 'recapitulation' is not given particular treatment here, but it is clearly earthed in a series of perceived 'types': Adam and Christ, Eve and Mary, tree and cross, etc. Christ 'replays' the story of fall and so achieves redemption. See standard histories of doctrine, G. Wingren, *Man and Incarnation. A Study in the Biblical Theology of Irenaeus*, ET R. Mackenzie (Edinburgh and London: Oliver & Boyd, 1959), and Denis Minns OP, *Irenaeus* (London: Geoffrey Chapman, 1994).

[24] *Church* 49.7; 51.8; quoted in Brock, *Luminous Eye*, p. 19.

Our Lord was stripped naked so that we be might clothed in modesty;
with gall and vinegar He made sweet
that bitter venom that the serpent had poured into humankind.[25]

It is in the *Hymns on Paradise* that we can observe the strangely
atemporal fusion of fall and redemption, and the deep sense that the
stories in fusion constitute the story of 'everyman'. Furthermore,
this story gives meaning to all other stories, stories which are types
of this fundamental story. In *Hymn XIII* for example, Ephrem speaks
of God creating the fountainhead of delights, a garden full of glory,
given to Adam, and then continues:

> The king of Babylon resembled
>   Adam king of the universe:
> Both rose up against the one Lord
>   and were brought low;
> He made them outlaws,
>   casting them afar.
> Who can fail to weep,
>   seeing that these free-born kings
> preferred slavery
>   and servitude.
> Blessed is He who released us
>   so that His image might no longer be in bondage.[26]

Then Ephrem turns to David, who wept for Adam and his fall, his
going astray and becoming like a beast in the abode of wild animals;
but

> In that king
>   did God depict Adam:
> since he provoked God by his exercise of kingship,
>   God stripped him of his kingship.
> The Just One was angry and cast him out
>   into the region of wild beasts;
> he dwelt there with them
>   in the wilderness
> and only when he repented did he return
>   to his former abode and kingship.
> Blessed is He who has thus taught us to repent
>   so that we too may return to Paradise.

---

[25] *Nisibis* 36.1; quoted in Brock, *Luminous Eye*, p. 20.
[26] *Hymns on Paradise* XIII.4; ET *St Ephrem. Hymns on Paradise*, introd. and trans. Sebastian Brock
(New York: St Vladimir's Seminary Press, 1990), p. 170.

> Because it was not easy
> for us to see our fallen state –
> how and whence we had fallen
> at the very outset –
> He depicted it all together
> in that king,
> portraying in our fall
> his fall,
> and portraying our return
> in his repentant return.
> Praise to Him who delineated
> this likeness for the repentant.[27]

As the hymn goes on, not only is Adam a type of David, and both are types of 'us', but Adam is a type of Samson, too, who falls, outwitted by Satan, but who is also a type of Christ whose death 'returned us to our heritage'.[28] Jonah and Joseph also exemplify the pattern of being cast out and rescued. Time and person are fused into exemplars of a single human narrative.

Other examples could be given, but this will suffice. In his introduction, Brock draws attention to the fact that Paradise, for Ephrem, is both primordial and eschatological, but also transcendent, located outside time and space, entered by resurrection, yet anticipated on earth in the Church and the lives of saints. Elsewhere he notes how traditional types like the Passover are fused not only with the cross but with the nativity, and how some of Ephrem's key imagery like that of the 'Robe of Glory' can 'link together in a dynamic fashion the whole of salvation history'.[29] But, I would add, this salvation history is not like our sort of history. The almost cinematographic way in which one exemplar or narrative fades into another belies a purely linear historical understanding of this typology, and the tension between the presence and transcendence, past, future and eternity of Paradise, provides a model for the interpenetration of types and symbols in Ephrem's poetry.

Two of Brock's observations concerning Ephrem's thought give us the clue to what is happening: one is his analysis of Ephrem's understanding of 'two times', what he calls 'ordinary time' and 'sacred time'. Ordinary time is linear and successive, but in liturgical time

---

[27] *Hymns on Paradise* XIII.5–7; ET in Brock, *Hymns*, pp. 170–1.
[28] *Hymns on Paradise* XIII.13; ET in Brock, *Hymns*, p. 173.
[29] Brock, *Hymns*, Introd. pp. 66–7.

the worshipper steps into the 'eternal now' where no 'before' and 'after' is known. Ephrem's 'types' belong to 'sacred time'. The other is his reference to 'the freedom with which, in Semitic thought, the individual can merge into the collective, and the collective into the individual'.[30] The collocation of these two elements means that there is little distinction between the kind of type drawn from nature and the kind of type drawn from the scriptural narratives. These narratives may succeed one another – must indeed succeed one another in a time-bound universe; but, like the bird (which is of course any bird and every bird) which represents the sign of the cross as it flies, so they represent in their particularity a universal and eternal human story which makes sense of each person's story. This confirms the view that it is not the 'historical event' as such which makes typology what it is; it is the sense of recapitulation, the 'impress' of one narrative or symbol on another, 'fulfilling' it and so giving it meaning.

III

For the moment we turn from Ephrem to reconsider, in the light of this part of our explorations, the nature of typology in the Christian tradition of exegesis.

'Typology' is a modern construct.[31] Ancient exegetes did not distinguish between typology and allegory, and it is often difficult to make the distinction, the one shading into the other all too easily. Allegory was often required to turn a scriptural oracle into a prophecy; allegory was also required to make a 'type' prophetic in its various respects. The modern affirmation of typology as distinct from allegory,[32] an affirmation which requires the historical reality of an event as a foreshadowing of another event, its 'antitype', is

---

30 Brock, *Luminous Eye*, p. 17. If that description is understood in terms of the old notion of 'corporate personality', it might be challenged; see John Rogerson, 'The Hebrew Conception of Corporate Personality: A Re-examination', *JTS* NS 21 (1970), pp. 1–16. However, I would suggest that this merging is also a 'liturgical' feature found in the 'I' of Psalms and hymns shared by a congregation. Rogerson's article does not exclude the common experience of ambiguity with respect to the individual and the collective in liturgical texts such as the biblical Psalms and later Christian hymns.

31 See below, ch. 9 note 20.

32 Associated with Jean Daniélou, *From Shadows to Reality: Studies in the Biblical Typology of the Fathers*, and G. W. H. Lampe and K. J. Woollcombe, *Essays in Typology*. See further ch. 9, pp. 192–6.

born of modern historical consciousness, and has no basis in the patristic material.

What the patristic texts describe as a 'type' is a mimetic 'impress' or figure in the narrative or action described: Moses' uplifted arms at the battle against Amalek[33] represent the cross in the same way as the outstretched wings of Ephrem's bird. Usually types and anti-types contribute to the prophetic understanding of scripture, and so past narrative points to present fulfilment, or present instance is prophetic of future reality. To that extent 'types' usually relate to the Christian sense of a providential history leading to a denoue-ment, but so did allegory, by facilitating the prophetic reading of texts. The word *typos* may be used for any 'model' or 'pattern' or 'parable' foreshadowing its fulfilment, whether an event or an oft-repeated ritual. It is not its character as historical event which makes a 'type'; what matters is its mimetic quality. Later, we will explore both the *Epistle of Barnabas* and Melito's *Peri Pascha*, and what we will find is a kind of interillumination as mimetic details in the narrative represent or signify what they were taken to prophesy.[34]

Typology is an important theme in Northrop Frye's literary approach to the Bible, *The Great Code*; his treatment of it has been taken up and explored further by a disciple of his, the Hungarian Tibor Fabiny.[35] In the introduction to his book, *The Lion and the Lamb*, Fabiny discusses what typology is. Though he states that he would regard typology as indicating a complex range of things, he is unfortunately misled by theologians into treating as traditional the use of the word typology when

certain real or supposedly historical events, persons or 'things' in the Old Testament were seen as being, in addition, prefigurative symbols – that is, 'types' of which the 'fulfilment' or 'reality' was given in the New Testament in the form of so-called 'antitypes'.[36]

This emphasis on history tends to dominate his discussion of typology in the Bible, and indeed, though often his material gainsays it, his fascinating examination of mediaeval art as a pictorial

---

[33] A 'type' found in the *Epistle of Barnabas*, and repeated regularly in patristic literature.
[34] See below, chs. 9 and 10.
[35] Fabiny held a Northrop Frye Fellowship, and has produced a book with typology as its theme, *The Lion and the Lamb, Figuralism and Fulfilment in the Bible, Art and Literature* (Studies in Religion and Literature, London: Macmillan, 1992).
[36] Ibid., p. 2.

expression of traditional types. It is when he comes to explore typology in literature that he allows himself to be freed of this distraction, and to discover another way of speaking of typology as a hermeneutical device.

The important shift he makes, one facilitated by recent emphasis on reader reception, is from the event behind the text to the text itself. Adapting a sentence of Auerbach's, he suggests that

Figural interpretation establishes a connection between two textual events or persons, the first of which signifies not only itself but also the second, while the second encompasses or fulfils the first.[37]

Typology thus becomes a form of intertextuality, the biblical text the 'architext',[38] the literary text a 'supertext'. The important point is that both texts are what he calls 'real'. One is not the pretext for the other.[39] Allegory involves one text being the pretext for the other, whereas typology gives both their integrity and validity, the architext retaining its own autonomy and yet the texts resonating together as the supertext fulfils or re-creates the architext. What he calls 'postfiguration' means that the supertext carries a surplus of meaning which is gained from the architext. Thus the important element in a 'type' is its integrity, its 'reality' whether as event or simply as narrative or character or act, its autonomy, and yet its capacity significantly, often prophetically, to mirror another event or narrative or character or act. Typology permits both setting side by side, as in the pictorial representations in the mediaeval *Biblia Pauperum*, and poetic superimposing, as in Ephrem's poetry.

Prophecy and fulfilment involve a successive time-frame, but superimposition shifts the 'type' into a different frame, what Brock called 'sacred' or liturgical time, suggesting a universal or eternal truth played out in time, time and again. Ephrem allows us to draw

---

[37] Ibid., p. 114. Fabiny has added the word 'textual'; he acknowledges the quotation as from Erich Auerbach, 'Figura', trans. Ralph Manheim, in *Scenes from Drama of European Literature* (New York: Merridian, 1959; German original in *Archivum Romanicum*, 1938).

[38] Here Fabiny acknowledges indebtedness to Julia Kristeva and Gerard Genette, notable contributors to twentieth-century literary theory.

[39] By contrast, Harold Bloom (*Ruin the Sacred Truths. Poetry and Belief from the Bible to the Present* (Cambridge, Mass. and London: Harvard University Press, 1987/89), p. 43) protests against Auerbach that 'in merest fact, and so in history, no text can fulfil another, except through some self-serving caricature of the earlier text by the later. To argue otherwise is to indulge in a dangerous idealization of the relationship between literary texts.' This would seem to presuppose that supersession is inevitable. That that often is the result of typology cannot be gainsaid, but need it be?

out implications from Frye's great study which neither he nor
Fabiny articulated. The characteristic of much Christian typological
narrative is that the linear sequence of particular narratives in time
is intersected by the cycle of universal, timeless myth.

Frye explored not only the fate of metaphor in his three phases,
but also that of *mythos*, which he wishes to understand in its proper
sense of 'significant story'. Story belongs to phase 1, phase 2 con-
ceptualises sequence and causality, dressing it in narrative, and
phase 3 distinguishes history from story, and is concerned with the
'facts', not with narrative truth. A myth in phase 1 is a sacred story
with special significance and import; in phase 3 it becomes 'not
really true'. Frye takes historico-critics to task for misreading the
Bible: 'If anything historically true is in the Bible, it is not there
because it is historically true, but for different reasons. The reasons
have to do with spiritual profundity or significance.'[40]

The boundary between the historical and the 'mythical' is not
clearly drawn in the Bible, he suggests, and credibility is not an
issue. The story of Doubting Thomas shows that the more trust-
worthy the evidence, the more misleading it is. History is irrelevant,
but story is not. The 'symbolic Egypt' is important not the
historical Egypt, important to the exiles who saw the exodus as type
of their return, important to Christians who saw the Passover as
type of Christ, important to the slaves of North America who
sang,

> Go down, Moses,
> Way down in Egypt land,
> Tell old Pharaoh,
> Let my people go.

'The symbolic Egypt is not in history: it extends over past, present
and future',[41] writes Frye. 'Myth redeems history: assigns it to its
real place in the human panorama.'[42]

So Frye argues that the narrative of the Bible is much nearer to
being a 'poetic universal narrative' rather than a 'particular
historical one'. Yet when he comes to speak of typology[43] he defines
it as a 'figure of speech that moves in time' and which involves a
theory of history. Like causality it requires sequence, though it

---

[40] Frye, *The Great Code*, p. 55.   [41] Ibid., p. 49.
[42] Ibid., p. 50.   [43] Ibid., pp. 80–3.

differs from causality in being future-directed rather than past-directed in its discernment of meaning: its meaning lies in vision, hope and faith. In the Bible, mythology is made diachronic, by contrast with the synchronic mythology of most other religions. But Ephrem, I suggest, encourages us to recognise that typology works at the intersection of the synchronic with the diachronic. Typology does not simply operate in the linear-eschatological time-frame, nor should we be tempted to bring back the historicity of event, as Fabiny does. The particularities of the earthly realm, whether those of nature or of scripture, become luminous of a hidden eternal reality.

In Ephrem, 'types', like symbols, become windows through bearing the 'impress' of eternal truth, which is what the word 'type' means.

> Joyfully did I embark
>   on the tale of Paradise –
> a tale that is short to read
>   but rich to explore.
> My tongue read the story's
>   outward narrative,
> while my intellect took wing
>   and soared upward in awe
> as it perceived the splendour of Paradise –
>   not indeed as it really is,
> but insofar as humanity
>   is granted to comprehend it.[44]

> A symbol of the divisions
>   in that Garden of Life
> did Moses trace out in the Ark
>   and on Mount Sinai too;
> he depicted for us the types of Paradise
>   with all its arrangements:
> harmonious, fair and desirable
>   in all things –
> in its height, its beauty,
>   its fragrance, and its different species.
> Here is the harbour of all riches,
>   whereby the Church is depicted.[45]

[44] *Hymns on Paradise* I.3; ET in Brock, *Hymns*, p. 78.
[45] *Hymns on Paradise* II.13; ET in Brock, *Hymns*, p. 89.

So Ephrem has helped us to notice two important features of typology: (1) 'Types' are often in narrative, but not just narrative, and certainly not just treated as historical event. Often they are more like what we would call symbols, though the borders of symbol and narrative are often blurred. (2) 'Types' belong to sacred time, and so they concur, they have a curious simultaneity as well as a fulfilment pattern. The womb of Jordan and the womb of Mary meld into one another; in them the purity made possible in Christ by baptism is conceived.[46] Mary and Eve in their symbols resemble a body one of whose eyes is blind and darkened, the other clear and bright providing light for the whole, and somehow that symbolises the condition of the whole world and each individual.[47] Ephrem speaks of the hidden power of the symbols and types, and our analysis would suggest that his poetic instinct means that he is close to Frye's phase 1 in his use of myth as of metaphor. His language and his symbols evoke presence, yet this is not quite the naivety of phase 1, for it is the presence of a mystery which cannot be reduced to words or narratives.

Ephrem also confirms for us that it is not for nothing that Fabiny speaks of fulfilment as to do with plenitude of meaning discovered in relationship with previous narrative. For Ephrem scripture is like a fountain and a treasury of riches: in comprehending a single utterance, we leave behind far more than we take from it, like thirsty people drinking from a fountain; anyone who encounters scripture should not think that the single one of its riches that he has found is the only one to exist.[48] Nor is it irrelevant to recall Fabiny's point that the previous narrative has its own autonomy and integrity, irrespective of the surplus discovered by typology. The plenitude of meaning in Ephrem arises from the contemplation of what I would call 'ikonic' relationships. Story and symbol alike are more than a pretext for the meaning with which they are invested. We are not dealing with story-myth that finds its true meaning in a conceptual or argumentative translation, which is Frye's way of distinguishing allegory, a feature of phase 2. As I have argued, we are dealing with a sacramental use of language that lies somewhere between Frye's two first phases.

---

[46] Brock, *Luminous Eye*, p. 71.
[47] Ibid., pp. 53ff.   [48] Ibid., pp. 35–6.

IV

In the next chapter, we shall take up again the issue of distinguishing allegory and typology as we examine the Antiochene reaction to
the Origenist tradition in the fourth century. Meanwhile, let me
refer back to the first part of this chapter, and observe that what we
have discovered is that Ephrem's understanding of types and
symbols is entirely coherent with his understanding of names and
metaphors. Language, whether verbal or narrative, is sacramental.
To see its significance involves contemplative insight. Scripture,
along with nature, the incarnation, baptism and eucharist, has the
quality of witness, revealing yet concealing the hidden reality to
which it points, evoking the powerful presence of transcendent
mystery. This contemplative insight is perhaps best illustrated by
Ephrem's five hymns on the Pearl: in scripture the pearl of great
price is a parable of the kingdom, but Ephrem takes a pearl in his
hand and sees in it symbols, images, types, and it becomes a fountain
from which he drinks the mysteries of the Son, of the Church, of
Mary, of the cross, of faith, of truth, of baptism and eucharist. The
multifaceted brightness of the pearl speaks of the incomprehensible
light of Christ, and as the daughter of the sea she speaks of the
crossing of the Red Sea and of Jonah.[49] Types, symbols and
metaphors are melded together through contemplative association.

Most important is the element of worship. It is because of the
worship context that the language of scripture thus becomes sacramental. Let us return to the Greek tradition. In the context of
worship, John Chrysostom is preaching. His theme is God's incomprehensibility,[50] his object an attack on the blasphemy of Arianism.
He begins with the well-known text from 1 Corinthians 13: 'we know
in part, we see in a glass darkly'. Knowledge is limited, he says; I
know God is present everywhere, and that he is without beginning
and eternal, but how I know not. Reason cannot know how God's
Being is. Prophets and Psalmists confess, 'Your knowledge is too
wonderful for me' (Ps. 139.6). Chrysostom draws a picture of the

---

[49] Ibid., pp. 83ff. The five hymns on the Pearl are found in the hymn cycle on Faith.
[50] The text of Chrysostom's homilies on the incomprehensibility of God is in *SC*: *Sur
l'incomprehensibilité de Dieu* (Introd. J. Daniélou, text and notes, A.-M. Malingrey, trans.
R. Flacelière, 1970); ET in *FC*. What follows is based on the first of this series of homilies. A
slightly fuller treatment is found in my article 'God: An Essay in Patristic Theology', *The
Modern Churchman* 29 (1981), pp. 149–65.

Psalmist looking down from a cliff-top onto the boundless and vast ocean of God's wisdom and going dizzy with vertigo. The Psalmist is at a loss, confused, dizzy: 'If I go up to heaven you are there; if I go down to hell, you are there' (Ps. 139.8).

The Psalmist also says, 'You have shown me the hidden secrets of your wisdom' (Ps. 50.8 LXX); but though knowing these secrets he also confesses that God's understanding is beyond measure. Chrysostom turns again to Paul: 'O the depth of the riches of the wisdom and knowledge of God. His judgements are unsearchable, his ways past finding out' (Rom. 11.33). So even God's providential activities are only partially discernible, and the human heart has not conceived what God has prepared for those who love him (1 Cor. 2.9). His peace passes all understanding (Phil. 4.7). His grace is inexpressible (2 Cor. 9.15). 'If all that is beyond our grasp, how can God be comprehensible?' asks Chrysostom. We know in part, not his essential Being but his *oikonomia*.

Here is a remarkably sensitive appeal to scripture. It is true that philosophical terms are drawn into a process of exegetical deduction, yet the outcome is surely a valid expression of the intent of scripture – for the aim is to evoke wonder and worship. This is enhanced by the exploitation of indirect and evocative language borrowed from the Psalms.

To turn to Chrysostom's *Homilies on the Psalms* is to discover the same atmosphere, but now in a non-polemical context. According to the *Homily on Psalm 9*,[51] God is worshipped in song and celebration. It is impossible to see God – so the prophet composes songs, through his songs communicating with God, kindling his own desire, seeming to see him, and even through singing songs and hymns, kindling the desire of many others. The Psalmist is like a lover; for lovers are always like this – singing love-songs when they cannot see the loved one. Praise comes from thinking the things of God – his wonders, what happens day by day to individuals, to people in general, the marvels of creation. The worshipper gets material from everything – heaven, earth, air, beasts, seeds, plants, the Law, grace – there is a whole sea of blessings to be told.

The fundamental principle in this homily, as in the *Homily on Psalm 42*[52] where the image of the lover drooling over everything connected with the loved one is beautifully exploited, is that praise

---

[51] Migne, *PG* 55.121–40. [52] Migne, *PG* 55.155–67.

requires elusiveness, yet scripture can evoke love. Catalogues of texts in this homily are summarised in these phrases:

God speaks of the love of birds for their young, the love of fathers for their children, the tenderness of mothers, not because he only loves like a mother loves her child, but because we have no greater proofs of love than these examples.

The burden of this chapter has been that, in the fourth century, circumstances, coupled with the traditions of the Church's worship, produced the articulation of an understanding of scriptural language concerning the divine which was not allegorical or merely metaphorical, and, despite the intellectual pressures, not metonymic on the one hand, nor literal on the other. Maybe it was the Arian desire to specify the nature of religious language in such unequivocal definitions that earned them the charge of borrowing too much philosophy. The Church's language – including that of someone like Cyril of Jerusalem in his Catechetical lectures[53] and despite the fact that his position in the fourth-century controversies was distinctly ambiguous – was sacramental in a way that acknowledged the poverty of human language to express the divine reality, yet retained the evocative power of the true metaphor. This was a linguistic possibility, I suggest, because the structure of Christian thought revolved around the notion of a transcendent God choosing to accommodate the divine self to the limitations of the human condition in incarnation and eucharist. Scriptural language, they recognised, belonged to the same fundamental pattern.

---

[53] *Cat. orat.* VI and IX; text in Migne, *PG* 33.331–1059; ET: Leo P. McCauley and Anthony A. Stephenson, *Catecheses* (2 vols. *FC*, 1968, 1970).

CHAPTER 8

Allēgoria *and* theōria

I

Towards the end of the last chapter, we began discussing how a 'sacramental' understanding of language might relate to the distinction between typology and allegory. Chapter 11 will show how ultimately typology and allegory contribute to Christian *mimēsis*, or figural representation, both being so interwoven that a firm differentiation is very hard to make. But meanwhile we must consider the explicitly exegetical debate which emerged in the fourth century, and which is often characterised in terms of a difference between typological and allegorical exegesis – I refer of course to the Antiochene reaction against Alexandrian allegory.[1]

Northrop Frye, whose book *The Great Code* provided some useful clues for us in the last chapter, speaks of allegory arising when the story-myth finds its true meaning in a conceptual or argumentative translation.[2] Allegory ceases to be story and becomes propositional; typology, on the other hand, retains the narrative and sequence. Building on Frye, we observed that by typological exegesis, meaning is discovered in 'universal' narrative patterns played out in past, present and future, the intersection of particular story and story-type. We also found non-narrative types, signs and symbols like the bird signing the cross as it flies, and Moses' arms doing likewise at the battle with Amalek. We decided that the important thing was the mimetic or ikonic quality of symbol or story. What I now propose

---

[1] Since producing this chapter I have discussed the matter further at the Oxford Patristic Conference, 1995. The paper, entitled 'The Fourth-Century Reaction against Allegory', will be published in *Studia Patristica*.

[2] Frye, *The Great Code*, p. 85.

is a distinction between ikonic and symbolic *mimēsis*,[3] associating the first with Antiochene exegesis, the second with Alexandrian allegory. The distinction lies in a different perception of how the text related to that to which it was taken to refer: what I call ikonic exegesis requires a mirroring of the supposed deeper meaning in the text taken as a coherent whole, whereas allegory involves using words as symbols or tokens, arbitrarily referring to other realities by application of a code, and so destroying the narrative, or surface, coherence of the text. This would account for the Antiochene acceptance of typology even as allegory was criticised and rejected.

This would appear to bear out Northrop Frye's way of making the distinction. Typology remains true to the narrative, allegory translates narrative into propositions. Unfortunately it is not quite as simple as that. Both sides equally turned out propositional translations:[4] Origen took the story of Christ's feeding the multitude as symbolical of spiritual feeding.[5] The desert place represented the desert condition of the masses without the Law and the Word of God, and the disciples were given power to nourish the crowds with rational food. The five loaves and two fish symbolised scripture and the Logos. Clearly the items in the story have become tokens, the text a code to be cracked. Chrysostom, on the other hand,[6] turned the story into proofs of dogma and moral lessons – Christ looked up to heaven to prove he is of the Father, and he used the loaves and fish, rather than creating food out of nothing, to stop the mouths of dualistic heretics like Marcion and Manichaeus. He let the crowds become hungry and only gave them loaves and fish, equally distributed, to teach the crowd humility, temperance and charity, and to have all things in common. He wanted to be sure they did not become slaves to the belly . . . This is not exactly typology, and it certainly lacks the imaginative richness of the sacramental language of Ephrem. It is intellectualising, and no less propositional than Origen's allegory. Doctrinal and moral lessons are to be drawn from the text, as in the allegorical tradition. What is different is the

---

[3] Here the terms 'ikon' and 'symbol' are used quite specifically, whereas in the previous paragraph 'signs' and 'symbols' were used in Ephrem's way as loosely corresponding. See further the definitions offered in ch. 9, pp. 210ff, and the discussion in note 53 of that chapter.

[4] The following example I used in my article 'Rhetorical Schools'; it is repeated as providing a particularly clear contrast.

[5] *Comm. Matt.* xi; *GCS* vol. x, pp. 34ff.; ET *ANCL*, addit. vol., pp. 431ff.

[6] *Hom. in Matt.* xlix on Matt.14.19; Migne, *PG* 58.496–7; ET *NPNF*, 1st series, vol. x, pp. 303ff.

assumption that the narrative provides a kind of 'mirror' which images the true understanding, rather than the words of the text providing a code to be cracked.

Confirmation of Antiochene interest in the narrative coherence of the text can be found if we examine the first anti-allegorical treatise, that of Eustathius *On the Witch of Endor*.[7] Eustathius begins by attacking Origen for paying attention to *onomata* (names, terms), not *pragmata* (deeds, things).[8] His ensuing discussion shows that his concern is with a lexical approach, treating words as tokens, by contrast with an approach which takes the thrust of the narrative seriously.

It appears that Origen had made certain deductions about the resurrection on the basis of the statement that the witch summoned up Samuel from Hades. Eustathius argues that only God can raise up the dead, therefore the witch cannot have done it, and Samuel was not raised at all. This is deductive argument on both sides, with a certain appeal on Eustathius' part to a priori theological consider-ations. Ironically, Origen would seem to have taken the story more literally than Eustathius.[9] Eustathius goes on to explain, however, that the devil used the witch to play upon the mad mind of Saul and induce him to believe that he saw Samuel,[10] displaying a reading of the story which respects its narrative coherence. According to Eustathius, the thrust of the whole tells against Origen's view.

The entire treatise is in fact a series of rationalistic arguments, bolstered by scriptural parallels, to prove Origen's lexical reading of the text is on the wrong lines, and so everything he deduces from it is unacceptable. There is no statement anywhere that Saul actually saw Samuel, Eustathius points out – he only thinks he did. Scriptures are cited to show that the devil is a consummate liar, and can even turn himself into an angel of light. To the objection that it cannot have been the devil because the prophecy was true, Eustathius replies that the prophecy was true only in so far as prophetic words of Samuel during his lifetime were quoted: the prediction of the deaths next day of Saul and Jonathan was wrong in

---

[7] Migne, *PG* 18.613–73. The argument that follows is summarised from my article, 'Rhetorical Schools'.

[8] *De engastrimytho* 1; Migne, *PG* 18.618.

[9] Cf. Patricia Cox, 'Origen and the Witch of Endor: Toward an Iconoclastic Typology', *Anglican Theological Review* 66 (1984), pp. 137–47.

[10] *De engastrimytho* 7; Migne, *PG* 18.625.

detail, because if you look at the text closely, it must have been the day after, and it was Saul and his three sons who actually died on the field of battle, not just Saul and Jonathan.[11] So it goes on: every detail of the conversation between Saul and the witch is exploited to show that it represents the dissimulations of the devil and makes no sense any other way. The scriptural laws against sorcery and consulting mediums confirm that the witch's words must be treated as false. At one level, Origen's verbal focus was, as we have noted already, more literal than Eustathius' narrative focus, at least in the sense of attending to the letter of the text. Indeed, Eustathius justifies his non-literal interpretation by giving examples of other scriptural narratives where details are not spelt out verbally but left to commonsense inference.

In a long aside, Eustathius objects to the fact that Origen allegorises Moses' accounts of creation, Paradise and many other things, including the Gospel-narratives.[12] In this context his point is that it is scandalous to allegorise those key narratives and then treat this story literally, especially when it leads to such blasphemous conclusions. The fundamental objection in all cases, it would seem, was to methods which fastened on words and ignored the sequence of the story and the coherence of the narrative, both with itself and with the rest of scripture. After all, as Eustathius points out, the very word *engastrimythos* shows that the story-writer meant to imply the witch was false.[13] She generates 'myths' in her inwards, her stomach rather than her mind, myths fathered by the devil.

In this treatise, Eustathius is concerned to counter a particular deductive reading of a particular text. He does not provide an alternative dogmatic, moral or spiritual exegesis. So the treatise gives us little further help with the supposed distinction between *allegoria* and *theoria*. What it does show, however, is that the challenge to allegory came from people who cared about the coherence of narrative, and resisted a tokenist exegesis. He also demonstrates that the Antiochene approach was as deductive and intellectualist as the Alexandrian – in fact, the two sides had much in common.[14]

---

11 *De engastrimytho* 12–14; Migne, *PG* 18.637–44.
12 *De engastrimytho* 21; Migne, *PG* 18.656.
13 *De engastrimytho* 26; Migne, *PG* 18.669.
14 Cf. J. Guillet, 'Les exégèses d'Alexandre et d'Antioche conflit ou malentendu?' *Recherches de Science Religieuse* 34 (1947), pp. 257–302.

II

Eustathius requires us to reconsider the standard exposition of the
Antiochene protest against allegory: his first distinction, we noted,
was between *onomata* (names or words) and *pragmata* (deeds or
things), and he speaks much of the *historia* to which Origen pays too
scant attention. Quasten's comment on Eustathius' treatise *On the
Witch of Endor* is as follows:

> Eustathius rejects not only Origen's interpretation of this particular
> passage but his entire allegorical exegesis, because it deprives scripture of
> its historical character.[15]

In a few sentences, R. M. Grant sums up the common estimate of the
Antiochene stance:

> The school of Antioch insisted on the historical reality of the biblical
> revelation. They were unwilling to lose it in a world of symbols and shadows
> ... Where the Alexandrians used the word *theory* as equivalent to allegorical
> interpretation, the Antiochene exegetes use it for a sense of scripture
> higher and deeper than the literal or historical meaning, but firmly based
> on the letter. This understanding does not deny the literal meaning of
> scripture but is grounded on it, as an image is based on the thing
> represented and points towards it. Both image and thing are comprehen-
> sible at the same time. There is no hidden meaning which only a Gnostic
> can comprehend. John Chrysostom observes that 'everywhere in scripture
> there is this law, that when it allegorises, it also gives the explanation of the
> allegory.'[16]

Some aspects of this account bear out what we have said so far, in
particular the emphasis on the coherence of deeper meaning and
literal meaning, described earlier as 'ikonic'. But the question is
whether the Antiochene concern with history is as paramount as this

---

[15] Quasten, *Patrology*, vol. III, p. 303. This is not borne out by the text. Rowan Greer, *The Captain
of our Salvation. A Study in the Patristic Exegesis of Hebrews* (Tübingen: J. C. B. Mohr (Paul
Siebeck), 1973), pp. 150–5, recognised this, but argued the key difference lay in theology,
rather than in exegesis or literary approach. However, he emphasises the insistence on the
proper *prosōpon* – in other words, attributing words in the narrative to the appropriate
character (here the devil), rather than suggesting that each proposition comes from the
Holy Spirit. This is the ancient way of recognising different 'points of view' or 'voices' in
texts – a matter of literary analysis, and a means of maintaining narrative coherence.

[16] Robert M. Grant with David Tracy, *A Short History*, p. 66. Rudolf Bultmann, *Die Exegese des
Theodor von Mopsuestia* (Habilitationsschrift, posthumously published, Stuttgart/Berlin/
Cologne/Mainz: Kohlhammer, 1984), p. 60, provides the Greek of the quotation and the
reference: In Isa. 5.3, Migne, *PG* 56.60 (Bultmann's 't.vi.54, 55' corrected).

account suggests – indeed, whether their preference for typology is rooted in that concern with history. The problems with the now traditional account lie, I suggest, in the assumption that Antiochene literalism meant something like modern historicism.[17] It assumes that their problems with allegory were just like ours, and their preference for typology rested on the same criteria as those advanced by such as Lampe and Woollcombe,[18] namely that typology works with historical events with a family likeness. It assumes that the Antiochenes regarded Origen's allegorical approach as out of tune with the Bible because he had no historical sense, thus anticipating the view of R. P. C. Hanson.[19] The historical earthing of the biblical material and the historical nature of the Christian religion Hanson took for granted – an unquestioned dogma. Now, however, we can see how this historical emphasis was recognisably culturally specific to the modern world, a novelty which is itself increasingly challenged in postmodern hermeneutics.

It is true that *historia* meant *pragmata* (deeds) or *res gestae* (things that happened); stories given this epithet were meant to be 'true', not *res fictae* or *res fabulosae* – that was the expectation raised in readers' minds by the genre.[20] But the distinctive thing about

---

[17] A. C. Charity, *Events and their Afterlife: The Dialectics of Christian Typology in the Bible and Dante* (Cambridge: Cambridge University Press, 1966), considers history important in the Bible, but is critical of the historico-critical impoverishment of 'typology'. It undermines the prophetic thrust in vague general ideas of 'providence', and obscures what he calls 'applied typology', the existential *mimēsis* by which believers 'work out' types in their lives. The point may be put by stating that the ancient (biblical and Antiochene) sense of history is *Geschichte* ('story') rather than *Historie*: cf. Wolfram Kinzig in van Oort and Wickert, *Christliche Exegese*, p. 113, notes 26 and 27.

[18] In *Essays on Typology*.

[19] In *Allegory and Event*.

[20] M. J. Wheeldon, '"True Stories": The Reception of Historiography in Antiquity', in Averil Cameron (ed.), *History as Text* (London: Duckworth, 1989). One of his sources is Lucian's essay, *How to Write History* (*LCL*, vol. VI of Lucian's works, ed.and ET K. Kilburn, pp. 2–72). This work illuminates the point very well: Lucian insists that there is a 'high wall' between history and encomium (§7, *LCL* p. 10), but clearly this implies that practitioners did not always observe it. Lucian's critique of flattery in history-writing, inappropriate *mimēsis* of Homer (§8, *LCL* pp. 10–11), and the use of conventions claiming to have seen things when the author had never set foot outside Corinth (§29, *LCL* p. 42) all presuppose certain expectations about 'factuality' rather than fiction, but also suggest that such expectations were often deliberately dishonoured (or even parodied: see Niklas Holzberg, *The Ancient Novel. An Introduction* (German 1986; ET London and New York: Routledge, 1995), for the way in which novels deliberately parodied history). For Lucian, the best writer of history had two qualities, political understanding and power of expression (§34, *LCL* p. 48), but an uncorruptible mind, prepared to sacrifice only to truth (§§38–40, *LCL* pp. 52–4), was also necessary. Still a plain catalogue of events was no good (§16, *LCL* pp. 24–6): history

historical writing was not 'single-minded pursuit of facts' but their presentation as morally significant, their interpretation in terms of 'virtue' and 'vice' and 'fortune'.[21] No Antiochene could have imagined the kind of critical stance of the Biblical Theology movement, explicitly locating revelation not in the text of scripture but in the historicity of events behind the text, events to which we only have access by reconstructing them from the texts, treating the texts as documents providing historical data. This is anachronistic, and obscures the proper background of the Antiochenes' protest. For them scripture was the Word of God, an unproblematic account of what had happened which pointed to the truths of Christian dogma.[22]

Dogmatic interests were certainly at play in the Antiochenes' insistence on what we might call the 'material facts' of the Gospel, and indeed of the story of God's creation and re-creation of the universe. The links between the exegetical debate and current doctrinal interests are evident,[23] and it seems to be no accident that the Christological and Origenist controversies emerged from the same stable as these anti-allegorical protests. Doing justice to the human birth of the Son of David, and to the reality of the bodily resurrection, were contemporary concerns which are surely linked with the rejection of allegory in the mind of Eustathius and

was intended to be 'useful' (and he quotes Thucydides' famous phrase, *ktēma es aei*, 'a possession for ever' (§42, *LCL* p. 56)), well arranged, with events clarified and expounded for posterity's benefit (§§ 47, 51–5, 61–3, *LCL* pp. 60, 64–6, 70–2). The subject-matter will speak for itself – it has already happened, so what to say is not so much the object as how to say it (§50, *LCL* pp. 62–4)! Even the odd 'myth' may be reported; the author should not believe it entirely, but make it known for the audience to make what they will of it (§60, *LCL* p. 70).

21 See Glenn F. Chesnut, 'Fate, Fortune, Freewill and Nature in Eusebius of Caesarea', *Church History* 42 (1973), pp. 165–82, and *The First Christian Histories*. As already noted, Momigliano long since drew attention to the rhetorical character of ancient historiography; see further above, ch. 5. A similar point is made about biographies by Patricia Cox, *Biography in Late Antiquity. A Quest for the Holy Man* (Berkeley: University of California Press, 1983) pp. 56–65: here the interest was in anecdotes illustrating particular virtues; there was no 'true historical criticism' though the authors referred to sources and sought credibility.

22 For the dogmatic thrust of Antiochene exegesis, see Rowan Greer, *Captain of our Salvation*. See also Silke-Petra Bergjan, 'Die dogmatische Funktionalisierung der Exegese nach Theodoret von Cyrus', in van Oort and Wickert, *Christliche Exegese*, pp. 32–48. Clearly in this period dogmatic concerns became paramount: other essays in the same volume draw attention to the dogmatic exegesis of Asterius, Apollinarius and Athanasius.

23 Greer, *Captain of our Salvation*, perhaps overplays the theological motivations, especially the Christological element, but they must be recognised as part of the total picture.

Diodore.[24] This aspect of Antiochene theology can be exaggerated, however: the texts of the Christological controversy reveal their primary interest in preserving the Nicene affirmation of the 'Godness of God' which they thought the Alexandrians were compromising.[25] The reality of the 'Son of David' was a necessary corollary, and not exactly parallel to modern interest in the full humanity of Jesus and the precise facts of his earthly career.

It is also true that the Antiochenes were fascinated by prophecy, and were particularly interested in the doctrine of providence;[26] they certainly had a sense of 'salvation-history' which explains their concern with the coherence of the biblical story and the narratives that contribute to it. But whatever they meant by 'literal', it was not exactly 'historical' in the modern critical sense. Josipovici can perhaps focus the difference for us:

[The Bible is] a magnificent conception, spread over thousands of pages and encompassing the entire history of the universe. There is both perfect correspondence between Old and New Testaments and a continuous forward drive from Creation to the end of time: 'It begins where time begins, with the creation of the world; it ends where time ends, with the Apocalypse, and it surveys human history in between, or the aspect of history it is interested in, under the symbolic names of Adam and Israel'. Earlier ages had no difficulty in grasping this design, though our own, more bookish age, obsessed with both history and immediacy, has tended to lose sight of it. Neither theologians nor biblical scholars have stood back enough to see it as a whole. Yet it is a whole and quite unlike any other book.[27]

Their sense of history belonged to the world of antiquity, where telling the story of the past was literary and edificatory. Their standpoint reflected the need to preserve the overarching plot of universal history as told in the Bible and summarised in the creeds.[28]

---

[24] That the protest against allegory is less methodological than doctrinal might be deduced from the material in Elizabeth A. Clark, *The Origenist Controversy. The Construction of an Early Christian Debate* (Princeton: Princeton University Press, 1992); the emphasis here is on issues like the 'body', the material creation, and physical resurrection.

[25] Clearly full justification of this lies outside the bounds of this work. For the arguments supporting this view see my book, *From Nicaea to Chalcedon*.

[26] Guillet, in his article 'Les exégèses d'Alexandre et d'Antioche conflit ou malentendu?', contrasts 'typisme prophétique' with 'typisme symbolique'. See further below, pp. 174–5 and 177, for the Antiochene interest in prophecy, especially note 56.

[27] Wayne Meeks, *The Origins of Christian Morality*, p. 192, reproducing Josipovici, *Book of God*, p. 42, where Frye, *The Great Code*, p. xiii, is quoted.

[28] See above, ch. 1.

That is why it is the allegorising of creation, Paradise and resurrection that most upsets these critics. They are anxious about precisely those stories which modern historians are most disposed to treat as mythological. So much for their interest in 'historicity'.

So what is the proper cultural background to the Antiochenes' protest, and how is its import to be understood? What we need to account for the debate between the two exegetical schools is some way of explaining the rise of a different intellectual approach to finding meaning in texts, one that wanted to relate text and reference in what I have described as an ikonic way rather than a symbolic or tokenist way.[29]

III

As has been stressed many times, early Christian exegesis is best understood by considering the function of literature in the culture of the Graeco-Roman world, and discovering the kind of debates about exegesis that were then current. The tension between the two schools has a parallel in the tension between sophists and philosophers in the classical tradition, a tension which continued in the rivalry between philosophy and rhetoric as ways of education and ideals for life in the Hellenistic and Roman appropriation of the classics.[30] Of course the contrasts can be overdrawn. Gregory of Nazianzus and Origen, not to mention characters such as Synesius of Cyrene and even Augustine, were the heirs of both traditions.

[29] Essentially the answer was given by my article, 'Rhetorical Schools'. The crucial points are repeated here.

[30] The tension between philosophers and sophists is evident in Plato, and explored by W. Jaeger in his classic work, *Paideia. The Ideals of Greek Culture*, ET 3 vols. Gilbert Highet (Oxford: Oxford University Press, 1943–5). It is standard in studies such as Marrou, *L'education*. Clearly there was much mutual influence in the Hellenistic and Roman periods, but also continuing rivalry. For a recent discussion, see Brian Vickers, *In Defence of Rhetoric*, (Oxford: Clarendon Press, 1988), chs. 1–3. Rosemary Radford Ruether used the contrast as a key in her book, *Gregory of Nazianzus. Rhetor and Philosopher* (Oxford: Oxford University Press, 1969), showing that Gregory never reconciled the two ideals – of public service and contemplative withdrawal. James L. Kinneavy, *Greek Rhetorical Origins of Christian Faith* (New York and Oxford: Oxford University Press, 1987), is at pains to draw on the educational ideals of the rhetorician Isocrates, as well as Aristotle, to counter the negative view of *pistis* and *doxa*, by comparison with knowledge (*epistēmē*, etc.), which is found in the philosophical tradition (pp. 36ff.). That different exegetical approaches also characterised philosophy and rhetoric and lay behind the differences between the two Christian schools of biblical interpretation is hinted at in Froehlich, *Biblical Interpretation* (e.g. p. 20), and developed in my article, 'Rhetorical Schools'.

Their confluence as well as their tension reaches back into the classical period. Aristotle and his successors had regarded all areas of research as open to the philosopher, and literary criticism, linguistic analysis and rhetorical techniques were placed on the philosopher's agenda. Indeed, the Stoics pioneered the classification and analysis of grammar and figures of speech which were used in the Hellenistic schools. Undoubtedly each had a profound effect upon the other and some important figures, long before the Christian examples mentioned, claimed both traditions: Cicero, Plutarch and Dio Chrysostom, for example.

Nevertheless, tension and accommodation oscillated in the relationship between philosophy and rhetoric: philosophy accused rhetoric of being merely an empty technique with no moral purpose, practised by those who wanted to get ahead in the world; rhetoric countered by emphasising its moral aspects, its aim being to prepare the pupils to play an active and effective role in civic and political life. On rhetoric's side, philosophy was sneered at as withdrawal from the world, or as useless speculation, the profound disagreements between philosophical schools only reinforcing the criticisms. My argument is that philosophy and rhetoric also represent different, though mutually interacting, approaches to texts.

The impression is often given that nearly all ancient interpretation was affected by the search for symbolical meanings.[31] Certainly everyone tended to look for the moral of the tale, but symbolical allegory was not universal. The tracing of doctrines, or universal truths, or metaphysical and psychological theories by means of allegorical reading was characteristic of philosophers, especially the Stoics, but was not the universal way of reading literature – indeed hardly characteristic of the grammar and rhetorical schools, whose influence was certainly more pervasive, since philosophy was the crown of education for a few, but many studied rhetoric. As we have seen, the rhetorical schools sought to derive moral principles, useful instruction and ethical models from their study of literature.[32] This approach, I suggest, informed Antiochene exegesis of the Bible with its reaction against Origenist allegory.[33]

---

[31] E.g. by Hatch, *Influence of Greek Ideas.*
[32] See above, ch. 4, p. 81.
[33] Christoph Schäublin, *Untersuchungen zu Methode und Herkunft der antiochenischen Exegese* (Cologne/Bonn: Peter Hanstein, 1974), anticipated my own argument that the Antiochenes were principally formed by exegetical practice in the schools. His study documents, with

It is worth observing that the principal Antiochene exegetes could have been expected to practice exegesis according to rhetorical conventions.[34] John Chrysostom, and his friend Theodore, who was probably Theodore of Mopsuestia, were educated by Libanius, the great fourth-century rhetorician used by Julian in his campaign to restore classical learning and pagan religion. Julian characterised Diodore, their Christian biblical teacher, as a sharp-witted sophist, who armed his tongue with rhetorical devices against the heavenly gods.[35] No wonder Julian wanted to banish Christians from the schools and deprive them of rhetorical education! Theodoret may protest that he received all his education from monks, but every word he wrote demonstrates his training in the classical *paideia*: he quotes Homer, Sophocles, Euripides, Aristophanes, Demosthenes and Thucydides, and his correspondents included distinguished sophists. The principal Antiochene exegetes undoubtedly had a rhetorical education.

Key features of the rhetorical approach to texts were outlined earlier.[36] Antiochenes clearly addressed the questions of subject-matter and of lexical analysis. Characteristic of both commentaries and homilies in the Antiochene tradition are opening paragraphs setting out the *hypothesis* of the text – they want to understand the subject-matter. Details of the text are then examined point by point. Comments range from discussion of alternative readings to matters like correct punctuation and proper construal of sentences. Questions of translation and etymology, explanations of foreign words, attention to metaphor and figures of speech all feature, as do mini-concordances arguing the special biblical flavour of particular words or phrases. Here is the *methodikon* of the schools.[37] Then they explore the sequence of thought, test text against text, and provide background material, often utilising other texts in the Bible to set

respect to Antiochene exegetical practice, a range of correspondences similar to those documented for Origen by Neuschäfer (see above ch. 4, note 18). Cf. also his 'Zur paganen Prägung der christlichen Exegese', in van Oort and Wickert, *Christliche Exegese*, pp. 148–73. This article covers the Cappadocians, Jerome and Augustine, with cross-reference to Origen and the Antiochenes.

[34] For these biographical details, see *From Nicaea to Chalcedon*, relevant sections.

[35] Julian, *Epistle* 55 (frag. from a letter to Photinus preserved by Facundus); text and ET in *LCL*, vol. iii.

[36] In ch. 4 above.

[37] Rudolf Bultmann documents Theodore's attention to grammatical, stylistic and rhetorical matters in *Exegese*, pp. 44–64.

the text in question in its appropriate context. Here they speak of the *historia*, and they were concerned to get it right – Theodoret argued that Paul had visited Colossae, though Theodore had denied this.[38] Yet what they are engaged in is the *historikon* of the schools. It is quite misleading to think they had developed a historical consciousness which their contemporaries did not have.

Summary and paraphrase are persistent techniques used by the Antiochenes to bring out the gist of the argument and the *hypothesis* usually includes this, together with circumstantial introductory material. This technique ensures that context and thrust were not lost under the mass of detailed commentary. Like school exegetes, they sought to discern the underlying idea dressed up in the words and style of the text. They often show concern with the *akolouthia*, or sequence, of argument or story. They also discussed genre and the particular literary characteristics of, for example, prophecy.[39]

One feature of rhetorical criticism not so far explored is its *krisis* – its judgement of literature. This could include rhetorical evaluation, questions of authenticity and so on, but it was principally concerned with discernment of the good – it was ethical criticism. Rhetoric, as Quintilian insisted, involved moral education, not just learning to make lies plausible as Plato and others suggested. Plutarch[40] allows us to see how ethical advice was extracted from literature, and how the potentially adverse effect of violent or immoral tales was neutralised. Poets tell lies, as Plato said, but in the invention of tales and myths as examples of good and bad conduct, admonition and instruction is implied. Poetry is true to life in its inextricable mixture of good and evil, and so the making of moral judgements as literature is read provides training for life. The young were to be urged to emulate the virtuous, and texts were to be subjected to a kind of moral pruning. Thus literature was supposed to provide

[38] Theodore of Mopsuestia (*In Ep. Col.*, Argumentum, in H. B. Swete (ed.), *Theodore on the Minor Epistles of St Paul* (Cambridge: Cambridge University Press, 1880–2) vol. 1, p. 254) assumes Paul has not seen the recipients, and explains his usual custom when addressing such people. Theodoret in his *Hypothesis* (Migne, *PG* 82.592) mentions that 'some say' Paul had not seen the recipients on the basis of Colossions 3.1, the text quoted by Theodore, but says one must understand the *dianoia* of the words, advancing the alternative view. I am indebted for this point to the D.Phil. thesis presented to Oxford University by Paul Parvis.

[39] See Bultmann, *Exegese*, pp. 64–7 for discussion of genre; pp. 69ff. for Theodore's concern with *akolouthia*, the sequence of argument; and pp. 128–34 for the parallels between Theodore's methods and those of 'profane exegesis'.

[40] *On the Education of Children*, and *How the Young Man should study Poetry* in *Moralia*, vol. 1, *LCL*.

moral lessons. It is instructive to note that it was precisely this tradition which enabled Basil to write his *Address to the Young on how they might derive Benefit from Greek Literature*.[41] He advises Christian parents and pupils to allow the usual (that is, the pagan) educational curriculum to train the mind while discriminating between the morally useful and the harmful. This was an ancient educational tradition, not some curious Christian double-think.

The narrative or argumentative coherence of the text was important to the Antiochenes, and it was from this that they deduced moral or dogmatic conclusions, again treating the text as texts were used for the education of youngsters in the schools. Chrysostom often notes differences between the Gospels, bringing out the point that they are complementary not contradictory, and each Gospel author tells the story with a particular 'lesson' in view. The kind of enquiry stimulated by *to historikon* results in drawing morals. Further illustration of this can be found at the beginning of this chapter as well as in chapter 11, where we will discover Chrysostom's remarkable adaptation of the typical 'audience-oriented' criticism to provide moral exhortation.

The Prologue to a *Commentary on the Psalms* attributed to Diodore, and certainly coming from the Antiochene school,[42] shows how much it was these standard exegetical practices which informed the Antiochene approach. According to this work, the book of holy Psalms 'teaches (*paideuei*) righteousness in a gentle and suitable manner to those willing to learn',[43] offering reproof and correction. The primary function of holy scripture is educational, an assumption adopted unquestioningly from the ancient view of literature as the core of the curriculum. Diodore wants to provide a 'concise exposition of the subjects (*hypotheseōn*)' of the book, both in general

---

[41] Text and ET in vol. IV of Basil, *Letters, LCL*.

[42] Froehlich, *Biblical Interpretation*, has performed an important service in making available in translation the key statements on exegesis found in the Prologue to the Psalm Commentary and the Preface to Ps. 118 (pp. 82–94). As he notes (in the introd. p. 21), the attribution to Diodore is highly probable, though the material comes from an eleventh century ms. under the name of Anastasius of Nicaea. The text of the former is found in *CC*, series Graeca VI; both were published by L. Mariès, 'Extraits du Commentaire de Diodore de Tarse sur les Psaumes', *Recherches de Science Religieuse* 9 (1919), pp. 79–101. See Froehlich's discussion and the article by Guillet, 'Les exégèses d'Alexandre et d'Antioche conflit ou malentendu?' The summary and exposition which follows shows that I would put a slightly different gloss on much of the Greek text from that implied by the choice of wording in Froehlich's translation.

[43] *Comm. in Ps.* Prologue; *CC* p. 3; Froehlich, *Biblical Interpretation*, p. 82.

and in relation to particular Psalms, and also 'an explanation
(*hermeneia*) of their plain text [*kata lexin* – perhaps better translated
"at the verbal level"]'. Thus those who sing the Psalms will do so
intelligently, grasping the 'logical coherence (*akolouthia*) of the
words' (that is, how to construe the sentences at the grammatical
level) and 'the depth of their mind (*dianoias*)'.[44]

The author proceeds to state[45] that the subject-matter (*hypothesis*)
of the whole Psalter can be divided into two categories: the ethical
and the doctrinal. As far as ethics is concerned, some of the Psalms
are there to correct individual behaviour, others apply to the Jews
only, others are universal. He proposes to make clear which are
which in his 'detailed [*kata meros* – "bit by bit"] commentary
(*hermeneia*)'. As for doctrine, what concerns him are issues of free will
and providence.

But there are also other *hypotheseis*.[46] One is the Babylonian
captivity; others are 'past events' recalled 'for the benefit of later
generations' – in other words, they function in an exemplary way.
The Psalmist, who is unquestioningly identified with David, is
understood to be the prophet *par excellence*, who speaks in the person
of specific individuals later than his own time, individuals like Onias
at the time of the Maccabees, or like Jeremiah or Hezekiah.[47]
Prophecy is disclosure, and may relate to past, present or future.
The 'detailed (*kata lepton*) commentary' will provide the keys to this
enormous variety of *hypotheseis*, and 'Diodore' refrains from holding
up the reader by introducing them all in the Prologue.

Here he wants to draw attention to the lack of chronological
sequence in the Psalter, offering the theory that the book was lost at
the time of the Babylonian captivity and only rediscovered bit by
bit: the collectors put them together as they were found, not in the
original order. The superscriptions he regards as inaccurate – not
according to knowledge (*epistēmē*); but with God's help he will try
and offer a *hermeneia* even of these errors.[48] This may seem like
historical interest, but the purpose is to elucidate the text by
relating each Psalm to its background, and, given the assumptions

[44] *Comm. in Ps.* Prologue; *CC* p. 4; Froehlich, *Biblical Interpretation*, p. 82.
[45] *Comm. in Ps.* Prologue; *CC* p. 4; Froehlich, *Biblical Interpretation*, pp. 82–3.
[46] *Comm. in Ps.* Prologue; *CC* p. 5; Froehlich, *Biblical Interpretation*, p. 84.
[47] Froehlich, *Biblical Interpretation*, p. 84, misreads *(h)Ezekia* as Ezekiel (Gk: *Iezekiel*).
[48] *Comm. in Ps.* Prologue; *CC* p. 6; Froehlich, *Biblical Interpretation*, p. 85.

about authorship, the interest is really focussed on prophecy, prediction and providence, the overall doctrinal *hypothesis* to which readers have already been alerted.

Diodore is determined to expound the text according to the *historia* and the actual wording (*lexis*), but without excluding *anagōgē* and higher *theōria*.[49] This is usually taken to contrast literal and spiritual senses. Diodore goes on to assert that the *historia* is not opposed to *theōria*, but is its foundation. *Theōria* never does away with the substance (*hypokeimenon*) – if it does it becomes allegory rather than *theōria*. This expresses precisely the 'ikonic' relationship we have proposed. But the terms are not about 'senses' of the text so much as activities of the exegete. The exegete attends to the wording and the 'story', the *methodikon* and the *historikon*; the exegete may then probe the narrative and by 'insight' (*theōria*) and 'elevation' (*anagōgē*) perceive the moral and spiritual import built into the text's wording and content. This way of understanding *theōria* is the proper understanding of Paul's procedure in Galatians, according to Diodore, and provides a middle way between a Hellenism which through allegory opposes wording and subject-matter, and a Judaism which concentrates too exclusively on the wording and disallows any higher import.

Antiochene exegesis, then, is grounded in the exegetical activities of the rhetorical schools. The objection to Alexandrian allegory is that it treats texts as a collection of arbitrary tokens, not as 'mirroring' in its narrative coherence the truths which may be discerned within it. *Mimēsis* was a key term in ancient literary criticism, and the Antiochene approach was to understand the wording and content of the scriptures as 'mimetic' of divine truths, thus providing moral and doctrinal teaching, and also prophecy. Even the most radical of the Antiochenes, Theodore, accepted that Jonah prefigures Jesus because the extraordinary events of his life signify by *mimēsis* Christ's rejection, resurrection, and conversion of the Gentiles.[50] Indeed, Theodore explicitly said[51] that every 'type' has a certain *mimēsis* with respect to that of which it is said to be the 'type', so confirming the view of 'types' taken earlier. The typology

[49] *Comm. in Ps.* Prologue; *CC* p. 7; Froehlich, *Biblical Interpretation*, p. 85.
[50] Theodore's *Hypothesis* on Jonah, *Comm. on Minor Prophets*; Migne, *PG* 66.320.
[51] Quoted in Bultmann, *Exegese*, p. 107, who refers to *Comm. in Mic.* 4.1–3, Preface to *Comm. in Jonah*, and *Comm. in Mal.* 3.2ff.

so often associated with the Antiochenes is rooted in the rhetorical commonplace that literature imitates life.

To return briefly to Eustathius, in arguing that *engastrimythos* indicates that the witch was false, he refers to the definition of myth in rhetorical textbooks as a fiction made up for pleasure and also for a purpose.[52] Fiction is a plausible *mimēsis* of reality, like painting, he says, but it creates unreal things. Myths are a way of educating children – Plato's advice to parents is here quoted – but Greek children, he says, are eventually taught to distinguish between truth and fiction.[53] The techniques of narrative criticism are no doubt in his mind. Eustathius' purpose is to prove his basic point about the *engastrimythos*, but in the process he uses standard etymological methods, explicitly refers to literary-critical observations about art being a *mimēsis* of life, makes a learned reference to Plato as any well-educated teacher would, and actually mentions rhetorical textbooks. His interpretation is rooted in the traditional *paideia* of the rhetorical schools.

So neither literalism as such, nor an interest in historicity as such, stimulated the Antiochene reaction against Origenist allegory, but rather a different approach to finding meaning in literature which had its background in the educational system of the Graeco-Roman world. Perhaps we could say that it was not 'allegory' as such that they objected to; for allegory was a standard figure of speech, and, if the text carried some indication of its presence, even allegory could be allowed. What they resisted was the type of allegory that destroyed textual coherence.

IV

The word *allēgoria* is derived from a Greek verb meaning 'to speak in public' compounded with the adjective *allos*, meaning 'other'. Ancient definitions all ring the changes on the same theme: allegory is 'to mean something other than what one says'. It is discussed in the rhetorical textbooks on style as a *tropē*, a 'turn' or figure of speech, and lies on a spectrum with metaphor and irony. By the time of Quintilian it was recognised that a continuous metaphor makes an allegory, and personification (of abstract qualities, for example)

---

[52] *De engastrimytho* 27; Migne, *PG* 18.669.   [53] *De Engastrimytho* 28–9; Migne, *PG* 18.669–72.

became an increasingly common feature of compositional allegory. In the rhetorical tradition, therefore, it might refer to deliberate obfuscation on the part of the author, implying the adoption of guarded or élite language, things only to be said in secret or unworthy of the crowd. It was at the very least a sophisticated conceit.[54]

One distinction to be drawn is between compositional allegory, a figure of speech deliberately adopted by the author for effect, and allegorical interpretation,[55] where the reader or interpreter suggests that a whole text has an 'undersense', or *hyponoia*, and should therefore not be read according to what might seem to be its obvious meaning. The Antiochenes would seem to want to make some such distinction: as Grant noted for us above, Chrysostom observed, 'everywhere in scripture there is this law, that when it allegorises, it also gives the explanation of the allegory'. Allegory as a figure of speech was recognised by any who engaged in literary analysis.[56] The point was, the text should give some sign to the reader that the figure of speech was in play.

In the *Commentary on the Psalms* attributed to Diodore,[57] it is made quite clear that some things in scripture are clarified by the

---

54 Jon Whitman, *Allegory. The Dynamics of an Ancient and Medieval Technique* (Oxford: Clarendon Press, 1987), Appendix I, 'On the History of the Term "Allegory"', pp. 263–8. Cf. H. N. Bate, 'Some Technical Terms of Greek Exegesis', *JTS* 24 (1923), pp. 59–66; he discusses *allēgoria* as *tropē*, together with *theōria* and *tropikōs*, distinguishing Antiochene and Alexandrian usage much as I do, though using the word 'literal' for Antiochene recognition of 'allegory' as a figure of speech. Also cf. Bultmann, *Exegese*, p. 60.

55 This distinction is emphasised by Whitman, *Allegory*.

56 A minor treatise by one Adrianos, entitled *Introduction to the Divine Scriptures* (found in Migne, *PG* 98.1273–312), is placed by Bultmann (*Exegese*) in the Antiochene tradition. This treatise clearly reflects 'rhetorical' hermeneutics; it distinguishes *dianoia*, *lexis* and *synthesis*, looking at each for the 'idioms' of scripture. In the final category, figures of speech (*tropoi*) are listed and illustrated, allegory receiving a mere four lines by contrast with, e.g., hyperbole, which has sixteen! This is particularly interesting in that it is not polemical, but (1) simply treats allegory as a standard figure of speech; and (2) reflects the relatively greater importance of hyperbole for the Antiochenes who regarded it as an indicator of prophecy inherent in words initially relating to the circumstance of their utterance. Adrianos also notes that there are only two genres in scripture, namely 'prophecy' and 'history', another point of interest in relation to Antiochene concerns. See further the paper referred to in note 1 of this chapter, and below, p. 178, with note 62.

57 *Comm. in Ps.* Preface to Ps. 118; text in Maries, 'Extraits', p. 90. Froehlich, *Biblical Interpretation*, p. 87, translates: 'In any approach to holy scripture, the literal reading of the text reveals some truths while the discovery of other truths requires the application of *theōria*.' What this misses is the important distinction between the wording or reading (*lexis*) and the subject-matter or 'mind' (*dianoia*) of the text. *Theōria* for the Antiochenes began with a perfectly straightforward application of normal 'reading' principles.

'wording' (*lexis*), but the 'mind' of some things has to be 'looked for' (*theoreitai*). The issue concerns the proper interpretation of figures of speech, which need to be carefully distinguished:

> since, by the grace of God, I intend to interpret the 118th psalm, I had to discuss in detail the above-mentioned modes of expression, as this psalm contains many of them . . . [A] clear statement [was needed] in order to alert [readers] to the fact that some parts of the psalms are meant to be taken literally (*pros lexin*) while others are figurative expressions (*tropologiai*), parables (*parabolai*) or enigmas (*ainigmata*).[58]

The author has explained *tropologia*[59] as being present when words with an obvious meaning are turned into illustrations, and gives examples showing he means 'metaphor'. *Parabolē*[60] he explains as introduced by 'like' or 'as', though sometimes scripture omits the introductory word – he clearly means 'simile'. 'Enigmas'[61] take careful differentiation from allegory: what he understands by this, it seems, is that something 'real' in the narrative points beyond itself, and has a kind of 'double' sense. Hyperbole[62] he regards as a 'sign' that prophetic words refer to the prophet's context, but also point beyond themselves, predicting the future.

What is emphatically not present is allegory. Of course, some interpreters have fancied that it is.[63]

Earlier in this preface,[64] however, allegory has been defined as a 'Greek' usage, whereby something is understood one way but said in another. He gives two examples: (1) The first is an allegorical interpretation of the story of Zeus changing himself into a bull and carrying Europa off across the sea. Since a real bull could not possibly swim so far across the ocean, it must mean Europa crossed the sea on a ship with a bull as figurehead! We might describe this as explaining away a miraculous event in a naturalistic way (inviting

---

58 Mariès, 'Extraits', p. 96; ET Froehlich, *Biblical Interpretation*, p. 91.
59 Mariès, 'Extraits', p. 92; ET Froehlich, *Biblical Interpretation*, pp. 88–9.
60 Mariès, 'Extraits', pp. 92–4; ET Froehlich, *Biblical Interpretation*, pp. 89–90.
61 Mariès, 'Extraits', p. 94; ET Froehlich, *Biblical Interpretation*, p. 90.
62 Mariès, 'Extraits', p. 96; ET Froehlich, *Biblical Interpretation*, pp. 91–2. A similar stress is put on hyperbole by Theodore: the words of the prophet are meant for his own time, but because they are exaggerated, they hint at something more than the *pragmata* – the immediate facts. See Bultmann, *Exegese*, p. 107, where this, alongside *mimēsis*, is admitted as a criterion for discerning a double-sense in scripture.
63 Mariès, 'Extraits', p. 96; ET Froehlich, *Biblical Interpretation*, p. 91.
64 Mariès, 'Extraits', p. 90; ET Froehlich, *Biblical Interpretation*, pp. 87–8.

comparison with the procedures of some historico-critics, who might be surprised to be associated with the allegorist!). (2) The second interprets in terms of natural forces ('scientifically', in our terms) mythological stories about divine intercourse – thus

> when ether, a fiery element, mingles with air, it produces a certain mixture which influences events on earth. Now since air adjoins ether, the text [about Zeus calling Hera his sister and his wife] calls these elements brother and sister because of their vicinity, but husband and wife because of their mixture.

Scripture does not allegorise in that way, asserts Diodore. It does not abrogate the *historia*, but 'theorizes' (*epitheōrei*),

> that is, it develops a higher vision (*theōria*) of other but similar events in addition [Froehlich's translation].

It is interesting that Asterius quotes an epigram to the effect that 'the exposition of the *historia* is the eye (*ophthalmos*) of *hermeneia*'.[65] Asterius the Sophist was, of course, a notorious Arian, but the saying may well reflect the standard outlook of the sophist or rhetor. Surely what the Antiochenes meant by *theoria* is the action of 'looking through' the *akolouthia* of the text to 'higher things'.

To say scripture does not use allegory, however, necessarily meant facing up to Paul's use of the term 'allegory' with respect to Sarah and Hagar in Galatians. This Diodore proceeds to do, indicating that what the apostle calls allegory is really this *epitheōria*. The example proves that what is really meant is insight into the way this narrative mirrors or coheres with others, which elevates the *pragmata* in front of one (in the text) to higher *pragmata* – the point is that both sets of *pragmata* are real and true, for no one would persuade Paul to suggest otherwise. In any case, Diodore will define history later[66] as 'a pure account of something that happened', 'pure' because it is not interrupted by authorial comments or dramatisations, the absence of which was one of the recognised stylistic devices for creating 'objectivity' in history-writing.[67] But the issue is not historicity: the reference of the text is taken to be 'real', but the point concerns the 'integrity' of the narrative which is

---

[65] Wolfram Kinzig, 'Bemerkungen zur Psalmenexegese des Asterius', in van Oort and Wickert, *Christliche Exegese*, p. 113, note 26.

[66] Mariès, 'Extraits', p. 94; ET Froehlich, *Biblical Interpretation*, p. 91.

[67] Cf. Wheeldon, '"True Stories"'.

undermined by the 'Greek' examples just given. Diodore[68] shows himself as much bothered by a talking, scheming serpent as ever Origen was – a serpent is not a rational animal and only rational animals can scheme. The 'serpent' points 'by an enigma' to the devil. But this is not an allegory: the story retains its integrity, while pointing beyond itself.

Still scripture itself uses the word 'allegory'. Origen had justified his practice on the basis of a series of Pauline texts, most notoriously Galatians 4.24.[69] Theodore of Mopsuestia protested at what had been built on Paul's use of the term there:

> There are people who take great pains to twist the sense of the divine scriptures and make everything written therein serve their own ends. They dream up silly fables in their own heads and give their folly the name of allegory. They misuse the apostle's term as a blank authorisation to abolish all meanings of divine scripture.[70]

Antiochene discussion shows how anxious they were to deal with the allegorists' claim that their methods were justified by scripture.

Diodore had said that the scriptural sense of the word is different from the 'Greek' sense, and that the story of Sarah and Hagar is not repudiated; rather *theōria* (insight) discerns a parallel: the *historia* provides a foundation on which the *theōria* is developed. Theodore now addresses the issue in his *Commentary on Galatians*. By implication both treat Paul as using a figure of speech by which Sarah and Hagar 'represent' the two covenants. For Theodore, Paul's statement, 'This is said by way of allegory', was explaining why he has rehearsed the Abraham story at this point in his argument.[71] He turns on the allegorists:

> They make a point to use the same expression as the apostle, 'by way of allegory', but fail to understand the great difference between that which they say and what the apostle says here. For the apostle neither does away with the *historia* nor [as Froehlich translates] elaborates on events that happened long ago [the Latin is *evoluit res dudum factas*]. Rather he states the

---

[68] Mariès, 'Extraits', p. 94; ET Froehlich, *Biblical Interpretation*, p. 90.

[69] Ron Heine, 'Gregory of Nyssa's Apology for Allegory', *VC* 38 (1984), pp. 360–70: Origen has eight Pauline texts which he repeatedly cites – Romans 7.14; 1 Corinthians 2.10; 2.16 and 12 (quoted in that order); 9.9–10; 10.11; 2 Corinthians 3.6; 3.15–16; Galatians 4.24.

[70] Swete, *Theodore of Mopsuestia on the Minor Epistles of St.Paul*, vol. 1, p. 73; ET Froehlich, *Biblical Interpretation*, p. 96.

[71] Swete, *Theodore on the Minor Epistles of St Paul*, vol. 1, pp. 73–4; ET Froehlich, *Biblical Interpretation*, p. 96.

events just as they happened and then applies the *historia* of what occurred there to his own understanding. For instance, he says at one point: 'She corresponds to the present Jerusalem', and at another: 'Just as at that time he who was born according to the flesh persecuted him who was born according to the Spirit'. Paul gives *historia* priority over other considerations.[72]

Theodore goes on to stress the impossibility of comparison being made if there are not two things to compare (*rebus non stantibus*).

It is easy to read this as if Theodore shared our concern with historicity, especially in a translation which encourages the assumption. But, surely, the passage is more concerned with the thrust of the narrative, because to lose that is to invalidate the comparison which is important for Paul's argument. The first thing to note is Theodore's concern to show that 'this is Paul's way of speaking':

He wants to say that by way of allegory one can liken the two covenants to those two women, Sarah and Hagar, with Hagar representing the order of the precepts of the law, for the law was given on Mount Sinai.[73]

In other words, Paul is making a point by using a figure of speech.

Theodore does have other concerns, however. The two covenants are essential to his own hermeneutical approach, and it was his sensitivity to the newness of the new covenant in Christ which led him to reject the Christological reading of the whole Old Testament.[74] This necessarily involved challenging the tradition of allegorical reading, reclaiming the eschatological perspective of the New Testament, and seeing a sequence of salvation-history made up of reliable stories, not mere parables.

Those people, however, turn it all to the contrary, as if the entire *historia* of divine scripture differed in no way from dreams in the night. When they start expounding divine scripture 'spiritually' – spiritual interpretation is the name they like to give to their folly – they claim that Adam is not Adam, paradise is not paradise, the serpent not the serpent. I should like to tell them this: If they make *historia* serve their own ends, they will have no *historia* left.[75]

---

[72] Ibid.
[73] Swete, *Theodore on the Minor Epistles of St Paul*, vol. I, p. 79; ET Froehlich, *Biblical Interpretation*, pp. 99–100.
[74] Ackroyd and Evans (eds.), *Cambridge History of the Bible*, pp. 489–510, on Theodore as representative of the Antiochene School, especially p. 504; *From Nicaea to Chalcedon*, pp. 199–213, especially pp. 200–1 and 204–6.
[75] Swete, *Theodore on the Minor Epistles of St Paul*, pp. 74–5; ET Froehlich, *Biblical Interpretation*, p. 97.

For Theodore, scripture could not simply be instructive myths representing spiritual reality, or the whole thing became a docetic charade. His interest in the *historia* was not exactly that of modern apologists worried about historicity. But he was opposed to the whole tradition of arbitrarily treating narratives as really about some hidden 'undersense'. The 'credal' story was essential to the truth.[76] Commenting on the Galatians passage, Theodoret[77] states that Paul does not remove the *historia*, but teaches those things prefigured (*protypōthenta*) in the *historia*. The significance lies in the impress, the mirror image provided by the narrative or *typos*. Chrysostom[78] suggests that Paul called the *typos* an allegory *katachrēstikōs*, improperly. This *historia* not only reveals what it describes, but also 'announces other things' – *alla . . . anagoreuei*; the Greek here consists of the very words from which 'allegory' was derived, and Chrysostom adds the comment, 'That is why it is called allegory.' They were not averse to allegory as a figure of speech. You might say they rejected the word *allēgoria* because it had been misappropriated by a particular tradition of exegesis which had a different background, and which shattered the narrative coherence of particular texts, and the Bible as a whole.

v

I have argued, then, that Antiochene exegesis is not simply according to the letter, nor was it an anticipation of historical criticism. Rather they used the standard literary techniques in use in the rhetorical schools to protest against esoteric philosophical deductions being made in what they regarded as an arbitrary way. One thing Eustathius was keen to show was that Origen appealed to other scriptures which were inappropriate and unconvincing while ignoring genuinely relevant passages. In other words Origen's methods were arbitrary and his conclusions unreliable: this story, he rightly insisted, is not about the resurrection. To prove this Eustathius interprets according to *to methodikon* and *to historikon* – not historically in the modern sense, nor literally, but according to the

---

[76] See above the discussion in Part I. The *regula fidei* as the overarching narrative from creation to End was an important *kanōn* for the unity of scripture. The Antiochenes are in that tradition.

[77] Theodoret on Galatians 4.24; Migne, *PG* 82.489.

[78] Chrysostom on Galatians 4.24; Migne, *PG* 61.662.

rationalistic literary-critical methods current in the contemporary educational practice of *grammaticus* and *rhētōr*. In this he was the precursor of Diodore, Theodore, Chrysostom and Theodoret, and perhaps the successor of that shadowy but influential biblical scholar, Lucian of Antioch.

But I have also argued that Origen was the first philologist who applied these scholarly methods to scripture. Origen, like the Antiochenes, made use of the standard techniques of *to methodikon* and *to historikon*, enquiring about the text, the language and the content, and practising narrative criticism. All that I have documented. There was far more overlap than most accounts of the controversy allow. They shared a common culture, and a lot of common assumptions. There was no hard and fast distinction between rhetorical and philosophical exegesis. Their common ground and common practices were very considerable, and they are certainly not to be distinguished by the simple opposition 'literal' and 'allegorical'. All alike were interested in features of style like metaphor; all alike were seeking the 'truth' conveyed in the 'dress' of the language. Challenging the term 'allegory' meant finding another to describe what those Antiochenes less radical than Theodore were doing when they followed long-standing traditions of finding prophecies, types, images and 'representations' in scripture. They chose to contrast *theōria* with allegory,[79] but this term was in fact also used by the Alexandrians. For the Alexandrians it was equivalent to allegory; for the Antiochenes it was not. Yet Theodoret, like Origen, could 'allegorise' the Song of Songs in terms of Christ and his bride the Church, even as the term 'allegory' was repudiated.

The difference, however, can be illustrated by consideration of how Origen and Theodore used the word *skopos*. As we noted in chapter 1, ancient literary criticism generally encouraged movement from one topic to another, and alternating tension and relaxation in composition, rather than a single aim or *skopos*. The notion of a single *skopos*, however, is found in both Origen and Theodore.

For Theodore, *skopos* referred to the aim or intent of a particular book or literary unit, such as a Psalm, and it was a way of guarding

---

[79] According to Suidas' list, 'On the difference between *theoria* and allegory' was the title of a work (now lost) by Diodore against the Alexandrians; Quasten, *Patrology* III, p.399.

against piecemeal interpretation.[80] The text in question had to have a single, coherent aim: notoriously he claimed that Psalm 22 could not refer to Christ, despite the fact it appears on the lips of Jesus at the passion, and this was the reason – a single *skopos* implies a single author, and since the Psalmist refers to his sins, that single mind cannot belong to the sinless Jesus Christ.[81] Rather David was lamenting Absalom.

For Origen, as we have seen, the intent of scripture lay not at the level of literary author but at the level of the inspiring Spirit: so consistency lay not in the text and its wording, but in the deeper spiritual realities to which the text referred. According to Origen, the *skopos* of the Spirit was, on the one hand, to enlighten, on the other hand, to conceal spiritual truth in a narrative dealing with the visible creation. Narrative criticism was one technique for revealing the stumbling-blocks in the letter of the text, so as to provoke exploration of what the narrative symbolised. The identification of metaphor was a technique for uncovering the symbols. Coherence lay not in the text or narrative itself, but in what lay behind it.

Origen was happy to decode symbols without worrying about textual or narrative coherence, and the symbols were tokens. His procedures were not entirely arbitrary, for two reasons: the symbols were consistent, each metaphor having a scriptural reference which could be consistently decoded; and there was an underlying spiritual coherence, guaranteed by the unity of scripture, and unveiled by allegory. But this meant the wording of the text found its significance in jots and tittles over-exegeted, rather than in context and flow. The Antiochenes sought a different kind of relationship between wording and content, style and meaning. The narrative sequence and flow of argument mattered. The text was not a pre-text for something else. It might pre-figure something else, but it would do so 'ikonically'. Ikonic exegesis, I suggest, implies some kind of genuine representation, by contrast with symbolic exegesis where the symbols are signs and tokens. So what was needed was insight (*theōria*) to discern the patterns and types, the images and parables.

---

80 For Theodore's interest in the unity of a text and his use of *skopos*, see Rudolf Bultmann, *Exegese*, p. 29, note 2, where it is linked with *hypothesis*; pp. 69ff. (especially note 1 on pp. 69–70) where it is linked with *akolouthia*; and pp. 87ff., especially note 1.
81 Cf. Ackroyd and Evans (eds.), *Cambridge History of the Bible*, p. 500.

The process of exegesis is rationalistic, and, to revert to the discussion of the last chapter, one cannot help feeling that both Antiochenes and Alexandrians were in Northrop Frye's 'metonymic' phase – the phase in which 'this stands for that', the phase which spawns commentary and deduction, where metaphor is recognised as a figure of speech, and metaphorical images illustrate a conceptual argument. Yet all of them put their scholarly techniques to the service of preaching, and there are many times when their exegesis leaves the pedestrian level of an explained joke, and facilitates a reading of scripture which is sacramental in the sense I have tried to elucidate. The most important thing these so-called schools had in common was a desire to foster the life of faith. The way in which exegesis served that end will be taken up in Part IV.

CHAPTER 9

The question of method

I

The discussion so far, especially in Part III, surely raises some questions for standard accounts of patristic exegetical method. It is time we took stock and faced the implications.

Patristic method is commonly characterised in terms of 'literal', 'typological' and 'allegorical' exegesis, the Fathers being understood as the precursors of the mediaeval fourfold sense.[1] Simonetti,[2] for example, tends to work with two senses, material and spiritual, but subdivides the latter into moral and typological. This threefold division, found he thinks in Origen, is then developed into a fourfold pattern by John Cassian.[3] Debate in the fourth century between the two great schools of Antioch and Alexandria is generally taken to focus on the merits of the 'literal' and 'allegorical' approaches, the 'literal' usually being equated with the 'historical'. Some of the great exegetes, like the Cappadocians, Jerome and Cyril of Alexandria, since they do not fit into these categories, are described as 'eclectic' in their method.[4] But not one of these conventional terms is univocal. A review of each will highlight the problems of treating them as methodological categories.

---

[1] See Henri de Lubac, *Exégèse mediéval: les quatre sens de l'écriture*, 4 vols. (Paris: Aubier, 1959–64); and discussion of de Lubac's work in Andrew Louth, *Discerning the Mystery. An Essay on the Nature of Theology* (Oxford: Clarendon, 1983), especially chapter v, 'Return to Allegory'.

[2] Simonetti, *Biblical Interpretation*.

[3] Ibid., p. 119.

[4] E.g. Kerrigan, *St Cyril of Alexandria*; M. Alexandre, 'La théorie de l'exégèse dans le *De Hominis Opificio* et l'*In Hexaemeron*', in Marguerite Harl (ed.), *Ecriture et culture philosophique dans la pensée de Grégoire de Nysse* (Actes du Colloque de Chevetogne 1969, Leiden: Brill, 1971), pp. 87–110. On Jerome's eclecticism, see Dennis Brown, *Vir Trilinguis. A Study in the Biblical Exegesis of Saint Jerome* (Kampen: Kok Pharos, 1992).

Literal meanings

The assumption that we know what 'literal' means conceals different usages, with different weightings in our world from the world of the Fathers. For us, 'literal' may mean the 'plain sense' of the words, taking full account of context and including metaphors such as 'God is my Rock'; by contrast the Fathers distinguished wording from sense, and the normal sense of a word from its use as a metaphor, so that they would argue that 'God is my Rock' is an absurdity 'according to the letter', and so one must take it *tropikōs*, that is, metaphorically or tropologically.[5] For us literalness is often associated with the claim to an inerrant report of historical fact, whereas for Origen inerrancy lay neither in the wording of the text, nor in the worldly fact behind the text, but in the 'undersense' intended by the Spirit.

The fact is that the Fathers had no single concept corresponding to our notion of literalness, and the wealth of terminology uncovered for the so-called 'literal sense' reflects that.[6] The majority of these

[5] Commenting on a passage in Clement of Alexandria (*Strom.* III, 38.1), W. den Boer ('Hermeneutic Problems in Early Christian Literature', *VC* I (1947), pp.150–67) wrote:

> Clement addresses himself to heretic sects which take passages from the Holy Scriptures, meant to be taken allegorically, in a literal sense ... Now it is curious to see that Clement himself gives an explanation of these words which follows the method of historical exegesis: he traces the connection in which the words were spoken and gives an explanation which suits the text. Yet he speaks disapprovingly of those who take these words literally, as it is meant allegorically. Hence we may conclude that by 'allegorical' Clement means: the text in its context, and by 'literal' the isolated text which is explained as if it were a word by itself.

This rather odd conclusion is better explained by the rhetorical distinction between examining the 'wording' and the 'sense'. Nevertheless, it shows that the difference between ancient and modern senses of 'literal' has long been recognised.

[6] Browsing through Origen, for example, one may find a whole list of terms which may be treated as rough equivalents to our term 'literal': *epi lexeōs, kata lexin, pros lexin, hypo tēs lexeōs; epi tō(i) rhētō(i), kata to rhēton, pros rhēta; pros to (psilon) gramma*, etc. These largely refer to the 'wording'; other terms indicate reference to sensible or physical things. Kerrigan, *St Cyril of Alexandria* (pp. 35–6, and footnote) lists many more terms, and observes that some concern the objects envisaged by the literal sense. In fact his list embraces terms referring to the 'plain sense', the 'letter', the sequence of the words, the 'obvious' or 'immediate' *logos*, the *logos* concerning 'sensible' objects, the things apparent, 'corporeal matters', and so on. Also included are phrases specifying the *hermeneia, theoria* or *nous* of what lies in front of the interpreter (*to prokeimenon*). It is questionable whether these were ever seen as alternative ways of speaking of the same thing, namely an univocal 'literal sense'. The same comment may be made about the parallel list of Latin terms used by Jerome assembled in Dennis Brown, *Vir Trilinguis*, pp. 124–5. In particular, his assumption that *historia* designates the literal sense is one that needs fresh examination in the light of the considerations advanced here.

terms refer to the wording, and, as we have seen, this was to be investigated through *to methodikon*, and the analysis could include etymology, lexical explanation of archaic terms, and so on. The wording was the dress for the idea. Interpretation 'according to the letter' could simply focus on the words; but one understood 'according to the letter' when idea and wording were taken to correspond straightforwardly without figures of speech, or other divergences between the expression and what it signified. This correspondence or divergence could operate at the level of individual word, the combination of words in sentences, or the sequence of sentences in argument or narrative, and these three levels are worth distinguishing.

Within modern hermeneutical discussion the relationship between sense and reference has been recognised as complex: some would defend the principle that texts are self-referential and have no reference to the external world, others debate the nature of the referential value of texts, thinking especially of the problems of fictional narrative. That was not exactly the problem for the Fathers, but they were aware of a difference between sense and reference. It was the potential for the same words to have multiple reference that created multiple meanings for such as Origen: words could be taken as referring to something immediate in the world of the text, or to a past or future event, or to an experience of the soul, or to a heavenly reality. These applications, as we might call them, could be treated as more or less plausible depending on the sense of the wording. This was the issue we touched on in chapter 6 when discussing Eusebius' treatment of the fulfilment of a riddling prophecy as 'literal'.[7]

Taking together the considerations in the last two paragraphs, it becomes clear that five distinguishable but overlapping kinds of 'literal' reading may be listed:

(1) attending solely to the wording;

(2) taking individual words in their normal sense;

---

[7] De Boer, 'Hermeneutic Problems', is concerned to show how indistinct is the terminology used by the Fathers, and he notes (p. 163) that Origen regarded Isaiah 53 as 'an example of clear and direct speech of the prophets'. His point is that typology is not properly distinguished as a category, and here belongs to the 'literal' rather than the 'allegorical' sense. The matter is clearer if one concentrates on the question of the reference of the prophecy: the wording implies a person (not a nation, as the Jews claim), and so for Origen the only possible person to which it can refer is Christ.

(3) attending to the 'plain sense' of words in combination (the sentence);

(4) discerning the overall logic of an argument or narrative;

(5) accepting the implied factual reference (whether carnal, earthly, historical, prophetic).

All of these presume correspondence between the wording and the idea expressed or reference intended, and that is why a literal reading might sometimes be dismissed as absurd. That is also how it was that Origen could regard Jewish interpretation as 'literal': he imagined they thought that the laws of scripture were to be obeyed 'according to the letter' rather than the spirit, and the prophecies were to be read according to their wording rather than their (true) reference.

Types of allegory[8]

As already observed, the word *allēgoria* is derived from a Greek verb meaning 'to speak in public' compounded with the adjective *allos* meaning 'other'. To quote Jerome:

Allegory is specially to do with the art of philology, and how it differs from metaphor or other figures of speech we learn as little children in school. It puts forward one thing in the words but means another in the sense. The books of the orators and poets are full of allegories.[9]

So, allegory, which is 'to mean something other than what one says', is a *tropē*, a turn or figure of speech,[10] involving deliberate

---

[8] Much of the following discussion is drawn from my article, 'Allegory and the Ethics of Reading', in Watson (ed.), *The Open Text*.

[9] Quoted by Dennis Brown, *Vir Trilinguis*, p. 146.

[10] E.g. Demetrius, *On Style* II. 99–102:

> There is a kind of impressiveness also in *allēgoria* . . . [Example given] In the phrase . . . used the speaker has shrouded his words, as it were, in an allegory. Any darkly-hinting expression is more terror-striking, and its import is variously conjectured by different hearers . . . Hence the Mysteries are revealed in an allegorical form in order to inspire such shuddering and awe as are associatd with darkness and night. Allegory also is not unlike darkness and night.' (ET W. Rhys Roberts, Loeb edition)

Cf. H. N. Bate, 'Some Technical Terms of Greek Exegesis', *JTS* 24 (1923), pp. 59–66, which discusses *allēgoria* as a *tropē*, essentially distinguishing Antiochene and Alexandrian usage of this term, together with *theōria* and *tropikōs*: his conclusion is that *theōria* and *allēgoria* are not distinguished in the Alexandrians, but *allēgoria* for the Antiochenes belongs only to the 'literal' sense, i.e. it is only a figure of speech See above the discussion on pp. 176–7, especially note 54.

obfuscation, the adoption of guarded or élite language. The difference between compositional allegory and allegorical interpretation is worth noting.[11] It is one thing for an author to adopt a particular figure of speech and develop it, and then for the reader to identify this process in exegetical analysis; it is another thing for a reader or interpreter to suggest a whole text has an 'undersense' or *hyponoia*, and should not be read according to what might be claimed to be its 'obvious' meaning. But there are reasons for suspecting that the distinction cannot hold for too long. One thinks of the ancient (and psychoanalytic) propensity to find meaning in dreams, and what might be called unauthored phenomena, understood as symbolic allegories.[12] Besides this, the distinction puts undue weight on authorial intention: 'postmodern' sensitivities and reader-response theories may help us to appreciate again the patristic tendency to think of language as indefinite, as transcending the conscious meaning of the human scribe, and as dependent for meaning on the inspiration of the interpreter. In any case, those engaged in allegorical interpretation usually thought that the *hyponoia* was what the author intended. Stoics thought that the original philosophical wisdom was known to Homer, and that he really meant what they thought he meant. Origen believed that the Holy Spirit had clothed the divine *skopos* in the dress of the wording, and that only those who probed for the deeper meaning really understood what the text was about. The Word of God used the conceit of allegory like a well-trained rhetorician!

Allegory in any case lies on a spectrum and cannot be sharply differentiated from other figures of speech. But there is allegory and allegory. Jon Whitman helps us to grasp the dynamics of allegory:

Our language is constantly telling us that something is what it is not . . .

All fiction . . . tries to express a truth by departing from it in some way. It may embellish its subject, rearrange it, or simply verbalize it, but in every case, that ancient dislocation of words from their objects will keep the language at one remove from what it claims to present. Allegory is the extreme case of this divergence . . . In its obliquity, allegorical writing thus exposes in an extreme way the foundation of fiction in general.[13]

---

[11] Jon Whitman, *Allegory*, pp. 3–4.
[12] Cf. above, ch. 4, p. 93, especially Lieberman's discussion of Artemidorus' *Oneirocriticon*.
[13] Jon Whitman, *Allegory*, pp. 1–2.

If we take this seriously, all reading of texts which involves entering the text-world, appropriating the perspective of the text, or reading ourselves into the text, is in some sense allegorical.[14] Just as drama involves its audience, so the scriptures demand response. Ancient literary critics recognised that this process depended on *mimēsis* – imitation or representation. Once admit this and the dialectic between similarity and difference is inevitable, and allegory becomes an extreme form of all forms of reading.

The more allegory exploits the divergence between corresponding levels of meaning, the less tenable the correspondence becomes. Alternatively the more it closes ranks and emphasizes the correspondence, the less oblique and therefore the less allegorical, the divergence becomes.[15]

Taking up this perspective, my suggestion would be that the crucial differences between forms of allegorical reading lie in the way in which the correspondences and divergencies are conceived. In fact, that is the kind of case argued in chapter 9 with respect to the Antiochene reacion against Alexandrian allegory. The question was whether the *mimēsis* happened through genuine likeness or analogy, an 'ikon' or image, or by a symbol, a token, something unlike which stands for the reality. One could argue that both are forms of allegory. Typology can also be understood simply in terms of *mimēsis*, and so in terms of allegory in its widest sense: Louth, following de Lubac, preferred to speak of *allēgoria facti* alongside *allēgoria verbi*.[16] In chapter 11, we will find allegory and typology running into each other again, and propose a form of 'figural allegory'.

There is then allegory and allegory. Indeed, allegory cannot be treated as a particular Hellenistic development foreign to the Jewish world, and therefore imported into interpretation of the Gospel parables, as Dodd and Jeremias[17] had taught us to believe. *Mashal* meant all kinds of riddles, fables, parables and allegories, and, as John Drury[18] pointed out,

---

[14] As I suggested in the *The Art of Performance*, ch. 7, *passim*.
[15] Jon Whitman, *Allegory*, p. 2.
[16] Andrew Louth, *Discerning the Mystery*, p. 119.
[17] The classic studies following Jülicher, *Die Gleichnisreden Jesus* (1899–1910), are C. H. Dodd, *The Parables of the Kingdom* (London: Collins, 1934), and J. Jeremias, *The Parables of Jesus* (ET London: SCM Press, 1954).
[18] 'Origins of Mark's Parables', in Michael Wadsworth (ed.), *Ways of Reading the Bible* (Brighton: Harvester, 1981), pp. 171–89.

The parables in Mark are, briefly and clumsily put, historical allegories mixing concealment and revelation in the sort of riddling symbolism which is an ingredient of apocalyptic.

So I would propose the following list of types of allegory:
(1) rhetorical allegory, where allegory is adopted as a figure of speech on a spectrum with irony and metaphor;
(2) parabolic allegory, of a kind found in fables and riddles;
(3) prophetic allegory, hidden and riddling revelation found in oracles, dreams, symbolic visions, or narrative signs;
(4) moral allegory, where the moral of a text is sought for paedeutic or paraenetic reasons, e.g. by particulars being universalised as examples;
(5) natural or psychological allegory, where a mythological text is read as referring to forces interacting in the world according to accepted scientific norms;
(6) philosophical allegory, where the transcendent world is revealed, in veiled fashion, through the material world, and/or a text employing earthly language to convey heavenly meanings;
(7) theological allegory, whereby Christ, or the creative and saving purposes of the Trinity, becomes the true meaning of life, the universe, the text and everything.

Clearly (3) and (4) overlap with features commonly treated as typological, and the overlap between typology and allegory will become even clearer if, in anticipation of chapter 11, we add
(8) figural allegory.
Nevertheless, it is worth considering typology further in its own right.

Types of typology[19]

The word *typos* means something like 'impress', the mark left by the imprint of a seal, for example. The one use of the word in the Gospels is with reference to the 'mark' of the nails (John 20.25). So when the word *typos* is used, it is intended to alert one to the presence of a correspondence of some kind which lends significance to the text. Often the word *eikōn* (ikon or image) is used synonymously. So it is not without reason that the Latin equivalent was *figura*, and a

[19] The following is largely abstracted from my article 'Typology', as is the material in note 23 below.

widespread alternative expression to 'typology' is 'figural interpretation' or 'figurative composition'.

The word 'typology' is a modern coinage.[20] Nevertheless, it is a useful term, and may be employed as a heuristic tool[21] for discerning and describing an interpretative device whereby texts (usually narrative but, as we have already seen, not exclusively so) are shaped or read, consciously or unconsciously, so that they are invested with meaning by correspondence with other texts of a 'mimetic' or representational kind. Typology, then, is not an exegetical method, but a hermeneutical key, and, taking our cue from places where the word 'type' is explicitly used, we may be able justifiably to identify other examples of the procedure where the terminology is not explicit.

The 'representational' character of the 'type' is clear in the way that the second-century bishop, Melito of Sardis, justifies in the *Peri Pascha*[22] his interpretation of Passover in terms of Christ's passion, so offering the only ancient discussion which could be regarded as in any sense a theoretical explanation of typology. Scripture provides a *parabolē*, a designer's sketch (*prokentēma*), a prefiguration (*protypōsis*), and he uses the analogy of an artist's model which 'represents' the finished product until such time as it becomes obsolete. He means the wax, clay or wooden mock-up used by architect or sculptor. This is a 'true representation' which outlives its usefulness, a sign which points beyond itself.

The historicity of the event behind the text is not at issue for

---

[20] A. C. Charity, *Events and their Afterlife*, p. 171, note 2, states that *typologia* appears for the first time in Latin in 1840, 'typology' in English in 1844; and argues that allegory and typology are only distinguished in the aftermath of the post-Reformation rejection of allegory. The definition of J. Gerhard (1582–1637) became more or less a classic, he suggests:

> *Typus est, cum factum aliquod Vet. Test. ostenditur, praesignificasse seu adumbrasse aliquid gestum vel gerendum in Nov. Test. Allegoria est, cum aliquid ex Vet. vel Nov. Test exponitur sensu novo atque accomodatur ad spiritalem collatione. Allegoria occupatur non tam in factis, quam in istis concionibus, e quibus doctrinam utilem et reconditam depromit.*

De Boer, in his article 'Hermeneutic Problems', confirms the difficulty of distinguishing 'typology' in both Clement and Origen.

[21] Michael Fishbane, in *Biblical Interpretation in Ancient Israel*, makes a similar move. He assumes that typology belongs to 'classical Christian exegesis' and therefore could be regarded as 'both anachronistic and methodologically problematic' if applied to 'inner-biblical exegesis', but suggests that 'the post-biblical phenomena . . . help to identify the inner-biblical phenomena'. See pp. 350–51.

[22] Melito of Sardis, *On Pascha and fragments*, ed. Stuart George Hall, Oxford Early Christian Texts (Oxford: Clarendon Press, 1979). See especially 39–45, pp. 20–3.

Melito[23] – in fact, Melito graphically retells the story according to rhetorical conventions, allusion and quotation 'mimicking' the scriptural narrative by creatively reminting it. According to Melito, the *typos* (consistently translated by Stuart Hall as 'model') is temporary, the grace eternal; yet the old has become new, the Law grace, the *typos* truth. In other words, the mock-up is superseded by the finished article, and each has its own *kairos*. Indeed, the mock-up

---

[23] It was Jean Daniélou (*The Lord of History*, ET by Nigel Abercrombie of *Essai sur le mystère de l'histoire* (London: Longmans, 1958)) who proposed a distinction between typology and allegory, intending to find a justification of the former in the modern climate, the latter being generally regarded as unacceptable. His distinction was grounded in 'historicity'. He speaks of

> a new kind of symbolism, which is characteristic of the Bible. Its specific difference is historicity, for it denotes a relationship between various events belonging to sacred history. It is called *typology* . . . This figurative sense of Scripture is grounded in the structural unity of God's design: the same divine characteristics are revealed in successive strata of history.   (p. 140)

He firmly distinguishes this 'typology' from 'the use of allegory by such as Philo, and some of the Fathers after him'. This he sees as 'a recrudescence of nature-symbolism, from which the element of historicity is absent'.

This insistence on the 'historical' character of typology was taken up by Lampe and Woollcombe (G. W. H. Lampe, 'The Reasonableness of Typology', and K. J. Woollcombe, 'The Biblical Origins and Patristic Developent of Typology', in *Essays on Typology*). These essays came to represent critical orthodoxy on the matter. Thus Lampe was concerned to reclaim the historic exegetical traditions of the Church in a responsible way, taking account of modern historical criticism. This meant that the arbitrariness of allegorical exegesis had to be repudiated, together with any form of typology which got tainted with the ahistorical symbolism that allegory represented. However,

> [i]f we admit the unity of scripture in the sense that it is the literature of a people whose thought was controlled by a single series of images . . . , and if, further, we hold that Christ is the unifying centre-point of Biblical history . . . , then we can have no objection to a *typology* which seeks to discover and make explicit the *real correspondences in historical events* which have been brought about by the recurring rhythm of the divine activity.   (p. 29; my emphasis)

With this 'historical typology' he contrasted another kind of typology which rests 'not on an interpretation of history, but on a particular quasi-Platonist doctrine of the relation of the literal sense of Scripture... to eternal spiritual reality'. It seems that this other typology conspires with allegory, and is not to be regarded as typology proper.

> Allegory differs radically from the kind of *typology* which rests on *the perception of actual historical fulfilment*. The reason for this great difference is simply that *allegory takes no account of history*.   (p. 31; my emphasis)

Woollcombe's conclusions are little different, though he is less concerned with legitimacy in the modern world, more with discerning what the ancients were really doing. He suggests that New Testament typology was 'to the Apostolic writers, what Biblical theology is to the modern exegete – an historical approach to the understanding of the saving acts of God' (p. 69). So he identifies the following principles as those which 'determined the use of historical typology in the Bible', as well as 'in the writings of those Fathers who followed the Biblical rather than the Hellenistic tradition of typological exegesis':

only has power because of its relationship with what it signifies: it is the blood of Christ which the angel of death sees on the Egyptian doorposts![24] There is an essentially 'mimetic' intent in Melito's treatment of scripture. The 'reality' (*alētheia*) lies in the fulfilment, not in an event whose occurrence in the past is its principal feature.

The point is that the narrative is prophetic and so its details are potentially oracular riddles to be unpacked by allegory. Richard Hanson in *The Cambridge History of the Bible* notes the extent to which, even in this, the earliest, Paschal Homily, allegory is attracted to the basic 'type', or, as he puts it, the

analogies (or fancied analogies) between the death and resurrection of Christ on the one hand, and on the other the events of the institution of the Passover and the Exodus from Egypt.[25]

Nor is the presence of allegory the only clue to the fact that Melito would seem to be providing an explanation for a Hellenistic audience: we have noted his use of rhetorical devices, and the word *parabolē* hardly has its biblical meaning – it is surely nearer to being used as rhetoricians used it, to refer to the

---

1 To confine typology to the search for historical patterns within the historical frame of revelation.
2 To reject spurious exegesis and Hellenistic allegorism as means of discerning the patterns.
3 To insist that the identity between the type and the antitype must be real and intelligible.
4 To use it solely for expressing the consistency of God's redemptive activity in the Old and in the New Israel. (p. 75)

Would that such principles could indeed be discerned in the Bible and the Fathers! In order to establish them, Woollcombe has both distinguished different uses of the word *typos*, so narrowing down actual usage to conform with his historical principles, and imported the notion of typology where the texts give no hint of its existence. His accusation that the Alexandrians confused historical with symbolic typology, and so with allegorism, undermines the very distinction that he, in common with Daniélou and Lampe, wishes to draw. Furthermore, on Lampe's own admission, 'it is very difficult to know where to draw the line in typological exegesis', much patristic typology is 'often little more than a rhetorical trick', and 'we ought not always to treat their fancies too seriously'. In other words, there are difficulties inherent in their endeavours to use history as the determining characteristic.

In fact the attempt to define typology through associating it closely with historicity and event must be deemed to have failed.

24 William Golding captures something of this power in his novel *The Spire*; the Dean of the Cathedral is 'taken over' by the vision of what is to be by contemplating the architect's model, and that 'inspiration' has a kind of demonic force which is played out in the rest of the novel.

25 Ackroyd and Evans (eds.), *Cambridge History of the Bible*, pp. 414–15.

brief comparisons, usually fictitious, that orators invent . . . to serve as proof or demonstrations in their speeches.[26]

Melito's 'type' belongs to the argument from prophecy, so prominent in Justin and other second-century apologists:[27] if you could prove that the scriptures were fulfilled, then you had demonstrated both the truth of the claimed fulfilment and the reliability of the supposed scriptural predictions.

Mimēsis was an important element in ancient discussion of literary texts.[28] Literature was supposed to 'represent' life, to provide moral examples to be 'imitated', to provide stylistic 'models' to be followed. One begins to suspect that Melito is trying to provide, in terms familiar to the culture shaped by Hellenistic rhetoric, a theory for a kind of prophecy which was unfamiliar,[29] and indeed more than mere prophecy.

This strange kind of prophecy, presented here in terms of Hellenistic *mimēsis*, must have had some kind of precedent. Melito has surely not invented it, but received it. To discover its background, it will be worthwhile to examine New Testament use of the words *typos* and *antitypos*. Here the most frequent use of *typos* is entirely in accord with standard Greek usage, and relates to the provision of moral example(s) (Phil. 3.17; 1 Thess. 1.7; 2 Thess. 3.9; 1 Tim. 4.12; Tit. 2.7; 1 Pet. 5.3; arguably also Rom. 6.17; and even possibly 1 Cor. 10.6). We also find the word introducing an 'exemplar' of a written document, the quotation of a letter (Acts 23.26). Nor is it particularly unusual to find the word being used in the plural (*typoi*) for the idols (i.e. casts or replicas made in a mould) worshipped by 'our ancestors' in the desert, and then for the 'pattern' (*typos*) according to which Moses was to make the 'tent of testimony'(Acts 7.43–4): both uses quote or allude to the LXX

---

[26] Quoted from David Stern, *Parables in Midrash. Narrative and Exegesis in Rabbinic Literature* (Cambridge, Mass.: Harvard University Press, 1991), p. 10. I am indebted to this work for alerting me to the difference between general Greek usage and the biblical adoption of the term as equivalent to *mashal*.

[27] See above ch. 6; also Hanson, in Ackroyd and Evans (eds.), *Cambridge History of the Bible*, pp. 414–16 and 420–1; and Oskar Skarsaune, *The Proof from Prophecy*.

[28] See further D. A. Russell, *Criticism in Antiquity*, especially ch. 7, and the selection of texts in D. A. Russell and M. Winterbottom, *Ancient Literary Criticism*. Also my own treatment of *mimēsis* in *The Art of Performance*, pp. 137ff.; in 'Rhetorical Schools', and in 'Panegyric and the Bible' (reproduced here as ch. 5).

[29] I am grateful to my research student, Rowena Edwards, for a conversation which generated this observation.

(Amos 5.26 and Exod. 25.40), and both are within the range of standard Greek usage. In the latter case we again have the 'architect's model', found also in Hebrews 8.5. This, however, is a 'heavenly' or 'eternal' model, revealed to Moses so that it could be realised on earth. It is hardly surprising that Philo and Platonising Christians could use 'type' for spiritual symbols, and to exclude this usage by using the criterion of 'history' is clearly problematic.

There are only two cases where the usage is at all exceptional. In 1 Corinthians 10.11 (where the word occurs in the adverbial form, *typikōs*) it might appear unusual, yet, if our reading were not affected by typological assumptions, it could be taken simply to mean that 'these things happened to them *by way of example*'. So, in terms of Greek usage in general, the one oddity is Romans 5.14 which speaks of Adam as the *'typos* of the one to come'. It is this kind of thing that Melito tries to account for, a peculiarity of usage reinforced by the two New Testament cases of *antitypos* (a word never used in Greek outside the biblical–Christian tradition in the kind of sense found here).[30] In Hebrews 9.24, the sanctuary made with human hands is an 'antitype' of the 'true' or 'real' one, which turns out to be heaven; and 1 Peter 3.20–1 treats the Flood as an 'antitype' of baptism, each saving by water. The interesting thing here is that while in some sense the antitype precedes the type, what is signified is something eschatological and transcendent. Furthermore there is a liturgical dimension in these last two cases, a dimension which pervades the Epistle to the Hebrews which is understandably regarded as 'typological' in its treatment of the scriptures, even though it uses the terminology but sparsely, and is not interested in historical 'events' at all, but rather the patterns of cultic rites.

Such usage is also found in the *Epistle of Barnabas*: Jacob blessed the younger son because 'he saw in the Spirit a *typos* of the people of the future'; the scapegoat is cursed and therefore bears the mark (*typos*) of Jesus. Somehow an 'impression' of the future is etched into the scriptural texts, so that the oracles are not just verbal riddles but 'representations' of what is to come. The element of *mimēsis* is what makes a 'type'. The other examples in the *Epistle of Barnabas*

---

[30] Normal Greek usage follows the general sense of 'repelled' or 'repellant', taking the literal sense of *typtō* – 'blow' and understanding the compound as 'counter-blow'. There are few cases of the word meaning 'corresponding', or 'an image' or 'an impression' outside biblical-Christian literature: see Liddell and Scott.

make this clear: the bronze serpent, and Moses stretching out his arms during the battle with Amalek, are models or parables with particular significations, not because of a dramatic replication of the event to which each belongs, but because of particular features which bear the same 'impress' – the arms outstretched on the cross enabling victory, the serpent placed on a tree giving healing and life. The features which go beyond general usage relate to the eschatological and dispensational claims of early Christianity. They also seem to have a rootage in liturgical associations, for, as in the Epistle to the Hebrews, so here there is an interest in showing that ritual requirements have been fulfilled and surpassed in Christ and the Church.

It is these features which Melito must have received and seeks to account for in his rhetorically rationalising way. Nor is it insignificant that his basic 'type' also has a liturgical context. There are good reasons, then, for thinking that Melito is familiar with a non-Hellenistic way of reading and shaping texts which invests significance through highlighting correspondences with sacred literature and ritual acts, and that he uses Hellenistic conventions to articulate this. But it is the correspondences which matter. And the 'production' of correspondences, whether or not the word 'type' actually appears, is what may constitute 'typology' as a particular definable form of the broader category 'allegory'.[31]

The production of correspondences is something we can trace not merely in early Christianity, but in the Hebrew Bible itself. Innerbiblical typologies are characterised by Fishbane,[32] and he finds that correspondences between narratives could even be retrospectively created, the Abraham stories, for example, 'typifying' the exodus and receiving the 'impress' of Israel's story.[33] In exploring such correspondences, Fishbane discerns a range of different types of typologies, each of which can be paralleled in patristic material.

His first category is remarkably like what we found in Ephrem, and he calls them 'Typologies of a Cosmological-Historical Nature'. Here there is 'a parallelism ... between the *Urzeit* of origins and the *Endzeit* of hope'; the

---

[31] See further my discussion of allegory in my article 'Allegory'.

[32] *Biblical Interpretation in Ancient Israel*, pp. 350–79.

[33] Ibid., pp. 372–9; cf. R. W. L. Moberly, *The Old Testament of the Old Testament: Patriarchal Narratives and Mosaic Yahwism* (Minneapolis: Fortress, 1992), pp. 142–6.

mythic prototype . . . enables the historical imagination to assess the significance of certain past or present events; and, correlatively, it projects a configuration upon future events by which they are anticipated and identified.

In other words, there is a kind of intersection of particular history with universal myth, and this requires a 'reconsideration of the common view that the Israelite apprehension of history is linear only'. Biblical examples include the pictures of restoration in Isaiah 51 and 65, where the return from exile is configured according to creation, Eden and the exodus. It is not simply Ephrem's types, but particularly Irenaeus' sense of Adam's creation and fall being 'recapitulated' and reversed in Christ that would seem to have roots here, with potential for the rich growth we observed in chapter 7.

Fishbane classifies his second group as 'Typologies of a Historical Nature', suggesting that a historical paradigm or prototype 'provides the terms or configuration for the way the later event is presented', or 'for the way a future hope is formulated'. The exodus motifs in Joshua 3–5, Psalm 114, and prophetic writings like Hosea, Micah, Isaiah and Jeremiah provide his biblical examples. Without the word 'type' being used, similar use of allusive motifs can be traced in Gospel-narratives, most obviously John 6. Such narrative patterns clearly anticipate the 'prophetic types' which we have found in *Barnabas* and Melito. 'Types' of this 'oracular' kind were certainly drawn into the apologetic reading of scripture and used in the defence of Christian claims to fulfilment, but these texts suggest that, like the first kind of typology, the initial flourishing lay in the liturgical and homiletic context. The *Peri Pascha* appears to be a Christian Haggadah which commemorated both the exodus and its eschatological replay in Christ.

Fishbane further identifies 'Typologies of a Spatial Nature', citing the arbitrary identification of Mount Moriah and the site of the Jerusalem Temple in 2 Chronicles 3.1, as well as the symbolic correlations made with Eden and Zion in a variety of texts. Ephrem provides instances in the Christian tradition, and such 'sacred geography' had an important role in Christian allegorical readings of scripture. Particular times and places, like events and persons, are overlaid by universal, mythical or cosmological 'types' and liturgically anticipate the eschaton.

But it is Fishbane's 'Typologies of a Biographical Nature' which provide a link between biblical typology and Hellenistic exemplarist reading of narrative. In their 'personal traits and personal behaviours', suggests Fishbane, Joshua and Moses are aligned; Noah is a new Adam, as is Abraham too; Elijah and Ezekiel bear the marks of a new Moses. The moralising tendency of rhetorical exegesis and composition turned such biographical typologies into 'types' of virtuous action, 'exemplars' presented for imitation. Already we can see this happening in Hebrews 11, and it rapidly becomes characteristic of Christian *paraenesis*.

But such biographical 'types' would easily become also prefigurations of Christ. Already in Matthew's Gospel, Christ is presented as a 'new Moses'. The identity of name in Greek would encourage the notion that Joshua was the 'type' of Jesus, and generate Origen's allegorical exegesis of the book of Joshua as predictive in its every detail of Christ. It is not surprising that the various kinds of typology identified by Fishbane acquired a prophetic and so Christological focus in early Christianity. We can see it happening in *Barnabas* and Melito.

This discussion of its biblical roots alerts us to the complexity of typology, and to the fact that allegory would easily be generated by it in the Hellenistic environment. Melito's theory captures it but partially. Yet in crucial ways Melito does anticipate the particular character of Antiochene theory, by contrast with the Origenist allegorical tradition.The notion of the text being 'parabolic' or 'ikonic' easily grows out of Melito's procedure and his description of it. The key thing is the imitative nature of the representational narrative which is seen as a model or *typos*. Origenist allegory, as we have seen, tended to take bits of the text piecemeal as more or less arbitrary symbols of truths which provided the underlying coherence. What the Antiochenes sought was a more integral relationship between the coherence of text or narrative and the truth discerned by *theōria* or insight: the kind of ikonic *mimēsis* Melito offered gave them a way of seeing parabolic possibilities, not only for oracular reference but for dogmatic reference.

Thus 'typology' may usefully be used as a heuristic term to distinguish interpretative or compositional strategies which highlight correspondences, not just at the verbal level, but at the level of mimetic sign. Within that broad definition, however, different types of typology can be discerned. Focussing on method of production, types of typology might be distinguished as functioning through mimetic symbols, parallel narratives, corresponding characterisations, exemplary patterns, or intertextual resonances. Focussing on content, they may be broadly distinguished in Fishbane's terms as cosmological, historical, biographical and spatial types, though in Christian texts these categories need to be extended to specify types of a predominantly prophetic, eschatological, liturgical, universal and Christological kind.

I therefore propose the identification of four broad categories of 'types' in patristic exegesis, all of which in some sense create intersections of time and eternity, particular and universal:

(1) exemplary (or biographical – potentially 'universal');
(2) prophetic (or 'historical' – narrative prefiguration);
(3) spatial or geographical;
(4) recapitulative (cosmological/eschatological).

Thus our review proves that to approach patristic exegesis through the 'senses' of scripture is not as straightforward or as illuminating as has generally been supposed. Each 'sense' is itself multivalent. The 'senses' are derived, I suggest, partly by reading back the mediaeval analysis of 'senses' of scripture, and partly by adaptation of Origen's (polemical) account of his exegetical procedures, an account which leaves unsaid a very great deal about the principles of exegesis because they were taken for granted and therefore not articulated. Besides, this whole approach to describing patristic exegesis overlooks the question how New Testament texts were interpreted. Here these categories scarcely apply, yet issues of meaning and implication, for Christology, for morality, fate and freedom, and so on, were crucial.[34] So what seem to be needed are new proposals about how to characterise the actual exegetical practices of the early Church. My contention is that neither the self-conscious practice of detailed exegesis, nor its broader hermeneutical principles, are properly attended to by the standard analysis into senses. It would seem that a more complex approach is needed for describing the process of biblical interpretation in the early church.

---

[34] See, for example, the studies of Maurice Wiles, *The Spiritual Gospel* (Cambridge: Cambridge University Press, 1960) and *The Divine Apostle* (Cambridge: Cambridge University Press, 1967); also Gorday, *Principles of Patristic Exegesis*.

II

Standard analyses in terms of 'literal', 'typological' and 'allegorical' (with perhaps the addition of 'moral' or 'tropological' or 'symbolical' or 'theoretic' so as to include the range of patristic terms) do not in fact constitute an approach to method at all. Method should surely address the mechanics employed to extract meaning, and those mechanics may be used in any of the approaches usually treated as 'methods'. Etymology, for example, may figure in explanatory exegesis of a 'literal' kind, or as the basis of allegory. Deductions may be made from texts by a logical method akin to the syllogisms of philosophy or the enthymemes of rhetoric, but the result may be literal, dogmatic or allegorical. The Rabbinic *middot* (exegetical rules),[35] which are more methodological in character, may yield *halakah* (rulings on how to keep the Law in daily life) or *haggadah* (narrative exposition), or, in a Christian context, similar moves may produce a typological, Christological or spiritual harvest. While it is important to be aware of the articulated 'rules' or 'methods' that can be found in the material with which we are concerned, such rules are not necessarily useful for characterising actual exegetical approaches, or 'reading strategies', to use terminology current in critical theory. Differences in stance and practice can be traced to different schools or contexts[36] – indeed, the standard terms may be seen as tools to describe those differences rather than methodological keys.

So can we provide a more adequate descriptive grid? To that end, a range of categories is now suggested. The history of patristic exegesis reflects an accumulation and overlay of these approaches, and the debate between Alexandria and Antioch is not a little to do with the appropriate relationship between them. The articulation of these different exegetical strategies is based on what can be observed in early Christian material, together with what can be gleaned about the approach to texts in antiquity. In other words, what follows does not pretend to reproduce their own accounts of scriptural interpretation but categorises practices observable in the texts.

---

[35] See Froelich, *Biblical Interpretation*, for translation, and above, ch. 4, for discussion.
[36] Simonetti, *Biblical Interpretation*, is recommended as an attempt to trace different exegetical 'schools'.

Producing paraenesis

In Christian circles the scriptures were always treated as the Word of God and as a guide to life. Even though Halakah was rejected by the increasingly Gentile Christian movement at a very early stage, the notion that moral teaching was enshrined in God's Word replaced it very rapidly. In practice Paul himself would have endorsed this process: he offers his own *paraenesis*. The ethical interest of the Apostolic Fathers was based in scripture, as we shall see in the next chapter. Their *paraenesis* was built up out of scriptural material in a way that presupposed that scriptural texts provided divine teaching of a moral nature.

It is therefore no surprise to find that Origen assumes the moral meaning of scripture in his hermeneutical discussion in *De principiis* IV. He begins his discussion by comparing the Law of Moses and the teaching of Jesus with the work of other lawgivers, celebrating the fact that whereas others have been merely local, these have proved potentially universal, despite the very real dangers of persecution involved in adopting allegiance to them. The subsequent chapters raise the question how the laws are to be read, and despite all Origen's arguments to the effect that scripture cannot always be read 'according to the letter' given the impossibilities and absurdities which arise, it becomes evident that a great deal is to be taken at face value, as noted earlier, especially the moral commands not to kill, not to commit adultery, not to steal, and the Gospel precepts concerning anger, lust and so on.[37] In the *Contra Celsum*,[38] Origen would celebrate the fact that, unlike philosophy, Christianity could make even the 'simple' good. Yet, for Origen, the Bible is without question a manual of morality, to be subjected, like the classical texts in the schools, to 'ethical criticism'. The conscientious interpreter has to distinguish those laws which are meant to be kept and those which have a deeper meaning because they are unreasonable or impossible.

Paraenetic exegesis runs right through the period and beyond. Like the sermonic material of every age, the moral exhortations of the great preacher, John Chrysostom, are more or less grounded in scriptural texts. Theologians like Gregory of Nyssa speak of human

---

[37] *De princ.* IV.3.4; *GCS*, vol. V, pp. 329–30; ET Butterworth, pp. 293–6.
[38] *C. Cels.* VI.1–3ff.; *GCS*, vol. II, pp. 70–3; ET: Chadwick, pp. 316ff.

beings having a choice between living like the beasts and living like the angels:[39] the nature of that choice and the moral characteristics of the two possibilities were drawn from reading the Bible, just as the *Epistle of Barnabas* and the *Didache* had found there the Two Ways, the way of darkness and the way of light.

The primacy of this way of reading scripture in the Christian tradition has been obscured by concentration on other features, such as the rejection of Halakah and the development of the Christological reading, or the supposed concern for history in the Antiochene reaction against Alexandria. Nor has enough been made of the background in the schools of grammar and rhetoric which read texts to find the moral of the tale, and engaged in necessary 'ethical criticism' to turn immoral myths into edificatory material. As already observed, Basil's *Address to the Young on how they might derive Benefit from reading Greek Literature* has fascinating precedents in the *Moralia* of Plutarch, and remarkable parallels in Christian interpretation of the Bible.[40]

Decoding oracles and unfolding prophecies

The Roman world was fascinated by oracles. Plutarch was writing *On the Cessation of Oracles* at a time when the imperial government consulted Sibylline Books, collections of oracular riddles, to determine policy. Jews and Christians would assemble Sibylline collections to suit their apologetic.[41] Oracles were traditionally in riddling form.

In the Hellenistic world, the prophetic books of the Jewish scriptures were treated as collections of oracles. The riddles were to be interpreted in order to understand the reference and discover the prophetic prediction. Inevitably this involved allegory of some sort. The 'pesher' found in the Dead Sea Scrolls applies texts to the present in that way, a usage found also in Matthew's Gospel and Justin's *Dialogue with Trypho*. Thus was initiated Christian 'oracular'

---

[39] E.g. *De opificio hominis;* see my article, 'Adam, the Soul and Immortality: A Study of the Interaction of "Science" and the Bible in some Anthropological Treatises of the Fourth Century', *VC* 37 (1983), pp. 110–40.

[40] Cf. my article, 'Rhetorical Schools'; also Dennis R. MacDonald, *Christianizing Homer.*

[41] H. W.Parke, *Sibyls and Sibylline Prophecy in Classical Antiquity*, ed. B. C. McGing (London: Routledge, 1988).

interpretation, encouraging piecemeal application of texts to supposed fulfilments and a disregard of context or unity of subject.

Irenaeus suggested that every prophecy before its fulfilment was full of enigmas and ambiguities, justifying this view with reference to the instruction given to Daniel to seal the book until the consummation, and Jeremiah's statement that in the last days they shall understand these things.[42] For Christians, he says, the Law is a treasure, hid in a field, but brought to light by the cross of Christ. With textual coherence rendered irrelevant, a new kind of unity is found in the Christological reading.

For Clement of Alexandria, prophecies and oracles were spoken in enigmas.[43] The mysteries were not profusely revealed to all and sundry, but only to the initiated. The Pythian Apollo, Isaiah, Orpheus, Homer, the Psalms, Pythagoras, Moses: they all spoke a common enigmatic language. Indeed, Clement affirmed that religious language consists in mystical symbols since the God of the universe is above all speech, all conception and all thought, and can never be committed to writing. The 'oracular' reading of scripture went beyond predictive prophecy to regarding riddles and symbols as constitutive of sacred texts. Only the 'illuminated' could see through the enigma.

We recall the *Rules of Tyconius*,[44] the Donatist treatise on exegesis which at the end of our period influenced Augustine and continued to be used in the Middle Ages in the West. He rationalises the long-accepted practice of applying texts to Christ, and then justifies distinguishing applications within the same text to Christ himself and to the Body of Christ, namely the Church, where passages could not easily be referred consistently to Christ's person. This is a systematisation of an essentially arbitrary process grounded in the assumption that oracles may mean anything because they are riddles and meant to be.

A series of notorious patristic doctrines and practices had their genesis in 'oracular exegesis': the notion that scripture was inspired by the Holy Spirit and 'dictated' to human scribes, who, as it were, mechanically recorded its riddles; the prophetic, indeed

---

[42] *Adv. haer.* 4.26.1, quoting Daniel 12.4, 7 and Jereremiah 23.20.; Harvey, vol. II, pp. 234–5; *SC* IV.2, pp. 712–13; ET *ANCL*, vol. I, p. 461.

[43] *Strom.* v.4ff.; *GCS*, vol. II, pp. 338ff.; ET *ANCL*, vol. II, pp. 232ff.

[44] Cf. ch. 6, pp. 137–9 above.

Christological meaning of the whole of scripture; and the use of the so-called allegorical method, treating scripture as a veiled symbol of the spiritual world.

Developing philological scholarship with respect to the scriptures, according to then current cultural norms

Prior to the advent of Christian scholarship in the third century, textual and grammatical analysis was employed only piecemeal and usually with a particular end in view, such as to score polemical or apologetic points. But the rise of a more 'professional' approach to exegesis meant recognition of the need to establish agreement about the wording of the text; to attend to the proper construal and correct reading of its sentences; to elucidate figures of speech; and to discuss particular words and their range of meaning, offering exposition of the meaning of uncommon words, or of special meanings in the biblical context – in other words, to make all the indispensable moves which writers of commentaries take for granted and analysts of exegesis forget to articulate!

Origen we have observed taking this lexical analysis very seriously, since every jot and tittle was significant. But this 'literal' level only dealt with the 'body' of the text. Just as rhetoricians distinguished the wording and the content, so Origen saw the letter as the 'dress' in which the true meaning came: 'we have this treasure in earthen vessels,' he quotes. 'By "earthen vessels"', he explains, 'we understand the humble diction of the scriptures.'[45] Where he probed and enquired for the hidden treasure, the Antiochenes would be more anxious to preserve the connection between the wording and the meaning.

Scholarship also assumed that to grasp the allusion was to enrich the reading of the text; consequently explanatory notes were generated, and Origen often employed his erudition in the provision of such material. What distinguished the Antiochene approach from the Alexandrian seems to have been not only a concern about the connection between the letter of the text and any other meaning attributed to it, but also an interest in the narrative coherence of the text both with itself and with the 'facts' which explanatory comment provided. A Theodore of Mopsuestia wanted to relate the message of

---

[45] Fragment of *Comm. Jn.* IV; *GCS*, vol. IV, p. 98; ET *ANCL*, addit. vol., p. 345.

each prophet to the time and events through which he lived; so the so-called historical books of the Bible were used to provide the necessary material for such explanatory comment. But without the modern historical consciousness, none of this prevented anachronistic reading, and the modern preoccupation with historicity was not the principal motive in providing straightforward and practical bits of useful information for understanding what was going on behind the text.

This illuminates the similarities and differences between modern historico-critical procedures and Antiochene commentaries. The roots of all commentary lie in the practices of the grammatical and rhetorical schools, and most material in a modern commentary, like most material in an Antiochene commentary, is a collection of odd bits of very different kinds of information, generally belonging to the spheres of *to methodikon* and *to historikon* distinguished by ancient practitioners, ordered only by the order of the words of the text being commented upon, and selected by the judgement of the commentator as to what requires elucidation. Sometimes this sinks to stating the obvious – Antiochene commentaries are often described as boring because they do precisely that. But that point immediately highlights the redundancy of exegesis if a text is transparent. Exegesis is bound to be concerned with the problems raised by a text. The difference between ancient and modern exegesis lies in the massive shift in what is found to be problematical. We have had problems about historical coherence; they had problems about doctrinal coherence. Doctrine figures large in all patristic exegesis of whatever so-called school.

Long before the Antiochenes, however, the need to provide background information had generated an interest in biblical geography, chronology, natural history, prosopography and so on. A notable collector of such scholarly information was Eusebius, the inheritor of Origen's famous library at Caesarea. Some of such information was undoubtedly gleaned from Jewish scholars,[46] and within the limits of the information available to the ancients, it was the precursor of the reference literature produced by modern scholars in atlases, encyclopedias and dictionaries, as well as commentaries.

---

[46] See de Lange, *Origen and the Jews*; and Adam Kamesar, 'The Narrative Aggada'.

Demonstrating divine truth and deducing doctrine

Deductive exegesis was the product of using reason to figure out the implications of scripture, as lawyers interpreted legal texts, philosophers Homer and Rabbis Torah. The application of reason to determining the implications of biblical texts was taken seriously. Origen encouraged enquiry; Tyconius insists that reason be used to relate text and interpretation. In debate, doctrinal deduction from texts was, of course, fundamental.

But the deductive process was more pervasive than that. Hippolytus, writing *On the Psalms*,[47] enquires why there are one hundred and fifty. That the number fifty is sacred he proves from the days of Pentecost. It signifies release from labour and fasting, liberty and joy, a point further deduced from the Jubilee year. It is therefore fitting that there be not just one set of fifty hymns celebrating liberation and the goodness of God, but three, for the name of the Father, the Son and the Holy Spirit. He goes on to find further saving significance in the position and numbering of particular Psalms. Questions and deductions of this kind were a feature of literary criticism in philosophical schools: Porphyry's *Homeric Questions* apparently used the method of explaining Homer by Homer, resolving problems by reference to other passages.[48] The same principle of deduction by comparison of texts is found among the Rabbinic *middot*.

Much that has been described as allegory is in fact deduction of this kind, through etymology, by *gematria* or number symbolism and other such techniques, or by the correlation of one text with another in a kind of syllogistic process: grant the premisses and the conclusions follow. Enough weight has not so far been given to the rationalistic character of much exegesis that may seem to us quite bizarre. The Rabbinic *middot* are a series of rationalistic rules of this kind: deduction from the 'light' case to the 'heavy'; deduction from the general to the specific; deduction from other passages, or adjudication of discrepancies between passages by reference to a third; or, finally, deduction from context. As far as method is concerned, Christians exercised the same kind of reasoning.

---

[47] Hippolytus, *On the Psalms*: *GCS*, vol. I, Frag. ix, p. 138; Frag. xvii, p. 145.
[48] Lamberton, *Homer the Theologian*.

Discovering the text's 'mimetic' representation of reality

Mimēsis was a key concept in ancient understanding of literature. The performance of epic or drama created a 'representation' of life from which the audience learnt.[49] In the ancient Church mimēsis or 'representation' was important. It underlay the enactment of the saving events in the sacraments, as well as the 'exemplary' use of scripture: great heroes were listed to illustrate a particular virtue, so a character like Job came to embody patience, and Christ's life and death were set forth as a way to be imitated. Such 'mimetic' use of literary heroes reinforced the paraenetic use of scripture with which we began, and provided 'types'. 'Mimetic exegesis' assumes the replay of a *drama* – an act or plot – and so had a place in forming ethics, lifestyle and liturgy.

As we have seen, *mimēsis* also provides a framework for understanding 'typology'. 'Types' are forms of *mimēsis*, the *mimēsis* of a story or act, of a *drama*, a thing done, a life lived.[50] Job was a 'type' prefiguring Christ: both are models of patience to be followed. When Cyril of Alexandria understands the Pentateuch as exemplifying exile and spiritual famine, followed by repentance and renewal, both Abraham's migration and the exodus being paradigms of God's grace effecting conversion, it is easy to see that

---

[49] Cf. *The Art of Performance*, ch. 7.

[50] I am somewhat sceptical of recent attempts to make a clear distinction in Christian usage between 'type' and 'exemplary model', and trace a development from one to another: see J.-N. Guinot, 'La typologie comme technique herméneutique', and F. Heim, 'Le figure du prince ideal au IVe siècle: du type au modele', in *Figures de l'Ancien Testament chez les pères*, Cahiers de *Biblia Patristica* 2 (Strasbourg: Centre d'analyse et de documentation patristiques, 1989). To quote my review in *JTS* NS 42.2 (1991), p. 707:

> the final paper is somewhat in tension with the first if one is looking for a consistent history of development. Guinot argues that typology is not characteristic of Homeric interpretation, that Odysseus provided a 'model' not a 'type'. How then, he asks, did typology enter Christian interpretation? He regards it as not properly defined within the New Testament, and in Origen not distinguishable from allegory. He concludes that as a theory, it was Antiochene, consciously developed and defined against allegory, though he admits the Jewish origins of typology, suggesting that it existed and functioned before becoming a rationalistic technique of exegesis. By contrast, Heim traces the development of Old Testament models in the post-Constantinian period, distinguishing them from earlier typologies. Both papers are well-argued, and the contrast highlights the complexity of the issues.

> As we have seen, the word 'type' appears with a very wide range of usages, which probably have differing roots, but certainly became compounded. The idea of 'types' of good conduct is a proper Greek usage whereas a tendency to develop parallel narratives probably has semitic roots.

mimetic exegesis is being practised, whereas the designation 'typology' might be debated. It is not after all 'prophetic' in the way 'types' of Christ have been taken to be; in a way it is more like Origen's universal spiritualising. Cyril himself calls it *ēthikē paraenesis*.[51] Yet it has a 'dramatic' quality.

For good reason, the narrative and moral focus of all these variants of typological *mimēsis* attracted the Antiochenes in their reaction against the speculative kinds of allegory associated with Origen. However, the various approaches outlined so far also find their place in the work of Origen. What is it then that distinguishes his so-called allegorical method and makes it problematical for many, both now and in the ancient church? I have suggested that the distinction between Origenist allegory and Antiochene *theōria* is best characterised in terms of a distinction between 'ikonic' and 'symbolic' *mimēsis* or representation.

The difference lay in the Antiochene desire to find a genuine connection between what the text said and the spiritual meaning discerned through contemplation of the text. I use the terms 'ikonic' and 'symbolic' to distinguish that difference. This terminology comes from a distinction drawn by Coulter:[52] representation (*mimēsis*) may be through genuine likeness, an analogy, 'ikon' or image, or it may be by a symbol, something unlike which stands for the reality. The 'ikon' will resemble the person or event which it represents, but symbols are not representations in that sense; symbols are 'tokens' or 'signs' whose analogous relationship with what is symbolised is less clear.[53] Indeed, whereas a text offers

---

[51] Migne, *PG* 69.383B. Kerrigan, *St Cyril of Alexandria*, describes examples of this kind as 'moral explanation of historical texts' (pp. 155ff.).

[52] J. A. Coulter, *The Literary Microcosm*.

[53] The term 'symbol' is open to many different definitions. In some discussions, 'symbol' has been contrasted with 'sign' but, by contrast with Coulter, 'sign' is treated as the equivalent of 'token', and 'symbol' is used much as we use 'ikon' here. For fuller discussion, see Weinsheimer, *Philosophical Hermeneutics and Literary Theory*, ch. 5, 'A Word Is Not a Sign', pp.87ff. He shows how semiotics since Saussure has emphasised the arbitrariness of the 'sign' and the disjunction between 'word' and 'world'; by contrast, 'symbol' is treated as never wholly arbitrary. Gadamer used 'symbol' to restore the connection between 'language' and reality, using aesthetics to demonstrate that symbol 'is not a subsequent coordination . . . but the union of two things that belong to each other'. Gadamer is further quoted as saying (in *Truth and Method*, p. 78): 'The possibility of the instantaneous and total coincidence of the apparent with the infinite in a religious ceremony assumes that what fills the symbol with meaning is that the finite and infinite genuinely belong together.' In other words, as already noted, 'symbol' is filled with the content given here to 'ikon'. Symbol is self-referential – at least signifier and signified are indivisible, whereas allegory, like sign,

internal clues to its 'ikonic' intention, the clues to 'symbolic' language lie in the impossibilities which cannot be taken at face value. That is precisely Origen's claim.

The Antiochenes criticised Origen for arbitrariness. They saw the biblical text as 'ikonic', as imparting dogma and ethics through 'images'. Chrysostom, for example, sees the Gospel stories of Jesus as endless moral teaching aids: Christ is unambitious and void of boasting, teaching on a mountain or a wilderness, not in a city or forum, 'instructing us to do nothing for display, and to separate ourselves from the tumults of ordinary life, and this most especially when we are to study wisdom and discourse of things needful to be done'.[54] Christ sleeps in the boat in the storm as a way of signifying freedom from pride, and teaching a high degree of austerity; he lets the disciples feel alarm and reproves them in order to rub home the lesson that they ought to be confident in all the trials and temptations to come.[55] The stories also teach dogma: Christ heals bodies as well as souls so as to 'stop the shameless mouths of heretics, signifying by his care of both parts of our being that he himself is the Maker of the whole creation. Therefore also on each nature he bestowed abundant providence, now amending the one now the other'.[56] This is not exactly typological exegesis as generally understood, but it has similar 'ikonic' features: paraenetic concerns and deductive methods facilitate the discernment of 'theoretic' meanings through the narrative conveyed by the text.

Coulter's analysis of Neoplatonic exegesis would seem to bear out my contention[57] that the Antiochenes prefer the literary criticism of the rhetorical schools, by contrast with Origen and the allegorists who prefer the approach of philosophers, exploiting the 'letter' to demonstrate that an alternative 'symbolic' reading is required. For the Antiochenes, the narrative logic, the plain meaning, the 'earthly' reality of the text read in a straightforward way, was the vehicle or 'ikon' of deeper meanings of a moral and dogmatic kind. What was needed was 'insight' – which might commend itself as a

---

is 'hetero-referential'. Despite the difference in terminology, Gadamer's position, as expressed in this discussion, would surely cohere with my discussion of language as sacrament in ch. 7.

54 *Hom. in Matt.* xv, on Matthew 5.1, 2; Migne, *PG* 57.223; ET *NPNF*, 1st series, vol. x, p. 91.
55 *Hom. in Matt.* xxviii on Matthew 8.23ff.; Migne, *PG* 57.351; ET *NPNF*, 1st series, vol. x, p. 190.
56 *Hom. in Matt.* xv on Matthew 4.23–4; Migne, *PG* 57.223; ET *NPNF*, 1st series, vol. x, p. 91.
57 See my article, 'Rhetorical Schools'.

better English equivalent to *theōria* than others such as 'contemplation'.

The famous exegetical debate was in a sense about method, but it is not well characterised by the distinction between typology and allegory. Both Origen and the Antiochenes incorporated all the previously discussed exegetical 'strategies' into their approaches. The debate was about the connections between different exegetical processes, about the coherence of different levels of reading, about the appropriate way of focussing on the text and its 'mimetic' relationship to reality. Both Origen and the Antiochenes believed scripture was about heavenly realities, but for Origen scripture was a veil, a shadow, which might obscure as much as reveal; for the reality behind the 'tokens' was not self-evident. The Antiochenes found this arbitrary and insisted on attending to what we might call the internal clues to the way the text or narrative 'mirrored' the truth. Both presupposed that every literary text clothed the 'mind' in its 'wording', and the issue was how the two related to one another.

So we may list a series of 'reading strategies':
(1) Paraenetic reading;
(2) Oracular exegesis;
(3) Lexical analysis;
(4) Explanatory comment;
(5) Deductive expansion;
(6) Mimetic reading:
    (a) for exemplary paraenesis;
    (b) to provide prophetic 'types';
    (c) to see how the text mirrors reality 'ikonically';
    (d) to uncover the underlying truth symbolically.

The 'senses' of scripture, 'literal', 'typological' and 'allegorical', are demoted from their position as keys to method, but we may chart (see Fig. 1) the relationship between these more traditional categories and our 'reading strategies', so providing the reconfigured and more complex picture that seems necessary.

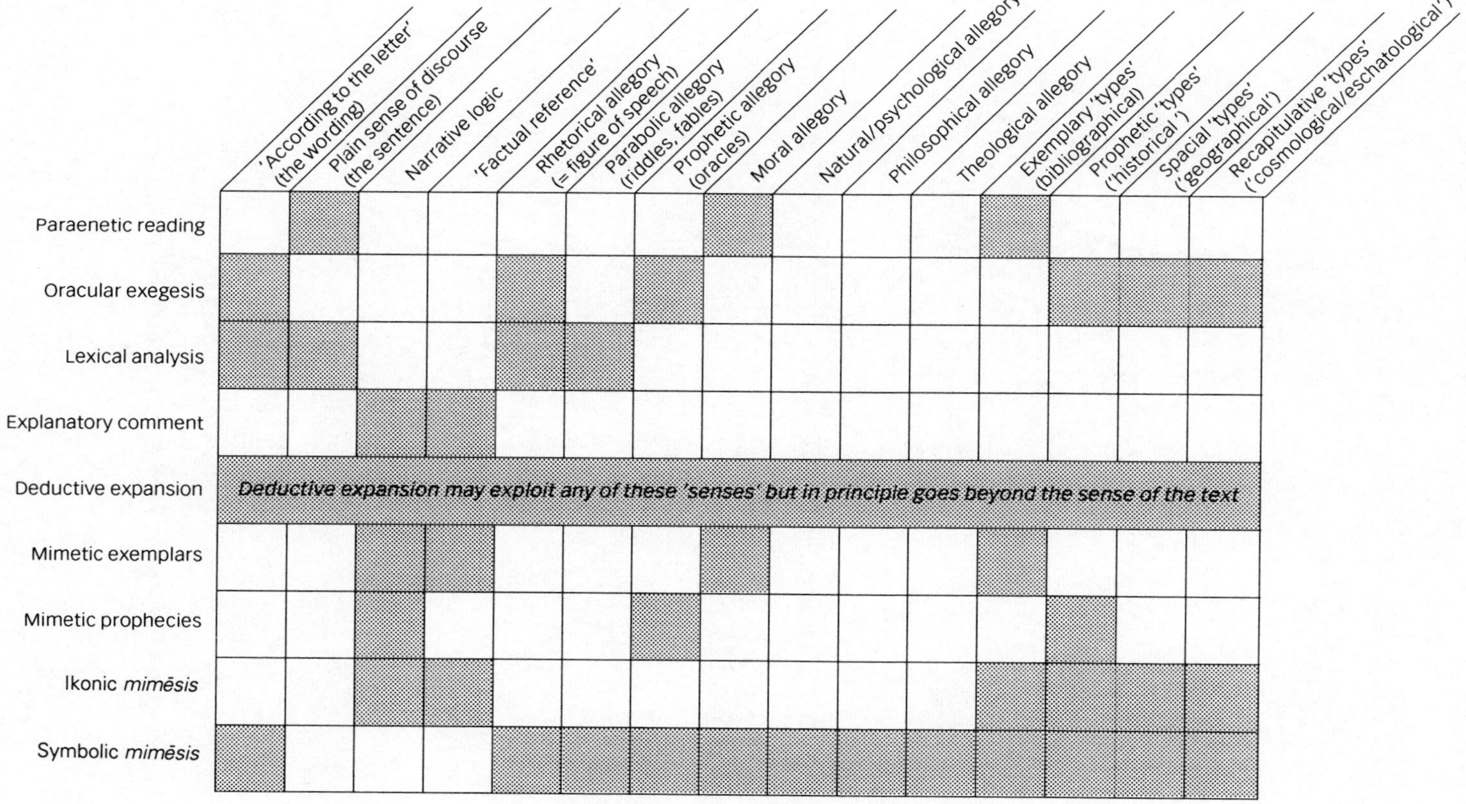

Figure 1

Row labels (methods):
- Paraenetic reading
- Oracular exegesis
- Lexical analysis
- Explanatory comment
- Deductive expansion
- Mimetic exemplars
- Mimetic prophecies
- Ikonic *mimēsis*
- Symbolic *mimēsis*

Column headings ('senses'):
- 'According to the letter' (the wording)
- Plain sense of discourse (the sentence)
- Narrative logic
- 'Factual reference'
- Rhetorical allegory (= figure of speech)
- Parabolic allegory (riddles, fables)
- Prophetic allegory (oracles)
- Moral allegory
- Natural/psychological allegory
- Philosophical allegory
- Theological allegory
- Exemplary 'types' (bibliographical)
- Prophetic 'types' ('historical')
- Spatial 'types' ('geographical')
- Recapitulative 'types' ('cosmological/eschatological')

Deductive expansion may exploit any of these 'senses' but in principle goes beyond the sense of the text

PART IV

The Bible and the life of faith

The use to which a work of literature is put surely influences the way it is understood. Technically speaking, exegesis is the self-conscious extension of translation which seeks to spell out meaning, and so might be confined to scholia, or the more elaborate commentary form. But, in practice, texts are interpreted in the context of polemic or debate, in homily or sermon, in liturgy, and by implication through quotation and allusion in all kinds of literary compositions. Does this make a difference? Is exegesis, especially of literature treated by the exegetes and their hearers as authoritative scripture, affected by the context in which the reading takes place, or by the interpretative genre in which it is incorporated or articulated?

The Bible's principal function in the patristic period was the generation of a way of life, grounded in the truth about the way things are, as revealed by God's Word. Exegesis served this end, whatever the context, and so, perhaps surprisingly, different interpretative genres did not produce distinguishable exegetical strategies. The heart of the matter lay in the many-faceted process of finding life's meaning portrayed in the pages of scripture.

CHAPTER 10

The contexts of interpretation

I

According to one broad-brush picture of the history of exegesis,[1] from Augustine to the Reformation,

theology was practised as the discipline of the sacred page (*sacra pagina*). The monastery became the place, and the monk's daily liturgy was the context, for the practice of theology.

The 'sacred page' 'bore the imprint of God', and to get home to God was the goal. So,

[t]heology as commentary served the purposes of the sacred page. Theology, whether expressed in doctrine, liturgy, or catechesis, was the discipline of the sacred page.

However, with the rise of the universities and of Scholastic theology in the twelfth century, there was a shift to 'sacred doctrine' (*sacra doctrina*). Here faith was seeking understanding. Theology took the form of a *Summa*, rather than a biblical commentary, though interpreting scripture. Then

with the printing press and the scholarship of the Christian humanists, theology shifted to the sacred letter as literature ... The study of the sacred letter of Scripture was to lead not so much to God as to a better society, church, education, and government . . . The rise of historico-critical methods ... continued Humanistic methods.

This account is drawn from an attempt to characterise sixteenth-century commentaries. The conclusion reached is that there was no

---

[1] Kenneth Hagan, 'What did the Term *Commentarius* mean to Sixteenth-century Theologians?', in Irena Backus and Francis Higman (eds.), *Théorie et pratique de l'exégèse*, Actes du troisième colloque international sur l'histoire de l'exégèse biblique au XVIe siècle (Geneva: Librairie Droz S.A., 1990), pp. 13–38.

clear understanding of what constituted a commentary over against
annotations, expositions, or paraphrases; but it is possible to
distinguish the three styles of interpretation outlined, and to see
that commentaries, though similar in being essentially notes on
scripture, differed widely according to the manner in which the task
was understood. Luther and Calvin approached it in terms of the
'sacred page'; Erasmus practised the 'sacred letter'; others
approached the text as vehicle for 'sacred doctrine'. In other words,
their commentaries envisaged different contexts, devotional,
academic or controversial, and for this reason reflected different
interests.

Clearly biblical interpretation in the twentieth century has
inherited this sixteenth-century legacy. A parallel spectrum of
interests is embodied in a range of different 'interpretative genres'.[2]
Thus, scholarship produces commentaries and theme-studies,
utilising the methods current in the humanities; church committees
produce doctrinal or ethical reports in which they seek to do justice
to modern demands without violating the authority of the scriptural
canon; while preachers find neither a satisfactory quarry for their
task of expounding scripture in the context of liturgy – the sermon is
a different interpretative genre, and the expectation that it might
gain from knowledge of scholarly commentaries is disappointed
time and again. To what extent was there a similar divergence of
exegetical interests in the patristic period?

As history, the broad-brush sketch we have borrowed is surely
somewhat problematical – the concurrence of different exegetical
interests, and the overlap of different genres of interpretation,
must have been a feature of Christian use of scripture from the
beginning. Then as now there were different contexts within which
interpretation was taking place: liturgy, catechesis, commentary,
homily, theological treatise, apology, collections of ecclesiastical
canons, hagiography and so on, not to mention the epistles and
apocryphal Gospels of the earliest period, and the monastic
apophthegms of a later time.[3] So was the exegesis of texts, implied

---

[2] See my paper, 'Interpretative Genres and the inevitability of Pluralism', given as the T. W.
Manson memorial lecture in the University of Manchester, 1993, published in *JSNT* 59
(1995), pp. 93–110.

[3] Most, but not all, of these genres will receive some mention in this chapter; for the last see
Douglas Burton-Christie, *The Word in the Desert. Scripture and the Quest for Holiness in Early
Christian Monasticism* (Oxford: Oxford University Press, 1993).

or explicit, distinctive in relation to such genres? Did context affect what readers looked for in texts and the way in which the text functioned in relation to the community which read it? Certainly a remark of Theodore of Mopsuestia might suggest so: 'I judge the exegete's task to be to explain words that most people find difficult; it is the preacher's task to reflect also on words that are perfectly clear and to speak about them.'[4] However, the argument developed here is that, despite a similar range of 'interpretative genres', divergence in exegetical practice is far less marked. Often the same person embodied scholarly interest and preacher's concern. Commentary would gather more problem-oriented notes, dogmatic treatise would argue from the Bible, homily and sermon would focus more on *paraenesis* and the spiritual journey. But the lines were not so clearly demarcated as to prevent vast areas of overlap, and commentary and treatise were meant to inform oral communication. Theology, spirituality and philology were integrally related to one another.

What, then, are the genres to be considered? They must include all forms of early Christian literature, since all in some way interpret scripture. As we have seen, scripture replaced the classics in the formation of a distinctive culture, which nevertheless assumed that texts were the source of cultural identity. So all early Christian literature has an intertextual relationship with the Bible. The genres of this literature may be conveniently mapped in concentric circles (see Fig. 2). At the heart lies worship, public worship in liturgy, private devotion in prayer and spirituality. Associated with them – indeed, generating appropriate attitudes and responses within them – are homilies which shape and reinforce the identity expressed at the heart of it all. Here too we may place works intended to foster Christian values and lifestyle – the narratives of apocryphal Gospels and Acts, later of hagiography – for all of these have intertextual resonances which make them 'interpretative' in their own way. Christian identity was formed by catechesis and safeguarded by canons – both assembling the *paraenesis* found in scripture in order to be effective. Other literary activities were intended to reinforce Christian teaching, both ethical and doctrinal, and cement the wider community, and

---

[4] Quoted by M. F. Wiles, 'Theodore of Mopsuestia as Representative of the Antiochene School', in Ackroyd and Evans (eds.), *Cambridge History of the Bible*, vol. I, p. 491.

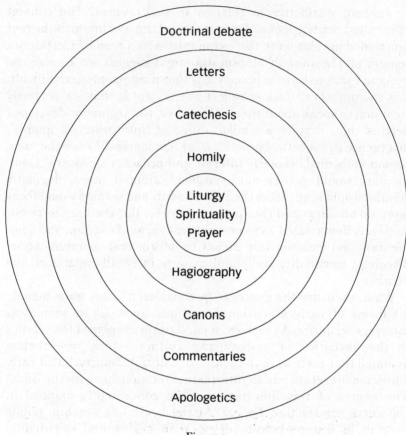

Figure 2

these became more sophisticated as scholarship emerged: epistles, treatises, commentaries. Finally there are works concerned with the community's boundaries, apologies, whether directed to rank outsiders or against dangerous heretics. In literary form they may conform to the type of treatise or letter, but still may be distinguished by their polemical focus, argument and tone.

Clearly these genres emerge and develop over the period with which we are concerned. Important continuities lie in their common inheritance from the earliest period. We will begin therefore by returning to the second century, endeavouring to discern what we can about the core use of scripture to form identity within the community.

II

It is often assumed that the earliest Christian use of scripture was apologetic, differentiation from others, especially the Jews, being the crucial factor in forming self-identity.[5] The really crucial setting for Christian use of scripture, however, was the reading and telling, explaining and exhorting, that went on in the Christian assemblies. There is little reason to doubt that the earliest communities functioned rather like synagogues, and the reading of scripture was central to their regular gatherings.[6]

Our earliest homily as such would seem to be the piece known as *II Clement*.[7] In one particular way it contrasts strikingly with the apologetic material: the prophetic passages of warning, rather than being directed at Jews, are taken as warnings to Christians who might fail in their profession of faith or way of life. Thus, the 'brethren' are those saved from perishing by the mercy of God, and prophetic texts such as Isaiah 54.1 are taken to refer to this saved community;[8] that means they should beware lest they deserve the words of Isaiah 29.13: 'this people honours me with their lips, but their heart is far from me'.[9] It is of those who have not kept the seal of baptism that Isaiah said, 'Their worm shall not die, and their fire shall not be quenched, and they shall be a spectacle for all flesh.'[10] A notable New Testament precedent for this is found in the Epistle to the Hebrews. Apologetic material of an anti-Jewish kind certainly had the function of giving Christians a sense of identity as the new 'replacement' people of God. In Hebrews and *II Clement*, however, this identity as God's people is presumed by the treatment of the Christian congregation as the recipient of the message, and it appears without the explicit anti-Jewish tone.

---

[5] Note the title of Barnabas Lindars' book on the use of scripture in the New Testament, *New Testament Apologetic* (London: SCM Press, 1961). It is perhaps surprising, especially in the structuralist days of 'binary oppositions', that definition over against others does not figure more than it does in the collection of papers, *Jewish and Christian Self-Definition*, 3 vols. (i: *The Shaping of Christianity in the Second and Third Centuries*; ii: *Aspects of Judaism in the Graeco-Roman Period*; iii: *Self-Definition in the Graeco-Roman World*), ed. E. P. Sanders (London: SCM Press, 1980, 1981, 1982).

[6] Burtchaell, *From Synagogue to Church*.

[7] Text and ET are conveniently found in *LCL*.

[8] *II Clem.* 2.1; *LCL*, p. 130.

[9] *II Clem.* 3.5; *LCL*, p. 132.   [10] *II Clem.* 7.6; *LCL*, p. 138.

Within the community, then, its identity as God's people meant that the words of scripture, even the harsh words, applied directly to Christians. The exegetical procedure is a kind of pastiche of texts and allusions which ensured that the prophetic warnings reinforced the predominant note of *paraenesis*:

The Lord says, 'Continually my name is blasphemed among the nations' . . . Wherein is it blasphemed? In that you do not do what I desire. For when the nations hear from our mouth the oracles of God, they wonder at these good and great sayings; then learning of our [unworthy] deeds . . . , then they are turned to blasphemy, saying this is some myth and delusion.[11]

It is a mistake simply to suggest that early Christian use of scripture is Christological and anti-Jewish, for in worship it is focussed on the congregation as the people of God.[12]

Meanwhile, the impression given by *II Clement* is borne out by other evidence. As New Testament scholars well know, in the earliest period much material of a confessional, liturgical or homiletic kind has to be deduced from texts whose surface-genre is quite different, things like letters, or apocalypses, or even Gospels. We will examine *I Clement*[13] as a kind of test case, and see if we can find traces of the use and interpretation of scripture found in this confessional context.

This document is so packed with scriptural allusion, or, if not allusion, language that can be paralleled in scriptural material, that a comprehensive examination is beyond our scope. We will first select sections[14] which belong to the genre of exhortation, *paraenesis*. What we immediately notice is that scriptural exhortations are simply 'compounded' out of allusive phrases, mixed quotations, echoes. When discussing cross-reference in chapter 6, we considered the 'Two Ways' tradition found in the *Didache* and the so-called *Epistle of Barnabas*. We discovered there a process of allusion and 'collage'. In *I Clement*, we find this same use of the Bible in *paraenesis*, together with the 'mimetic' use of scriptural heroes as exemplary of particular qualities or virtues.

The opening words of our example are words of warning: 'beware

---

[11] *II Clem.* 13.2–3; *LCL*, p.148. (My ET.) Cf. 17.4–5; *LCL*, p. 156.
[12] Melito's *Peri Pascha*, on the other hand, is notoriously anti-Jewish. We will return to that later.
[13] Text and ET are available in *LCL*; ET also in Louth, *Early Christian Writings*.
[14] *I Clem.* 21–3; *LCL*, pp. 46–50. ET Louth, *Early Christian Writings*, pp. 32–3.

lest God's many blessings turn into a judgment on us'. One is reminded of the implications, if not the actual words, of texts like 2 Corinthians 6.1ff. Such judgement would be the result of 'not doing what is good and well-pleasing in his sight with concord'. This is clearly allusive material applied to the particular situation the epistle is addressing, namely the breakdown of concord in the Corinthian church. There follows an acknowledged quote ('it says somewhere'). This seems to be a version of Proverbs 20.27, though the text is interestingly different from the LXX:[15]

> *1 Clement*: The Spirit of the Lord is a lamp searching the secret places of the stomach.
> *LXX*: The breath of the Lord is the light of human beings which searches the secret places of the bosom.

On the basis of this text, the reader is exhorted to note 'how near God is – nothing escapes God's notice, even thoughts and intentions'. One is reminded of Psalm 139. The section goes on to enjoin reverence, purity, meekness and gentleness, specifying the proper qualities for the young, for wives and for children. The following section[16] confirms these general exhortations from scripture, quoting Psalm 33.12–17 (LXX numbering) at length, and appending a stray verse from Psalm 31.10 (LXX) as a contrasting warning to sinners.[17]

Clement then speaks of the all-merciful and beneficent Father having compassion on those that fear him:[18] the scriptural language is again evident. Sometimes the exact reference is untraceable – here an extensive quote, found also in *II Clement* 11.2, would appear to come from a lost apocalypse: the image of a tree with ripening fruit leads into witness from scripture that God will quickly accomplish his purpose, this time conflating Isaiah 13.22b (LXX) and Malachi 3.1.

---

[15] The translations are my own, and are meant to bring out the differences. Clement has *pneuma* (spirit) where Proverbs has *pnoe* (breath); Clement has *lychnos* (lamp) where Proverbs has *phos* (light); Clement has *gastros* (stomach) where Proverbs has *koilias* (bosom). The ET also reflects the fact that Clement has no *anthropōn*, and uses a participle where LXX uses a relative clause.

[16] *1 Clem*. 22; *LCL*, p. 48; Louth, *Early Christian Writings*, p. 32.

[17] Not surprisingly some manuscripts have substituted Psalm 33.19 instead: both verses begin in a similar way, 31.10 speaking of the sinner's many scourges, contrasted with the mercy surrounding those who hope in the Lord; 33.19 speaking of the many afflictions of the righteous, from all of which the Lord saves.

[18] *1 Clem*. 23; *LCL*, pp. 48ff.; Louth, *Early Christian Writings*, p. 33.

This process of assembling collages is characteristic of early Christian *paraenesis*. It has been observed that one result of Paul's insistence on accepting Gentiles without requiring that they adopt the ethnic marks of a Jew was that early Christianity had no Halakah. But as Wayne Meeks has shown,[19] a distinct Christian morality rapidly developed and was claimed as a mark differentiating the 'third race' from Jew and Greek. The kind of scriptural *paraenesis* we have discovered generated this morality. Furthermore, it enabled the Bible to become the source of canonical rulings.

To turn for a moment to the *Didache* is to move into that other genre, namely the literature of ecclesiastical canons. Yet the exegetical manner appears largely similar to the features of scriptural *paraenesis* we have been exploring in *I Clement*. It is worth digressing for a moment to look further at this material. Interestingly enough, Clement's name came to be attached to the largest collection. The *Apostolic Constitutions*[20] is highly composite, the end-product of a long literary development; so, by attending to this work, we can reasonably claim to have considered a representative sample of this genre. The bulk of it is an enlarged version of the earlier work known as the *Didascalia,* now extant only in Syriac; Book VII incorporates and expands the *Didache*, adding also a collection of model prayers, in the midst of which are inserted instructions for training catechumens and for baptism; the final book is a version of the *Apostolic Tradition* of (Ps.-) Hippolytus. This last book ends with a list of canons or rules, but the bulk of the material is more like an ever-expanding ecclesiastical handbook.

The work opens by identifying the catholic Church as God's plantation, his beloved vineyard,[21] and the whole of the first book is devoted to outlining what we might call the 'lifestyle' of Christian believers, their characteristic behaviour and 'culture', first in general, then specifically for men[22] and women[23] respectively. As previously hinted, the parallels with the kind of paraenetical

---

[19] In his Speaker's lectures, *The Origins of Christian Morality.*

[20] Text in *SC*; ET in *ANCL*, vol. xvii. A good introduction is found in Paul Bradshaw, *The Search for the Origins of Christian Worship* (London: SPCK, 1992), ch. 4 'Ancient Church Orders: A Continuing Enigma', pp. 80–110.

[21] *Apost. Const.* I. Prologue; *SC* I, p. 102; ET *ANCL*, p. 15.

[22] *Apost. Const.*I.3–7; *SC* I, pp. 110–22; ET *ANCL*, pp. 17–22.

[23] *Apost. Const.*I.8–10; *SC* I, pp. 124–32; ET *ANCL*, pp. 22–6.

collages of quotation and allusion to scriptural commands, proverbs or sayings found in the Apostolic Fathers is striking.

Succeeding books characterise church officers and others with specific roles in the community, bishops and deacons, widows and virgins. Mixed up with these are parents and children, masters and servants. Here is not just a Church Order, but a pattern of *paraenesis* with roots in the so-called 'Household Codes' of the New Testament. Indeed, it is particularly striking that priority is given to outlining not the precise duties or tasks so much as the character and manner of figures such as the bishop, as in the Pastoral Epistles which clearly provided the basis on which this material expanded.[24] Overlapping vocabulary, and clear allusion to what was believed to be Paul's advice, are filled out with quotations from the Gospels and other scriptural material.

Clearly the bishop[25] exercises discipline over the community, and the parameters of his authority are provided by scriptural precepts and patterns. He is the 'watchman' and the 'shepherd'. Absolute fairness and integrity, with mercy for the penitent, are grounded in biblical texts. Administration of resources as a good steward, remembering the poor, orphans, widows, the afflicted and the stranger, is to be modelled on the scriptures: for the bishop receives tithes and offerings as priest and Levite, and he is also prophet, ruler, governor, king – the mediator between God and God's faithful people. He must imitate Christ, and so provide an example to others.

Inevitably this is but a sketch of a huge deposit of material. Clearly the core of the Christian lifestyle, at every level of the community's hierarchy, is obedience to the Ten Commandments, understood through Wisdom's proverbs and the sayings of Christ. The laity are told not to roam the streets, but stay at home to read the scriptures;[26] the bishop is told to study the scriptures so as to expound them to others.[27] Pagan literature and heretical teachers

---

[24] See my *Theology of the Pastoral Letters*.

[25] *Apost. Const.* II *passim*; *SC* I, pp. 144–339; ET *ANCL*, pp. 26–92.

[26] *Apost. Const.* I.4–6; *SC* I, pp. 114–20; ET *ANCL*, pp. 19–20. Joshua 1.8 and Deuteronomy 6.7 are conflated to form an injunction to meditate on the Law day and night, when walking in the field, sitting in the house, etc. At home, the Law, Kings and Prophets are to be read, the hymns of David sung, and the Gospel perused. There must be abstention from heathen books.

[27] *Apost. Const.* II.5.4–7; *SC* I, p.152; ET *ANCL*, p. 29. John 5.39 and Hosea 10.12 appear here to reinforce the injunction.

are to be avoided, and the 'handbook' indicates how to identify these heretics,[28] as well as offering guidance about martyrs and festivals.[29] Carefully, and largely on the basis of scriptural texts, Christian practice is distinguished from Jewish in the matter of Sabbath, Passover and Pentecost, for example, as well as advice given as to how to distinguish commands that belong to Jewish Law and those which constitute Christian morality.

It would appear that part of the process whereby this literature expanded was the addition of further biblical validation; for this literature seems to become increasingly packed with scriptural language, allusion and quotation. Apart from the Two Ways tradition, the *Didache* is relatively free; the *Apostolic Constitutions* saturated. That in itself points to the developing status of scripture as moral guidebook, even 'law-book', within the Church's institution. Above all, here is material that shows how a whole Christian identity was built up out of the biblical books by the construction of the kind of textual collages already exemplified in the *Apostolic Fathers*.

Intermingled with the quotations and allusions are exemplary figures, stories, or acts, also drawn from the approved literature of the Christian *ethnos*. We began our examination of *paraenesis* in *1 Clement* by observing that it used two techniques, the collage and moral 'types'. To return to *1 Clement*, we find that, in fact, this exemplary use of scripture is even more pervasive than the paraenetical collages on which we have been focussing. A few examples must suffice:

(1) Section 4 gives instances of jealousy: Cain and Abel, Jacob and Esau, Joseph, Moses, Aaron and Miriam, Dathan and Abiram, David and Saul. The first is developed a bit, but most of the examples are conjured up through brief allusion.[30]

(2) Sections 7–8 give instances of preaching repentance: Noah, Jonah, and a quotation from Ezekiel 33.11, followed by other quotations, one unidentified, the other Isaiah 1.16–20. Thus exemplary allusion is integrated with the 'collage' procedure we have already instanced.[31]

[28] *Apost. Const.* vi *passim*; *SC* ii, pp. 294–394; ET *ANCL*, pp. 143–77.
[29] *Apost. Const.* v *passim*; *SC* ii, pp. 202–84; ET *ANCL*, pp. 115–43.
[30] *1 Clem.* 4; *LCL*, pp. 14–15; ET Louth, *Early Christian Writings*, pp. 24–5.
[31] *1 Clem.* 7–8; *LCL*, pp. 18–22; ET Louth, *Early Christian Writings*, pp. 25–6.

(3) Section 9ff. provides examples of obedience, faith and hospitality: Enoch and Noah provide one-line references, Abraham is more fully developed in section 10, with Lot and his wife providing material for section 11, and Rahab for section 12.[32] The examples of Abraham's obedience, faith and hospitality are assembled with textual quotations in a way that would become classic. Rahab's hospitality is celebrated, again with relevant quotations, but the section ends with the 'sign' given to her, the scarlet thread, which is taken to foreshadow redemption through the blood of Christ: so, it is stated, Rahab is an instance not only of faith, but also of prophecy. A new feature seems to have entered the picture: but the word 'sign' is used rather than 'type'.

(4) Sections 17–18 treat of humility: Abraham, Job, Moses and David appear, the latter for his prayer of abasement, Psalm 51, now quoted at length.[33]

These exemplary catalogues are connected by exhortatory material of the kind we have already explored. Between sections 12 and 17, for example, humblemindedness is enjoined[34] using Gospel sayings along with texts from the Jewish scriptures already used by Paul in the Corinthian correspondence, and peaceable behaviour is suggested by quotations from wisdom material together with the Psalms. On this occasion, the character of Christ is delineated in an exemplary way,[35] with Isaiah 53 and Psalm 22 providing the portrait. In a later section,[36] a kind of panegyric on love is built up by appeal to Christ, together with quotation of 1 Corinthians 13.

So, by ranging fairly widely in the traditionally 'Clementine' literature, we have found that in ethical exhortation, scripture not only provided the maxims and material for assembling collages of precepts and building up character-sketches, but it could also function as the provider of moral examples for imitation, rather as the classics did in Hellenistic culture. One element embraced by the term 'typology' is present, but studies of exegesis have rarely drawn attention to the manner by which a whole lifestyle is constructed on the basis of scripture.

---

[32] *1 Clem.* 9–12; *LCL*, pp. 22–8; ET Louth, *Early Christian Writings*, pp. 26–8.
[33] *1 Clem.* 17–18; *LCL*, pp. 38–40; ET Louth, *Early Christian Writings*, pp. 30–1.
[34] *1 Clem.* 13–16; *LCL*, pp. 28–36; ET Louth, *Early Christian Writings*, pp. 28–30.
[35] *1 Clem.* 16; *LCL*, pp. 34–6; ET Louth, *Early Christian Writings*, pp. 29–30.
[36] *1 Clem.* 49; *LCL*, pp. 92–4; ET Louth, *Early Christian Writings*, p. 43.

III

Liturgy is also introduced by *I Clement*, since the final sections[37] constitute an explicit prayer. This is another genre to be considered, touched on a little in our earlier study of Ephrem.[38] As we shall see, both moral exhortation and prayer facilitate the same hermeneutical procedures. The prayer in *I Clement* is not unlike the extemporary prayers of old-fashioned nonconformists in the sense that though almost certainly not a fixed liturgical form, it is built out of flexible liturgical conventions and phrases culled from the largely scriptural 'in-language' of the community.

The prayer is introduced by a warning to those who are not persuaded by the words taken to be spoken by Christ through the writer.[39] The readers are then assured that urgent prayer will be offered that

the Creator of all things may guard unharmed the number of the elect counted in all the world through Jesus Christ, his beloved servant [or child; the Greek is *pais*, a word found in Acts].[40]

This leads into a description of their calling: from darkness to light, from ignorance to knowledge of the glory of his name, and so into petition. Already without identifying particular texts, the allusively scriptural language is apparent, and we begin to sense the difficulties of deciding which if any New Testament documents are already known to the author. We are hearing echoes.

Moving into the prayer proper,[41] we continue to experience the same sensation of hearing echoes which are difficult to pin down. The petition begs 'to hope on your name, the source of all creation', asks for the opening of 'the eyes of our heart to know you the only Most High among the highest, eternally holy among the holy ones'. This God to whom the prayer is offered is the one who humbles the proud, destroys the imaginations of the nations, lifts up the humble on high and reduces the lofty, makes rich and makes poor, sees into the abysses, observes human works, helps those in danger, saves those without hope, and is the creator and overseer (*episcopos*) of

---

[37] *I Clem.* 59–61; *LCL*, pp. 110–16; ET Louth, *Early Christian Writings*, pp. 47–8.
[38] See above ch. 7.
[39] *I Clem.* 59.1–2; *LCL*, p. 110; ET Louth, *Early Christian Writings*, p. 47.
[40] *I Clem.* 59.2; *LCL*, p. 110; ET Louth, *Early Christian Writings*, p. 47. (My ET.)
[41] *I Clem.* 59.3; *LCL*, pp. 110–12; ET Louth, *Early Christian Writings*, p. 47.

every spirit. This God multiplies the nations on earth and from all of them has 'chosen those who love [him] through Jesus Christ, [his] beloved *Pais*'. God teaches, sanctifies, grants honour to us. One is reminded of Hannah's song and the Magnificat, of phrases in Isaiah, the Psalms, Job and so on.

Having characterised the God addressed, the prayer turns to specific request:[42] for help and succour, salvation for those in affliction, mercy for the lowly, lifting up for those fallen, revelation to those in need, healing for the sick. Those who have wandered away are to be turned again, the hungry filled, our prisoners ransomed, the weak lifted up, the faint-hearted encouraged. And then for the first time the allusions become a bit more definite: Let all the nations know you, that you are God alone (LXX 3 Kings 8.60; 4 Kings 19.19; Ezek. 36.23), and that Jesus is your *Pais* and we are your people and the sheep of your pasture (LXX Ps.78.13; 94.7; 99.3). Yet the multiple references offered here indicate that the kind of phrases employed are not text-specific, but rather scriptural refrains, somewhat comparable to the standard repeated epithets of Homeric verse. There is here a 'playing' with the tradition in which the Bible has had a formative role.

Throughout the prayer such echoes go on. What one needs to recognise the process is a finely tuned ear rather than marginal references:

You, Lord, created the world (*oikoumenē*). You are faithful in all generations, righteous in judgement, marvellous in strength and majesty, wise in creating, understanding in establishing your works . . . ; as one gracious to those who trust in you, merciful and compassionate, forgive us our sins and wickednesses, our transgressions and shortcomings. Do not reckon up every sin of your slaves and maidservants, but purify us with the purification of your truth.[43]

And then[44] once more allusions become apparently more definite and marginal references helpful, though yet again the references are multiple, the quotations not exact and often more than one text is moulded together into a new sentence: 'Guide our steps to walk in holiness of heart and to do what is good and well-pleasing in your sight' is LXX Psalm 118.133 combined with 3 Kings 9.4;

---

[42] *1 Clem.* 59.4; *LCL*, p. 112; ET Louth, *Early Christian Writings*, pp. 47–8.
[43] *1 Clem.* 60.1; *LCL*, p. 112; ET Louth, *Early Christian Writings*, p. 48. (My ET.)
[44] *1 Clem.* 60.2; *LCL*, pp. 112–14; ET Louth, *Early Christian Writings*, p. 48.

Deuteronomy 12.25, 28; and 21.9.[45] The following petitions[46] request
that the Lord make 'his face to shine upon us in peace for our good',
that 'we may be sheltered by your mighty hand and delivered from
sin by your uplifted arm', with prayer for deliverance from those who
hate us, and a general prayer for peace rounding off this section.
Again allusions could be specified and multiplied, but surely the
point is already effectively illustrated.

A classicist might call this procedure a *cento*, at least in parts –
certainly the *mimēsis* of scriptural language fits Hellenistic cultural
patterns of the kind already observed. Whatever label we might
choose, the process is certainly not adequately described by the
standard distinction between literal, typological and allegorical, for
it is none of them. It is a 'taking over' of the language of scripture.
The language is made 'one's own'. Hermeneutically there is no
perceptible gap between text and reader, for reader is assimilated to
text and text creatively taken over and adapted by reader. Those
praying stand before God in community with others who have stood
before God.

Treatises on prayer from the early Church invariably concentrate
on exegesis of the Lord's Prayer as the pattern given by the Lord
himself.[47] Other evidence shows that regular use of the Psalter
provided a staple prayer-diet, certainly among monks and ascetics
at a later date, but one suspects from earliest times also.[48] The
prayers of the Bible thus moulded the praying of the Church, and
both the developing liturgies and the traditional synagogue service
reveal in their different ways the extent to which scripture shaped
liturgical life in both communities. Explicit exegesis only happens
when a text is not patently obvious. In this context, the exegesis is
implicit, taken for granted, unproblematic. The problems that
emerge are those of the analyst of this material, who may want

---

[45] The author appends 'and our rulers' – that is, what is good and well-pleasing to God is also
what will please 'our archons', though whether this refers to kings and emperors, or church
leaders, or perhaps even angels, is by no means obvious, though most probably the
reference is political.

[46] *I Clem.* 60.3; *LCL*, p. 114; ET Louth, *Early Christian Writings*, p. 48.

[47] E.g. Origen, *De oratione, GCS*, vol. II, pp. 295–403, ed. Koetschau; ET in *LCC* and *ACW*. Also
Tertullian, *De Oratione*, Latin text with ET and notes, ed. Ernest Evans (London: SPCK,
1953).

[48] See Douglas Burton-Christie, *The Word in the Desert*. Cf. Athanasius, *Letter to Marcellinus on the
Interpretation of the Psalms*, Migne, *PG* 27.11–45; ET in *CWS* and in Charles Kannengiesser
(ed.), *Early Christian Spirituality. Sources of Early Christian Thought* (Philadelphia: Fortress,
1986), pp. 56–77.

to understand what justifies the selection, what criteria were in operation, what distinctive interests led to the difference between the worship traditions of synagogue and Church, what common interests are reflected in their appropriation of scripture.

Two other texts from the second century give us a rather different window on the liturgical context, the so-called *Epistle of Barnabas* and the *Peri Pascha* of Melito of Sardis.[49] It would seem likely that though in form a letter, *Pseudo-Barnabas* has homiletic roots; the precise genre of the *Peri Pascha* has been the subject of debate – the notion has been developed that it is the Haggadah or liturgy for the Quartodeciman Passover rather than a homily. In any case, both seem to emerge from the community's internal homiletic, confessional or worship activity. Both seem to betray close proximity with Jewish traditions, but, unlike *I* and *II Clement*, they are explicitly anti-Jewish – indeed, *Barnabas* quite explicitly contrasts texts which are taken to refer to 'them' and texts fulfilled in 'us'. These texts show that Christianity, in claiming the arrival of the fulfilment, effectively took over typological thinking to establish its supersessionary claims. They also confirm the links between liturgy and typology which we discovered in chapter 7, and demonstrate how the liturgical formation of Christian identity as the new people of God could fatefully reinforce anti-Jewish tendencies, even where the material betrays its Jewish roots.

In the *Epistle of Barnabas*, the word *typos* appears twelve times, and each 'type' has a 'prophetic' dimension. Of these, ten occurrences describe signs of Christ, while the two remaining instances point to the future 'people of God'. Each of the latter is integrated into a collage of prophetic texts. The first[50] develops the salvific notion of new creation through relating the earth (*gē*) out of which Adam was created and the promised land (*gē*) flowing with milk and honey for the nourishment of children to be fashioned in the image and likeness of God. Here 'we' are made into 'another *typos*'.[51] The

---

[49] As it happens I have had research students working on each of these texts, and their work bears on the provenance and genre of each: Alistair Stewart-Sykes, 'The Quartodeciman Paschal Liturgy in the light of Melito's *Peri Pascha* formcritically examined' (University of Birmingham Ph.D. thesis, 1992); and Lynne Wall, 'The *Epistle of Barnabas* and early Rabbinic exegetical traditions' (University of Birmingham Ph.D. thesis, 1993).

[50] *Ep. Barn.* 6.8–19; *LCL*, pp. 360–2; Louth, *Early Christian Writings*, pp. 165–6.

[51] *Ep. Barn.* 6.11; *LCL*, p. 360; Louth, *Early Christian Writings*, p. 166. (Louth's translation does not take *typos* as 'type', but uses the word 'stamp' – thus, 'he made us into men of a wholly

implication is that 'we' are heirs of the promised land and newly
created. In the second passage,[52] the issue is the covenant, whether
it is 'for us' or 'for them'. Of Rebecca's children the younger is the
heir. Jacob blessed the younger son because 'he saw in the Spirit a
typos of the people of the future'. The deduction from such prophetic
signs is confirmed by 'Abraham, the father of the Gentiles who
believed in God in uncircumcision'. These cases confirm our distrust
of modern definitions of typology[53] – the emphasis is not on any past
event, but rather a mimetic sign or 'parable' is discerned which,
properly understood, has a prophetic reference.

Such is also a better way of describing the 'types of Christ' to be
found in this Epistle. These are concentrated in two passages. The
first[54] weaves together the Akedah (Binding of Isaac), the scapegoat
and sacrificial goat of the Day of Atonement, and the scarlet wool of
the red heifer ritual; the second[55] focusses on Moses, first stretching
out his arms during the battle with Amelek, then lifting up the
bronze serpent in the wilderness, and finally naming Joshua
(= Jesus in Greek). Thus an 'impression' of the future is etched into
the scriptural texts. It is discerned through overlaying images. The
element of *mimēsis* makes the 'types', but their effect is produced by
collage, as two examples demonstrate:

(i) Joshua is urged by Moses to take a book and write a prediction
about tearing up Amalek.[56] It is implied that in a riddling way this
refers to the Son of God shattering the strength of kings as predicted
in Isaiah 45.1 and Psalm 110.1. This is a kind of prophetic *cento*,
though described as a 'type': 'See Jesus [= the Greek form of
Joshua], not as Son of Man, but as Son of God manifested in flesh by
a "*typos*"' – by means of a model, figure or outline.

(ii) The single point of comparison with Isaac is his being offered
on the altar, but this is integrated with the more elaborate exploration of the Day of Atonement ritual. Here both goats are significant. The one is offered on the altar (like Isaac), the other is cursed

different stamp'. This may well be a better way of construing the sentence, given the
context, especially the first part of the sentence which speaks of renewal through
forgiveness of sins. If so, *typos* is far from being in any sense a technical term.)

52 *Ep. Barn.* 13; *LCL*, pp. 386–8; ET Louth, *Early Christian Writings*, p. 175 (Louth omits the word
'type' in 13.5).

53 Cf. ch. 9, note 23.

54 *Ep. Barn.* 7–8; *LCL*, pp. 364–70; ET Louth, *Early Christian Writings*, pp. 167–8.

55 *Ep. Barn.* 12; *LCL*, pp. 382–6; ET Louth, *Early Christian Writings*, pp. 173–5.

56 *Ep. Barn.* 12.9–11; *LCL*, p. 386; ET Louth, *Early Christian Writings*, pp. 174–5.

and therefore bears the mark (*typos*) of Jesus. The cursed one is crowned with scarlet wool, and the mocking-scene of the passion-story is drawn into the picture. The two goats are alike, and both represent Jesus in different ways, as does also the sacrifice of the red heifer, which also involved scarlet wool; the various details of the latter are allegorically referred to purification through the cross.[57]

What we see in all these cases is a kind of inter-illumination as mimetic details in the narratives represent or signify what they are taken to prophesy. And in every case in this epistle, this kind of discernment or *gnōsis* is linked with the Christian claim to supersede the Jewish people as God's chosen. Rabbinic parallels often cast light on extra-biblical details which are drawn into the development of these mimetic clues, but can hardly be the direct source of these particular typological insights. So such exegesis is neither a straight inheritance from Jewish exegetical precedent, nor can it be clearly separated out, at least in this text, from the range of other methods used to unpack texts treated as oracles or prophetic riddles: gematria, etymology, deduction, and the recognition of symbol, mimetic sign or type imprinted in ancient narratives – all had precedents outside the Christian context, all served the same ends of discerning prophetic reference. What is evident in this text is that the Christian eschatological and supersessionary claim has provoked the kind of 'oracular' reading of Jewish festivals and rituals that Melito would provide with a kind of theoretical justification.

As noted earlier,[58] the 'representational' character of the 'type' is clear in the way that Melito of Sardis justifies his interpretation of Passover in terms of Christ's passion. In the *Peri Pascha*, he graphically retells and develops the story of Passover and exodus, intoning it in rhetorical, almost hymnic, style. The presentation is 'mimetic' in more senses than one: a dramatic effect is deliberately created by the use of evocative language, drawing the hearer imaginatively into the 'pity and terror'[59] of the story, and allusion and quotation suggest a 'mimicking' of the scriptural narrative

---

[57] See note 54 above for references, and Lynne Wall, 'Barnabas and early Rabbinic traditions', for the intriguing way in which Jewish midrashic material parallels some of the extra-biblical details found in *Barnabas*' development of these types.

[58] See above, ch. 9, pp. 193ff, and references to Hall's edn and ET of the text.

[59] I deliberately allude here to Aristotle's famous phrase from the *Poetics* about the effect of tragedy.

with much rhetorical reminting. Yet reality lies in the mimetic fulfilment, not in the past event.

There is a particular quality to this dramatic *mimēsis* arising from the eschatological claim – the evident fact that the narrative is treated as oracular and the *mimēsis* as prophetic fulfilment. As with *Barnabas*, so here we find extended both the range of texts which can become oracular, and the range of techniques for seeing the 'true' reference and unpacking the riddles of scripture: these now include mimetic narrative such as Melito produces. And the narrative being essentially prophetic, its details are potentially oracular riddles to be unpacked by allegory.

In describing Melito's procedure (both here and in chapter 9), I have deliberately hinted that Hellenistic rhetorical *mimēsis* has made a considerable contribution, and that Melito was explaining an unfamiliar form of prophecy to his audience. The obsolescence of the 'type' means that it almost becomes a 'pretext' for its fulfilment. Melito thinks his 'types' belong to the argument from prophecy so prominent in Justin and other second-century apologists. But he actually produces a text which could be heard, not diachronically, but synchronically, Passover and passion through *anamnēsis* resonating with each other in 'liturgical time'. As in the case of the exemplary use of scripture already observed, the essentially mimetic intent in Melito's treatment of the scripture is in accord with Greek usage. Yet there is something here which transcends Melito's explanation – something not unlike the dynamic liturgical replays of Ephrem.[60] Both Ephrem and recent biblical scholarship have provided the evidence that patristic 'types' had precedents in the Semitic world: Melito alerts us to the way Hellenistic *mimēsis* provided a way of justifying a Christian reading of scripture which had roots in the scriptures themselves.

The context of liturgy produces exegetical practices closely parallel to those found in *paraenesis*. On the one hand, the language of scripture is taken over and re-formed into collages; on the other hand, scripture provides 'types', which are themselves compounded with other 'types' and texts. Such material creates identity, by being exemplary or by enhancing the prophetic reading of the biblical texts, but 'types' would also increasingly 'represent' the whole drama of salvation in the sacraments. The connections between

[60] See above, ch. 7.

typology and liturgical *anamnēsis* need further consideration, but clearly liturgical 'replay' and figural *mimēsis* are fundamental to the formation of Christian worship and lifestyle.

IV

So Christian reading of the scriptures for homiletic and liturgical purposes tended to develop an embracing mimetic quality, and ranges over several of the exegetical 'strategies' noted. The exemplary *mimēsis* is integrated with a *paraenesis* in which the text is taken to refer directly to the reader, whose life is supposed to fulfil the proverbs and patterns of scripture. The 'typological' *mimēsis* overlaps with the oracular in understanding the text in some way to represent in advance the reality which is to be fulfilled. In these ways the identity of Christians was formed.

And this generated new texts, texts dependent upon the Bible for plot and diction and evidencing the kind of allusive intertextuality so evident up to now in this chapter. I refer to the apocryphal and hagiographical literature. These two genres should certainly be distinguished, but they have similar features in so far as they are narrative in form, and, despite the presence in some cases of novelistic motifs and even imitation of Homer,[61] both are imitative of biblical story-telling. Here the kind of *mimēsis* which models lifestyle, event and language on sacred precedent, integrating allusions and occasional quotations, takes another literary form, not immediately recognised as exegetical. Yet such narratives portray the ideals believed to be enshrined in the Bible, and spell out a reading of scripture not all that dissimilar from the panegyrical portraits explored in chapter 5, or the paraenetical collages in the earliest Christian texts.

To provide exemplary narratives was an important element in Graeco-Roman literature. It was a prime motive for history-writing, and especially for biography such as Plutarch's *Lives*:

---

[61] Dennis R. MacDonald, *Christianizing Homer*. A good introduction to novels is found in Niklas Holzberg, *The Ancient Novel* (ET London and New York: Routledge, 1995), which has a helpful discussion of genre; he does not include Christian narratives in the genre 'ancient novel', though recognising the influences – he prefers to regard Christian works as the beginnings of the reception and influence of the novel genre, the ideological climate having undergone radical change (p. 23).

Plutarch insists frequently on a double purpose: he wishes to demonstrate the character of his subjects, and to bring himself and his readers to imitate them.[62]

As Wayne Meeks observed, this moralising biography had long since been adopted by Jewish writers. With his famous introduction, 'Let us now praise famous men', Ben Sirach presents as models Enoch, Noah, Abraham, Moses, Aaron, Joshua, the judges, Samuel, David, Solomon, Elijah, Hezekiah, Josiah, Ezekiel and the high priest Simon, son of Onias. Philo

introduces his stories of the Patriarchs by propounding the notion of persons who are 'living laws', 'archetypes' of which particular laws and customs are but 'copies'. 'These are such men as lived good and blameless lives, whose virtues stand permanently recorded in the most holy scriptures, not merely to sound their praises but for the instruction of the reader and as an inducement to him to aspire to the same.'[63]

This is the background to much early Christian narrative. It would be impossible here to review this huge range of literature, some extant, much lost or fragmentary. We will take a small sample, beginning with the *Martyrdom of Polycarp*. Here is our earliest account of Christian martyrdom, dating from the late second century, and its features contribute to an emerging genre. It takes the form of a letter, but its intention is to assist in the celebration of Polycarp's memory, and already the beginnings of a cult can be discerned – the preservation of relics, the celebration of the anniversary, the 'heavenly birthday' of the martyr. Andrew Louth has written:[64]

The manner of his death sets the seal on his life, so that even his earthly utterances are endowed with infallibility (ch. 16.2). And the manner of his death is sharply etched out, so that we see in it an imitation of Christ (a feature so marked that some have suspected interpolations by a 'Gospel'-redactor, but the original writer, Marcion, could have done it himself, and Polycarp anyway was acutely aware that he was following his Lord on the path of martyrdom): the upper room, Polycarp's prayer, the ass on which he rides to the proconsul and many other touches. But perhaps the most impressive act of identification with Christ, in a way that reaches beyond

---

[62] Quoted by Wayne Meeks, *The Origins of Christian Morality*, p. 190, from C. P. Jones, *Plutarch and Rome* (Oxford: Oxford University Press, 1971), p. 103.

[63] Wayne Meeks, *The Origins of Christian Morality*, quoting Philo, *Life of Abraham* 4, ET Colson, LCC.

[64] *Early Christian Writings*, p. 117.

imitation, is his prayer before the pyre is ignited (ch. 14), which seems to echo the eucharistic prayer Polycarp would have said Sunday by Sunday and echoes that prayer in such a way as to suggest that now Polycarp is the offering, incorporated into Christ, whose offering is represented in the bread and wine offered and consecrated at the eucharist.

We only have to look at the opening section to see how this is built into the narrative from the start, and how it has an exemplary intent: Polycarp's

witness set the seal, so to speak, on the persecution and brought it to an end. It was almost as though all the preceding events had been leading up to another Divine manifestation of the Martyrdom which we read of in the Gospel [i.e. the Passion]; for Polycarp, just like the Lord, had patiently awaited the hour of his betrayal – in token that we too, taking our pattern from him, might think of others before ourselves. This is surely a sign of a true and steadfast love, when a man is not bent on saving himself alone, but his brethren as well.[65]

It is striking how sacrificial language is used in description of the death that follows, thus justifying the implication here that Polycarp died for others.

Bound like that, with his hands behind him, he was like a noble ram taken out of some great flock for sacrifice: a goodly burnt-offering all ready for God.[66]

The fire gave off 'a delicious fragrance, like the odour of incense'. When the fire failed to consume him, he was stabbed, and a dove flew out, 'together with such a copious rush of blood that the flames were extinguished'.[67] Christian narrative draws on biblical narrative to create exemplary heroes, and reinforce the particular features of Christian identity.

The apocryphal Gospels and Acts have similar features. Gaps in the biblical narrative may provide their starting-point; oral traditions not recorded may contribute to their content. But their purpose is exemplary, and their narrative develops aspects of Christian lifestyle by allusive reference to scripture. Again we can

---

[65] *Mart. Pol.* 1; text in *The Acts of the Christian Martyrs*, p. 2, ed. with introd. and ET H. Musurillo, Oxford Early Christian Texts, (Oxford: Clarendon, 1972); ET Louth, *Early Christian Writings*, p. 125.
[66] *Mart. Pol.* 14; *Acts of the Christian Martyrs*, p.1 2; ET Louth, *Early Christian Writings*, p. 129.
[67] *Mart. Pol.* 15–16; *Acts of the Christian Martyrs*, p. 14; ET Louth, *Early Christian Writings*, p. 130.

take but one example, the *Acts of Paul*,[68] but it may be the more telling for its inevitable association with the New Testament book of Acts, for much of which Paul also figures as the principal hero.

The most substantial extant section of the *Acts of Paul* is, of course, the *Acts of Paul and Thecla*. The opening paragraphs[69] are full of names, of places and persons, which recall those in Acts and the Pauline Epistles, but this is a different story. A physical description of Paul introduces the comment, 'For now he appeared like a man, and now he had the face of angel', an allusion to Acts 6.15. From the beginning the narrative is one of conflict, for Paul's critics, Demas and Hermogenes, are in the wings. The issues concern differing views of the resurrection and of Christian lifestyle. Paul becomes the spokesman of 'continence' (*encrateia*) in a remarkable collection of Beatitudes, clearly modelled on the Gospel:

Blessed are the pure in heart, for they shall see God.
Blessed are they who have kept the flesh pure, for they shall become a temple of God.
Blessed are the continent, for to them will God speak.
Blessed are they who have renounced this world, for they shall be well pleasing unto God.
Blessed are they who have wives as if they had them not, for they shall inherit God...
Blessed are they who tremble at the words of God, for they shall be comforted.
Blessed are they who have received (the) wisdom of Jesus Christ, for they shall be called sons of the Most High...
Blessed are they who through love of God have departed from the form of this world, for they shall judge angels and at the right hand of the Father they shall be blessed.
Blessed are the merciful, for they shall obtain mercy, and shall not see the bitter day of judgment.
Blessed are the bodies of the virgins, for they shall be well pleasing to God, and shall not lose the reward of their purity.[70]

The overall effect is to put a very different emphasis on the scriptural material from that we imagine to be appropriate. But the compounding of phrases nevertheless makes this deeply biblical.

---

[68] Text in *Acta Apostolorum Apocrypha* I, ed. R. A. Lipsius (Hildesheim: George Olms, 1959, photocopy of 1891 edn); ET *New Testament Apocrypha*. vol. II, pp. 322–90, ed. E. Hennecke and W. Schneemelcher, ET R. McL. Wilson (London: Lutterworth Press, 1965).
[69] *Acts of Paul and Thecla* 1–4; Lipsius, pp. 235–8; ET Hennecke, pp. 353–4.
[70] *Acts of Paul and Thecla* 5–6; Lipsius, pp. 238–40; ET Hennecke, pp. 354–5.

There are two direct quotations of the Matthaean Beatitudes, without modification (in the case of Matt. 5.8) except by addition (in the case of Matt. 5.7); others are half quoted (Matt. 5.4; 5.9), or alluded to (Matt. 5.5 where 'the earth' is to be inherited rather than 'God'). There are allusions to the Pauline Epistles: God's Temple – 1 Corinthians 3.16, 2 Corinthians 6.16; having wives as though not having them – 1 Corinthians 7.29; being heirs of God – Romans 8.17; judging angels – 1 Corinthians 6.3. And this deeply biblical injunction to continence is crucial to the ensuing narrative. For Thecla commits herself to following Paul's teaching, with disaster for her family who have ensured a good marriage alliance through her betrothal.

The scene is set for dramatic conflict and pursuit as her betrothed allies himself with Paul's opponents. An Acts-like trial scene[71] enables Paul to make a speech full of biblical allusions, and then he is visited in prison by Thecla;[72] the prison scenes in Acts seem not too far away. In another trial scene attention shifts to Thecla, who is condemned to be burned. 'But Thecla sought for Paul, as a lamb in the wilderness looks about for the shepherd.'[73] No specific biblical text can be footnoted, but it is an allusive image. When the fire refuses to consume her, we are reminded of Polycarp, though in this case a great hailstorm quenches it and she is miraculously saved. We could go on, but suffice it to say that the narrative goes on displaying this subtle but transformed intertextuality. Quotations and allusions are placed in a different context, so that the biblical style of narrative seems curiously unbiblical, the adventures of a 'romance', enjoining a Christian lifestyle sharply differentiated from the 'world'.

The following, sadly fragmentary, incident[74] confirms this: Paul heals Hermocrates in Acts-like fashion, and gives him bread to eat, an act full of symbolical links with the Gospels and the eucharist. But the thrust of the story lies in the sequel. The elder son, Hermippus, wanted to inherit, and so objected to the fact that his father was healed. Probably the missing bit tells how he plotted to get rid of Paul. The younger son, Dion, heard Paul gladly, but died (probably as the result of a fall, but this is also in the missing section). Apparently Hermippus tried to prevent Dion's body being

---

[71] *Acts of Paul and Thecla* 15–17; Lipsius, pp. 245–7; ET Hennecke, p. 357.
[72] *Acts of Paul and Thecla* 18; Lipsius, p. 247; ET Hennecke, p. 358.
[73] *Acts of Paul and Thecla* 20–2; Lipsius, pp. 248–51; ET Hennecke, pp. 358–9.
[74] *Acts of Paul in Myra*; ET Hennecke, pp. 364–7, from Coptic Heidelberg Papyrus, pp. 28–35.

taken to Paul, but nevertheless Paul raises the dead son. In a dramatic confrontation Hermippus and his friends come upon Paul with sword and cudgels, and Paul addresses them in a rather wordier and less resigned version of Christ's statement at his arrest in Gethsemane: Paul expects God to come to his assistance, and God does so by striking Hermippus blind as he lifts his sword against him. The story will eventually end with his healing too. The speeches draw out the lessons: Hermippus learns that the world is nothing, gold is nothing, all possessions nothing, as he faces being a blind beggar for mocking the one who saved his father and raised up his brother.

Christian narrative was mimetic of scripture, and intended to inspire *mimēsis*. In this way it contributed to the formation of Christian identity. The next chapter will be concerned with the way in which the Bible continued to function in this way, contributing to the Christianising of the Roman world in the post-Constantinian period.

V

So far we have largely concentrated on the central core of our map of interpretative genres, those concerned with identity and community formation. As we move outwards we reach genres which have in fact received substantial treatment in earlier chapters. The features of commentary, for example, have figured large, and there is little need to speak again of the philological procedures whereby aspects of the language and content of biblical texts were elucidated. But for the sake of completeness, we will sketch in the rest of the map.

A great deal of Christian use of the Bible in the second century was demonstrably apologetic:[75] the first debates about text arose because the traditional text-form of Christian testimonies proved to be different from the rolls of the LXX. Assumptions or arguments about reference were affected by commitments which dramatically refocussed the spectacles with which the text was read. Deductions were made, whether from the plain meaning of the text or its metaphorical suggestiveness, and those deductions were inevitably coloured by the need to persuade, or the need to authorise a

---

[75] See above, ch. 6, pp. 122ff.

particular claim. Christian identity was being formed by differentiation from Jews on the one hand, pagans on the other, and Gnostics within the gates. The argumentative context of apologetic moulded much of the earliest Christian exegesis and had an important legacy in the way scripture was handled in other contexts and other interpretative genres – not least because here the interpretation of texts as riddling oracles set fundamental assumptions about how particular passages were to be read for centuries to come.

The advent of scholarship meant that the now traditional Christian ways of interpreting the Bible, forged first in confessional and apologetic use of the scriptures, were taken up into more systematic scholarly exegesis.[76] Grammatical and explanatory comment entered the exegetical process more formally. The 'school' context became important, and school methods were introduced. This also meant that new interpretative genres began to appear: patronage, like that of Ambrosius for Origen, produced the commentary, regular instruction in church the more systematic homily series.[77] As noted, Theodore would later see the difference between these two forms as lying in the problem-oriented character of the former, and the latter's role in underlining what was already clear and obvious. But both in fact drew on the patterns of exegetical comment developed in Graeco-Roman schools.

Homilies, recorded by stenographers, are a reminder of the essentially oral process. Just as *paideia* in the schools was based on exegesis of texts and their appropriation by critical *mimēsis* of style or ethics, so Christian *paideia* took place through reading texts and discerning their appropriate application. The synagogue, we noted, was a place for reading texts and forming a culture based on a rival literature to the pagan classics. The corresponding analogy between Church and school became more apposite as a scholar like Origen

---

[76] See above, ch. 4.

[77] The question what difference there is between Origen's Homilies and Commentaries is asked by E. Junod in his article, 'Wodurch unterscheiden sich die Homilien des Origenes von seinen Kommentaren?' in E. Mühlenberg and J. van Oort (eds.), *Predigt in der alten Kirche* (Kampen: Kok Pharos, 1994), pp. 50–81. He supports my conclusion that there are no differences in method. There is a difference in audience, he suggests, which affects the content and to some extent the purpose: commentaries, composed in private, were meant to cover every aspect of the text with great thoroughness for the serious searcher after spiritual matters, whereas homilies, delivered extempore, respected a mixed audience, limited time, and the need to build up the Church.

engaged in systematic exegetical activity rooted in a paideutic understanding of providence and Gospel.

The work of Karen Jo Torjesen has highlighted this feature of Origen's work. There has long been debate as to how Origen's theory, as outlined in the *De principiis*, relates to his actual exegetical practice in commentaries and homilies. Torjesen[78] has shown that for Origen the task of the exegete was to enable scripture to function pedagogically for the hearer, assisting the journey of the soul. The soul's journey is conceived in three stages, the stage of purification, then knowledge of the Logos, then union with God. This journey is the means of redemption, and the saving work of the Logos is essentially educative, leading from one level to another. The three aspects of scripture corresponding to body, soul and spirit are understood in terms of this underlying vision, not as intended for distinct grades of Christian from *simpliciores* to spiritual élite, nor as corresponding to literal, typological and allegorical, nor as distinctively three 'meanings' for each text, but rather as the stages of the journey in which all Origen's hearers were engaged at some level or another. Something is offered in each homily for those at each stage.

In the light of this, the problem whether Origen was really head of a catechetical school, or of a centre of more advanced study following the usual cycle of educational studies but with a Christian slant, may perhaps appear in different perspective. Origen prided himself in the *Contra Celsum* on belonging to a community whose doctrines could make simple people good,[79] not just the élite like the philosophical schools. For him the whole Christian life was an educational process[80] revolving around the proper exegesis of texts whose diction veiled the deeper intent, namely knowledge of the divine. But the basic moral teaching of scripture was accessible to

---

[78] In *Hermeneutical Procedure and Theological Method in Origen's Exegesis* (Berlin and New York: de Gruyter, 1985), and ' "Body", "Soul", and "Spirit" in Origen's Theory of Exegesis', *Anglican Theological Review* 67 (1985), pp. 17–30.

[79] *C. Cels.* VI.1–3ff.; *GCS*, vol. II, pp. 70–3; ET Chadwick, pp. 316ff.

[80] See further my article, '*Paideia* and the Myth of Static Dogma', in Sarah Coakley and David Pailin (eds.), *The Making and Remaking of Christian Doctrine. Essays in Honour of Maurice Wiles* (Oxford: Clarendon, 1993). It is interesting that Christoph Schäublin, in his article 'Zum paganen Umfeld der christlichen Predigt' in Mühlenberg and van Oort (eds.), *Predigt in der alten Kirche*, pp. 25–49, also notes the analogies between the homily and the exegetical exercises of the schools, in his case working largely from Latin evidence, Jerome and Augustine.

anyone as the starting-point. His homilies were intended to feed a varied audience at a range of different stages in the journey.

The result appears to us chaotic and lacking in structure or criteria, but is not dissimilar to the preaching now heard in many a Black Pentecostal church. The point would appear to be not that everyone hears everything and follows a logical sequence, but that, as attention switches on and off, each catches the word specially directed at them for that moment. Origen's work is not exactly analogous, but such a hearer's perspective may tell us some things about the genre which have not been noted before. Origen is offering different kinds of titbits, from milk to solid food, so that babies and infants will sample some, mature athletes will digest more. Thus, the context affects the exegesis, and the proffering for different hearers of different possibilities of understanding demands multiple meanings.

In the post-Nicene period, the homily became, if anything, more assimilated to school exercises: Chrysostom went through texts like a *grammaticus* or *rhētōr*; he and the Cappadocians adopted the forms of panegyric.[81] It is probably incorrect to think that this 'school' perspective was entirely new with Origen. It has been suggested[82] that Paul exchanged the profession of Rabbi for that of sophist. Certainly Justin and the Gnostic teachers, like Arius at a later date,[83] appear as teachers with pupils and disciples, interpreting texts and offering 'doctrines', like rhetors and philosophers. Literature was vital for the process of educating people into a particular culture and the Church was a kind of 'comprehensive school', with a body of literature rather different from the élite texts of the classical tradition. It is in this overall context that the significance of the Bible and its interpretation in the early Church becomes the more evident.

The 'school' character of early Christianity appears again in the

---

[81] See above, ch. 5, and below ch. 11. Also the study by Schäublin, 'Zum paganen Umfeld der christlichen Predigt', which notes both the development of panegyric (pp. 26–7) and the way in which homilies reflect school instruction rather than declamation – delivered extempore, sitting down with text in hand, offering comments on figures of speech, argumentation etc. to different grades of hearers (pp. 38ff.).

[82] E. A. Judge, 'The Early Christians as a Scholastic Community', *Journal of Religious History* 1 (1960–1), pp. 4–15, 125–37; cf. Judge, 'St Paul and Classical Society', *Jahrbuch für Antike und Christentum* 15 (1972), pp. 19–36, and Abraham J. Malherbe, *Paul and the Popular Philosophers* (Minneapolis: Fortress Press, 1989).

[83] See Rowan Williams, *Arius. Heresy and Tradition* (London: Darton, Longman & Todd, 1987).

development of catechetical lectures delivered through Lent. These might be regarded as another interpretative genre, given that, rather than being specifically exegetical, their focus was on expounding the doctrines derived from scripture and their summary in credal form. But their essential purpose was to initiate converts into a learning community, and, if space permitted some treatment of the material, we would find that methods of citing and exegeting scripture show similar patterns to those already explored.

There are, then, many reasons for supposing that the early Church was more like a school than a religion in the social world of antiquity. The emphasis on morals and lifestyle, even the controversial and apologetic ways of differentiating their own 'dogma' from other 'options' (*haereseis*),[84] bespeaks a school-like activity. The appeal to scripture in doctrinal controversy belongs to the same cultural phenomenon as its other uses. So is Simonetti right when he suggests that the use of scripture in the definition of doctrine through argument and controversy

determined a style of reading and interpretation which had its own distinctive characteristics, compared with the interpretative methods usual in a specifically exegetical setting?

In other words, can we posit a sharp differentiation between exegesis of texts found in doctrinal debate and that found in other interpretative genres?

In the appendix to his historical introduction,[85] Simonetti suggests that one obvious difference between exegesis in doctrinal controversy and other forms of scriptural interpretation lies in the fact that

scripture passages used for doctrinal ends were normally taken out of their original context and considered in isolation, producing results sometimes quite foreign to the sense which they would have if interpreted in their proper context.[86]

---

[84] Cf. my article, 'Did Epiphanius Know What he Meant by Heresy?'
[85] Simonetti, *Biblical Interpretation*, p. 121ff., an article originally published in *Orpheus* NS 2 (1981). Quote above from p. 121.
[86] Simonetti, *Biblical Interpretation*, p. 122. Cf. Pollard's argument (in 'The Exegesis of Scripture in the Arian Controversy') that Athanasius 'refutes Arian arguments based on literal interpretation of isolated verses of scripture. No doctrine, he argues, can be based on an isolated verse of scripture unless it is in harmony with the general teaching of the whole of scripture' (quoted above, ch. 2, note 2).

So texts abstracted for use in doctrinal controversy, being

isolated from their original context, take on a life of their own and are often interpreted in the most diverse ways by different parties in controversy, but always in terms of the new doctrinal and polemical contexts into which they are inserted and which condition their meaning.[87]

But this is likewise true of all the evidence he himself reviews in tracing Christian exegesis of the first and second centuries. Second-century material predates the first formal commentaries, and tended to be piecemeal as testimonies were abstracted from context and reinterpreted as 'oracles' pointing to Christ. The apologetic needs of the earliest Christian communities had already established a tradition of controversial argument about reference which usually ignored context, and the resultant understanding was more often than not taken over into more formal exegetical activity when the writing of commentaries began. Indeed, commentaries themselves often focussed on piecemeal particularities. Thus it is simply not possible to claim, as he does, that

the hermeneutical procedures which are employed to accommodate them to their new needs entirely abandon the interpretative structures normally used in specifically exegetical settings.[88]

Others have suggested that doctrinal debate induced appeal to the literal sense of texts, as if the Fathers instinctively sensed that, while it was legitimate to let the imagination run in spiritual meditation or exhortation, texts had to be treated more seriously when issues of truth were at stake:

It is as a matter of fact noticeable that, where they are discussing strictly theological issues with a view to stating doctrine, Fathers like Hippolytus and Hilary and Augustine (to give but three examples) tend to adopt much more straightforward, rigorous methods of exegesis than when edification or ascetical instruction is their aim.[89]

---

[87] Simonetti, *Biblical Interpretation*, p. 122.
[88] Ibid.
[89] J. N. D. Kelly, 'The Bible and the Latin Fathers', in D. E. Nineham (ed.), *The Church's Use of the Bible Past and Present* (London: SPCK, 1963). Cf. Pollard, 'The Exegesis of Scripture in the Arian Controversy', an article which takes as its presupposition the notion that both sides were arguing from the 'literal' sense, and the essential difference was that Athanasius took the unity of scripture and the context seriously, unlike the piecemeal text-citing of the Arians. Cf. ch. 2, notes 2 and 3.

However, we should not by now be surprised to find that this too proves to be quite misleading. We have discovered that the meaning of 'literal' is problematic, and that allegory was not perceived as producing other than truth. In any case, we recall the points made in chapter 2, where Athanasius demanded a more 'elevated' sense and was less literal than Arius. Often the use of texts in doctrinal debate presupposes typological, allegorical or Christological senses which had developed in the contexts of liturgy or apologetic, and which we would not recognise as 'literal'. The understanding of texts used in debate is not generally other than in other contexts.[90]

So the treatment of texts in doctrinal controversy cannot be regarded as any different in principle from the exegetical activity observable in homily and commentary. Edwin Hatch argued one hundred years ago that the roots of patristic exegesis lie in the ancient educational system, the schools of *grammaticus* and *rhētōr*; this applies with increasing force as one moves from the centre to the periphery of our map (see fig. 2). In the schools, texts were exploited to illustrate grammatical usage and rhetorical devices, rationalistic enquiries sought meanings through etymology, synonyms, literary usage elsewhere and so on; and exegetical comments elucidated the import of figures of speech and explained allusions to narratives common or uncommon, mythical or historical. Discerning morals, references and deeper meanings was commonplace, though mystical allegory seems to have been characteristic not so much of the sophists and rhetors as of philosophers, at whose feet some, though by no means the majority, might subsequently sit. In the light of this, I would suggest that the search for meaning and truth in texts, whether overtly exegetical or employing exegesis in debate, followed essentially similar lines, and that in both contexts, certainly by the fourth century, the procedures of the grammatical and rhetorical schools were the source for patristic exegetical techniques.

VI

We have surveyed, with varying intensity, the diverse genres or interpretative contexts in which the Bible was read. We find that

---

[90] This was argued with more evidence in my paper 'Exegetical Method and Scriptural Proof', but see here the discussion of Proverbs 8 in ch. 2.

there does not seem to be any evidence that particular 'reading strategies' were confined to particular genres, or that distinct genres produced distinctive methodologies. Some things are genre-specific: a commentary follows through the text line by line rather than constructing collages such as we have found in letters, homilies and prayers. Nevertheless, there is a rather remarkable continuity in the modes of exegetical practice found in the various different sorts of contexts in which early Christians were engaged in interpreting the scriptures. The basic lines of approach were set early and became traditional, being taken up and developed by more professional procedures as the exegetical literature became more sophisticated. Now we embark on some more detailed case-studies of how the Bible, in the post-Constantinian world, formed the believer's life and the Church's teaching.

CHAPTER II

The life of faith

I

It might be said that paraenetic exegesis had primacy of place. The scriptures were always treated as the Word of God and as the guide to life. Even though Halakah was rejected by the increasingly Gentile Christian movement at a very early stage, the notion that moral teaching was enshrined in God's Word replaced it very rapidly. As we have seen, the pervasive exhortation not only compounded sayings from Psalms, Proverbs and the Gospels into new expressions of the character to be fostered by the Christian, but also drew on biblical models who exemplified particular virtues or lived a life worth imitating. Furthermore, the common assumption of the surrounding culture was that literature was read for the sake of moral improvement. It was characteristic of the Antiochene school to follow the practice of the rhetorical schools in seeking the moral import of the text. Generally, the expectation that a tale had a moral, that the text's intention was the improvement of the reader, encouraged ways of reading the text, especially in the homily genre, that had a practical outcome with respect to lifestyle, interior attitude and ethical choice.

It is against that background that we turn to examine the exegetical homilies of John Chrysostom. John drew huge crowds as the leading rhetorical speaker of the time, offending people in high places by his rigorous puritanism and moral outspokenness, but delighting the populace with the message of God's mercy and love and the call for repentance. Many homilies for specific occasions are extant, but the largest bulk of extant material is sets of consecutive homilies which provide a kind of recording of an oral commentary on whole books of the Bible. It is not exactly clear how they were produced and published. Certainly some seem to have been taken down by stenographers, given the topical asides. It has often been noted that on the whole these exegetical homilies fall into two parts: the first follows through the text providing commentary, then, after a certain time, Chrysostom abandons the text and develops a long exhortation on one of his favourite themes, the latter bearing precious little relation to the text or commentary preceding it. The themes are repeated over and over again: in the ninety *Homilies on Matthew*, it has been reckoned that he spoke on almsgiving forty times, poverty thirteen times, avarice over thirty times, and wealth wrongfully acquired or used about twenty times. Chrysostom was repetitive, frequently digressed, and often covered many, unrelated, topics in a single rhetorical piece. He sometimes justifies himself against those very criticisms: like a doctor, he says, picking up an old philosophical commonplace, he does not imagine the same medicine is suitable for all his patients.

My intention is to examine a few homilies from the exegetical set on Corinthians, to show that the whole process of exegesis is paraenetical, and that the one aim of Chrysostom's preaching is the paideutic one – to foster in his hearers the life of faith which is set forth in scripture, which is the Word of God.

Chrysostom, like any good commentator, especially one in the kind of literary-philological tradition of the rhetorical schools, prefaces his collection of homilies on 1 Corinthians by setting out the Epistle's 'argument' (*hypothesis*). He explains[1] that Corinth, then as now, was the first city of Greece, wealthy, a good trading position on the isthmus of the Peloponnese, and full of orators and philosophers; indeed, he thinks one of the seven wise men came from Corinth. This little bit of background information has parallels with, perhaps allusions to, classical texts, but Chrysostom disclaims any intention of mentioning these points for ostentation's sake, or to make a display of great learning. They are points which he affirms will be of use in understanding the Epistle's argument.

He then adds material about Paul's connection with Corinth culled from Acts, and creates a kind of narrative within which Paul's letter fits. The success of the Gospel led the devil to cause division, since the strongest kingdom of all, divided against itself, cannot stand. The wealth and wisdom of the inhabitants made the devil's project that much easier. There were rival parties, self-elected

---

[1] *Hom. 1 Cor.* Prol.; Migne, *PG* 61.9–12; ET *NPNF*, 1st series, vol. XII, pp. 1–2.

leaders, and the apostle hints at the problems when he says, 'I was not about to speak to you as spiritual' (1 Cor. 3.1) – evidently, Chrysostom comments, it was not his inability but their infirmity that prevented their instruction. So the church was torn asunder.

Chrysostom goes on to introduce other specific problems, like the one who had intercourse with his stepmother, the gluttony of those eating idol-meat, the contentiousness in going to court over money, wearing long hair, not sharing with the needy, being arrogant and jealous over spiritual gifts, and weak on the doctrine of resurrection because of the madness of heathen philosophy. They were at variance with one another because of ambition and *kenodoxia* (empty glory) – a particular moral concern of Chrysostom's in a society where reputation (*doxa*) was a key motivation.[2] They were contradicting one another's opinions and trusting in their own reason.

Chrysostom notes that they had written to Paul by the hand of Fortunatus, Stephanas and Achaicus, and that the letter is a reply, giving injunctions concerning the points they had raised and others. Paul had learned all about their failings, and sent the letter by Timothy. Paul sets himself against the fundamental disease which they were trying to conceal by claiming to teach better doctrines, namely the spirit of separation, and he uses the boldness appropriate to his relationship with them, as apostle. Chrysostom notes, however, that it is not probable that they were all as bad as all that: some were very holy, as is implied by Paul in certain comments he makes in the middle of the Epistle. With this background clarified, Chrysostom is able to launch into the text, beginning with the opening greeting.[3]

So far then we have a neat example of the exegete's *historia*, nicely eschewing excessive erudition as the true rhetorician should, carried just far enough to highlight the context of what Chrysostom reads as a text of moral philosophy. Already, by implication, the vices to be opposed have been spelled out, and the intent of the author to correct the problems provides the analysis of what the Epistle's 'argument' is all about.

Commenting on the opening greeting Chrysostom immediately calls attention to the way the text functions in relation to the problems he has outlined:

---

[2] See Frances Young and David Ford, *Meaning and Truth in 2 Corinthians*, pp. 12–13.
[3] *Hom. 1 Cor.* 1; Migne, *PG* 61.11; ET *NPNF*, 1st series, vol. XII, p. 3.

See how immediately, from the very beginning, he casts down their pride, and dashes to the ground all their fond imagination. He speaks of himself as 'called'. What I have learned, he suggests, I discovered not myself, nor acquired by my own wisdom. While I was persecuting and laying waste the church, I was called.[4]

Chrysostom contrasts the nothingness of the one called – all he does is obey – with the fact that the one who calls is 'all', then moves on to comment on 'Jesus Christ'. 'Your teacher is Christ', he says; 'and do you register the names of human beings as patrons of your doctrine?'[5] We have shifted from 'their' failings to direct address. Of course, at one level it is deductive paraphrase – Chrysostom putting words into Paul's mouth – but, at another level, his own congregation is drawn into the text, and addressed. The phrase 'through the will of God' is proposed for comment, and the same conflation occurs even more ambiguously – for from 'you' we move to 'we':

For it was God who willed that you should be saved in this way. We ourselves have produced no good thing, but by the will of God we have attained to this salvation; and because it seemed good to him, we were called, not because we were worthy.[6]

Certainly at this point it sounds as if Chrysostom with his 'we' might well be speaking for Paul after all. But the comment on the next lemma shifts the point of view:

'And Sosthenes our brother.' Another instance of his modesty; he puts in the same rank with himself one inferior to Apollos; for great was the interval between Paul and Sosthenes. Now if where the interval was so wide he stations with himself one far beneath him, what can they have to say who despise their equals?[7]

Here is subtle, but quite definite moral exhortation built into the process of exegesis, even where the 'third person' is adopted, and a notional distance from the text preserved.

So, phrase by phrase Chrysostom works through the words of greeting: 'To the Church of God' – of God, he emphasises, not of this or that human person. 'Which is at Corinth' – see how with each word, he says, Paul puts down their swelling pride: the Church is

---

[4] *Hom. 1 Cor.* 1; Migne, *PG* 61.11–12; ET *NPNF*, 1st series, vol. xii, p. 3 (altered).
[5] *Hom. 1 Cor.* 1; Migne, *PG* 61.12; ET *NPNF*, 1st series, vol. xii, p. 3 (altered).
[6] *Hom. 1 Cor.* 1; Migne, *PG* 61.12–13; ET *NPNF*, 1st series, vol. xii, p. 3 (altered).
[7] *Hom. 1 Cor.* 1; Migne, *PG* 61.13; ET *NPNF*, 1st series, vol. xii, p. 3.

God's, so it ought to be united, and it is one, not just in Corinth but throughout the whole world. The very word *ekklēsia* implies not separation but unity and concord. 'To the sanctified in Christ Jesus' – synonyms for sanctification highlight Paul's reminder to them of their own uncleanness, from which he had freed them, and so persuade them to lowliness of mind. Not by their own good deeds, but by the loving-kindness of God, had they been sanctified. 'Called to be saints' – Paul indicates that being saved is not 'of yourselves', for you did not first draw near, but were called. Here are two things to notice: first the switch in person again, suggesting Chrysostom in Paul's person addressing his own congregation through Paul's address to the Corinthians; second the allusion back to Paul's call and obedience, thus making Paul exemplary.

It is the phrase 'in every place both theirs and ours' which lets Chrysostom make explicit what has been implicit.

Although the letter be written to the Corinthians only, yet he makes mention of all the faithful that are in the earth; showing that the Church throughout the world must be one, however separate in diverse places ... And though the place be separate, the Lord binds together ... [8]

Chrysostom sums up the details of his working through the text by offering two alternative paraphrases to the opening greeting,[9] stressing this point – that grace and peace are wished not only on the Corinthians but on all Christians. It is this which allows the transition from what is formally exegesis to what is formally exhortation:

Now if our peace be of grace, why do you have high thoughts? Why are you so puffed up ... ?[10]

Suddenly the faults and failings of the Corinthians become the very things that prevent peace with God for the person Chrysostom addresses. Being in favour with God is contrasted with being in favour with men, and David exemplifies the one, where Absalom typifies the other; Abraham the one, Pharaoh the other; the Israelites the one, the Egyptians the other ... No matter who we are, slave, or wife, or soldier, we are to prefer favour with God, rather than the human master, husband, king or commander.

[8] Ibid.
[9] *Hom. 1 Cor.* 1 ; Migne, *PG* 61.13; ET *NPNF*, 1st series, vol. XII, p. 4.
[10] *Hom. 1 Cor.* 1; Migne, *PG* 61.14; ET *NPNF*, 1st series, vol. XII, p. 4 (altered).

And the way to favour with God is lowliness of mind.[11] God resists the proud (James 4.6); the sacrifice of God is a broken spirit and heart brought low (Ps. 51). Chrysostom has now abandoned exegesis of the Corinthians text, and he is developing a moral theme. As he does so scripture is exploited in the ways we have explored in earlier texts: examples catalogued, citation added to citation, and some illustrated by allusive retelling of key biblical narratives. Of Moses God said he was the meekest of all men (Num. 12.3), and Chrysostom explains that nothing was ever more humble than he, who, being leader of so great a people, and having overwhelmed the king and host of Egypt by the Red Sea, and done so many miracles, and so on, yet felt exactly like an ordinary person, and as son-in-law was humbler than his father-in-law, taking advice from him . . . (He alludes to the tale in Exodus 18 where Jethro gives Moses the sensible advice not to imagine he is indispensable but to delegate.)

We need not follow Chrysostom further in detail. Rather we should reflect on the exegetical processes we have traced. The fact that ancient literary criticism had no sense of anachronism or historical distance is again borne out by what we have seen: while there was the kind of interest in illuminative detail and circumstance which belonged to *to historikon* – as indeed this excursion into Chrysostom has itself shown – clearly the Antiochenes' interest was not the same as the modern historico-critic's. Chrysostom's exegesis, even at the philological level, even as he explores *to historikon*, is coloured principally by his ethical interest, long before he launches on the specifically hortatory development which emerges from it.

This is effected by implicit conflation of two situations; by the exegete's empathy, we might say, with the rhetorical intent of the text. Yet Chrysostom is not unaware that the text belongs to another 'narrative' from that to which he and his congregation belong. The narrative implied by the text is to be respected. The Corinthians are not the Antiochenes; Paul is not John the Goldenmouth. But the two narratives, while each having its own autonomy, somehow interpenetrate. They relate to one another as 'interillumination'. They have a mimetic quality.

Now, in noting that, we find ourselves not far from the kind of thing that has been said about typology – though I doubt if anyone

[11] *Hom. 1 Cor.* 1; Migne, *PG* 61.15; ET *NPNF*, 1st series, vol. XII, p. 4.

would apply that term to what Chrysostom is doing here. It is like but unlike the definition of figural interpretation derived from Auerbach:

Figural interpretation establishes a connection between two textual events or persons, the first of which signifies not only itself but also the second, while the second encompasses or fulfils the first.[12]

The sense of prophetic sign and fulfilment is missing, but not the perception of intertextual connection, or the sense of each implied narrative being 'real'. One is not the 'pretext' for the other. Allegory may treat a text as a pretext for moral or spiritual *paraenesis*; what Chrysostom is doing gives both textual context and exegetical context its own integrity and validity, yet the one resonates with the other.

In an earlier study[13] I noted the phenomenon of empathy or conflation which we have just tried to characterise. At that time, without having reached the point of challenging the assumption that the Antiochenes' interest in history was analogous to ours, I posed the question how it was that Chrysostom could understand the text as both historical and contemporary, how Chrysostom closed what we have come to call the hermeneutical gap. I noted how constantly Chrysostom read between the lines to bring out Paul's tone of voice or highlight his use of tactics to win over his hearers, thus re-creating for his own audience a drama of pastoral handling, observing the way Paul oscillated between praise and blame, mixed severity with tenderness, humility with assertion. One minute he scares them, next minute he softens his words to win them; he praises them *oikonomikōs*, preparing for reproofs to come, and so on. I suggested that

In the exegetical sections of his sermons, there is no explicit drawing of morals – there is no need for any. The empathy of Chrysostom the pastor with Paul the pastor produces a creative but non-explicit interplay between the two different audiences who, by implication, share the same shortcomings. So there is an entirely unconscious 'hermeneutic of retrieval'.[14]

---

[12] See above, p. 154.
[13] 'John Chrysostom on I and II Corinthians', a brief paper given at the 1983 Patristic Conference, and published in *SP* 18.1 (1986), pp. 349–52.
[14] Ibid., p. 351.

That description remains valid, but the process can now be seen as significantly mimetic or figural. Furthermore, we can understand it against the background of rhetorical exegesis: what did the rhetor do but help budding orators to observe the tactics of the speaker in the text being studied, and what were the tactics for but to persuade? Chrysostom has brilliantly adapted all that to provide a subtle *paraenesis*.

If we turn to the thirteenth homily on 1 Corinthians we can see even more clearly how this is the case. Resuming[15] his discourse on 1 Corinthians 4.10, Chrysostom summarises what has gone before – Paul has filled his speech with much severity, which delivers a sharper blow than any direct charges, he suggests, recapitulating the contrast Paul has drawn between their wisdom, glory, wealth, and his persecution, insult, suffering. He notes Paul's irony (as a good rhetor would) and amplifies Paul's meaning in paraphrase:

you disciples have become no less than kings, but we apostles and teachers, entitled to receive the reward before everyone else, not only have fallen very far behind you, but even, as persons doomed to death, in fact convicted criminals, spend our lives entirely in dishonours, dangers, and hunger: indeed insulted as fools, and driven about, and enduring all intolerable things.[16]

According to Chrysostom, Paul's intent here is to cause them to consider the point that they should zealously seek the condition of the apostles, their dangers and indignities, not honours and glories – for the former, rather than the latter, are what the Gospel requires. But he notes that Paul does not do this directly. He wants to avoid appearing disagreeable to them, and, characteristically, he uses irony to avoid offensive rebuke which might have compounded their errors by causing a fierce reaction. Chrysostom imaginatively composes alternative, and sharper, ways in which Paul might have expressed himself if he had not used irony. Here surely we can hear the rhetor demonstrating various techniques of persuasive discourse to his class, though Chrysostom is using it for a kind of indirect *paraenesis*, sketching the apostolic life to which Christians are called.

Chrysostom then moves[17] to phrase-by-phrase exegesis of verses

---

15 *Hom. 1 Cor.* 13; Migne, *PG* 61.107; ET *NPNF*, 1st series, vol. XII, p. 72.
16 Ibid. (ET altered).
17 *Hom. 1 Cor.* 13; Migne, *PG* 61.107; ET *NPNF*, 1st series, vol. XII, p. 73.

11–13, unpacking that life of hardship, indicating that it is to be expected of his congregation ('Don't you see that the life of all Christians must be like this?'). Oscillating between such address to his congregation and speaking paraphrastically in Paul's person, he again turns exegesis into implied *paraenesis*.

But before long we find Chrysostom drawing attention once more to Paul's rhetorical intent. Paul's phrase 'the offscourings of all', he describes as a vigorous blow.[18] It is, he says, the expression of one seriously concerned. Paul must have been hinting that he suffers not just from his persecutors, but from the very people on whose behalf he accepts suffering. Christ's teaching about bearing insults meekly, suggests Chrysostom, was both to get us to exercise ourselves in high virtue, and also to put the other party to shame. But then, he notes, Paul realises that that blow was hard to bear, and rushes to heal it, saying in verse 14 that he did not write these things to put them to shame.[19] Chrysostom points out that the very thing which he had done by his words, he claims not to have done! Chrysostom is not bothered by the question of contradiction or truth, for he has a rhetorical justification which doubles as a moral: Paul allows that he has done it, but not with an evil or spiteful mind.

Not to speak was impossible, since they would have remained uncorrected; on the other hand, after he had spoken, to leave the wound untended, was hard. So along with his severity he apologises: for this so far from destroying the effect of the knife, rather makes it sink deeper in, while it moderates the full pain of the wound. When someone is told that things are said not in reproach but in love, they receive correction more readily.[20]

From this point, the homily becomes a reflection on proper training in virtue.[21] For the moment Chrysostom remains close to the text on which he is commenting, for the text is about Paul's relationship with the Corinthians as father to children, with an implied contrast with certain other teachers. Verse 16 triggers the climax of the homily: 'be imitators of me, as I am of Christ'. A rhetorical portrait of Paul becomes the point at which strict exegesis is abandoned, and the exhortation grows out of this exemplary

---

[18] *Hom. 1 Cor.* 13; Migne, *PG* 61.108; ET *NPNF*, 1st series, vol. XII, p. 73.
[19] *Hom. 1 Cor.* 13; Migne, *PG* 61.109; ET *NPNF*, 1st series, vol. XII, p. 73.
[20] Ibid. (ET altered).
[21] *Hom. 1 Cor.* 13; Migne, *PG* 61.110 ff; ET *NPNF*, 1st series, vol. XII, pp. 73–4.

servant of God, the great athlete struggling against the powers of evil through his ascetic hardships.

We turned to this homily to illustrate Chrysostom's adaptation of the typical interests of the rhetor to the moral interests of the preacher. But it also instances the commonplace of antiquity that relationships such as father–son or teacher–pupil rested on example and imitation,[22] and the fact that *mimēsis* lay at the heart of apprenticeship, whether in skills leading to a trade or profession, or in those virtues which shaped a moral and spiritual life. It was the potential of the text to act as a 'mirror' that enabled the kind of quasi-typology we observed in the first homily. Paraenetic exegesis encouraged the creation of models out of assumed parallels.

II

In her remarkable book *Christianity and the Rhetoric of Empire*,[23] Averil Cameron sets out to explore, as the subtitle suggests, the development of Christian discourse. The underlying assumption, deriving from the sociology of knowledge and literary theory, is that human socio-cultural groups 'create' the universe in which they dwell through discourse, and the claim is that the control of language was at the heart of the struggle between pagan and Christian culture. Christianity is particularly 'word-oriented' and text-based, and this enabled the formation of a powerful 'totalizing discourse' enshrining an encompassing world-view or ideology. The value judgements in the old attempts to explain the decline of paganism she dismisses: what we need is an explanation of a 'paradigm shift'. The attempt to separate the Greek elements in Christianity, or distinguish the influence of the supposed Graeco-Roman background, she finds misleading.

Out of the framework of Judaism, and living as they did in the Roman Empire and in the context of Greek philosophy, pagan practice, and contemporary social ideas, Christians built themselves a new world.[24]

There is a process of interpenetration to be traced.

---

22 Cf. *The Theology of the Pastoral Letters*, ch. 4, pp. 88–91, with references.
23 Referred to previously in the Introduction.
24 Cameron, *Christianity and the Rhetoric of Empire*, p. 21.

The reason for turning to this book at this point is to highlight her emphasis on figural representation and narrative in this developing Christian discourse. As we have already found, the language of the Bible is parable, sign and symbol, and Christian religious language remained metaphorical, even though it was the language of representation. Cameron highlights the tension between the mystery and the definition, both features of Christianity's essentially linguistic nature. But it is the figurality of Christian discourse which gives it power, and she demonstrates how deep-seated this was by using an example she admits is paradoxical, Eusebius' *Life of Constantine*.[25] However opposed Eusebius may have been to images in Christian art, 'his literary presentation of Constantine is figural to a high degree'. She goes on to acknowledge the debt to pagan panegyric, but also to note how 'the emperor assumes a role in the divine dispensation akin to Moses, if not Christ himself'.[26]

Conversely, Gregory of Nyssa's *Life of Moses* presents Moses as a figure of Christian spirituality.

It is characteristic of Christian writing in general . . . that he should have chosen to express himself in just such a way, through the presentation and interpretation of a figure conceived as a 'pattern' or image of spiritual virtue. Elsewhere, Gregory conceives the Christian self in terms of painter, paint and image: the self-conscious Christian creates his own self, and does so through the medium of texts, which in turn assume the function of models.[27]

It is easy to see how the paraenetic exegesis we have been exploring was designed to facilitate that. The only element to which Cameron might have done more justice is the role of the 'educator' who is the interpreter and creator of these models – the exegete and preacher.

Cameron thinks it not at all surprising that Christians wrote *Lives*, forms of spiritual biography. As Patricia Cox had demonstrated, biographies in Late Antiquity, whether pagan or Christian, were generally meant to be 'literary celebrations of the virtues of eminent individuals'; their heroes were seen 'through ideal traits' which 'worked to distort the historical situation of the hero' so as to emphasise 'the ideal facets of his life'.[28] So *Lives* were exemplary:

[25] Ibid., p. 53.   [26] Ibid., p. 54.
[27] Ibid., pp. 56–7.   [28] Patricia Cox, *Biography in Late Antiquity*, p. 134.

In a concrete sense . . . written *Lives* provided the guidelines for the construction of a Christian life, and the ascetic . . . model provided the guidelines for the construction of a specifically Christian self . . . Written *Lives* were mimetic; real ascetic discipline in turn imitated the written *Lives*. Like visual art, early Christian discourse presented its audience with a series of images.[29]

Cameron recognises that scripture had an enormous role in the development of this discourse, but it was an aspect of the subject which she did not pursue in any depth. Her analysis coheres strikingly with the kind of figural and mimetic emphasis I have been developing in this consideration of paraenetic exegesis.

But it also alerts us to the fact that figural representation belonged to all forms of early Christian exegesis, and was as much a part of the allegorical tradition as of the Antiochene. Her examples are drawn from those who were without question influenced by Origen, namely Eusebius and Gregory of Nyssa. Gregory provides particularly striking examples of how biblical models provided the shape of the life of faith, a life which was a matter not just of moral conduct, but of pursuing purity and truth. Yet the allegorical element is undeniable, interwoven with the kind of figurality which often goes by the name typology.

For Gregory the spiritual life is essentially a journey, and orthodoxy provides the intellectual framework which is necessary for progression.[30] Eunomius thought he could define the nature of God, and his cleverness led to presumption, an over-wise philosophy which fixes a gulf between him and the saving faith of Abraham, who

went out by divine command from his own land and kindred on an 'exodus' befitting a prophet set on understanding God . . . For going out from himself and his country, by which I understand his lowly and earthly mind, he raised his conception as far as possible above the common bounds of nature and forsook the soul's kinship with the senses, so as to be troubled by none of the objects of sense and blind for the purpose of contemplating invisible things, there being neither sight nor sound to distract the mind; so walking, as the Apostle said, by faith not sight, he was lifted so high by the sublimity of his knowledge that he came to be regarded as the acme of human perfection, knowing as much of God as it was possible for finite human capacity at full stretch to attain.[31]

29 Cameron, *Christianity and the Rhetoric of Empire*, p. 57.
30 See my article, '*Paideia* and the Myth of Static Dogma'.
31 *C. Eunom.* II.84ff; Jaeger, pp. 251ff.; ET *NPNF*, 2nd series, vol. v, p. 259 (altered).

That is why, according to Gregory, God is called the God of Abraham. Abraham was able to soar above sense-objects and the beauty of objects of contemplation to behold the archetype of all beauty. He could use various human conceptions, such as God's power, goodness, being without beginning, infinity, or whatever, as stepping-stones for the upward course, and yet recognise that all fall short of what he was seeking, so that

when he had outstripped every supposition with respect to the divine nature, every single conception of God suggested by any designation, when he had thus purged his reason of all such fancies and arrived at a faith unalloyed and free from all prejudice, he produced an evident and unmisleading sign of the knowledge of God, namely the conviction that God is greater and more sublime than any known signification.[32]

So, for Gregory, Abraham is the type of a faith which recognises it is but dust and ashes, and that the curiosity of human knowledge betrays an inappropriate empirical disposition.

Knowing then how widely the divine nature differs from our own, let us quietly remain within our own proper limits.[33]

Let us return to his *Life of Moses*, a more explicitly exegetical work than the controversial text against Eunomius where Abraham is thus exploited. As Cameron observed, it is essentially figural, and, we may add, paraenetically so. Gregory wrote a number of works on the virtuous life, some intended for all Christians, like the *De professione Christiana*, others for monks, like the *De instituto Christiano*. Ron Heine[34] has argued that the *De vita Moysis* was written for priests. It is addressed to a young friend who has enquired about the perfect life, and it is intended to provide a model. If, as Heine argues convincingly,

Gregory's young friend were a priest and Gregory wrote the treatise with the priesthood specifically in view, we can then explain both why themes from Gregory's polemical theology are woven into the treatise and why these particular themes were chosen. Virtue, for a man who led and taught in the church, had to be carefully regulated by the rule of orthodoxy. Both his belief and his life had to be correct by this standard.[35]

---

[32] *C. Eunom.* II.89; Jaeger, p. 252; ET *NPNF*, 2nd series, vol. v, p. 259 (substantially altered).

[33] *C. Eunom.* II.96; Jaeger, p. 252; ET *NPNF*, 2nd series, vol. v, p. 260.

[34] *Perfection in the Virtuous Life: A Study in the Relationship between Edification and Polemical Theology in Gregory of Nyssa's De Vita Moysis*, Patristic Monograph Series, no. 2 (Philadelphia: Philadelphia Patristic Foundation, 1975).

[35] Ibid., p. 25.

Gregory intended the exegesis of the scriptural material to provide a pattern of life for the priestly vocation.[36]

Gregory's introduction recalls the anti-Eunomian figure we have already noted, but also, as Heine shows, directly addresses the problems of the Origenist understanding of perfection.[37] Gregory suggests that perfection in sensible objects involves limitations or boundaries; but virtue is not like that.[38] Like the nature of the infinite God, perfection is boundless, and there is no stopping-place of final attainment. Growth in goodness constitutes human perfection. So examples to be followed are such as Abraham and Sarah, or Moses. Gregory promises to outline Moses' life as a 'pattern', and then, through contemplation of it, reach an understanding of the perfect life.[39]

Moses' life was characterised by journeying, by watching the mysterious cloud that guided the people and teaching them to keep it in sight. Food was miraculously provided, enemies were overcome. At Mount Sinai he and the people were initiated, passing through purification to revelation. Moses had to ascend beyond the visible and enter the inner sanctuary of divine mystical doctrine. Gregory has summarised the story,[40] yet amplified it to bring out its spiritual intention. He goes on to probe its exemplary character more deeply.

Book II is entitled *theōria*. Expounding details allegorically,[41] Gregory delineates the continuous progress upwards that constitutes perfection; Heine would argue that he follows the biblical text in its order, seeing each episode as a progressive step in the virtuous life.[42] Moses' life is a series of ascending steps up Jacob's ladder, as it were.[43] The process involves both doctrine and discipline. *Eusebeia* implies a proper sense of God which produces appropriate worship and an appropriate lifestyle.

---

[36] I believe Heine has successfully challenged Daniélou's 'mystical' interpretation of this work. The introduction to the *CWS* translation does not seem to have noticed Heine's work, and suggests the *Life of Moses* was written for ascetics. That may be equally plausible, but the point is that ethical and doctrinal concerns are paramount.

[37] Heine, *Perfection in the Virtuous Life*, pp. 71ff.

[38] *Life of Moses* 1.5; Jaeger, vol. VII.1, pp. 3–4; ET *CWS* p. 30.

[39] *Life of Moses* 1.7–15; Jaeger, vol. VII.1, pp. 5–7; ET *CWS* pp. 31–3.

[40] *Life of Moses* 1.16–77; Jaeger, vol. VII.1, pp. 7–33; ET *CWS* pp. 33–51.

[41] *Life of Moses* II; Jaeger, vol. VII.1, pp. 33ff.; ET *CWS* pp. 55ff.

[42] Heine, *Perfection in the Virtuous Life*, p. 100.

[43] Ibid., p. 102; *Life of Moses* II.227; Jaeger, vol. VII.1, p. 113; ET *CWS* pp. 113–14.

These two are the pursuits by which virtue is constituted: both the faith concerning deity and conscience concerning life.[44]

Gregory's moral ideals, here as elsewhere, are rigorous and ascetic. Self-control and austerity of life lie at the heart of the purification which must accompany developing spirituality. And that spirituality discovers a progressively deepening piety, related to the doctrinal issues already noted. If at first religious knowledge comes as light, further progress and deeper penetration discover the invisible and incomprehensible, the darkness in which seeing consists in not seeing, for 'no one has ever seen God'.[45] Later[46] Moses enters the luminous darkness of the cloud of the presence. He is transformed by God's glory so that no one could look at him; he speaks with God as one speaks with a friend. Yet to see God is not attainable, and God hides him in a cleft in the rock, allowing him only to see his back-parts – the point being not just the absurdity of a literal seeing of the invisible, but the recognition of God's infinity, indefinability. For 'this truly is the vision of God: never to be satisfied in the desire to see him',[47] and Moses 'is now taught how he can behold him: to follow God wherever he might lead is to behold God ... He who follows will not turn aside from the right way if he always keeps the back of his leader in view.'[48]

Gregory's *Life of Moses* is a classic example of allegorical exegesis – Gregory states[49] that to look just at the *gramma* is to fail to understand the *dianoia*. But it is also to miss the *akolouthia* – Gregory's exegesis is not arbitrary, but paraenetic in intent and figural in its fundamental stance. The same essential approach to exegesis is to be found in Cyril of Alexandria's exegesis of the Pentateuch. His work *On Worship in Spirit and in Truth* is a series of dialogues between himself and a certain Palladius, largely exploring the proper Christian attitude towards the Law.[50] Much is conventional: righteousness comes not through the Law but Christ. The Mosaic

---

[44] *Life of Moses* II.192; Jaeger, vol. VII.1, p. 99; ET *CWS* p. 104 (ET quoted here from Heine, *Perfection in the Virtuous Life*, p. 120). Cf. *Life of Moses* II.166; Jaeger, vol. VII.1, p. 88; ET *CWS* p. 96.

[45] *Life of Moses* II.162ff.; Jaeger, vol. VII.1, pp. 86–8; ET *CWS* pp. 94–6.

[46] *Life of Moses* II.217–55; Jaeger, vol. VII.1, pp .110–22; ET *CWS* pp. 111–20.

[47] *Life of Moses* II.239; Jaeger, vol. VII.1, p. 116; ET *CWS* p. 116.

[48] *Life of Moses* II.252; Jaeger, vol. VII.1, p. 121; ET *CWS* p. 119.

[49] *Life of Moses* II.221–3; Jaeger, vol. VII.1, pp. 110ff.; ET *CWS* pp. 112–39.

[50] For a slightly fuller account of this work, see from *Nicaea to Chalcedon*, pp. 246–8; cf. Kerrigan, *St Cyril of Alexandria Interpreter of the Old Testament*.

covenant is a type and shadow. So its prescriptions work at two levels, at the literal level for the Israelites, but as image and type for the spiritual law of the Church. So by allegory the legal prescriptions are turned into meaningful spiritual commands, and the Law is holy if its double significance is properly appreciated.

But alongside this, Cyril has perceived that the true meaning of the Law is to be expounded in terms of the drama of fall and redemption. The pattern of exile and spiritual famine, followed by repentance and return to a better life, is traced in various biblical narratives: Abraham's migration and the exodus are taken as paradigms of God's grace bringing conversion. What Cyril gives us is a kind of thematic treatment – not verse-by-verse commentary; it aims to expose the human predicament and its solution in Christ, showing how the Christian use of the Jewish scriptures is an integral part of the whole theological construction. This is no word-by-word allegory, but a sort of biblical theology emerging from a kind of figural allegory which permits the two Testaments to cohere. The particular narratives are intersected by the universal narrative of fall and redemption, and the recapitulation theme undergirds both Cyril's exegesis and his Christology. But the universal narrative is the narrative of 'everyman' – so the implied *paraenesis* draws reader or hearer into the story.

The figural form of Christianity's 'totalizing discourse' was largely drawn from the Bible, and reflects the assumption that 'types' were represented in literature as patterns to be followed.

III

In *The Art of Performance*[51] I explored the importance of readers being drawn into the story for any text or drama to relate to its audience, and suggested that this essentially mimetic process implies some degree of allegory. Earlier I proposed a list of various types of allegory.[52] To that list I now suggest we should add figural allegory, noting its essentially paraenetic character. Its purpose was to provide patterns on which people could model their lives. And this means that the apparently non-allegorical readings of a preacher like Chrysostom are also by implication quasi-allegorical, as they are quasi-typological. Sharp differentiations are over-simplifications.

---

[51] *The Art of Performance*, ch. 7.   [52] Above, p. 192.

So the question is posed again: are there not such congruences between allegory and typology that attempts at distinction are problematic? Both are fuelled by the need to develop paraenetic exegesis. 'Types' often correspond by being particular instances of universal narrative; allegory tends to abstract eternal truths from narrative, and lose the narrative coherence. But both are woven together in developing a figural reading which can map the journey which constitutes the life of faith. The richly figural exegesis that developed is not something that can be traced to roots in a particular cultural background. Some Jewish precedents, together with the assumptions involved in treating a text as prophetic and referring to its fulfilment, made an important contribution. But so did the kind of *mimēsis* commonly attributed to literature in Graeco-Roman literature, and the rhetorical traditions of reading texts for their moral value and for their ability to create models to be imitated. The figural tendencies of Christian exegesis were the result of a remarkable cultural interpenetration.

CHAPTER 12

The theologian as exegete

I

By now it should be evident that patristic study is most significant for the discovery of the inseparability of theology, exegesis of scripture and spirituality, an integration by no means apparent in the modern world. This is borne out by turning to Augustine and focussing on the theologian as exegete. With Augustine, the quantity of material, both primary and secondary, is formidable: here is just a selective dip into a vast textual deposit. His work provides a fitting climax to this study, and, together with the earlier excursion into the work of Ephrem, allows me the satisfaction of having put the Greek tradition in context between both East and West.

Augustine fascinates, not least by reason of his lifelong intellectual development.[1] It is not really possible to speak of 'his theology' as if it were a single coherent entity. He was always on an intellectual and spiritual journey, and the later stages of the journey made him see the earlier stages in different perspective.[2] He was capable of changing his mind, of arguing one thing in one context, another in another. So one witnesses a mind at work, a mind increasingly formed by the reading of scripture, especially the Psalms and the

---

[1] There are many biographies and studies which provide insight into this: an excellent brief introduction is provided by Henry Chadwick, *Augustine* (Past Masters Series, Oxford: Oxford University Press, 1986). The classic biography is Peter Brown, *Augustine of Hippo* (London: Faber & Faber, 1967). Other studies include Gerald Bonner, *St Augustine of Hippo. Life and Controversies* (London: SCM, 1963; revised, Norwich: Canterbury Press, 1986), Eugene Teselle, *Augustine the Theologian* (London: Burns & Oates, 1970), and Christopher Kirwan, *Augustine* (London: Routledge, 1989).

[2] His writing of *Retractiones* (text in *CC*, vol. 57; ET in *FC*, vol. 60) is clear evidence of this.

Pauline Epistles. Christiaan Beker[3] has argued that in considering Paul's theology, one has to take account of both contingency and coherence, as his thought develops and responds to new situations; much the same can be said of Augustine, and the same kind of questions arise about where the coherence is to be located. The problem of interpretation in both cases is not dissimilar to the philosophical problem of locating the identity of an individual over a lifespan from babyhood to old age. The possibility of self-identification with such an evolving process is perhaps what makes Augustine so intriguing, and indeed disturbing. For one may claim, as Burnaby did,[4] that his organising theological idea, arising from both spiritual experience inspired by Neoplatonism and the reading of the scriptures, was the love and the grace of God, and yet, under the pressures of episcopal responsibility and doctrinal controversy, rationalistic argument led him to conclusions that later generations have judged a betrayal of that fundamental insight.[5] Be that as it may, we content ourselves here with a few observations on the exegetical formation of Augustine the theologian.

II

The *Confessions*[6] presents itself as the obvious starting-point. Yet how is the *Confessions* itself to be read? Is this disingenuous testimony to how it was? Or is it a re-reading of the author's past in the light of new perspectives?

There is again an instructive parallel with the interpretation of Paul. Romans has in the past been read as a sequential argument reflecting Paul's own thought-processes: he began in a plight, needing salvation, and Christ provided the solution. But E. P.

---

[3] J. Christiaan Beker, *Paul the Apostle. The Triumph of God in Life and Thought* (Philadelphia: Fortress, 1980; Edinburgh: T. & T. Clark, 1989); and *The Triumph of God. The Essence of Paul's Thought* (Minneapolis: Fortress, 1990).

[4] John Burnaby's *Amor Dei. A Study of the Religion of St. Augustine* (originally published London: Hodder & Stoughton, 1938; reissued in paperback, Norwich: Canterbury Press, 1991) remains an important exposition of Augustine's thought.

[5] I refer to the Donatist controversy, in which Augustine eventually took the position that state force might 'compel' the heretics 'to come in'; and the Pelagian controversy, which was the context of the development of his extreme doctrines of predestination. These are well treated in standard studies, such as Peter Brown, *Augustine*.

[6] Probably the most studied and translated of Augustine's works, the text may be found in *CC, series Latina*, vol. 27, text and ET in *LCL*, and ET by Henry Chadwick in World's Classics (Oxford: Oxford University Press, 1992).

Sanders[7] has obliged us to consider another approach. Suppose Paul means what he says in Philippians: 'I was a Pharisee of the Pharisees, blameless according to the Law.' Suppose Paul's exposition in Romans is not the way he came to faith, but the result of the new perspective on the past provided by newness of life in Christ. Whatever the course of the Romans argument, Paul himself moved, Sanders suggests, not from plight to solution, but from solution to plight.

A similar argument has been mounted with respect to Augustine. It was a new reading of Paul that gave him insight into the human moral predicament, and the *Confessions* makes his own life a paradigm of the life of 'everyman' as he now understood it, from being in Adam to being in Christ. This kind of thesis has been advanced by Paula Fredriksen:[8]

> The *Confessions* is a tremendously complicated book, and the temptation to see it primarily as autobiography should be resisted. It is rather, Augustine doing theology in a new key, using his own past experience as privileged evidence for his new theological propositions. Its true autobiographical status, in fact, may lie less in the particulars of its historical narrative than in the biographical fact to which it attests: in denying man's ability to do anything towards his own salvation, Augustine had broken completely with the classical ideal of virtue by which he had been reintroduced to Catholicism back in Milan. Enmeshed in ecclesiastical responsibilities, struggling almost as much with his own congregation as with schismatics and heretics, aware – through his dream life – of the deeper struggles continually going on within himself, Augustine now found such an ideal dangerous, ridiculous, and puerile. He ruthlessly renounces it in the *Confessions*.[9]

Of course, Augustine had previously read Paul, but, Fredriksen suggests, he had read Paul in another way, as had most other people in the first generations of Christianity. Her primary concern is with the question why Augustine changed his interpretation, considering various possible sources and influences. Babcock,[10] in reply, would

---

[7] See *Paul and Palestinian Judaism* (London: SCM, 1977), pp. 442ff. He argues particularly against scholars such as Bultmann.

[8] 'Beyond the Body/Soul Dichotomy: Augustine's Answer to Mani, Plotinus, and Julian', in William S. Babcock (ed.), *Paul and the Legacies of Paul* (Dallas: Southern Methodist University Press, 1990), pp. 227–51. Cf. 'Paul and Augustine: Conversion Narratives, Orthodox Traditions, and the Retrospective Self', *JTS* NS 37 (1986) pp. 3–34.

[9] Fredriksen, 'Beyond the Body/Soul Dichotomy', p. 243.

[10] Babcock, *Paul and the Legacies*, p. 256.

be 'inclined to give rather more weight . . . to Augustine's reading of Paul himself'. He suggests that 'it was precisely in his repeated reading and interpretation of Paul in the years from 394 to 396, and not in some other forum, that Augustine invented, perhaps with some help from Tyconius, Paul's augustinianism'. If that is correct, it provides us with a particularly good indication of how a theologian was formed by his reading of scripture.

Fredriksen stresses that 'Augustine's views change more drastically between 394 and 396–8 than between 398 and 430.'[11] According to the *Confessions*, Paul played an important role in the conversion-experience in Milan in 386, and the Pauline material may have been familiar earlier during the Manichaean period. But it was after 392, back in Africa, that Augustine was provoked by debate with Fortunatus to use exegetical tools against the Manichees. Prior to this he had argued in philosophical terms against moral determinism and in favour of free will. Now he needed to show that the apostle 'neither condemns the Law nor takes away man's freewill'. He wrote his commentaries on Romans and Galatians, added the third book of his work on free will (*De libero arbitrio*), and wrote his work *Ad Simplicianum*. Here lies the 'drastic shift in Augustine's assessment of the process of salvation'.[12]

Fredriksen has no doubt the process was complicated. Many have pointed to the social situation – Augustine, faced with the intractable habits of his congregation, 'within a very short time, . . . moved from the quiet of lay piety as a *servus dei* to the rough and tumble world of North African ecclesiastical politics'. Literary influences have been suggested: Ambrosiaster's commentary provided Augustine's interpretation of Romans 5.12: 'In quo – id est in Adam – omnes peccaverunt . . . Manifestum est itaque omnes in Adam peccasse quasi in massa' ('In whom – that is in Adam – all sinned . . . So it is clear that all have sinned in Adam as if *en masse*'). Here is the mistranslation of *eph' ho*, and the source of the *massa perditionis*. The other significant literary factor is that it was in this period that Augustine became acquainted with Tyconius' *Liber regularum*.[13]

---

11 Fredriksen, 'Beyond the Body/Soul Dichotomy', p. 228.
12 Ibid., p. 238.
13 See above, ch. 6, pp. 137–9. Also Henry Chadwick, 'Tyconius and Augustine', in the collection of his reprinted papers, *Heresy and Orthodoxy in the Early Church* (Aldershot: Variorum, 1991).

The latter source Fredriksen thinks was crucial, along with Augustine's attention to the life of Paul, as depicted in Acts and in the Pastoral Epistles. The converted Paul, 'the blasphemer and persecutor (1 Tim. 1.13), the foolish, impious and hateful man enslaved to various pleasures (Titus 3.3), imposed himself'.[14] The paradox of grace in Paul's case is expressed in the work *Ad Simplicianum*, according to Fredriksen:

> What did Saul will but to attack, seize, bind and slay Christians? What a fierce, savage, blind will was that! Yet he was thrown prostrate by one word from on high, and a vision came to him whereby his mind and will were turned from their fierceness and set on the right way towards faith, so that suddenly out of a marvellous persecutor of the Gospel he was made a still more marvellous preacher of the Gospel.[15]

'The essentially classical model of self-improvement and moral freedom . . . could not withstand Augustine's double encounter with Tyconius' emphasis on God's absolute omnipotence and his own growing sensitivity to Paul's past as a persecutor', concludes Fredriksen. Both Paul's own writings and Augustine's lifelong struggle with the problem of evil provide Babcock with a more satisfactory account: Augustine struggled not so much with *unde malum?* (whence evil?) as *unde male faciamus?* (whence our evil-doing?)[16]

The function of scholarly discussion and debate is surely to sharpen our awareness, not to settle questions which are ultimately unsettleable – no doubt these and many other factors contributed. But we should not underestimate the difference that exegetical engagement made. One knows the experience of accepting traditions of interpretation, until one engages specifically with a text for oneself. Then things emerge from the text that one had not imagined before, though one may have read it many times. And this is especially true if there is something in one's own intellectual or spiritual struggle that suddenly chimes with the text, and the two-way process of illumination brings a breakthrough in understanding. We can empathise with the kind of mental process which may plausibly be attributed to Augustine at this point, and affirm the vital importance of his engagement with the text. In the *Confessions*, the biblical text 'creates' a life – indeed, creates a self.

---

[14] Fredriksen, 'Beyond the Body/Soul Dichotomy', p. 240.
[15] Ibid., p. 241, quoting *Ad Simpl.* 1.2.22.   [16] *Paul and the Legacies*, p. 257.

Where Gregory Nyssen had created a paradigm out of the life of Moses, Augustine shapes his own life as a paradigm by seeing it afresh in the light of scripture.

III

But there is more to the *Confessions* than that. In chapter 11, we considered Averil Cameron's insight into how Christians were building a new world for themselves by the creation of a new discourse, and we explored the interpenetration of Bible and culture to provide a discourse steeped in figural representation. We have noted how the scriptures became part of a new *paideia*. All of this contributes to our evaluation of the *Confessions*, and of Augustine as theologian and exegete. It is worth considering the nature of a work begun between the *Ad Simplicianum* and the *Confessions*, namely the *De doctrina Christiana*.[17]

The title of the work might lead us to suppose that it is about doctrine as such, and parts of the first book almost seem to encourage that view. However, Augustine, followed by the majority of scholars, introduces it as a work on scriptural interpretation, however surprising that may be at first sight. The book's true nature is recognised if we remember that Augustine was by profession a rhetor, an educator. What he was providing was a Christian *Institutio oratoria* – to borrow the title of Quintilian's treatise on education.[18] The literature on which this Christian education was based was the scriptures, and Augustine begins by stating that scriptural interpretation depends on two things: the means of ascertaining the proper meaning, and the way in which that meaning is then communicated.

Augustine began this work in 397, and it was not for another twenty years that he completed it. The communication of meaning

---

[17] Text in *CC*, *series Latina*, vol. 32; ET in *FC*, vol. 2. For discussion of this work, see H.-I. Marrou, *S. Augustine et la fin de la culture antique* (Paris: de Boccard, 1938); Peter Brown, *Augustine*, pp. 259–69; Carol Harrison, *Beauty and Revelation in the Thought of Saint Augustine* (Oxford: Clarendon, 1992), especially ch. 2. In Mühlenberg and van Oort (eds.), *Predigt in der alten Kirche*, the papers by Ekkehard Mühlenberg, 'Augustins Predigen' (pp. 9–24), and Christoph Schäublin, 'Zum paganen Umfeld der christlichen Predigt' (pp. 25–49), draw from this work in discussing the importance of, and distancing from, rhetorical traditions which characterised Augustine's preaching.

[18] See above ch. 4. Marrou, *S. Augustine et la fin de la culture antique*, sees this work as developing 'une culture Chrétienne'.

was finally addressed in Book IV, which belongs to the second stage of composition. There he was careful to

> put a stop to the expectations of readers who may think I am about to lay down rules of rhetoric such as I have learnt, and taught too, in the secular schools.[19]

All that means is that Augustine was no longer sold on the schoolbook rhetorical tricks, recognising that true fluency is a gift – for the eloquent are eloquent because they instinctively exemplify the rules of the art. In practice, he regarded the study of good examples as being as important as it is for children to hear adults speak a language so as to learn to communicate.[20] Thus Augustine's concern in spelling out the duty of the Christian teacher is modelled on what he had known professionally as a rhetorician.

Because the Christian teacher has to communicate what scripture is about, rhetoric belongs to Augustine's subject-matter. He is concerned to show how the scriptures unite wisdom and eloquence, so themselves providing the exemplary material the Christian teacher needs.[21] There follows a remarkable examination of several passages of scripture, simply to demonstrate in the texts all the rhetorical devices an educated person would recognise. As for Cicero, so for Augustine, the aim should be to teach, delight and persuade; the hearer must be moved as well as instructed. The style should be in keeping with the subject-matter, and scripture provides examples of different styles, as do Cyprian and Ambrose. Variation in style is important, but so are the exemplary life and the prayer of the teacher.[22] Interpretation is about communication, not just ascertaining what the meaning is.[23] Scripture has to be performed.

Augustine always meant to lead up to this area of the subject. Whether he would have treated it in exactly the same way if he had written the final book twenty years earlier is a moot question, but perhaps not important. The final book helps us to see the nature of the whole. The educator whom Augustine now seeks to form has replaced the classical canon with the biblical canon, but the shape of

---

[19] *De doct. Christ.* IV.i.2; *CCL*, vol. 32, p. 116; ET my own, but passage may be found in context in *FC*, p. 168.

[20] *De doct. Christ.* IV.iii.4–5; *CCL*, vol. 32, pp. 118–19; ET *FC*, pp. 170–1.

[21] *De doct. Christ.* IV.vi.9–10; *CCL*, vol. 32, p. 122; ET *FC*, pp. 175–7.

[22] *De doct. Christ.* IV.xxvii.59–60; *CCL*, vol. 32, pp. 163–4; ET *FC*, pp. 229–31.

[23] *De doct. Christ.* IV.xv.32; *CCL*, vol. 32, pp. 138–9; ET *FC*, pp. 197–8.

that education lies in the classical *paideia*. As Peter Brown puts it, commenting on a letter to a young pagan written in 411,

Augustine implied that the Christians, too, possessed a classic as inexhaustible and as all-absorbing as Vergil or Homer had been to the pagans. Their Bible also, could form a man for all he needed in this life . . . In an age when culture was thought of exclusively in terms of the understanding of a classical text, the Bible was nothing less than the basis of a 'Christian culture', a *doctrina Christiana*.[24]

So the work given this title is meant to form the 'experts' who will communicate the scriptures to the Christian community. Now we understand why Augustine opens this work as if it were a system of rules for interpretation of scripture, and then spends the first book doing what to our eyes looks like something quite different. Augustine's mind is formed by the distinction between subject-matter and words: the terms he uses here are *res* and *signa*, things and signs.[25] So the first book is about the 'things' of which scripture speaks. The second and third books then deal with the 'signs', mostly verbal, through which scripture communicates its subject-matter.

Book I gives us what Augustine regards as the essential subject-matter of scripture. Like earlier exegetes he can speak of this as the rule of faith, but his account bears the stamp of his particular theological insights. He divides 'things' into two categories, those to be used and those to be enjoyed.[26] The problem is that human beings confuse the two. To enjoy a thing is to rest with satisfaction in it for its own sake. To use a thing is to employ whatever means are at one's disposal to obtain what one desires. The true objects of enjoyment are the Father, Son and Holy Spirit, the Trinity, the one Being who is the living God.[27] From this point, an exposition of the Trinity and the incarnation proceeds in a fairly systematic way, with a few allusions to scripture, such as 'the Word became flesh':[28] Wisdom assumed our humanity to heal it, and Christ holds together his Church in the bond of unity and love, while purging it with afflictions. The exposition of credal affirmations is there to

---

[24] Peter Brown, *Augustine*, p. 263. Cf. Marrou, *S. Augustine et la fin de la culture antique*, p. 403, where it is suggested that the Bible replaces, for Christians, Homer for the Greeks and Vergil for the Latins.

[25] *De doct. Christ.* I.ii.2; *CCL*, vol. 32, p. 7; ET *FC*, p. 28.

[26] *De doct. Christ.* I.iii.3ff.; *CCL*, vol. 32, pp. 8ff.; ET *FC*, pp. 29ff.

[27] *De doct. Christ.* I.v.5; *CCL*, vol. 32, p. 9; ET *FC*, p. 30.

[28] *De doct. Christ.* I.xiii.12; *CCL*, vol. 32, p. 13; ET *FC*, p. 36.

demonstrate the argument:[29] God alone is to be enjoyed and the things of this world are to be used to ensure our arrival at the full enjoyment of God. Augustine proceeds to speak of the human as a great 'thing', made in God's image with respect to the rational soul.[30] So should we use or enjoy ourselves? Humanity is to be loved, not for its own sake, but for God's.

If a person loves the self for the self's own sake, he does not look at the self in relation to God, but turns the mind in upon the self . . . This is the law of love that has been laid down by divine authority: 'Thou shalt love thy neighbour as thyself'; but, 'Thou shalt love God with all thy heart, and with all thy soul, and with all thy mind.' So you are to concentrate all your thoughts, your whole life, and your whole intelligence upon the one from whom you derive all that you bring.[31]

The rest of Book I could be described as an exploration of the law of love. The fulfilment of scripture is the law of love, and any interpretation that does not build up the twofold love of God and neighbour is mistaken. The person who is mature in faith, hope and love does not need the scriptures, except for the purpose of teaching others. Again we see how the scriptures are tied into a whole pedagogical programme, which has a moral and spiritual end.

This theological perspective is of course a key theme in the *City of God*,[32] one of the many works, large and small, which Augustine will compose before completing this treatise. There are two loves, love of God and love of self, and all human history bears witness to the struggle between them. In the *Confessions* the same struggle is evidenced in Augustine's own life. In all of these, and the *De Trinitate*, we see Augustine exploring the priority of God: 'you have made us for yourself, and our heart is restless until it rests in you'.[33] God is so deeply the principle of existence that no other starting-point is possible than the Being of God, and yet access to that Being

---

[29] *De doct. Christ.* I.xiv.13–I.xxi.19; *CCL*, vol. 32, pp. 13–16; ET *FC*, pp. 36–40.

[30] *De doct. Christ.* I.xxii.20; *CCL*, vol. 32, p. 16; ET *FC*, p. 41.

[31] *De doct. Christ.* I.xxii.21; *CCL*, vol. 32, p. 17; ET my own, but passage may be found in context in *FC*, p. 42.

[32] This other classic among the works of St Augustine is found in *CCL*, vols. 47–8; ET by Henry Bettenson in Penguin Classics (Harmondsworth: Penguin, 1972). Augustine's views on history and eschatology, particularly as expressed in this work, are discussed by R. A. Markus, *Saeculum. History and Society in the Theology of St Augustine* (Cambridge: Cambridge University Press, 1970).

[33] *Confessions* I.i.1; *CCL*, vol. 27, p. 1; ET Chadwick, p. 3.

is by turning inward, and inward turning is turning away from love of self, because love of self is lust for fulfilment through outer things, riches, friends, sex, or whatever. Love of God puts everything into proper perspective, including the self.

It is strangely difficult to identify and articulate clearly the difference between Augustine and Eastern Fathers, such as the Cappadocians. Neoplatonism had an effect on them all. Yet somehow there is a different centring: a shift from the shared search to know the unknowable God, from the shared recognition of the immense infinity of the mystery beyond the grasp of the human mind, to an experience of being known by God. Paradoxically the one who is apparently self-absorbed is the one overwhelmingly God-absorbed, and it is this which rules out Eastern synergism for Augustine. The absolute priority of God could be described as the hallmark of Augustine's theology. What the *De doctrina* indicates is that Augustine believes that theology, the theology of the inexorable love of God demanding love in return, to be what scripture signifies.

Scripture signifies these things, however, through signs, and these signs are the subject of Books II–III. It is the discussion of signs which comes closest to what we would expect to find in a treatise on interpretation. The important thing about signs is that they signify – they are not to be attended to in themselves, as things are, but only as they point to something else. Augustine distinguishes between natural and conventional signs.[34] Smoke indicates fire, an angry countenance indicates anger in the soul. These are natural and unintentional signs. Conventional signs belong to human culture. The principal example is language, followed by writing.[35]

But Augustine recognises that human discord has prevented any signs being common to all. The translation of the scriptures into various human languages has been a necessity to provide the remedy for the diseases of the human will; the object of interpretation is to find out the thought and will of those who wrote them, and through this to find out the will of God.[36] In the *Confessions*, Augustine sits rather lighter to the quest for the mind of the Moses, the author, since it is impossible sometimes to ascertain which

---

[34] *De doct. Christ.* II.i.1–2; *CCL*, vol. 32, pp. 32–3; ET *FC*, pp. 61–2.
[35] *De doct. Christ.* II.ii.3 ff; *CCL*, vol. 32, pp. 33ff.; ET *FC*, pp. 63ff.
[36] *De doct. Christ.* II.v.6; *CCL*, vol. 32, p. 35; ET *FC*, p. 64.

interpretation coheres with authorial intention.[37] But there as here the important quality is humility of mind before the text. Augustine recognises that the signs are not all transparent: the scriptures contain many obscurities. He thinks that this is to prevent pride and stimulate the intellectual appetite.[38]

The interpreter needs a number of characteristics: fear of the Lord, piety, knowledge, strength and resolution, purity of vision, wisdom.[39] The knowledge required includes basic information such as the books included in the canon, and experience of the language of scripture.[40] Augustine approves some skill in Hebrew and Greek, and finds a variety of translations helpful for discerning the meaning of the original. The rest of Book II covers difficulties in translation and interpretation. Figurative signs are elucidated by etymology and numerology. Knowledge of music and other liberal arts may also help, and should not be given up because of pagan superstition. Idolatry and astrology are to be rejected, but historical enquiry, chronology, natural science, technology and so on may provide important information for exegesis. Once again we see how important was commenting *historike*, and how much the various arts were in the curriculum of the rhetorical schools primarily for the purpose of learned exegesis.[41] Dialectics and logic are also required to ascertain valid processes of reasoning and deduction, and identify

---

[37] *Confessions* XII.xiii.16–end; *CCL*, vol. 36, pp. 223–41; ET Chadwick, pp. 253–72. This is a lengthy and important discussion of the problem of conflicting exegeses.

[38] *De doct. Christ.* II.vi.7; *CCL*, vol. 32, p. 35; ET *FC*, p. 65. Compare the importance of *aporiai* in Origen; see above, ch. 4, pp. 88–9 and 94ff. Cf. pp. 24 and 211. See also the discussion of the relationship between Origen and Augustine in Henry Chadwick, 'Christian Platonism in Origen and Augustine', reprinted in *Heresy and Orthodoxy*.

[39] *De doct. Christ.* II.vii.9–11; *CCL*, vol. 32, pp. 36–8; ET *FC*, pp. 66–8.

[40] On canon: *De doct. Christ.* II.viii.13; *CCL*, vol. 32, pp. 39–40; ET *FC*, pp. 70–1; on language: *De doct. Christ.* II.xi.16; *CCL*, vol. 32, p. 42; ET *FC*, p. 73.

[41] Marrou, S. *Augustine et la fin de la culture antique*, argues that all the liberal arts and sciences are in this period subordinated to rhetorical interests: 'Le grammairien commentant les classiques, devait, en même temps qu'il expliquait les faits relevant des diverses sciences, donner aussi tous les renseignements historiques nécessaires à l'intelligence du texte. Dans cette conception de l'histoire, comprise comme un aspect du labeur grammatical, la mythologie vient s'adjoindre à l'histoire au sens moderne et occupe bientôt une place d'honneur' (pp. 116–17). Later he shows how Augustine utilises the standard components of the *encyclios paideia* in the interests of scriptural exegesis: dialectic, mathematics, arithmetic, music, geometry, astronomy, geography, natural history. History itself is less 'le fait d'assiler une certaine conception de l'évolution de l'humanité, qu'une série d'*exempla*, de précédents utile de citer' (p. 119). Everything is reduced to an accumulation of 'souvenirs, citations, anecdotes, à propos de mille petits problèmes qu'on prend plaisir à resoudre en passant' (p. 121). Thus our argument about 'history' in earlier chapters based on the Greek tradition is borne out by Augustine.

false inference. In other words, the standard school methods are to be appropriated for scriptural exegesis. All this is fine, Augustine says, provided the right attitude of humility and purity of heart informs the analysis.

In Book III, Augustine deals with *to grammatikon*, as examples of problems with punctuation, pronunciation and correct construal are worked through. The rule is asserted that whatever there is in the Word of God that cannot, when taken literally, be referred either to purity of life or soundness of doctrine, should be treated as figurative.[42] At this point, the law of love becomes a crucial criterion. Augustine goes on to exercise ethical criticism, considering how stories like that of David's adultery are to be understood.[43] He shows that figures do not always mean the same thing, but that obscure passages should be illuminated by the clearer parallels. He lists the various figures of speech identified by grammarians, recognising that they are to be found in scripture and need to be identified for proper exegesis. These include allegory, enigma, parable, metaphor, catachresis, irony and antiphrasis.[44]

Somewhere in the middle of all this is the seam between his writing in 397 and his continuation in 426. The survey is brought to a conclusion with a critical review of the *Rules of Tyconius*.[45] This material belongs to his later additions, yet his discovery of Tyconius would seem to have occurred about the time of his earlier composition. Tyconius purported to provide keys to open the secrets of scripture, or, as we found in chapter 6, tried to establish criteria for determining the reference of figurative texts. Typical of the procedure is the first rule, which refers texts to Christ or to his Body, the Church: Augustine's *Enarrationes in Psalmos*[46] display this as a consistent exegetical principle. The seven rules in Augustine's view are not comprehensive, and yet many have noted the influence of Tyconius on Augustine's exegetical practice, and here he takes the trouble to list and discuss them.

For Augustine, the work of the exegete is the fundamental task of the ecclesiastical educator, and thus of the theologian. The

---

[42] *De doct. Christ.* III.x.14–16; *CCL*, vol. 32, pp. 86–7; ET *FC*, pp. 129–30.
[43] *De doct. Christ.* III.xxi.30–31; *CCL*, vol. 32, pp. 95–6; ET *FC*, pp. 141–2.
[44] *De doct. Christ.* III.xxix.40–41; *CCL*, vol. 32, pp. 100–2; ET *FC*, pp. 148–9.
[45] *De doct. Christ.* III.xxx.42ff.; *CCL*, vol. 32, pp. 102ff.; ET *FC*, pp. 150ff.
[46] See further below, p. 282, and notes.

techniques are those he practised long in the rhetorical schools. The convergence of cultures as educational custom takes over a different canon of literature is evidenced in the West as in the East. He too is contributing to the creation of a new discourse in which scripture has a vital role. But let us return to question how far the theologian is formed by the canonical texts.

IV

Augustine shared with Plotinus a concern with the status of 'signs', and the books of the Platonists had an incontestable influence on his intellectual move away from Manichaeism, whatever we make of the autobiographical character of the *Confessions*. For Augustine, as for Gregory of Nyssa and Ephrem, the words of human language are simply inadequate, and yet essential, for the expression of the divine.[47] As Henry Chadwick puts it:

The acute sense of the inadequacy of words explains why Augustine at the beginning of the *Confessions* experiences difficulty in finding any way of addressing God intelligibly, or speaking about God correctly. The answer to the question he finds in the reception of scripture in the Christian community. The Bible consists of words, human indeed but for the believing community a gift of God so that within the sign there is also the divine reality...

From the first paragraph of the *Confessions* onwards, Augustine can express Neoplatonic themes in language which sounds like a pastiche of the Psalter.[48]

Speaking of the problem of making sense of the last four books, when autobiography has given way to a variety of philosophical and exegetical topics, Chadwick suggests that these last four books

make explicit what is only hinted at in the autobiographical parts, namely that the story of the soul wandering away from God and then in torment and tears finding its way home through conversion is also the story of the entire created order. It is a favourite Neoplatonic theme...

So Augustine's personal quest and pilgrimage are the individual's experience in microcosm of what is true, on the grand scale, of the whole creation. Augustine found his story especially symbolized in St Luke's account of the parable of the prodigal son. But that parable also mirrors

---

[47] See the important discussion in Harrison, *Beauty and Revelation*, ch. 2.
[48] Introduction to ET of *The Confessions*, p. xxii.

the evolutionary process of the world as understood by the Neoplatonic philosophers of the age. So the autobiographical books I–IX are more than a memoir: they illustrate a universal truth about human nature.[49]

In the midst of this account, Chadwick refers to Romans 8 as a New Testament passage expressing a parallel motif, yet basically he offers an interpretation rather different from the one noted earlier from Fredriksen, an alternative construal of the *Confessions* as the construction of a life to instantiate a theme: Neoplatonic descent and return rather than human perdition and salvation read from Paul. Plotinus, we are told, had

provided Augustine with a model and a vocabulary for a mystical quest directed to the union of the soul with God in a beatific vision.[50]

The interpenetration is profound, for the work is on page after page a collage of scriptural texts, Augustine exploiting the Bible for allusion and quotation in the way explored in earlier chapters of this book. One suspects that, despite Augustine's awareness of differences between the books of the Platonists and the Bible, his theological mind, consciously or unconsciously, had made so many connections that true differentiation was beyond him. The Prologue of John taught the essentials of Platonism, and the Psalms provided the language for expressing Plotinian union with God in love and praise. So was Paul all that significant after all?

The reading of the apostle was undoubtedly formative at key moments in Augustine's intellectual and spiritual formation. Nothing for Augustine happened by chance. Providentially the voice of the child sang out 'Tolle, lege' ('Pick up and read').[51] It was Paul's words which struck home and changed Augustine's life. Studying Paul later, Augustine was struck by passages which illuminated his deepest question: why do we human beings do what is evil? Like Paul, Augustine moved from solution to plight. Reviewed in the presence of God, whose sovereign love is overwhelmingly holy and aweful, his own life becomes a case-history of human failure and sin.

Language, even the language of the scriptures, belonged to a world of signs, a world of indirect knowledge occasioned by the Fall. What the theologian craved was a more immediate access to the real

---

[49] Ibid., p. xxiv.   [50] Ibid., p. xxi.
[51] *Confessions* VIII.xii.29; *CCL*, vol. 27, p. 131; ET Chadwick, pp. 152–3.

world of 'things', of God's very self. Behind the signs of scripture was the reality of God, known in flashes of direct awareness. Augustine speaks of us being like people recovering from blindness, brought by their physician into the light to see how much healing has happened, and repulsed by the glare. They say, 'Just now I did see, but now I cannot.' The physician applies stinging eyesalves to foster their hope of seeing.[52] As Peter Brown puts it:

Wise men, pagan as well as Christian, had been able to rise above material things to 'an ineffable reality grasped by the mind alone', 'for a moment, like a blinding light, a lightning flash through heavy darkness.' (De civ. Dei ix.16). Yet Augustine had found such experiences painfully transient: 'You did beat back the weakness of my gaze, blinding me too strongly, and I was shaken with love and dread . . . And I learned that *Thou hast corrected men for iniquity and Thou didst make my soul shrivel up like a moth*' (Conf. vii,x,16).[53]

One feels the moth image is all too appropriate: for Augustine God sometimes seems so much the light that both attracts and dazzles, bringing its creatures to destruction as well as fulfilment. Yet the problem is that the light is too often obscure, and people prefer the comfort of the dark. The Word has to provide sharp salves, the medicine that hurts to heal. But the desire is to gaze on the brightness of God's glory.

'For the meantime', however, Augustine would 'let the Scriptures be the countenance of God'.[54] He 'had come to believe that the understanding and exposition of the scriptures was the heart of the bishop's life'.[55] He saw the scriptures as a witness to truth, indeed as expressive of the proper relationship to reality and truth. So, perhaps inconsistently, the *res* of which scripture spoke could be spoken of in distinction from the scriptural sign-language which referred to them. Hence Book 1 of the *De doctrina Christiana*, and the *De Trinitate*.

To get behind the 'signs' to some kind of conception of the *res*, the reality, required a process of deduction. In chapter 2, we explored Athanasius' appeal to the mind of scripture behind the words; Augustine belongs to the same intellectual tradition. By now it was an established part of the rule of faith that the reality of the God

---

[52] *Tractates on Jn.* xviii.xi.1–2; *CCL*, vol. 36, p. 187; ET *FC*, vol. 79, pp. 136–7.
[53] Peter Brown, *Augustine*, p. 262.
[54] Ibid., quoting *Serm*. 22.7. [55] Ibid., p. 162.

to whom scripture pointed was trinitarian. If scripture was God's countenance, it was necessary to discern through its expressions the mind behind the face. This is the work of the theologian. And yet far more deeply than in Athanasius, or even the Cappadocians, the priority of God dominates the life and thought of Augustine. No exegesis, no argument, no text can delimit that reality by containing it. It can but point to the divine *res* behind the signs, before which no creature has a leg to stand on.

In the final book of the *De Trinitate*,[56] Augustine reviews what he has done in the process of the argument. He had begun in Book I with the testimony of scripture to the unity and equality of the supreme Trinity. The following three books had continued the same process, concentrating on the missions of the Son and the Holy Spirit. Scripture had been the starting-point of the argument. Then in Books V–VII, he had undertaken a series of deductive arguments in response to questions and difficulties in the notion of a Triune God, dealing with substance, generation and so on, and showing that there are not three powers or three wisdoms or three loves, nor can one be regarded as 'greater' than another. God is essentially simple. So far the ground is familiar. Augustine shares the arguments of his Greek counterparts and Latin predecessors.

Book VIII had introduced Augustine's psychological analogies. In human reasoning and loving, he discerned a trinity of knower, known and knowledge, lover, beloved and love. Book IX had justified such analogies on the ground that humanity is made in God's image, and the following books developed the theme, discovering a clearer trinity in the mind, namely memory, understanding and will, and investigating the functioning of sense-perception and imagination. These explorations were presented as seeking an understanding of what has been believed, and betrayed Augustine's interest in current epistemological questions.

But all of this led up to the subject-matter of the final book. Now Augustine shows how the search for the Trinity means directing the mind to God. There is a difference between the reality of the Trinity and its image in another subject, and Augustine expends much effort in pointing out such difficulties as the contrast between

---

[56] Text in *CCL*, vol. 50; ET in *FC*, vol. 45; and *LCC*, vol. 8 has ET (quoted below with second person pronouns altered) of Books VIII–XV.

discursive reasoning in human knowing and God's total, immediate knowledge.[57] The analogies he has used are imperfect.

When the promised vision, 'face to face' has come, we shall behold the Trinity . . . far more clearly and surely than we now behold its image in ourselves. This present vision, through a mirror and in an enigma, . . . belongs . . . to those who see the mind as an image, and so are able to achieve a certain relating of what they see to the one whose image it is.[58]

Augustine presses Paul into service to support this: the apostle does not say, 'We see now a mirror', but 'We see now through a mirror.'

Augustine wants to move from reasoning to contemplation, though his argument goes on being a deductive process into which scriptural passages are drawn. At the end when he turns to prayer he begins to evoke a different level of understanding. Reason moves beyond rationalisation, and the *res* confronts through the verbal signs. Quotes from scripture and parables, mingled with Augustine's ever-elusive mental construct, draw the reader into his sense of humiliation before the mystery – indeed, Augustine demonstrates that knowing God, far from leading to the pride of achievement, rather means 'being known', as Paul indicates at the end of 1 Corinthians 15:

I have desired greatly to see with my understanding that which I have believed; I have made much discourse, and much toil therein. O Lord my God, my one hope, hear me, that weariness may not lessen my will to seek you, that I may seek your face evermore with eager heart . . . In your hands are my knowledge and my ignorance: where you have opened to me, receive my entering in; where you have shut, open to my knocking. Let me remember you, understand you, love you: increase in me all these, until you restore me to your perfect pattern . . .

O Lord, one God, God the Trinity, whatsoever I have said in these books that comes of your prompting, may your people acknowledge it; for what I have said that comes only of myself, I ask of you and of your people pardon.[59]

There is in this work a curious, indeed fascinating, interpenetration not just of Bible and culture, but of text and theological

[57] *De Trin.* xv.xiii.22ff.; *CCL*, vol. 50A, pp. 494ff.; ET *LCC*, vol. VIII, pp. 151ff.; *FC*, vol. 45, pp. 484ff.

[58] *De Trin.* xv.xxii.44; *CCL*, vol. 50A, p. 522; ET *LCC*, vol. VIII, p. 171; *FC*, vol. 45, p. 511.

[59] *De Trin.* xv.xxviii.51; *CCL*, vol. 50A, pp. 534–5; ET *LCC*, vol. VIII, pp. 180–1; *FC*, vol. 45, pp. 523–5.

construct. Augustine contrives to speak of the *res* to which the signs point, treating as signs not just scripture but the whole creation, particularly the apex of that creation, the rational human creature. Along the way the techniques of exegesis appear, sometimes explicitly discussed, but this is not 'mere' exegesis – it is hermeneutics. We see yet more clearly what Augustine was after in the *De doctrina Christiana*. The theologian is exegete; the exegete is theologian.

v

Finally we dip into what happens when such a theologian acts as exegete. Like the *De doctrina*, the collection of *Enarrationes in Psalmos*[60] was long in its formation, belonging indeed to much the same period. The first contributions were written in 392, the last in 418. Some pieces are brief exegetical notes, others more detailed commentaries; some are expositions in sermon form, perhaps read aloud by his priests, others sermons proper. We will look at the discourses on Psalm 30 (29 LXX).

The first discourse consists of exegetical notes, short, sharp and to the point. The comment on the title is enough to show how Augustine refers the Psalms to Christ and the Church:

A joyful song of the resurrection which has renewed the body, not only of our Lord but also of the whole church, and has altered its condition to one of immortality.[61]

Augustine states that it is Christ speaking in the Psalm. So the meaning of verse 3, 'O Lord my God, I have cried to you and you have healed me', is 'I have called on you, O Lord my God, and I am no longer burdened with a feeble body subject to death and disease.'[62] But soon the Church, or the Christian, is drawn in:

When I recall my days of trouble and misery, as if still plunged therein, I hear the voice of your first-born, my Leader who is about to die for me, crying aloud (the words of verse 9), 'To you, O Lord, will I cry, and I will make supplication to my God'.[63]

---

[60] Text in *CCL*, vols. 38–40; ET in *ACW*, vols. 29–30.
[61] *In Ps. 29*: 1.1; *CCL*, vol. 38, p. 171; *ACW*, vol. 29, p. 289.
[62] *In Ps. 29*: 1.3; *CCL*, vol. 38, p. 172; *ACW*, vol. 29, p. 289.
[63] *In Ps. 29*: 1.9; *CCL*, vol. 38, p. 172; *ACW*, vol. 29, p. 291.

When we reach verse 12, Augustine comments:

I, your church, imitating this first-born from the dead, now sing at the dedication of your house: 'You have turned for me my mourning into joy. You have cut off my sackcloth and girded me with gladness.' You have ripped away the covering of my sins, the sadness of my mortal existence, in order to clothe me in the best robe, and in never-ending joy.[64]

The subject of the Psalms is Christ and the Church.

The more elaborate homily on the same Psalm[65] spells out this perspective. This time Augustine fastens on the 'enemies' in the opening verse, enlarging on the humanity of Christ who really suffered. But could it be about Christ, for the enemies here are not allowed to rejoice over the speaker, whereas the enemies of Christ certainly did? Is it then about humanity, or the church, because in Christ all are one? But given the persecution of Christians the same difficulty arises.

Augustine reverts to the title to find the solution.[66] It is a Psalm of David at the dedication of the house. The house to be dedicated is the church, but it is still under construction. At the time of dedication, the splendour of the Christian people, as yet invisible, will burst forth in glory. The present triumph of enemies is in God's providence, and the Lord set a pattern of humility and patience, Christ being the foundation of the Church.[67] So, verse by verse, Augustine is able to draw the listener into the overarching story of fall and redemption, passion and resurrection,

'To the end that my glory may sing to you, and I may not be pierced.' As with the Head so with the Body . . . I may no longer undergo death. For our Lord was pierced as he hung on the cross . . . If the glory is ours, it is also Christ's, because we are the Body of Christ . . .

And finally: 'O Lord my God, I will confess to you forever' . . . there is confession of praise as well as of sins. Confess then today what you have done against God, and you will confess tomorrow what God has done in return for you . . . And God? God forgives your sins as soon as you confess your guilt, to free you from the remorse of sin, that you may confess God's praise hereafter forever and ever.[68]

---

[64] *In Ps. 29*: I.12; *CCL*, vol. 38, p. 173; *ACW*, vol. 29, p. 291.
[65] *In Ps. 29*: II.1; *CCL*, vol. 38, pp. 173ff.; *ACW*, vol. 29, p. 292.
[66] *In Ps. 29*: II.6; *CCL*, vol. 38, p. 178; *ACW*, vol. 29, p. 299.
[67] *In Ps. 29*: II.9; *CCL*, vol. 38, p. 180; *ACW*, vol. 29, p. 303.
[68] *In Ps. 29*: II.22; *CCL*, vol. 38, pp. 185–6; *ACW*, vol. 29, pp. 311–12.

A brief consideration of the discourse on Psalm 38 (37 LXX) confirms this exegetical stance.[69] The 'I' who laments for sin, and fears chastisement, turns out to be every human being who suffers for the sin of Adam. Some of the phrases in the Psalm, however, are predictive of Christ and his passion. So how could this be, if Christ is sinless?[70] Once more Christ and his Body are incorporated in one another, so that the Head saves and the Body is saved. The sufferings of Christ are our sufferings. The Son of God died the real death which is the lot of mortal flesh, and he was cast forth and forsaken. So God becomes the Lord of salvation.

In preaching and commenting on the Psalms, Augustine draws his hearers into a totalising discourse, a universal plot, the drama of salvation. He does this by applying the first rule of Tyconius, inheriting both the traditional Christological reading of the scriptures and the Rule of Faith. The drama of salvation is at the core of his theological reading of the Bible, and the 'paraenetic strategy' is once again integrated with this as the congregation is drawn into the text and inspired to new life. In almost every way, Augustine the theologian beautifully exemplifies the characteristics of Christian use of scripture which have been the subject of these studies.

---

[69] *In Ps. 37; CCL*, vol. 38, pp. 382ff.; *ACW*, vol. 30, pp. 328ff.
[70] *In Ps. 37.6; CCL*, vol. 38, pp. 386ff.; *ACW*, vol. 30, pp. 334ff.

Conclusion and retrospect: towards
an outline historical account[1]

Can a revised history of exegesis now be sketched? Origen, who really did build an alternative *paideia* based on the alternative biblical literature, pirating all the methods used in the Hellenistic schools for the exegesis of barbarian books and defending that position against the criticisms of Celsus, will clearly provide an important pivot, but the attempt here is to offer a chronological account.

In such a history, the New Testament's use of the Jewish scriptures cannot be passed over, for here the initial lines were laid down. The letters of Paul, our earliest Christian writer, are steeped in scriptural language and allusion.[2] Paul was a Jew who knew his Bible at the deep, almost unconscious, level in which its language and perspective, especially but not solely that of Psalms and Prophets, created his world. His writing is in part collage, his argument is given authority by quotation. Along with some other New Testament writers who are on occasion contrasted with him – the authors of Hebrews and of Matthew's Gospel, and even those who produced the Johannine material – Paul evidences an exegesis of scripture which is unselfconscious, entirely taken for granted. There is, of course, a different perspective from most Jews, yet here we seem still to be reading the work of Jews with a new perspective on their own heritage. Their prophecies, they believe, have been fulfilled, and that gives a new focus, namely Jesus the Christ; their covenant has been renewed, and that gives a different approach

---

[1] In this final survey, I eschew footnotes, except where points are made which are not standard, or not justified elsewhere in this volume.

[2] As I have argued in *Meaning and Truth in 2 Corinthians*, ch. 3, and as Richard Hays has explored more widely in *Echoes of Scripture in the Letters of Paul*. Previous work has tended to concentrate mainly on quotations and clear allusions in scriptural argument, especially in Galatians and Romans.

to the true import of their law. But the crucial transformation, I suggest, does not lie here.

The crucial shift happens with Luke and the author of the Pastoral Epistles, Gentiles who mediate the Pauline tradition to a community which is increasingly distanced from its Jewish roots. For, building on the new perspectives, such followers are engaged in universalising a national and literary heritage, in such a way as potentially to challenge both Jewish and Gentile identity and make the cultural 'take-over bid' which was described in chapter 3 and developed in subsequent studies. Already the ancient literary inheritance belonging to others is, we might say, misappropriated by upstarts, and, in the case of the author of the Pastorals, by one who knows only what the previous generation has mediated rather selectively, though Luke knows his scriptures rather better. Certainly Paul paved the way by embracing Gentiles within the community, and relativising Jewish culture in the light of Christ. But Paul, though a convert in one sense,[3] remained deeply formed by his Jewish roots as Gentile converts never could be.

In the New Testament documents, then, we find what I have called a 'reading of oneself' into the texts naturally employed, alongside collages of allusion which construct new visions, apocalyptic perhaps in 1 Thessalonians and Revelation, or parabolic and mystic in John's Gospel where the good shepherd, for example, must relate to Ezekiel 34. We also find examples of deduction and application which are methodologically similar to the Rabbinic *middot* (these may be found in Paul, Matthew and John's Gospel), together with two other approaches, the oracular and paraenetic. The latter two deserve further consideration.

(1) The belief that the reference of prophecy was now clear *post factum* was bound to change the perceived focus of the texts. Different techniques are used to demonstrate that this fulfilment has occurred. One has become known as *pesher*, on the basis of the Qumran discoveries, where prophetic texts are provided with commentary which takes each text piecemeal and discovers the reference of individual verses in current events affecting the community. The piecemeal use of verses understood in this way is

---

[3] I have long preferred to speak of Paul's prophetic/apostolic 'call' rather than his conversion, but concede conversion in the sense taken in Alan F. Segal, *Paul the Convert. The Apostolate and Apostasy of Saul the Pharisee* (New Haven and London: Yale University Press, 1990).

evident in Matthew's Gospel and elsewhere. Other kinds of material provide prophetic 'signs' which are now said to have been fulfilled: in standard New Testament commentaries some are described as allegorical or typological, but the 'signs' adduced by the author of Hebrews are not strictly speaking past events typologically replayed; for the most part they are ritual provisions in the scriptures, theoretical rather than actual, and recognised by the text as recurring – in fact that is one reason for their ineffectiveness! The problem of deciding whether Sarah and Hagar are typologically or allegorically paralleled with Israel and the Church in Galatians is, I suggest, a fruitless discussion. These are prophetic 'signs' which have their image or counterpart in the alleged fulfilment.

(2) In treating the scriptures as the Word of God which conveyed God's will and so spelt out the way of life, Paul and others were not doing anything novel. That the Law had a moral dimension and was to be not just outwardly practised but interiorised was accepted within Jewish circles. By deductive argument, Paul proclaimed a new covenant and therefore the end of the old Law, the end of the ethnic marks of a Jew as qualification for entry to the people of God, and the acceptance of righteous Gentiles within the very fold of the people of God. That argument, however, so far from meaning the end of a scripture-based morality, in fact enhanced the need for *paraenesis*, drawing from the scriptures the moral qualities and pattern of living appropriate to the universal people of God. True, the imitation of Christ and the teaching of Jesus appear alongside this, but only to some extent. Christian living was grounded in the summary of the law provided by Jesus on the basis of the Law itself: you shall love God, and your neighbour as yourself. It was spelt out in paraenetic material which was compounded of proverbs, maxims and wisdom drawn from such sources as the teaching attributed to Jesus, but predominantly from the scriptures.

All of these features of New Testament use of the scriptures can be paralleled in Jewish texts. There is nothing methodologically novel; the novelty lies in the focus on Christ, and the potential for relativising not merely the traditional Jewish interpretation of the texts, but the texts themselves, in the light of that refocussing. It should be evident that the exegetical approaches adopted by the first Jewish Christians provided the heritage picked up and developed as the Church moves on. But the Church's history was dramatically affected by progressive disengagement with its Jewish roots. I have suggested that the crucial shift comes with Luke. Luke in fact knows the scriptural narratives quite well. His models in writing his story lie not only in Graeco-Roman conventions, which he at least knows from textbooks and compendia, but also from the Jewish historical books. These he almost mimics, like a budding young rhetorician mimicking the classics; for some of the Gospel-narratives imitate narratives about prophets like Elijah, or the birth of Samuel, creating correspondences which we might grace with the label 'typology'. He develops such narratives, it would seem, to support the argument from prophecy. Luke is not obviously different from his Jewish teachers. Yet can there be any doubt that Luke's outlook is that of a convert who has become convinced that this message of the kingdom of God is for the whole earth, that the universalising community of the Church rightfully inherits the literature and history that once belonged to another community? It is this which points the way to the second-century issues, in particular the need apologetically to defend this cultural take-over.

In the New Testament, the scriptures were searched for the clues to the unexpected aspects of Jesus' career. The problem was to prove that the Messianic claim was not disallowed by his apparent failure and death. But already for Matthew and Luke the need to show that the traditional Messianic prophecies applied to this Christ had become apparent. Increasingly the right reference of scripture passages becomes the central issue. Scripture was mediated to Christians of the second century through Christianising Targums collected in notebooks, and by the time of Justin, these apparently had hermeneutical authority over against scrolls with the full text – for these derived from the Jewish community and were suspected of offering hebraising recensions. Textcritical issues emerged.

The transmission of the texts in codices is an important indicator, not only of the social status of the majority of Christians (clearly they belonged to urban business classes which were literate rather than literary), but also of the status accorded these books. Since their importance lay in their testimony to Jesus, they had a secondary function. As Papias put it, he preferred the living and abiding voice to books. But clearly testimonies, both oral and written, were valued in the new communities of believers; and doubtless, partly for convenience, but also because these believers were practical people who used notebooks every day for their business dealings, these testimonies were committed to codices.

The community may have owned 'official' rolls from which readings took place in the Christian assemblies, but ordinary people had indirect and selective access. In time, Christians would begin to produce their own copies of the scriptures, but they would be non-professional and adopt the codex rather than the roll, so anticipating a major technological change which lay well in the future as far as the general culture was concerned. Jews have never transferred their sacred texts from the scroll format. The Christian 'take-over' involved a blasphemous relativising of the texts.

Yet the texts retained their status as the Word of God, not only because they were testimony to Christ but also because they set out the way of righteousness. Christian *paraenesis* continued to be based in the traditions of the Jewish scriptures, from which were constructed collages of proverbs and maxims, and to which congregations were referred for examples of meritorious conduct. Already these writings were used in practice rather as the classics were in schools. They were creatively drawn upon to provide moral guidance. This respect for the scriptures was enhanced by the claim that the new covenant promised by God through the prophets had come into effect through Christ. For this enabled interpreters to interiorise and universalise the moral teaching of scripture while assigning to the Jews only the specific commandments which gave them their ethnic identity. It also justified the expropriation of Jewish history and literature by an alien group which could claim it was really all leading up to fulfilment in their community, and enabled the reading of prophetic warnings in two contrasting ways: as directed against unbelievers, Jews, deviants and heretics, or as *paraenesis* to which believers should give heed in fear of judgement. The tension between respect and relativising is evident in the Apostolic Fathers.

The collection of oracles in codices must have encouraged esoteric groups to search for the appropriate discernment, and the obverse of Justin's proof-text tradition is the development of gnostic readings. The assumption behind both is that the reference of the text lies behind the words. What is different is the kind of reference perceived. For Justin, the fulfilment of prophecy was a key argument producing conviction about the truth of Christian claims. Gnostics abandoned that tradition, finding in Jesus Christ a revelation of transcendent realities, a spiritual world from which they had originated and to which they were called back. Alienated from the material world, they radicalised Paul's apparent spiritualising of the Gospel and his rejection of the Law. Interested in cosmology, they read Genesis, but used it to construct their own account of cosmic origins, turning the Creator into a fallen Demiurge and the serpent into the embodiment of the female principle of Wisdom who rescued Adam and Eve from the inferior God. The relativising of the Jewish scriptures had the effect of providing licence to read them how you liked. Perhaps it is not altogether surprising that Marcion argued they were irrelevant, or even harmful, portraying as they did a God of merciless judgement and wrath, not the God of love revealed in Jesus Christ.

So debate about the authority and meaning of scripture was at the heart of the fragmentation of Christian networks in the second century. What seems to have happened, at any rate in Rome, is that the 'public' community gatherings continued to operate rather like a synagogue, reading the Jewish scriptures and interpreting them on the assumption that the God revealed by Jesus was the God of the Jewish people. In this context, because the lectionary passages were virtually unintelligible without an overall perspective, or perhaps in response to challenge, a kind of Rule of Faith emerged spelling out the *hypothesis* of scripture. But, meanwhile, esoteric study-groups pursuing the interests of Valentinus or Marcion, gradually found themselves excluded as the community perceived the implications of their attempts to divert it from its traditional practices and assumptions. Other Christian teachers like Justin, although practising a kind of freelance philosophical teaching activity, were seen to enhance rather than undermine the community's emerging sense of identity.

It was the contribution of Irenaeus to make all this explicit, claiming the public tradition of the Church over against private teachings, eschewing speculation yet articulating beyond the existing tradition the first systematic account of Christian theology and the first biblical canon which explicitly related old and new scriptures. In the thick of this debate, the unity of the enlarged scriptures, with the fourfold Gospel and the Apostle to parallel the fivefold Law and the Prophets, was asserted, and its basis in the one God who was both Creator and Redeemer firmly established. This canon of written testimony inevitably took precedence over oral traditions whose reliability became suspect in the face of competing claims, and the once relativised scriptures returned to an authoritative position. Origen provides evidence that all truth was believed to lie in scripture, and that Jewish views concerning the inerrancy of scripture and the significance of every jot and tittle were re-established. Ignatius had affirmed that his *archeiai* were Jesus Christ, and he claimed not to share the view of others that they would believe nothing unless it were to be found in the ancient testimonies. A considerable shift has taken place. But it was rooted in the cultural 'take-over' implied from the time of that earlier shift made in Luke–Acts.

Meanwhile the prophetic reference of the scriptures had been more fully developed by Justin, and the scene was set for a fully oracular approach to the whole Old Testament to emerge. This is set forth in theory by Clement of Alexandria, who thought that all religious truth was to be found in prophecies and oracles spoken in enigmas; the mysteries were not to be conveyed to all and sundry, but only imparted after certain purifications and previous instructions. He pointed out that symbols were characteristic of Egyptian religion, the mysteries and Pythagoreanism, and that in the Old Testament the tabernacle and its furniture have mystical meanings. Plato composed myths which should be interpreted allegorically; myriads of enigmatical utterances by poets and philosophers are to be found. So it is proper that the 'barbarian philosophy' (his name for Christianity) should prophesy obscurely and by symbols. The truth of scripture comes through a veil; an interpreter and guide is needed. The language of scripture is an expression of the inexpressible God in a very indirect way. Yet Clement is confident that somehow the hidden mysteries have been unlocked; for the key is Christ.[4] Clement's account of this position indicates how the kind of allegory we find in Origen emerged from the process whereby the prophetic fulfilment of the text was taken to be its reference.

This is an important observation. For despite Irenaeus' criticisms of the Gnostics for allegorical interpretation, he indulges in allegory himself. Oracular exegesis was bound to be allegorical, unpacking the riddles and signs. The non-Gnostic tradition remained wedded to prophecy, for prophecy enabled the interlinking of Old and New Testaments in an overarching providential plan. Apocalyptic writings, which to a large extent used sign and symbol to speak of

---

[4] *Strom.* v.4.20–10.66 and 12.82; *GCS*, vol. II, pp. 338–70, 380; ET in *ANCL*, vol. II, pp. 232–61 and 267ff.

hidden realities, undoubtedly contributed to the reading of the scripture in this way. Typology is integral to this approach, and not as neatly distinguishable from allegory as some modern scholars have supposed. There were many ways of discerning the reference, many different clues for discovering that the text spoke of something other than its immediate wording might have suggested. What distinguishes Irenaeus and the Gnostics is not so much allegory in itself, as the task to which allegory is put. Irenaeus recognised a coherent overarching narrative within which the signs and symbols made sense; the Gnostics had no interest in the *hypothesis*, only (at least as Irenaeus saw it) in piecemeal abstraction of hidden enigmas which point to their own alien perspective on God and the world. This debate has its counterpart in the Antiochene reaction to Origen.

With Origen we reach what I have called the 'pivot' of the story. Despite all the material that has been lost, there is extant more of Origen than any previous writer and here scholarship enters the Christian exegetical tradition. The traditions of exegesis outlined already provided the accepted norms that Origen inherited: namely that scripture as the Word of God provides moral guidance and prophesies the Christ. Scripture is a sacred text containing revelation of hidden mysteries. As Clement has suggested, this was the common attitude to texts treated as ancient, sacred and revelatory, particularly among philosophers. Origen's treatment of the Bible bears comparison with Neoplatonic treatment of Homer. Yet he also had some contact with Jewish scholarship, and was less keen than Clement to adopt the language of mysteries, Gnostics and theosophists. His use of allegory is rooted in inherited church traditions. What Origen did was to professionalise the exegesis of scripture and adopt methods from the schools so as to turn scripture into the basis for a complete educational system with primary, secondary and tertiary levels.

Once this occurred, the Christian Bible had truly become a classical canon, replacing for Christian pupils the texts which traditionally had pride of place in the schools of the Hellenistic world. The cultural 'take-over bid' was, at least in part, realised. There was no need to read Homer and Plato because they had in any case got all their best ideas from Moses. Rather, there was a need to read this new literature according to the norms of standard professional and educational approaches to literature.

Inevitably the techniques of textual criticism, attention to the letter of the text, the meanings of words and the construction of sentences (the work performed in the elementary school) provided a properly developed 'grammatical criticism' as the technical starting-point. Then followed the kind of exegetical comment which may enhance understanding or bemuse. Much 'explanatory comment' might fall into the trap of showing off the erudition of the commentator without furthering the meaning or impact of the text. But that would be a stimulant to Origen: to find the significance of the etymology or the extraneous fact he had to hand. Grammatical problems and exegetical research could themselves produce allegorical deductions once the principle that every jot and tittle was significant was granted.

Already, prior to Origen, deductive exegesis had used rational principles to arrive at conclusions relevant to the reader. These procedures were systematised by Rabbis and Hellenistic and Roman legal exegetes. Such rationalistic procedures could also be used to deduce the meaning of dreams, riddles and oracles. If a text was authoritative, its authority had to be evidently applied to the problems to hand. If a text was testimony, its testimony had to be 'proved'. Techniques developed in the schools for legal training were adapted to literary exercises, assessing the reliability of narratives. Origen bears the marks of this kind of education, and again uses such techniques to further his own perspective on the nature and importance of scripture. If the narrative were shaky as a true account of an event, if scripture contained impossibilities, then these stumbling-blocks pointed to deeper meanings. The unity and reliability of scripture lay in the Spirit's intent, not in the letter.

So Origen developed a pedagogical approach to the scriptures which closely paralleled the exegetical procedures of the ancient educational system. For the babes in Christ, milk was needed, but once weaned, the child needed to progress. The letter of the text was usually reliable, and much of the *paraenesis* of scripture was to be taken at face value. Examination of the letter of the text was important, for detail did indeed have significance, and this was the starting-point for more advanced study. The trouble with the Jews, according to Origen, was that they got stuck with the letter. Christians had to move on to the moral and spiritual meaning. As in the rhetorical schools, moral criticism had to be brought to the text. For not all its precepts were applicable at the level of the flesh, especially the particular provisions made in the Mosaic covenant that apply to Jews alone. So all Christians were to move further along the educational path, taught by the true Logos of God, abandoning the elementary stage of attending to the letter. Furthermore, the impossibilities at the level of the wording (*aporiai*) were there simply to provoke the necessary progress.

Origen, then, leads his hearers and readers from the letter to the moral. But he clearly intends them to advance beyond the rhetorical school's approach of finding morals in the text, to the philosophical or tertiary level of discovering spiritual truths revealed through symbols. Such truths might be the traditional prophetic signs understood through deducing the reference and unpacking the riddle, thus finding in the Jewish scriptures the hidden allegorical expression of the new covenant in Christ, whether by 'typology' or other techniques such as etymology, numerology and so on. But the truths unfolded might also be about the soul's progress, back to the perfection from which it has fallen, through purification and progressive reintegration with the true Logos of God. Platonic perspectives and Christian perspectives were deeply intertwined in a complex vision of God's providential purposes in which the exegesis of scripture played a major salvific role.

None of Origen's exegetical techniques are unique to him. To a greater or lesser extent, they are all found in Christian exegesis prior to his work. They have roots in Hellenistic literary exegesis as well as Jewish exegetical traditions. Origen's approach to the Bible reflects the contemporary approach to literature of all kinds in this period, his greatest precursor being Philo.[5] Here the exegetical approaches categorised in chapter 9 are employed alongside one another in an attempt to produce a convincing alternative pedagogy based on the Christian scriptures rather than the classical canon. Origen produces *paraenesis*, discerns oracles and prophecies, practices the specific exegetical techniques of *to grammatikon* and *to historikon*, deduces teachings of a moral and doctrinal kind, and reads the text symbolically. The more 'literal' strategies, as we have seen, feed the process whereby deeper meanings of a symbolic kind are

---

[5] The importance of Philo as an influence on Origen has not received much emphasis in this study. However, it was undoubtedly significant, and Christian exegesis is illuminated by studies devoted to Philo, such as David T. Runia, *Exegesis and Philosophy. Studies on Philo of Alexandria* (Aldershot: Variorum, 1990).

discovered. For every text clothes its 'mind' in its 'wording', and the wording may be a veil rather than a window.

It was tempting to say 'all' the approaches categorised, but of course 'ikonic' and 'symbolic' *mimēsis* were distinguished specifically in order to characterise the difference between Origen and the Antiochenes. There is a sense in which later exegesis cannot escape Origen, either being indebted to his work, or reacting against it.

Eusebius first self-consciously inherited his mantle, and indeed his library, in Caesarea. The puzzle as to why an Origenist should be a historian must surely now be dissolved. Eusebius picked up the scholarly curiosity that led Origen to investigate not just textcritical problems but other questions, about the compatibility of the Gospel-narratives, for example, or geographical locations: *historia* embraced all kinds of subjects, not least 'natural history', and served the ends of textual exposition. Eusebius also inherited Origen's apologetic concerns, and re-formed the genre of 'history' in the interests of telling a convincing story about the Church's origin and tradition. But moving on a little from Origen, Eusebius was interested in God's providential oversight of the world more than of the individual soul, and it was this that generated chronological interests and history-writing, as well as reinforcing an exegetical interest in the prophetic reference of scripture (the *Demonstratio evangelica* proved from scripture the truths for which, according to the *Praeparatio evangelica*, God had prepared the Greeks through philosophy). Eusebius was a scholar like Origen, and continued, even in the heat of controversy, to use scholarly methods to elucidate the language and reference of scripture.[6]

Others, too, inherited Origen's mantle. Didymus the Blind, once known but indirectly because of the destruction of his works in later Origenist controversies, has recently come to attention because of the rediscoveries at Tura. He seems to present a more systematic development of the allegorical tradition,[7] and was renowned in his

---

[6] Simonetti's study of the exegesis of Proverbs 8.22 (in *Studi sull' Arianesimo*, ch. 1) demonstrates that Eusebius alone used philological arguments to meet the Arian challenge, appealing to both context and word-usage; cf. my article 'Exegetical Method and Scriptural Proof'.

[7] See *From Nicaea to Chalcedon*, pp. 83–91, with references there to the work of W. A. Bienert, *'Allegoria' und 'Anagoge' bei Didymos dem Blinden von Alexandria* (Berlin: de Gruyter, 1972); and J. Tigcheler, *Didyme l'Aveugle et l'exégèse allégorique, son commentaire sur Zacharie* (Nijmegen: Dekker & van de Vegt, 1977). Further work has recently been done by my postgraduate

own day. Jerome and others both studied with him in Alexandria and borrowed from him. Through Jerome, he had a considerable, but at the time largely undetected, influence on mediaeval exegesis in the West. An Origenist tradition flourished in Egyptian monasteries, and the controversies that arose as a result were much more significant than histories of doctrine usually convey. Nor were they unrelated to the more well-known struggles over Arianism and Christology.

The fourth-century Origenist controversy directly involved not just the Westerners Jerome and Rufinus, but also Epiphanius and, fatefully, John Chrysostom in the East. It came somewhat later than the attacks on allegory from Eustathius, Diodore and Theodore. We should not, however, underestimate the doctrinal dimensions of the Antiochene reaction against allegorical readings, and it must be recognised that, in the period of Arian and post-Arian conflict, Origen's 'playing' with the text became less and less viable. Maybe Arius' problem was that he failed to recognise that the old-style Christian 'philosopher', such as Justin and Origen had been, could not survive the institutional consolidation that was already happening and would be reinforced by imperial patronage.[8] Certainly the *hypothesis* of scripture as a whole became the focus of a struggle for clearer and clearer specification in credal form, and that struggle challenged free-floating exegetical speculation. But it also encouraged the development of techniques to make individual texts conform, by hook or by crook, to the perceived 'mind' of the scriptural canon. Thus it is simplistic to suggest that in doctrinal debate, or indeed in the Antiochene reaction to Alexandrian allegory, we have a 'reversion' to the literal sense. What we do have is an important stress on the 'reality' of the overarching narrative from creation through fall to incarnation and redemption.

The 'reality' of the *oikonomia*, God's providential activity with respect to the world, meant that spiritualising away the body, the material world, the 'flesh' of the Christ in the story of his birth, life or passion, or indeed in the eucharist, had to be deemed heretical. The symbolic allegory of Origen seemed to undermine the core by

---

student, Hazel Sherman: 'Reading Zechariah: An Attempt to Assess the Allegorical Tradition of Biblical Interpretation through the Commentary of Didymus the Blind' (University of Birmingham Ph.D. thesis, 1995).
[8] See Rowan Williams, *Arius*.

encouraging such spiritualising. The key moments at the beginning and end, the story of Adam and Paradise, the resurrection of the body and judgement, not to mention the incarnation, were endangered. So was the concrete assimilation of the genuinely divine through the food of the eucharist; for was not the rite but a symbol of receiving the Word, according to Origen, and the Logos but the first and greatest of eternally created rational souls, temporally imprisoned in the body? Overall, Origen's *hypothesis*, for all his protestations that he speculated only on matters not determined by the Rule of Faith, did not correspond with what most people saw as the *hypothesis* of scripture, and was perceived to encourage heresy, anticipating Arius. Therefore his verbal allegory could not be accepted as getting to the heart of the matter. Yet Origen's scholarship had set the standards for biblical exposition. Many, like the Cappadocians, would continue to be indebted, even as they passed over his name in silence and repudiated his excesses. For the Antiochenes the answer was to be the more rigorous in following the practices of philological exegesis.

So allegory was to be admitted only as figure of speech, and only where the text indicated that this figure of speech was in play. Figures of speech were to be carefully identified: discerning metaphor or irony does, after all, make a difference to perception of meaning, and scripture has its own 'idioms'. The narrative logic of the story, whether on the large scale or the small scale, was to be preserved. Witches and talking serpents must be identified as mediums of the devil. Indeed, the reading of scripture could not be reduced to mere enjoyment of story or interest in the record of past events, for it was a deadly serious business. Its purpose was to understand one's place in the great scheme of things, and to learn how to live and act. No one questioned the ancient assumption that literature belonged to pedagogy, that it was the source of 'teaching' (*dogma* or *doctrina*); so the text was didactic. It was therefore incumbent upon the exegete to have insight (*theōria*) into the theology and the moral meaning even of passages where nothing of the kind was obvious. The key thing was to see how the text pronounced or 'mirrored' ecclesiastical and moral truth. Antiochene exegesis was always fundamentally moral and dogmatic, not 'historical' in the modern sense. And in the end Theodoret, like Origen and Gregory Nyssen, would celebrate the marriage of Christ and Church through an allegorical reading of the Song of Songs.

Despite the debate about allegory, in the end most exegetes proceeded in essentially similar ways. As Origen had taken up into his work all the paraenetic, prophetic and typological meanings inherited from a less self-conscious period, so the exegetes of the fourth and early fifth centuries inherited most of their material, and their differences were within a coherent tradition. That tradition largely drew on the standard procedures of Graeco-Roman schools. Some, like the Cappadocians and Augustine, were well aware of this, and not ashamed to claim that the tools of rationality were ultimately given by God for the understanding and celebration of the divine condescension in speaking with mere creatures through the Logos. But after Constantine there had been one significant shift: the Bible may have had primacy, but it was now recognised that it could not really replace pagan literature in the rhetorical schools. The traditional literary texts were required to hone rhetorical, stylistic and dialectic skills, even if the content had to be treated critically, and the Bible preferred for teaching about truth and ethics. Ironically the Christianising of the Roman Empire did not effect the cultural 'take-over bid' made in the second century and all but achieved by Origen – at least, not in the Byzantine East; one might argue that it was effected in the mediaeval West after Augustine.

As in the earlier period, the exegesis of scripture went on in many contexts which were not formally exegetical. Doctrinal debate is an obvious area in which appeal was made to scripture. Here it was a case not just of proof-texts, but of arguing about the 'mind' of scripture; it was a case not just of literal reading, but of finding the appropriate way of understanding finite human language when used of the infinite, or of testing the meaning of scripture against scripture. Traditional types and allegories went unquestioned, as did the Christological reference of the Old Testament. Much exegesis was simply inherited. But the stories and language of the Bible increasingly functioned to produce for society a new culture, a new 'totalising discourse', as art and mosaics presented the Virgin in place of the Goddess, and Jesus in place of Hercules, while panegyric for feast days and saints' days celebrated new virtues and new heroes with biblical allusion and biblical characters as models. The Bible engaged the imagination as an increasingly powerful and suggestive typology developed, especially in poetry and art; for it fostered the creative correlation of narratives. And allegory remained the principal way of probing beneath the wording of scripture to its theological reference and deeper spiritual sense in the exegetical traditions of both East and West.

The most striking thing, in fact, is the consistent way in which the Bible was read in differing contexts. If commentaries were meant to deal with problems in the text and homilies to focus the more obvious features, still one has an overriding feeling of similarity in the kinds of senses discerned and the 'reading strategies' adopted. For the whole enterprise embraced the concerns we tend to separate out into scholarship, theology, *praxis* and spirituality. The purpose of biblical exegesis, implicit and explicit, was to form the practice and belief of Christian people, individually and collectively. In so far as there was contention about belief or practice, the Bible was at the heart of the debate. But its most important contribution was that it provided a literature which shaped Christian discourse and fed the Christian imagination.

Bibliography

TEXTS AND TRANSLATIONS

Apocryphal New Testament
   Acta Apostolorum Apocrypha I. Ed. R. A. Lipsius. Hildesheim: George Olms,
      1959 (photocopy of 1891 edn).
   New Testament Apocrypha. 2 vols. Ed. E. Hennecke and W. Schneemelcher,
      ET R. McL. Wilson. London: Lutterworth Press, 1963, 1965.
   *The Apocryphal New Testament, A Collection of Apocryphal Christian Literature
   in an English Translation based on M. R. James*. Ed. J. K. Elliott. Oxford:
      Clarendon Press, 1993.
Apostolic Constitutions
   Text ed. M. Metzger. *SC*, vols. 320, 329, 336, 1985–7.
   ET in *ANCL*, vol. XVII.
Apostolic Fathers
   The Apostolic Fathers. 2 vols: Clement of Rome, 3 vols: Ignatius. Texts ed.
      with introd., notes and ET by J. B. Lightfoot. London: Macmillan,
      1885, 1890.
   The Apostolic Fathers. 1 vol., including *I* and *II Clement*, Ignatius, Polycarp
      (*Epistle* and *Martyrdom*), *Didache, Barnabas, Hermas, Diognetus*, Papias,
      Reliquaries of the Elder from Irenaeus. Texts and ET by J. B. Lightfoot.
      London: Macmillan, 1912.
   The Apostolic Fathers, with ET by Kirsopp Lake. 2 vols. *LCL*, 1930.
   ET *Early Christian Writings*. Trans. Maxwell Staniforth, rev. with introd.
      and notes Andrew Louth, London: Penguin Classics, 1987.
Aristeas
   Lettre d'Aristée à Philocrate. Introd., text, trans., notes, A. Pelletier. *SC*,
      vol. 89, 1962.
   H. B. Swete, *Introduction to the Old Testament in Greek*. Appendix: 'The
      Letter of Aristeas', text ed. and introd. by H. St J. Thackeray.
      Cambridge: Cambridge University Press, 1902.
Aristotle
   The Art of Rhetoric, with ET by John Henry Freese. *LCL*, 1967.
   Poetics. Ed. D. W. Lucas. Oxford: Oxford University Press, 1968.
   ET with commentary, Stephen Halliwell. London: Duckworth, 1987.

Athanasius
  De decretis. Ed. H.-G. Opitz, *Athanasius Werke ii. 1; Die Apologien: De Decretis Nicaenae Synodi*. Berlin and Leipzig: Walter de Gruyter, 1935–41.
  The Orations of St Athanasius against the Arians according to the Benedictine text. Ed. William Bright. Oxford: Clarendon Press, 1873.
  Migne, *PG*, 25–8.
  ET in *NPNF*, 2nd series, vol. IV.
  ET of *Life of Antony* and *Letter to Marcellinus* in *CWS*.
Augustine
  Aurelii Augustini opera, CCL:
    Vol. 27: *Confessionum libri XIII*. Ed. L. Verheijen. 1981.
    Vol. 32: *De doctrina Christiana/De vera religione*. Ed. J. Martin, 1962.
    Vol. 36: *Tractatus in Evangelium Joannis*. Ed. D. R. Willems. 1954.
    Vols. 38, 39, 40: *Enarrationes in Psalmos*. Ed. D. E. Dekkers and I. Fraipont, 1956.
    Vols. 47, 48: *De civitate Dei*. Ed. L. Verheijen. 1981.
    Vols. 50, 51: *De Trinitate*. Ed. W. J. Mountain, 1968.
  ET in NPNF, 1st series, vols. I–VIII.
  ET of *Confessions* by Henry Chadwick. World's Classics. Oxford: Oxford University Press, 1992.
  ET of *De doctrina Christiana* in *FC*, vol. 2, entitled *Christian Instruction*.
  ET of *Enarrationes in Psalmos* in *ACW*, vols. 29 and 30.
  ET of *City of God* by Henry Bettenson. Harmondsworth: Penguin Classics, 1972.
  ET of *Tractates on John* and *De Trinitate* in *FC*, vols. 78, 79, 88, 90, 92 and 45; and of *De Trinitate* Books VIII–XV in *LCC*.
Barnabas
  (see Apostolic Fathers)
Basil
  Letters. 4 vols. (Vol. IV includes *Address to Young Men on how they might Derive Benefit from Greek Literature*). Trans. R. J. Deferrari. *LCL*, 1926–39.
Cicero
  De natura deorum. Ed. A. S. Pease, 2 vols. Cambridge, Mass.: Harvard University Press, 1955.
  ET H. C. P. McGregor. Harmondsworth: Penguin Classics, 1972.
Clement of Alexandria
  Clemens Alexandrinus: GCS.
    vol. II: *Stromata I–VI*. Ed. O. Stählin, 1906.
  ET in *ANCL*, vol. XII.
I/II Clement
  (see Apostolic Fathers)
Cyril of Alexandria
  De adoratione in spiritu et veritate. Migne, *PG* 68.
Cyril of Jerusalem
  Catecheses. Migne, *PG* 33.331–1059.

ET *Catecheses*. 2 vols. Leo P. McCauley and Anthony A. Stephenson. *FC*,
    vols. 61, 64, 1968, 1970.
ET in *NPNF*, 2nd series, vol. VII.
Demetrius
    On Style. Text ed. and ET by W. Rhys Roberts,(together with Aristotle,
        The Poetics and Longinus, *On the Sublime*). *LCL*, 1965.
Didache
    (see Apostolic Fathers)
Diodore of Tarsus
    Diodorus Tarsensis. Commentarii in Psalmos. Vol. 1: Pss. 1–L. Ed. J.-M. Olivier,
        CC Series Graeca 6, 1980.
Dionysius of Halicarnassus
    Dionysii Halicarnassei opuscula. 2 vols. Ed. H. Usener and L. Radermacher.
        Leipzig: Teubner, 1929, 1933.
    The Three Literary Letters. Ed. and trans. by W. Rhys Roberts. Cambridge:
        Cambridge University Press, 1901.
    On Literary Composition. Introd., trans. and notes by W. Rhys Roberts.
        London: Macmillan, 1910.
    Critical Essays. ET Stephen Usher. *LCL*, 1974.
    De Thucydide, Ed. and trans. W. Pritchett. Berkeley/Los Angeles/Oxford:
        University of California Press, 1975.
Ephrem Syrus
    Syriac texts in *CSCO*.
    ET *St Ephrem. Hymns on Paradise*. Introd. and trans. Sebastian Brock. New
        York: St Vladimir's Seminary Press, 1990.
    ET *Ephrem the Syrian. Hymns*. Trans. and introd. Kathleen E. McVey.
        CWS, 1989.
Epiphanius
    Ancoratus and Panarion. GCS, 2 vols. Ed. Karl Holl. 1915, 1922.
Eusebius
    Eusebius Werke, GCS.
      Vol. 1: *Über das Leben Constantins*, etc. Ed. F. Winkelmann, 1975.
      Vol. II.1 and 2: *Kirchengeschichte*. Ed. E. Schwartz, 1908.
      Vol. IV: *Gegen Marcell*. Ed. Erich Klostermann, 1972.
      Vol. VI: *Demonstratio Evangelica*. Ed. I. A. Heikel, 1913.
      Vol. VIII.1 and 2: *Praeparatio evangelica*. Ed. K. Mras and E. des Places,
        1982, 1983.
    ET of *The History of the Church* by G. A. Williamson. Harmondsworth:
        Penguin Classics, 1965.
Eustathius
    Contra Origenem de engastrimytho. Migne, *PG* 18.613–74.
Gnostics
    The Nag Hammadi Library in English. Ed. James Robinson. Leiden: Brill,
        1977.
    The Gnostic Scriptures. Ed. Bentley Layton. London: SCM Press, 1987.

Gregory of Nazianzus
Grégoire de Nazianze. Discours funèbres. Ed. F. Boulenger. Textes et documents pour l'étude historique du Christianisme. Paris: Alphonse Picard et fils, 1908.
Discours 1–3, SC, vol. 247. Ed. Jean Bernardi. 1978.
Discours 4–5, Contre Julien, SC, vol. 309. Ed. Jean Bernardi. 1983.
Discours 20–23. SC, vol. 270. Ed. J. Mossay. 1980.
Discours 24–26. SC, vol. 284. Ed. J. Mossay. 1981.
Discours 38–41. SC, vol. 358. Ed. C. Moreschini. 1990.
Migne, *PG,* 35–8.
ET of Select Orations in *NPNF,* 2nd series, vol. vii.
Gregory of Nyssa
Gregorii Nysseni opera. Ed. W. Jaeger *et al.* Leiden: Brill.
  Vols. i and ii: *Contra Eunomium.* Ed. W. Jaeger. 1960.
  Vol. vii.1: *De Vita Moysis.* Ed. H. Musurillo. 1964.
  Vol. x.1 and 2: *Sermones.* Ed. G. Heil, J. P. Cavernos, O. Lendle. 1990.
De opificio hominis. Migne, *PG* 44.
ET *Gregory of Nyssa. The Life of Moses.* Trans., introd. and notes by Abraham Malherbe and Everett Ferguson in *CWS.*
ET of Select Works in *NPNF,* 2nd series, vol. v.
Hippolytus
Hippolytus Werke, GCS.
  Vol. i: *Exegetische und Homiletische Schriften.* Ed. G. N. Bonwetsch and Hans Achelis. 1897.
(Ps.-)Hippolytus
The Treatise on the Apostolic Tradition of St Hippolytus of Rome, Bishop and Martyr. Ed. Gregory Dix and Henry Chadwick. London: The Alban Press, 1992 (reprint of 2nd rev. edn, London: SPCK, 1968).
Ignatius
(see Apostolic Fathers)
Irenaeus
Sancti Irenaei libros quinque adversus haereses. 2 vols. ed. W. W. Harvey. Cambridge: Cambridge University Press, 1857.
Contre les hérésies. 10 vols. *SC,* vols. 263–4, 293–4, 210–11, 100, 152–3. Ed. A. Rousseau, L. Doutreleau, *et al.* 1969, 1974, 1979, 1982.
The Demonstration of the Apostolic Preaching. Trans. from Armenian with introd. and notes, J. A. Robinson. London: SPCK, 1920.
ET in *ANCL,* vols. v and ix.
John Chrysostom
Panégyriques de S. Paul. SC, vol. 300. Ed. A. Piédagnel. 1982.
Sur l'incomprehensibilité de Dieu. SC, vol. 28. Introd. J. Daniélou, text and notes A.-M. Malingrey, trans. R. Flacelière. 1970.
On the Incomprehensible Nature of God. ET in *FC,* vol. 72.
Homilies on the Psalms. Migne, *PG* 55.

Homilies on the Corinthian letters. Migne, *PG* 61.
ET in *NPNF*, 1st series, vols. IX–XIV.
Julian the Apostate
The Works of the Emperor Julian. 3 vols. Ed. Wilmer C. Wright. *LCL*, 1913, 1923.
The Emperor Julian. Panegyric and Polemic. Ed. Samuel N. C. Lieu. Liverpool: Liverpool University Press, 1986. (This includes translations of works for or against Julian by Mamertinus, Chrysostom and Ephrem).
Justin
Migne, *PG* 6.
ET in *ANCL*, vol. II.
ET *The Writings of St Justin Martyr. FC*, vol. 6. Trans. Thomas B. Falls. 1948.
Heraclitus
Quaestiones Homericae. Ed. Societas Philogae Bonnensis. Leipzig: Teubner, 1910.
Longinus
On the Sublime. Ed. D. A. Russell. Oxford: Oxford University Press, 1964.
On the Sublime. Text with ET by W. Hamilton Fyfe (together with Aristotle, *The Poetics* and Demetrius, *On Style*). *LCL*, 1965.
Lucian
Peregrinus and *Alexander of Abounoteichos.* Ed. and ET: A. M. Harmon, K. Kilburn, M. D. McLeod. *LCL*, 1911–67.
Lucretius
De rerum natura. 3 vols. Ed., trans. and comm. C. Bailey. Oxford: Clarendon, 1947.
ET R. E. Latham. Harmondsworth: Penguin Classics, 1951.
Melito of Sardis
On Pascha and Fragments. Texts and translations ed. by Stuart George Hall. Oxford Early Christian Texts. Oxford: Clarendon, 1979.
Menander Rhetor
Menander Rhetor. Ed. with trans. and commentary D. A. Russell and N. G. Wilson. Oxford: Clarendon, 1981.
Origen
Origenes Werke, GCS.
    Vol. I: *Der Schrift vom Martyrium. Buch I–IV Gegen Celsus.* Ed. P. Koetschau. 1899.
    Vol. II: *Buch V–VIII Gegen Celsus. Die Schrift vom Gebet.* Ed. P. Koetschau. 1899.
    Vol. III: *Jeremiahomilien. Klageliederkommentar.* Ed. E. Klostermann. 1901.
    Vol. IV: *Der Johanneskommentar.* Ed. E. Preuschen. 1903.
    Vol. V: *De Principiis.* Ed. P. Koetschau. 1913.
    Vol. X: *Matthäuserklarung.* Ed. E. Klostermann. 1935.

Philocalie, 1–20, Sur les Ecritures. Introd., text and trans. Marguerite Harl.
 Lettre à Africanus, Sur l'histoire de Suzanne. Introd., text and trans.
 Nicholas de Lange. *SC*, vol. 302, 1983.
 ET *ANCL*, vols. x, xxiii.
 NB: the additional vol. published 1897, containing selections from the
 Commentary on John and the *Commentary on Matthew*.
 ET of *On Prayer* in *LCC*, vol. ii and *ACW*, vol. 19.
 On First Principles. ET with introduction and notes, G. W. Butterworth;
 Introduction to Torchbook edn by Henri de Lubac. (Originally
 published London: SPCK, 1936) Gloucester, Mass.: Peter Smith,
 1973.
 Origen. Contra Celsum. ET and ed. H. Chadwick. Cambridge: Cambridge
 University Press, 1965.
 Commentary on the Gospel according to John, Books 1–10. ET Ronald E. Heine.
 FC, vol. 80, 1989.
 Commentary on the Gospel according to John, Books 13–32. ET Ronald E. Heine.
 FC, vol. 89, 1993.
 Selections from the Commentaries and Homilies of Origen, ET R. B. Tollinton.
 London: SPCK, 1929.
Philostratus
 The Life of Apollonius of Tyana. Ed. and ET: F. C. Conybeare. *LCL*, 1912.
Plutarch
 Moralia. Vol. i (including *De liberis educandis* and *Quomodo adolescens poetas
 audire debeat*), vol. ii (including *De Superstitione*) and vol. v (including
 De Iside et Osiride and *De defectu oraculorum*), text and ET by F. C.
 Babbitt. *LCL*, 1965.
Ptolemy
 Letter to Flora, SC, vol. 24. Ed. and trans. G. Quispel. 1949.
Quintilian
 The Institutio Oratoria of Quintilian. 4 vols. Ed. and trans. H. E. Butler. *LCL*,
 1920, 1921, 1922.
Sozomen
 Kirchengeschichte. Ed. J. Bidez and G. C. Hansen. *GCS*, 1960.
 ET in *NPNF*, 2nd series, vol. ii.
Tatian
 Tatian: Oratio ad Graecos and Fragments. Ed. M. Whittaker. Oxford Early
 Christian texts. Oxford: Clarendon, 1982.
Tertullian
 Opera, CSEL.
 Vol. ii.1: *Apologeticum*. Ed. H. Hoppe. 1939.
 Vol. ii.2, pp.1–58: *De praescriptione haereticorum*. Ed. A. Kroymann.
 1942.
 Vol. iii, pp.290–650: *Adversus Marcionem*, Ed. A. Kroymann. 1906.
 Adversus Marcionem. 2 vols. Ed. and trans. E. Evans. Oxford Early
 Christian Texts. Oxford: Clarendon, 1972.

De oratione. Latin text with ET and notes, ed. Ernest Evans. London: SPCK, 1953.
ET in *ANCL*, vols. VII, XI and XVIII.
Theodore of Mopsuestia
Commentary on the Minor Epistles of St Paul. 2 vols. Ed. H. B. Swete. Cambridge: Cambridge University Press, 1880–2.
Theodoret
Eranistes. Ed. Gerard H. Ettlinger. Oxford: Oxford University Press, 1975.
Theophilus of Antioch
Ad Autolycum. Text and translation by Robert M. Grant. Oxford Early Christian texts. Oxford: Clarendon, 1970.
Theophrastus
Characters. Ed. and ET: J. M. Edmonds. *LCL*, 1929.
ET Philip Vellacott. Harmondsworth: Penguin Classics, 1967.
Thucydides
Thucydides' History. Text and ET: Charles Forster Smith. *LCL*, 4 vols., 1919–23.
ET R. Warner. Harmondsworth: Penguin Classics, 1954.
Tyconius
The Book of the Rules of Tyconius. Ed. F. C. Burkitt. *TS*, vol. 3. Cambridge: Cambridge University Press, 1894.
ET in Froehlich, *Biblical Interpretation.*
The Church Fathers on the Bible.
Selected Readings, ed. by Frank Sadowski. New York: Society of St Paul, 1987.

SECONDARY LITERATURE

Ackroyd, P. and C. F. Evans (eds.), *The Cambridge History of the Bible*, vol. 1. Cambridge: Cambridge University Press, 1970, pp. 412–end.
Babcock, William S. (ed.), *Paul and the Legacies of Paul.* Dallas: Southern Methodist University Press, 1990.
Barrett, C. K., 'Pauline Controversies in the Post-Pauline Period', *NTS* 20.3 (1974), pp. 229–45.
Bate, H. N., 'Some Technical Terms of Greek Exegesis', *JTS* 24 (1923), pp. 59–66.
Bauer, Walter, *Orthodoxy and Heresy in Earliest Christianity.* ET London: SCM, 1972.
Beker, J. Christiaan, *Paul the Apostle. The Triumph of God in Life and Thought.* Philadelphia: Fortress, 1980; Edinburgh: T. & T. Clark, 1989.
The Triumph of God. The Essence of Paul's Thought. Minneapolis: Fortress, 1990.
Bienert, W. A., *'Allegoria' und 'Anagoge' bei Didymos dem Blinden von Alexandria.* Berlin: de Gruyter, 1972.

Bloom, Harold, *Ruin the Sacred Truths. Poetry and Belief from the Bible to the Present.* Cambridge, Mass., and London: Harvard University Press, 1987/89.

Boer, W. den, 'Hermeneutic Problems in Early Christian Literature', *VC* 1 (1947), pp. 150–67.

Bonner, Gerald, *St Augustine of Hippo. Life and Controversies.* London: SCM, 1963; revised, Norwich: Canterbury Press, 1986.

Bonner, S. F., *The Literary Treatises of Dionysius of Halicarnassus.* Cambridge: Cambridge University Press, 1939.

Bonsirven, J., *Exégèse patristique et rabbinique.* Paris: Beauchesne, 1939.

Boularand, E., *L'hérésie d'Arius et la 'foi' de Nicée* (2 vols). Paris: Letouzey & Ane, 1972.

Bowersock, G. W., *Julian the Apostate.* London: Duckworth, 1978.
    Hellenism in Late Antiquity. Cambridge: Cambridge University Press, 1990.

Bradshaw, Paul, *The Search for the Origins of Christian Worship.* London: SPCK, 1992.

Brock, Sebastian, *The Luminous Eye.* Rome: Centre for Indian and Inter-Religious Studies, 1985.

Brown, Dennis, *Vir Trilinguis. A Study in the Biblical Exegesis of Saint Jerome.* Kampen: Kok Pharos, 1992.

Brown, Peter, *Augustine of Hippo.* London: Faber & Faber, 1967.

Bultmann, Rudolf, *Die Exegese des Theodor von Mopsuestia.* Habilitationsschrift, posthumously published. Stuttgart/Berlin/Cologne/Mainz: Kohlhammer, 1984.

Burnaby, John, *Amor Dei. A Study of the Religion of St Augustine.* Originally published London: Hodder & Stoughton, 1938; reissued in paperback, Norwich: Canterbury Press, 1991.

Burtchaell, James Tunstead, *From Synagogue to Church. Public Services and Offices in the Earliest Christian Communities.* Cambridge: Cambridge University Press, 1992.

Burton-Christie, Douglas, *The Word in the Desert. Scripture and the Quest for Holiness in Early Christian Monasticism.* Oxford: Oxford University Press, 1993.

Cameron, Averil (ed.), *History as Text.* London: Duckworth, 1989.

Cameron, Averil, *Christianity and the Rhetoric of Empire. The Development of Christian Discourse.* Sather Classical Lectures. Berkeley/Los Angeles/Oxford: University of California Press, 1991.

Campenhausen, Hans von, *The Formation of the Christian Bible.* ET: J. A. Baker. Philadelphia: Fortress, 1972.

Chadwick, Henry, *Augustine.* Past Masters Series, Oxford: Oxford University Press, 1986.
    Heresy and Orthodoxy in the Early Church. Aldershot: Variorum, 1991.

Charity, A. C., *Events and their Afterlife: The Dialectics of Christian Typology in the Bible and Dante.* Cambridge: Cambridge University Press, 1966.

Chesnut, Glenn F., 'Fate, Fortune, Freewill and Nature in Eusebius of Caesarea', *Church History* 42 (1973), pp. 165–82.

The First Christian Histories. Théologie Historique 46. Paris: Beauchesne, 1977.

Clark, Elizabeth A., *Ascetic Piety and Women's Faith*. New York: Edwin Mellen, 1986.

The Origenist Controversy. The Construction of an Early Christian Debate. Princeton: Princeton University Press, 1992.

Coggins, R. J., and J. L. Houlden (eds.), *A Dictionary of Biblical Interpretation*. London: SCM, 1990.

Coulter, J. A., *The Literary Microcosm. Theories of Interpretation of the Later Neoplatonists*. Leiden: Brill, 1976.

Cox, Patricia, *Biography in Late Antiquity. A Quest for the Holy Man*. Berkeley: University of California Press, 1983.

'Origen and the Witch of Endor: Toward an Iconoclastic Typology', *Anglican Theological Review* 66 (1984), pp. 137–47.

Crouzel, Henri, *Origen*. ET by A. S. Worrall. Edinburgh: T. & T.Clark, 1989.

Daniélou, J., *Origène*. Paris: La Table Ronde, 1948. ET New York: Sheed & Ward, 1955.

The Lord of History. ET by Nigel Abercrombie of *Essai sur le mystère de l'histoire*. London: Longmans, 1958.

From Shadows to Reality: Studies in the Biblical Typology of the Fathers. London: Burns & Oates, 1960.

Daube, David, 'Rabbinic Methods of Interpretation and Hellenistic Rhetoric', *Hebrew Union College Annual XXII* (Cincinatti, 1949), pp. 239–64.

Dawson, David, *Allegorical Readers and Cultural Revision in Ancient Alexandria*. Berkeley/Los Angeles/Oxford: University of California Press, 1992.

Devréesse, R., *Essai sur Théodore de Mopsueste*. Studi e Testi. Vatican: Biblioteca Apostolica Vaticana, 1948.

Dodd, C. H., *The Parables of the Kingdom*. London: Collins, 1934.

Dowden, Ken, *Religion and the Romans*. London: Bristol Classical Press (an imprint of Duckworth), 1992.

Drake, H. A., *In Praise of Constantine: A Historical Study and New Translation of Eusebius' Tricennial Orations*. Berkeley: University of California Press, 1976.

Droge, Arthur J., *Homer or Moses? Early Christian Interpretations of the History of Culture*. Hermeneutische Untersuchungen zur Theologie 26. Tübingen: J. C. B. Mohr (Paul Siebeck), 1989.

Dunn, J. D. G., *Jesus, Paul and the Law*. London: SPCK, 1990.

The Parting of the Ways Between Christianity and Judaism and their Significance for the Character of Christianity. London: SCM Press, 1991.

Ehrman, Bart D., *The Orthodox Corruption of Scripture. The Effect of Early Christological Controversies on the Text of the New Testament*. Oxford: Oxford University Press, 1993.

Fabiny, Tibor, *The Lion and the Lamb, Figuralism and Fulfilment in the Bible, Art and Literature.* Studies in Religion and Literature. London: Macmillan, 1992.

Fishbane, Michael, *Biblical Interpretation in Ancient Israel.* Oxford: Clarendon, 1985.

Fleury, E., *Hellénisme et Christianisme. S. Grégoire de Nazianze et son temps.* Paris: Beauchesne, 1930.

Fox, Robin Lane, *Pagans and Christians in the Mediterranean World from the Second Century AD to the Conversion of Constantine.* Harmondsworth: Penguin, 1988.

Fredriksen, Paula, 'Paul and Augustine: Conversion Narratives, Orthodox Traditions, and the Retrospective Self,' *JTS* NS 37 (1986), pp. 3–34.

'Beyond the Body/Soul Dichotomy', in William S. Babcock (ed.), *Paul and the Legacies of Paul,* pp. 227–51.

Froehlich, K., *Biblical Interpretation in the Early Church.* Sources of Early Christian Thought. Philadelphia: Fortress Press, 1984.

Frye, Northrop, *The Great Code. The Bible and Literature.* New York and London: Harcourt Brace Jovanovich Publishers, 1981.

Gamble, Harry Y., *Books and Readers in the Early Church.* New Haven and London: Yale University Press, 1995.

Goodman, Martin, *Mission and Conversion. Proselytizing in the Religious History of the Roman Empire.* Oxford: Clarendon Press, 1994.

Gorday, Peter, *Principles of Patristic Exegesis. Romans 9–11 in Origen, John Chrysostom and Augustine.* New York and Toronto: The Edwin Mellen Press, 1983.

Grant, R. M., *The Letter and the Spirit.* London: SPCK, 1957.

The Earliest Lives of Jesus. London: SPCK, 1961.

Gods and the One God. Christian Theology in the Graeco-Roman World. London: SPCK, 1986.

Grant, Robert M., with David Tracy, *A Short History of the Interpretation of the Bible.* 2nd edn, revised and enlarged. London: SCM Press, 1984 (chapters 1–15 originally published in 1963).

Greer, Rowan A., *Theodore of Mopsuestia. Exegete and Theologian.* Westminster: Faith Press, 1961.

The Captain of our Salvation. A Study in the Patristic Exegesis of Hebrews. Tübingen: J. C. B. Mohr (Paul Siebeck), 1973.

Guignet, Marcel, *Saint Grégoire de Nazianze et la rhétorique.* Paris: Alphonse Picard & fils, 1911.

Guillet, J., 'Les Exégèses d'Alexandre et d'Antioche conflit ou malentendu?', *Recherches de science religieuse* 34 (1947), pp. 257–302.

Guinot, J.-N. 'La typologie comme technique herméneutique', in *Figures de l'Ancien Testament chez les Pères,* Cahiers de *Biblia Patristica* 2. Strasbourg: Centre d'analyse et de documentation patristiques, 1989.

Hadas, Moses, *Hellenistic Culture, Fusion and Diffusion.* New York: Norton, 1972.

Hagan, Kenneth, 'What did the term *Commentarius* mean to Sixteenth-century Theologians?' in Irena Backus and Francis Higman (eds.), *Théorie et pratique de l'exégèse*, Actes du troisième colloque international sur l'histoire de l'exégèse biblique au XVIe siècle. Geneva: Librairie Droz S.A., 1990.

Hanson, A. T., *Studies in Paul's Technique and Theology*. London: SPCK, 1974.

Hanson, R. P. C., *Allegory and Event*. London: SCM, 1959.

The Search for the Christian Doctrine of God. Edinburgh: T. & T. Clark, 1988.

Harl, Marguerite (ed.), *Ecriture et culture philosophique dans la pensée de Grégoire de Nysse*. Actes du Colloque de Chevetogne 1969. Leiden: Brill, 1971.

Harnack, Adolf, *The Mission and Expansion of Christianity*, vol. 1. London: Williams & Norgate, 1908.

Harris, William V., *Ancient Literacy*. Cambridge, Mass.: Harvard University Press, 1989.

Harrison, Carol, *Beauty and Revelation in the Thought of Saint Augustine*. Oxford: Clarendon, 1992.

Hatch, Edwin, *The Influence of Greek Ideas on Christianity*. New York: Harper, 1957 (reprinted by arrangement with Williams & Norgate, London).

Hays, Richard B., *Echoes of Scripture in the Letters of Paul*. New Haven and London: Yale University Press, 1989.

Heath, Malcolm, *Unity in Greek Poetics*. Oxford: Clarendon, 1989.

Heim, F., 'Le figure du prince idéal au IVe siècle: du type au modèle', in *Figures de l'Ancien Testament chez les Pères*, Cahiers de *Biblia Patristica* 2, Strasbourg: Centre d'analyse et de documentation patristiques, 1989.

Heine, Ron, *Perfection in the Virtuous Life: a study in the relationship between edification and polemical theology in Gregory of Nyssa's De Vita Moysis*. Patristic Monograph Series, no. 2. Philadelphia: Philadelphia Patristic Foundation, 1975.

'Gregory of Nyssa's Apology for Allegory', *VC* 38 (1984), pp. 360–70.

Hengel, Martin, *Judaism and Hellenism*. 2 vols. ET London: SCM Press, 1974.

Holzberg, Niklas, *The Ancient Novel. An Introduction*. ET London and New York: Routledge, 1995.

Jaeger, Werner, *Paideia. The Ideals of Greek Culture*. ET 3 vols. Gilbert Highet. Oxford: Oxford University Press, 1943–5.

Jeanrond, Werner, *Text and Interpretation as Categories of Theological Thinking*. ET by Thomas J. Wilson. Dublin: Gill & Macmillan, 1988.

Jeremias, J., *The Parables of Jesus*. ET London: SCM Press, 1954.

Josipovici, Gabriel, *The Book of God*. New Haven and London: Yale University Press, 1988.

Judge, E. A., 'The Early Christians as a Scholastic Community', *Journal of Religious History* 1 (1960–1), pp. 4–15, 125–37.

'St Paul and Classical Society', *Jahrbuch für Antike und Christentum* 15 (1972), pp. 19–36.

Kamesar, Adam, 'The Evaluation of the Narrative Aggada in Greek and Latin Patristic Literature', *JTS* NS 45 (1994), pp. 37–71.

Kannengiesser, Charles (ed.), *Politique et théologie chez Athanase d'Alexandrie*. Paris: Beauchesne, 1974.

Kannengiesser, Charles, 'Athanasius' *Three Orations against the Arians*: A Reappraisal', in *Arius and Athanasius. Two Alexandrian Theologians*. Aldershot: Variorum Reprints, 1991 (originally published in *SP* 18.3 (1982)).

Early Christian Spirituality. Sources of Early Christian Thought. Philadelphia: Fortress Press, 1986.

Kannengiesser, Charles, and William L. Petersen, (eds.), *Origen of Alexandria. His World and His Legacy*. Notre Dame, Indiana: University of Notre Dame Press, 1988.

Katz, Peter, 'The early Christians' Use of Codices Instead of Rolls', *JTS* 46 (1945), pp. 63–5.

Kelly, J. N. D., *Early Christian Creeds*. London: Longmans, 2nd edn, 1960.

Jerome. London: Duckworth, 1975.

Kennedy, George, *The Art of Rhetoric in the Roman World*. Princeton: Princeton University Press, 1972.

Classical Rhetoric and its Christian and Secular Tradition from Ancient to Modern Times. Chapel Hill and London: University of California Press, 1980.

Greek Rhetoric under Christian Emperors. Princeton: Princeton University Press, 1983.

New Testament Interpretation through Rhetorical Criticism. Chapel Hill and London: University of North Carolina Press, 1984.

Kerrigan, Alexander, *St Cyril of Alexandria. Interpreter of the Old Testament*. *Analecta Biblica* 2. Rome: Pontifical Biblical Institute, 1952.

Kinneavy, James L., *Greek Rhetorical Origins of Christian Faith*. New York and Oxford: Oxford University Press, 1987.

Kirwan, Christopher, *Augustine*. London: Routledge, 1989.

Koen, Lars, *The Saving Passion. Incarnational and Soteriological Thought in Cyril of Alexandria's Commentary on the Gospel according to St John*. Uppsala: Acta Universitatis Upsaliensis, 1991.

Koester, Helmut, *Synoptische Überlieferung bei den Apostolischen Vätern*. TU 65. Berlin: Akademie-Verlag, 1957.

Lamberton, Robert, *Homer the Theologian*. Berkeley and Los Angeles: University of California Press, 1986.

Lampe, G. W. H. and K. J. Woollcombe, *Essays in Typology*. Studies in Biblical Theology 22. London: SCM Press, 1957.

Lange, Nicholas de, *Origen and the Jews*. Cambridge: Cambridge University Press, 1976.

Lieberman, Saul, *Hellenism in Jewish Palestine*. New York: Jewish Theological Seminary of America, 1950.

Liebeschutz, J. H. W. G., *Continuity and Change in Roman Religion*. Oxford: Clarendon Press, 1979.

Lindars, Barnabas, *New Testament Apologetic*. London: SCM Press, 1961.

Lodge, David (ed.), *Modern Criticism and Theory: a Reader*. London: Longman, 1988.

Louth, Andrew, *Discerning the Mystery. An Essay on the Nature of Theology*. Oxford: Clarendon Press, 1983 (especially chapter 5, 'Return to Allegory').

Lubac, Henri de, *Exégèse mediéval: les quatre sens de l'écriture*, 4 vols. Paris: Aubier, 1959–64.

MacDonald, D. R., *The Legend and the Apostle: The Battle for Paul in Story and Canon*. Philadephia: Westminster, 1983.

   Christianizing Homer. The Odyssey, Plato and the Acts of Andrew. Oxford: Oxford University Press, 1994.

Malherbe, Abraham J., *Paul and the Popular Philosophers*. Minneapolis: Fortress Press, 1989.

Markus, R. A., *Saeculum. History and Society in the Theology of St Augustine*. Cambridge: Cambridge University Press, 1970.

Marrou, H.-I., *L'éducation dans l'antiquité*. Paris: Editions du Seuil, 1948; ET London: Sheed & Ward, 1956.

   S. Augustine et la fin de la culture antique. Paris: de Boccard, 1938.

Martin, Luther H., *Hellenistic Religions*. Oxford: Oxford University Press, 1987.

Massaux, Edouard, *The Influence of the Gospel of Saint Matthew on Christian Literature before Saint Irenaeus*. ET of thesis of 1950. Macon, Ga.: Mercer University Press; and Leuven: Peeters, 1990.

McFague, Sallie, *Metaphorical Theology. Models of God in Religious Language*. London: SCM Press, 1983.

McKnight, Edgar V., *Postmodern Use of the Bible. The Emergence of Reader-Oriented Criticism*. Nashville: Abingdon, 1988.

Meeks, Wayne, *The Origins of Christian Morality. The First Two Centuries*. New Haven and London: Yale University Press, 1993.

Minns OP, Denis, *Irenaeus*. Outstanding Christian Thinkers Series. London: Geoffrey Chapman, 1994.

Moberly, R. W. L., *The Old Testament of the Old Testament: Patriarchal Narratives and Mosaic Yahwism*. Minneapolis: Fortress, 1992.

Momigliano, Arnaldo, 'Pagan and Christian Historiography in the Fourth Century AD', in *The Conflict between Paganism and Christianity in the Fourth Century*. Oxford: Clarendon, 1963, pp. 79–99.

Mühlenberg, E., 'Marcion's Jealous God', in Donald F. Winslow (ed.), *Disciplina Nostra. Essays in Memory of Robert F. Evans*. Cambridge, Mass.: The Philadelphia Patristic Foundation, 1979.

Mühlenberg, E., and J. van Oort (eds.), *Predigt in der alten Kirche*. Kampen: Kok Pharos, 1994.

Neuschäfer, Bernhard, *Origenes als Philologe*. Basel: Friedrich Reinhardt Verlag, 1987.

Neusner, Jacob, *A Midrash Reader*. Minneapolis: Fortress, 1990.

Nineham, D. E. (ed.), *The Church's Use of the Bible Past and Present*. London: SPCK, 1963.

Oort, J. van, and U. Wickert (eds.), *Christliche Exegese zwischen Nicaea und Chalcedon*. Kampen: Kok Pharos, 1992.

Pagels, Elaine, *The Gnostic Paul. Gnostic Exegesis of the Pauline Letters*. Philadelphia: TPI, 1992 (originally, Fortress, 1975).

Adam, Eve and the Serpent. London: Penguin, 1988.

Parke, H. W., *Sibyls and Sibylline Prophecy in Classical Antiquity*. Ed. B. C. McGing. London: Routledge, 1988.

Pétrement, Simone, *A Separate God? The Christian Origins of Gnosticism*. ET by Carol Harrison. London: Darton, Longman & Todd, 1991.

Pollard, T. E., 'The Exegesis of Scripture in the Arian Controversy', *BJRL* 41 (1958–9), pp. 414–29.

Quasten, J., *Patrology*. 3 vols. Utrecht and Antwerp: Spectrum, 1962–4.

Ricciotti, G., *Julian the Apostate*. ET by M. J. Costeloe. Milwaukee: Bruce, 1960.

Ritchie, B., 'The Emergence of *skopos* as an Important Technical Term in Patristic Exegesis', unpublished paper given at the Eleventh International Conference on Patristic Studies, Oxford, 1991.

Roberts, C. H., 'The Codex', in *Proceedings of the British Academy* 40 (1954), pp. 169–204.

'Books in the Greco-Roman World and in the New Testament', in P. Ackroyd and C. F. Evans (eds.), *The Cambridge History of the Bible*, vol. 1, pp. 48–66.

'The Writing and Dissemination of Literature in the Classical World', in David Daiches (ed.), *Literature and Western Civilisation*, vol. 1. London: Aldus, 1972.

Manuscript, Society and Belief in Early Christian Egypt. Oxford: Oxford University Press for British Academy, 1979.

Roberts, C. H. and T. C. Skeat, *The Birth of the Codex*. London: Oxford University Press for the British Academy, 1983.

Rogerson, John, 'The Hebrew Conception of Corporate Personality: A Re-examination', *JTS* NS 21 (1970), pp. 1–16.

Rokeah, David, *Jews, Pagans and Christians in Conflict*. Leiden: Brill, 1982.

Rudolf, Kurt, *Gnosis*. ET by R. McL. Wilson. Edinburgh: T. & T. Clark, 1983.

Ruether, Rosemary R., *Gregory of Nazianzus. Rhetor and Philosopher*. Oxford: Clarendon, 1969.

Runia, David T., *Exegesis and Philosophy. Studies on Philo of Alexandria*. Aldershot: Variorum, 1990.

Russell, D. A., *Criticism in Antiquity*. London: Duckworth, 1981.

Russell, D. A. and M. Winterbottom, *Ancient Literary Criticism. The Principal Texts in New Translations*. Oxford: Oxford University Press, 1972.

Sanders, E. P., *Paul and Palestinian Judaism*. London: SCM, 1977.

Sanders, E. P. (ed.), *Jewish and Christian Self-Definition*, 3 vols. London: SCM Press, 1980, 1981, 1982.

Sanders, Jack T., *Schismatics, Sectarians, Dissidents, Deviants. The First One Hundred Years of Jewish–Christian Relations*. London: SCM Press, 1993.

Schäublin, Christoph, *Untersuchungen zu Methode und Herkunft der antiochenischen Exegese*. Cologne and Bonn: Peter Hanstein, 1974.

'Zum paganen Umfeld der christlichen Predigt', in E. Mühlenberg and J. van Oort (eds.), *Predigt in der alten Kirche*, pp. 25–49.

Schürer, Emil, *The History of the Jewish People in the Age of Jesus Christ*, vol. II, new edition ed. by Geza Vermes, Fergus Millar and Matthew Black. Edinburgh: T. & T. Clark, 1979.

Segal, Alan F., *Paul the Convert. The Apostolate and Apostasy of Saul the Pharisee*. New Haven and London: Yale University Press, 1990.

Sévrin, J.-M., *The New Testament in Early Christianity*, Papers from the Leuven Colloquium of 1986. Leuven: Leuven University Press, 1989.

Sherman, Hazel, 'Reading Zechariah: An Attempt to Assess the Allegorical Tradition of Biblical Interpretation through the Commentary of Didymus the Blind'. University of Birmingham Ph.D. thesis, 1995.

Shotwell, Willis A., *The Biblical Exegesis of Justin Martyr*. London: SPCK, 1965.

Simonetti, M., *Studi sull'Arianismo*. Rome: Editrice Studium, 1965.

Biblical Interpretation in the Early Church: An Historical Introduction to Patristic Exegesis. ET by John A. Hughes, with Anders Bergquist and Markus Bockmuehl as editors, and William Horbury as Consultant Editor. Edinburgh: T. & T. Clark, 1994.

Skarsaune, Oskar, *The Proof from Prophecy. A Study in Justin Martyr's Proof-Text Tradition: Text-Type, Provenance, Theological Profile*. Leiden: Brill, 1987.

Soskice, Janet Martin, *Metaphor and Religious Language*. Oxford: Clarendon, 1985.

Steiner, George, *Real Presences*. London: Faber, 1989.

Stern, David, *Parables in Midrash. Narrative and Exegesis in Rabbinic Literature*. Cambridge, Mass.: Harvard University Press, 1991.

Stewart-Sykes, Alistair, 'The Quartodeciman Paschal Liturgy in the Light of Melito's *Peri Pascha* Formcritically Examined'. University of Birmingham Ph.D. thesis, 1992.

Teselle, Eugene, *Augustine the Theologian*. London: Burns & Oates, 1970.

Tigcheler, J. H., *Didyme l'Aveugle et l'exégèse allégorique, son commentaire sur Zacharie*. Nijmegen: Dekker & van de Vegt, 1977.

Torjesen, Karen Jo, *Hermeneutical Procedure and Theological Method in Origen's Exegesis*. Berlin and New York: Walter de Gruyter, 1985.

'"Body", "Soul", and "Spirit" in Origen's Theory of Exegesis', *Anglican Theological Review* 67 (1985), pp. 17–30.

Torrance, T. F., *The Trinitarian Faith. The Evangelical Theology of the Ancient Catholic Church*. Edinburgh: T. & T. Clark, 1988.

Divine Meaning. Edinburgh: T. & T. Clark, 1995.

Trigg, Joseph Wilson, *Origen. The Bible and Philosophy in the Third-century Church*. London: SCM Press, 1985.

Vickers, Brian, *In Defence of Rhetoric*. Oxford: Clarendon Press, 1988.

Wadsworth, Michael (ed.), *Ways of Reading the Bible*. Brighton: Harvester, 1981.

Wall, Lynne, 'The *Epistle of Barnabas* and Early Rabbinic Exegetical Traditions'. University of Birmingham Ph.D. thesis, 1993.

Wallace-Hadrill, D. S., *Christian Antioch. A Study of Early Christian Thought in the East.* Cambridge: Cambridge University Press, 1982.

Watson, Francis (ed.), *The Open Text. New Directions for Biblical Studies?* London: SPCK, 1993.

Weinsheimer, Joel, *Philosophical Hermeneutics and Literary Theory.* New Haven and London: Yale University Press, 1991.

Whitman, Jon, *Allegory. The Dynamics of an Ancient and Medieval Technique.* Oxford: Clarendon Press, 1987.

Wiles, Maurice, *The Spiritual Gospel.* Cambridge: Cambridge University Press, 1960.

The Divine Apostle. Cambridge: Cambridge University Press, 1967.

Wilken, R. L., *Judaism and the Early Christian Mind. A Study of Cyril of Alexandria's Exegesis and Theology.* New Haven and London: Yale University Press, 1984.

The Christians as the Romans Saw Them. New Haven and London: Yale University Press, 1984.

Williams, Rowan, *Arius. Heresy and Tradition.* London: Darton, Longman & Todd, 1987.

Wingren, G., *Man and Incarnation. A Study in the Biblical Theology of Irenaeus.* ET by R. Mackenzie. Edinburgh and London: Oliver & Boyd, 1959.

Young, Frances M., 'The God of the Greeks and the Nature of Religious Language', in W. R. Schoedel and Robert Wilken, *Early Christian Literature and the Greek Intellectual Tradition. Festschrift for R. M. Grant.* Théologie Historique 53. Paris: Editions Beauchesne, 1980.

'God: An Essay in Patristic Theology', *The Modern Churchman* 29 (1981), pp. 149–65.

'Did Epiphanius Know What he Meant by Heresy?' *SP* 18 (1982), pp. 199–205.

From Nicaea to Chalcedon. London: SCM, 1983.

'Adam, the Soul and Immortality: A Study of the Interaction of "Science" and the Bible in some Anthropological Treatises of the Fourth Century', *VC* 37 (1983), pp. 110–40.

'John Chrysostom on I and II Corinthians', *SP* 18.1 (1986), pp. 349–52.

'Allegory and atonement', *Australian Biblical Review* 35 (Festschrift vol. for E. F. Osborn, 1987), pp. 107–14.

'The Rhetorical Schools and their Influence on Patristic Exegesis', in Rowan Williams (ed.), *The Making of Orthodoxy. Essays in honour of Henry Chadwick.* Cambridge: Cambridge University Press, 1989, pp. 182–99.

'Exegetical Method and Scriptural Proof: The Bible in Doctrinal Debate', *SP* 24 (1989), pp. 291–304.

The Art of Performance. Towards a Theology of Holy Scripture. London: Darton, Longman & Todd, 1990.

'Allegory and the Ethics of Reading', in Francis Watson (ed.), *The Open Text*, pp. 103–20.

'Panegyric and the Bible', *SP* 25 (1993) pp. 194–208.

'*Paideia* and the Myth of Static Dogma', in Sarah Coakley and David Pailin (eds.), *The Making and Remaking of Christian Doctrine. Essays in Honour of Maurice Wiles*. Oxford: Clarendon, 1993.

The Theology of the Pastoral Letters. Cambridge: Cambridge University Press, 1994.

'Typology', in Stanley E. Porter, Paul Joyce and David E. Orton (eds.), *Crossing the Boundaries. Essays in Biblical Interpretation in Honour of Michael D. Goulder*. Leiden: Brill, 1994, pp. 29–48.

'Interpretative Genres and the Inevitability of Pluralism', T. W. Manson lecture, *JSNT* 59 (1995), pp. 93–110.

Young, Frances, and David Ford, *Meaning and Truth in 2 Corinthians*. London: SPCK, 1987.

Zaidman, Louise Bruit, and Pauline Schmitt Pantel, *Religion in the Ancient Greek City*. ET by Paul Cartledge. Cambridge: Cambridge University Press, 1992.

Index of biblical references

Index of modern scholars

Aland, Barbara 133
Auerbach, Erich 154, 254

Babcock, William S. 267, 269
Beker, J. Christiaan 266
Bowersock, G. W. 70, 72–3
Brock, Sebastian, 149, 151–2
Brown, Peter 279

Cameron, Averil 257–60, 270
Chadwick, Henry 277–8
Coulter, J. A. 210–11
Cox, Patricia 258–9

Daube, David 91
Dawson, David 59–62, 68
Dodd, C. H. 191
Droge, Arthur 51–7
Drury, John 191–2

Fabiny, Tibor 153–7
Fishbane, Michael 198–201
Fleury, E. 75
Frederiksen, Paula 267–9, 278
Froehlich, K. 91
Frye, Northrop 144–5, 147, 153–7, 161–2, 185

Grant, R. M. 165, 177

Hall, Stuart 194
Hanson, R. P. C. 166, 195
Hatch, Edwin 3, 246
Hays, Richard B. 130–1
Heine, Ron 260–1

Jeremias, J. 191
Josipovici, Gabriel, 168

Kelly, J. N. D. 18, 71
Kennedy, George 11

Lampe, G. W. H. 166
Lieberman, Saul 91–5
Louth, Andrew 191, 236–7
Lubac, Henri de 191

Meeks, Wayne 224, 236
Momigliano, A. 79–80

Pagels, Elaine 63
Pétrement, Simone 62

Quasten, J. 165

Roberts, C. H. 12, 13–14
Russell, D. A. 76

Sanders, E. P. 266–7
Simonetti, Manlio 1, 37, 186, 244–6
Skarsaune, Oskar 122–4
Steiner, George 119–20

Torjesen, Karen Jo 242

Whitman, Jon 190–1
Winterbottom, M. 76
Woollcombe, K. J. 166

Index of subjects